TV Formats Worldwide

TV Formats Worldwide

Localizing Global Programs

Edited by Albert Moran

intellect Bristol, UK / Chicago, USA

First published in the UK in 2009 by
Intellect, The Mill, Parnall Road, Fishponds, Bristol, BS16 3JG, UK

First published in the USA in 2009 by
Intellect, The University of Chicago Press, 1427 E. 60th Street,
Chicago, IL 60637, USA

A catalogue record for this book is available from
the British Library.

Cover designer: Holly Rose
Copy-editor: Sue Jarvis
Typesetting: Mac Style, Beverley, E. Yorkshire

ISBN 978-1-84150-306-6

Contents

Part I

Introduction

Chapter 1

Introduction: 'Descent and Modification'

Albert Moran

In the sesquicentennial anniversary year of the publication of Charles Darwin's *The Origin of Species*, I begin with Darwin's felicitous phrase regarding the basic mechanism of adaptation in the natural world. This collection deals with cultural reproduction, not biological copying and change. Nevertheless, Darwin's phrase is significant in helping to orient us towards the fact of television program seriality in general, and format adjustment and production in particular. Like other cultural institutions, television's appetite for content is voracious. Helping to meet such an ever-increasing demand, the medium *inter alia* feeds off itself as well as finding other ways to generate new outputs. In turn, semiotics helps identify repetition as a recurring feature of popular fiction and entertainment, whether the form be printed stories, popular song or television program production. The serial principle has to do with the ongoing recourse to a framing mechanism that yet permits and invites the deliberate variation embodied in the instalment, the verse or the episode. The latter are all offspring of one kind or another, whether the features of the forebearer program are easy or difficult to recognize in a descendant program instalment.

The same ambiguity is presented by the recent formalization and recognition of the practice of television program format franchising. The format inaugurates program descent and modification as a formal principle of television production. As an industry practice, it seeks to bolster its significance by elaborating successive activities and material resources, not least to secure and enhance its legal safeguards and monetary rewards. But action also invites reflection, the development of critical consciousness concerning practice, both as a means of developing greater insight for purposes of industry, management and production clarification and as a means of extending greater cultural understanding.

The enigmatic format

Accordingly, this collection provides the opportunity for sustained engagement with the puzzle that is TV format program franchising. The collection's motivation is twofold. On the one hand, authors seek to analyze the program format franchising phenomenon. This practice is sometimes bracketed with a complementary form of program provision labelled the 'finished' program. The latter is thought to be complete and ready for broadcast (even if subtitling or dubbing is necessary to help make the program more intelligible for particular viewers). On the other hand, presumably the format program must need to be 'finished' in some specific way or set of ways to be capable of being broadcast in a particular regional or national market. The authors in this volume are all concerned to investigate the pattern and meaning of this kind of process. As I have noted elsewhere, broadcasters in national television markets who are licensing in program material for broadcast frequently face the dilemma of whether to choose a finished program or a format (Moran 1998). The finished program is usually less expensive to license and involves far less bother than having to arrange for a format production based on a franchise. However, broadcasters and producers very often choose to license a program format on the assumption that the format can be finished or completed in such a way that its broadcast will achieve greater audience appeal than a finished counterpart is likely to gain. The demonstrated success of a forebearer program in another television market helps provide this confidence and insurance.

What, then, is involved in finishing a format program? How is it modified for its new circumstances and what does it retain from its previous manifestation? In this collection, this matter is explored through a variety of approaches or research strategies on the part of both emerging and established media scholars and critical researchers. Altogether, some eighteen chapters are brought together in the volume representing critical research being pursued in North and South America, the United Kingdom and Western Europe, the Middle East, East Asia and the South Pacific. Coincidentally, the volume also appears at the same time as another collection, *Global Television Formats: Understanding Television Across Borders*, where the emphasis primarily falls on a US perspective, although again various of its contributors hail from other places around the world (Oren and Shahaf 2009).

Taken together, these two volumes might be seen as inaugurating an important, newly emerging field of contemporary study. TV format studies is set to become a significant sub-field of present-day research in media and communications, in cultural studies, in creative industry research, and in a set of allied fields including international studies, globalization studies, business and commerce, legal and policy studies, and management studies. TV format studies represents the conceptual end of practices of content franchising as they are pursued by TV production and broadcasting professionals. As a field of inquiry, it can help inform and illuminate the activities of format professionals just as the practice of professional scan test and modify the understandings and insights developed by critical investigators. TV format studies engages with a series of different phenomena, including the political economy of franchising, the textual consequences of remaking, the legal and governmental frameworks within which such practices occur, the prehistory of such activities and the routines and self-understandings of format professionals as they go about their business. Various universities and centres such as the Institute for Media and Communication Research at the University of Bournemouth in the United Kingdom and the Erich Pommer Institute at the University of Potsdam in Germany have now made formal commitments to ongoing involvement in the area of TV format studies in conjunction with different professional format organizations.

Familiarizing formats

Besides the troublesome notion of format adaptation, authors in this volume have had to grapple with the difficulty of applying a suitable term to the broad cultural result of such a process. Many different names can be given to the practice of changing a program to enhance its appeal in a particular territory elsewhere in the world. Synonyms include adapting, remaking, copying, imitating, mimicking, translating, customizing, indigenizing and domesticating. Few, if any, of these terms have a spatial dimension, although this aspect of variation and alteration is highlighted in the title of this collection. Descent and modification of TV programs are contextualized in terms of perceived levels of a multi-level television world. As outlined by O'Regan (1993), Straubhaar (1997) and Chalaby (2005), television is a diverse phenomenon which characteristically exists on several spatial tiers. Although the terms are relative, nevertheless at least five different levels have been identified. Moving up a (televisual) Great Chain of Being, one can perceive levels that can be labelled the local, the national-regional, the national, the world-regional and the global. Each of these tiers has its own distinct history and all have experienced degrees of significance over time. The names of the levels also carry a good deal of vagueness and imprecision. Frequently, over the past 80 years, television appears to have had very little existence or presence at different tiers at different times. Equally, developments at other levels often appear to have overwhelmed or even obliterated some of the other tiers of television's existence. Hence the development of, first, landline systems and, second, satellite broadcasting capacity seemed to herald the permanent triumph of national television services at the expense of local and regional-national services. More recently, arguments concerning massive cross-border connection and penetration have flourished under the impact of a perceived globalization of communications and culture. One ancillary argument regarding this effect has had to do with political and cultural changes at the sub-national tier having to do with community and locality. However, the world of television does not exclusively consist of that which might be labelled the 'global' and the 'local'. Not only are these problematic terms in themselves, but they are also nagged by the bracketing out of the other levels, most especially that of the national. One of the most persistent notes in the chapters that follow is the issue of whether national television remains important, and indeed whether a term such as 'local' is only another way to refer to the national level of television.

In fact, it might be argued that there is little that answers to the name of local or localized television, or a global or globalized television. The notion of the local conjures up ideas of that which is proximate, nearby, immediate, handy, concrete, tribal, homeland-based, communal, and so on. While the medium has, at times – largely for reasons having to do with technology policy and social outlook – been answerable to the name of local television, nevertheless it is debatable whether the kind of customized programming that results from TV format adaptation is usefully understood in this kind of way. This is also the case with the binary opposite form, global television. The term carries suggestions that have to do with the transnational, that which is worldwide, cross-border, international, planetary, universal or even transcultural. Again, there is very little that actually conforms to such a designation in the field of television. What Dayan and Katz (1992) label media events are often of considerable interest to many populations. One thinks of such exceptional events as the first moon walk, the funeral of Princess Diana or more regular international sporting events such as the televising of the Olympic Games or the Soccer World Cup. While the collective audience for such events falls into the billions, nevertheless there are viewers and even nations bypassed by such coverage. Global television seems as much a phantom as local television.

Format trade development

One way in which the interrogation of terms such as 'local', 'national' and 'global' might more usefully be pursued is by adumbrating a short history of the deliberate transfer of television program and radio program prototypes. The recontextualization of industry and cultural know-how involved in the adaptation of broadcast programs from one place to another is neither new nor novel. Consideration of the development of TV production knowledge transfer gives the lie to the claim – less frequent nowadays – that television is national whereas cinema is international (Ellis 1982). Such a formula is only half true. In the era of radio broadcasting between 1939 and 1942, for instance, Australian commercial networks saw the systematic importation and redevelopment for broadcast of such US wireless forerunners as *Lux Theatre, Big Sister* and *When a Girl Marries*. BBC Radio paid a licence fee to the US originators and producers for its adaptation of the panel show *What's My Line?* In Chapter 12, by Gabriele Cosentino, Waddick Doyle and Dimitrina Todorova, the authors speculate that the format of television news was probably widely imitated and adapted from one place to another as television services began in the years after World War II, although little in the way of formal licensing or authorization was involved.

The developments in mainstream radio broadcasting were harbingers of what was to happen in television. The fact that British television began operation in 1936 while US network broadcasting commenced in 1940 meant that other national television systems would, variously, be influenced and shaped by these English-language forerunners. This was certainly the case with Australian television, which on its first night of official transmission in 1956 put to air a remake of a US game show, *What's My Line?* Much more of the same kind of thing was to follow. Between 1962 and 1964, for example, Australian commercial television was involved in remaking such daytime 'reality' series as *People in Conflict* and *Divorce Court* by adapting their American scripts for local circumstances. One of the first deliberately formatted television programs to emerge from the United States in the 1950s, the children's show *Romper Room*, was licensed to several regional broadcasters in Australia around the same time. Meanwhile, the public service television broadcaster the Australian Broadcasting Corporation (ABC) set about re-customizing British Broadcasting Corporation (BBC) programs for its television service following its long-standing practice in radio broadcasting. Beginning in 1963, it has continued down to the present to remake the BBC current affairs series *Panorama* as *Four Corners*. This development was quite unexceptional so far as the BBC and the ABC were concerned. In the time before legal authorization and fee payment became part of the process whereby program knowledge was transferred from place to place, the ABC long believed that imitating the BBC's program formats was a mark of cultural respect on the part of the institutional offspring towards its symbolic parent. None of these developments outlined in connection with Australian broadcasting is unique to that history. Broadcasting has always been an international as well as a national affair, so the sketch of program knowledge transfer outlined here is repeated again and again in many parts of the world. Broadcasting in radio and television, whether on the part of commercial organizations, public service bodies or state authorities, has never placed unique emphasis on program originality. The high number of broadcast hours needing to be filled has never allowed such a luxury. Hence, copying and customizing program production knowledge has been ongoing, widespread and persistent over the past 80 years.

Nevertheless, it is only in more recent times that a formal international system for the transfer and redeployment of TV formats has begun to emerge. For the most part, the different knowledges accumulated by the original producers remained scattered and undocumented. Format knowledges had to be inferred from the residual traces available in broadcast episodes of the program and, with fiction, from scripts. The situation continues in the present when formats are pirated from their owners. By contrast, it has only been relatively recently – some date the change to around 1990 – that producers have begun to systematize and document various production knowledges that come together under the name of the program format (Moran and Malbon 2006). Product branding and intellectual property recognition have played an important role in this development. Obviously, though, the seeds of the format trade's evolution lie back in the 1950s and 1960s with programs such as *Romper Room* and the emergence of service franchising industries.

TV format studies

If tracing the historical development of TV program franchising is a useful way of throwing more light on the puzzling matter of how programs are reshaped to suit audiences in different places, then mapping the emergence of TV format studies as a sub-field of knowledge in media and cultural studies is also valuable. The documentation and analysis of TV format programming presuppose the accessibility of cross-border comparison. Studying format adaptation and production is, at the very least, an international activity if not a global one. Just as the worldwide television trade itself demands the ready availability of such services as lower-cost international travel and telephony, not to mention backup resources such as email, digitalization storage and transmission, and the Internet, so those who would engage in the critical study of the phenomenon and meaning of TV program formats require some of these same facilities. One is reminded that Raymond Williams' famous analysis of television news on US networks compared with that available on a public service broadcaster such as the BBC was based in part on a trans-Atlantic crossing to the United States that he made by ocean liner some time in the early 1970s (Williams 1974).

Even when these resources of transport and communications are available, various cultural capital and aesthetic and social competences are still required for undertaking this kind of investigation. This truism is variously demonstrated by several of the authors found in this volume. Edward Larkey (Chapter 11), for instance, is a US citizen by birth but is a Professor of German Studies and speaks the language fluently. Thus, he has been in position to undertake the investigation of a TV comedy program format's adaptation in the United States and in Germany. Pia Majbrit Jensen (Chapter 10) has studied television systems in both her native Denmark and in Australia, and is therefore well placed to discuss the situation of formats in these two national settings. Collaborative research also comes into its own when the subject is TV program franchising in different places. Hence, in Chapter 12, Cosentino, Doyle and Todorova investigate the advent of parody news programs in Italy and Bulgaria sharing linguistic, cultural and political competencies, as well as particular geographical proximities.

These competencies, resources and linkages that are at the heart of TV format studies are worth underscoring because they help emphasize the modern cosmopolitanism that contextualizes this kind of investigation. They also assist in beginning to date the advent of this type of inquiry. Although there may turn out to be forerunner studies in earlier times, the systematic inquiry into the redeployment and localization of TV programs from one place to another only seems to have got underway in the 1980s and 1990s. Perhaps a paradigmatic moment for such study was the collection edited by Alesandro Silj that appeared in English in 1988. Entitled *East of Dallas*, the collection was intended as a critical contribution to the '*Dallas*ization' (or 'Americanization') debate. This occurred among European media researchers following the startup of private television channels in Western Europe and the importation of US prime-time soap opera series such as *Dallas* as programmers sought to fill their expanded broadcast hours. While various national studies investigated viewer responses to the series in particular European countries such as the Netherlands and Sweden, the *East of Dallas* investigation focused on the generic program response to *Dallas* on the part of several European broadcasters. Various new soap operas in television systems such as those of France and Germany were examined as generic spinoffs of the US program. These clones or copycats were, in effect, format remakes or adaptations of *Dallas, Dynasty, Knot's Landing* and other programs, although they were loosely based on these predecessors and therefore did not require any kind of format licensing for their development. Needless to say, the term 'format' was not used by broadcasters or scholars at this time.

By the 1990s, however, there was increasing recognition that television program adaptation and remaking were far from occasional or accidental. This was documented in relation to several television genres. With TV game shows, for example, Skovmand used the term 'syndicated' in his 1992 analysis of several licensed adaptations of the US *Wheel of*

Fortune by various Nordic broadcasters, while Cooper-Chen (1994) tracked a large number of such formats from the United States and elsewhere across 50 different television markets across the world. My own study of international format trade in the areas of game shows and soap opera, *Copycat TV*, was published in 1998 (Moran 1998).

This last-mentioned investigation was mostly based on interview with figures in the TV format industry in various parts of the world. But it also drew on a developing trade literature on the phenomenon of TV formats. One writer deserves special mention because of his recognition of the emerging importance of the trade in TV formats. From the early 1990s, London-based television journalist Chris Fuller devoted ongoing attention to format trade news in the pages of industry publications such as *Variety* and *TV World*. This coverage in the trade press was to continue during the decade and explode in 1999 with the international success of both *Survivor* and *Big Brother*. Fuller's untimely death in the first years of the new millennium curtailed his coverage of the phenomenon, but by then there were plenty of journalists in various parts of the world who were keenly interested in format programming, especially in the genre of reality television.

Structure of the book

The aim of this collection is to explore the paradox of the local–global duality as it has to do with television program formats. As an industry, this form of transaction appears to promote the global at the expense of the national. As a form of cultural practice, though, it asserts the continuing importance and centrality of the national in the everyday lives of viewing publics. Television format exchange and adaptation point simultaneously to a locally conditioned globalism and a globally constructed localism. While this kind of contingency may appear new and novel, it simply highlights the fact that the local and the national have always been complexly mediated by larger cultural, economic and political forces. The challenge in the present undertaking is to understand how these forces operate in relation to television program formats.

As befits a comparatively new field of media research, it pays not to be too prescriptive so far as the investigation of TV program formats is concerned. Not only are methodological flexibility and imagination necessary for such a task, but so too is the involvement of researchers from fields other than media and cultural studies. Hence, the present volume contains work not only from those involved in television and media studies but also from other fields including economic geography, journalism and communication studies, management studies, and creative industry studies. Various possibilities have also arisen, having to do with likely chapter groupings. There are, for example, three chapters in the collection that have to do with the talent show *Idol* that might have been bracketed together. Equally, chapters dealing with news, infotainment and news show parody might also have been assembled alongside each other. These arrangements have not been followed. Instead, the emphasis in the grouping of parts of the book falls on the critical approach taken to the overall subject of television program franchising. Four interpretative strategies provide the book's scaffolding. These have to do with explicit attempts to develop general conceptual models regarding format adaptation, to understand format franchising from an institutional perspective, to connect adaptations occurring in different places, and to investigate program franchising in specific television territories where the intention is to ensure that home audiences find such programs familiar and accessible. Further detail on the individual chapters follows.

Generalizing

Part II has to do with modelling and theory-building. Authors here are concerned with developing conceptual maps of format adaptation. Elsewhere, I have discussed the contribution that various structural, semiotic and translation theories offer for the study of television program format adaptation. Based on their own field of study, authors such as Levi Strauss, Bakhtin, Lotman, Venuti, Trussig and Taylor have provided highly illuminating insights into the cultural processes involved in adaptation. This philosophical tradition certainly warrants extended engagement so far as achieving greater understanding of the phenomenon and meaning of TV format adaptation is concerned. The authors in this part postpone this general engagement in favour of an emphasis on more middle-range, concrete theory-building.

Chapter 2, by Marwan Kraidy, suggests a larger social context in which to understand the dramatic popular impact of format-driven reality programming on Middle Eastern television. Television has shifted to accord a significant place to the franchising of program formats from the West, and the reality programs so adapted make manifest competing forces that are remoulding Arab identities and societies. Format reality TV offers women, youth and other minorities some of the cultural and even political tools with which to engage in this debate. Kraidy has coined the term 'hypermedia space' to describe the arena in which this kind of viewer can link mobile phones, email and television in a fluid, interactive form that bypasses censorship and political control. Thus, the recontextualization of a format program is always intimately linked to domestic currents in culture, religion and politics.

Chapters 3 and 4 are concerned with the systematic understanding of adaptation whereby formats are remade to suit particular national television contexts. Focusing on the interactive process of exchange that occurs in the production setting where the wishes of both the licensor owner of a format and the licensee adapter of that format have to be satisfied, the two chapters have recourse to a long-standing conceptual tradition in media and communications studies associated with the 'gatekeeper' figure and function in production research. Chapter 3 suggests that the person of the visiting producer who offers a consultancy service to licensing companies in different places qualifies as just such a figure. She or he is, in effect, a translator so that various elements of translation theory having to do with different levels of textual coding becomes a very useful way of approaching the broader matter of TV format adaptation. Chapter 4, by Sonia Jalfin and Silvio Waisbord, complements this approach. These authors focus on the adaptation and production of program formats in Argentina. Their interest lies with the other parties in the format-production negotiation process, namely the local or national producer, writer, broadcaster and executive, who act as mediators of global industry and cultural knowledges. Finding parallels between this work and that of journalists involved in adapting news from elsewhere for local audiences, Jalfin and Waisbord adopt the metaphor of the 'journalistic prism'. This refers to the fact that local media professionals scan potential materials (whether news events or format programs) as proxy for reality, as a means of monitoring potential audience interest and involvement.

From inside the business

Part III of the book groups together chapters that have to do with television formats as business and social practices on the part of the media institution. The latter term refers to television not only as an industry but also as a culture, conjuring up notions of organization, technology, professional worker, work practice, business outlook and content production, as well as social engagement, fans, media events, and so on. Television formats are multi-level entities themselves, so an institutional engagement can and does focus on diverse but equally significant components of the practice of program franchising. Four chapters target the matter of how television formats are handled at different levels of the institution. Chapter 5, by Katja Lantzsch, Klaus-Dieter Altmeppen and Andreas Will, is written from a management studies perspective. It focuses on the international level of media institutions and is concerned with the inter-organizational networks of television program format licensor and licensee. Television format franchising is a worldwide business. Highlighting network and structuration theory, these authors see such a connection as itself a complexly patterned structure of more discrete connections. These include the network of the licensing trade, the network of content production, the network of format adaptation, and the interlinking network of knowledge transfer.

At the national level of the media institution, Raymond Boyle in Chapter 6 sees the television program format as a useful means of understanding shifts in British society and the related media ecology. He is particularly concerned with the role played by business and finance, and especially the way public service television – particularly the BBC – has accommodated this development. In the increasingly competitive digital world of multi-platform delivery, the public broadcaster has tended to recontextualize business and finance from a factual domain to an entertainment milieu. Thus, international formats such as *The Apprentice* from the United States and *Dragon's Den* from Japan are presented as infotainment, to help meet the BBC's public broadcasting obligations.

With new media, new actors and new audience attractions, the public is now pressed into more active and interventionist roles in the institution. Yngver Njus, in Chapter 7, is concerned with the managerial and production process whereby a local version of a format program such as *Pop Idol* is made for a particular national audience (in this case, that of Norway). He identifies the format script or the 'bible' as a key element in stabilizing and varying the program format in its different national manifestations. The (format) 'bible' is neither fixed or rigid, but is itself in dialectic relationship with national productions of the franchised program. Hence, successful local variations in different territories across the world are progressively incorporated in the overall format script of a program such as *Idol*. Chapter 8 also has to do with the audience as an increasingly important component of the media institution so far as format localization is concerned. Doris Baltruschat adds to an understanding of the 'conversation' between the *Idol* format and its local inception with her chapter concerning participants in the *Canadian Idol* production. Here, the audience was not only 'active' but might be said to have become 'productive', turning into a vital component of the overall institutional context. Thanks to mobile phone technology and the Internet, as well as live staging, members of the public help redefine the value chain of content production through contributing their labour and thus enhancing the overall program structure.

Close and distant cousins

The matter of television localization can also be approached by means of cross-border comparisons and contrasts. Accordingly, the chapters in Part IV of the book have to do with analyses of adaptation industries and cultures that span two or more territories. Such an approach is concerned not only with the details of specific correspondences and contrasts but also with the larger set of social, political and cultural arrangements that they both project and represent. In Chapter 9, Amos Owen Thomas argues that television programming available on various national and regional channels points to a situation of considerable cultural heterogeneity across the Middle East. The reception of TV format remakes by audience markets of the affluent Gulf sub-region has been uneven, variously gaining new audience segments and/or alienating others. Echoing Kraidy's findings in Chapter 2, Thomas reports that these adaptations form another proxy arena of contestation about Arab identity between cultural progressives and conservatives.

Pia Majbrit Jensen's chapter (Chapter 10) may be regarded as transitional, moving as it does between an institutional approach and a comparative, cross-border orientation. Her object of attention is the television systems of Denmark and Australia, which have several features in common including their origination in the 1950s, the fact of being dual or mixed systems of public service and commercial broadcast networks, and their willingness to embrace format programming. However, the public service sector has been much stronger in Denmark than in Australia. On the other hand, format program adaptation has had a much longer history in Australia. Yet another difference lies in the fact that Danish television enjoys linguistic autonomy while Australia is part of a larger Anglophone region with intimate links to the television systems of the United States and the United Kingdom. These commonalities and variations have resulted in two quite different television ecologies so far as the importation and deployment of television formats are concerned. Jensen suggests that particular developments in the recent present relating to formats such as Danish public service broadcasting's greater preparedness to deploy imported formats than its Australian counterpart suggest both a different sense of public service broadcasting and further diverging developments between the two systems.

The British sitcom *The Office* has given rise to several program offspring. These include a US remake of the same name and a German copycat entitled *Stromberg*. Recognizing that these adaptations will fall under the rubric of 'cultural proximity', which reinforces their common format origins, Edward Larkey in Chapter 11 offers a close analysis of the pilot episodes of the two series. Rather than argue for any overall cultural process that equates with an 'Americanization' or 'Germanification' of the original, his chapter locates these variations of *The Office* within a more general globalized movement in the institution and culture of office administration and management. In particular, he suggests that both adaptations can be seen to represent and affect what he calls 'global network capitalism'. Over the past two decades, a new administrative elite, termed 'global networkers', has progressively been replacing an upper echelon of management which itself had earlier ousted an owner-manager hierarchy. Larkey presents a persuasive argument regarding the place that various figures in the US and German versions of the program occupy, most especially the pivotal figures of Michael Scott in the former adaptation and Stromberg in the latter. Many of the articles in this collection have to do with the various genres and forms of entertainment or infotainment television, whether this be drama, reality, makeover or game shows. With the exception of Chapter 6 by Boyle and Chapter 13 by Sosale and Munro, news and information genre programming are not featured prominently in this book. Nevertheless, Chapter 12 by Cosentino, Doyle and Todorov focuses on a modern variant of the television news genre, namely the parody news program. These authors see this emerging genre as an important sign of the times, asserting that, just as the national news program helped fix the idea of the nation state in the mind of a population, so this kind of comedy news constitutes a response to a new geo-political viewing situation. In Italy and Bulgaria, in particular, the international flow of people means that sub-national and supra-national identities are increasingly important within national political and cultural frontiers. Cosentino, Doyle and Todorov offer a particular example of program format transfer to flesh out this assertion. This involves the movement of one such format from Italy to Bulgaria where elements to do not only with genre, but also those to do with law and political economy, came into play. The authors point to a specific historical moment involving broader social developments, including those to do with political forces, economic developments and cultural formations wherein the commercial opportunity and political and cultural need for a particular format program happen.

Talking to ourselves

Part V has to do with processes whereby formats and genres are given homegrown accents and images. They are reconstituted in such a way as to develop a recognizability so far as the domestic viewing public is concerned. They are reconfigured to speak to an 'us', on behalf of an 'us' and about an 'us'. Coining various national neologisms, one can say that this part of the format franchising operation sees the coming together of a version of the global and the local so that programs are variously 'Italianized', 'Australianized', 'New Zealandized', and so on. Four chapters trace such processes in concrete detail and distil them for the insight they yield into the dialectic of the television local and global.

In Chapter 13, Sujatha Sosala and Charles Munro take up the matter of television news not so much at the national level, but rather at a sub-level of the regional-national. Their concern is how the BBC in Northern Ireland, the only part of the Irish island that remains part of the political settlement that is the United Kingdom, shapes its television news coverage to appeal to its homegrown audience and, at the same time, differentiates itself from its commercial television competitor, formerly Ulster Television (UTV). Besides the cultural and political elements in play in this situation, there are also economic factors operating. National and even world news packages are more financially attractive than are the costs of gathering Northern Ireland news. Given these pressures, Sosala and Munro argue that studying the BBC news-gathering and operation arrangements against those of UTV helps sharpen understanding of how local news values are articulated in this particular situation.

In turn, in Chapter 14, Michael Keane and Bonnie Liu examine the situation of the television format industry in a rapidly emerging post-broadcasting era in contemporary Mainland China. More satellite channels are available as provincial broadcasters seek to carve out positions of independence in relation to the national broadcaster, China Central Television (CCTV). Digital TV exacerbates the search for content in this more open system. Production units are no longer linked directly to television stations, and new ideas – as well as older ideas that can be reformatted to fill an expanding content vacuum – are at a premium. Although TV serial drama remains dominant, reality TV and infotainment programming are seen as easy ways to produce TV that is cheaper and with less risk attached. The problem, however, is that much of the current output is of variable quality.

TV formats are more than program prototypes. They are complex, comprehensive bodies of industrial and cultural knowledge that have developed in a particular context. When they are transferred to another television setting, they add up to a valuable resource to be exploited on the part of the importing culture and industry. This was the case in Italy in the early 1990s, when the Australian soap opera genre embodied in series such as *Neighbours* was reformatted for the Italian public broadcaster, RAI. Milly Buonanno takes up this story in Chapter 15, which examines the development of the first Italian soap opera, *A Place in the Sun*. The serial constituted a production collaboration between the Australian-born company Grundy World Wide and the Italian public broadcaster RAI as an instance of the global and the local in fruitful interaction with each other. Far from representing any kind of global cultural homogenization, the startup of this Italian serial represented a complex cultural process whereby an Italian sound and image in fictional drama were able to find an ongoing place on television and in the everyday life of the Italian public. This infusion of soap opera genre and format know-how breathed new life into Italian television drama, both as cultural form and as an industrial institution. In Chapter 16, Barry King returns to the *Idol* format, and especially to its New Zealand offspring. This was an unlikely licensing for the New Zealand public broadcaster TVNZ, given the very small size of the local television and music industry market, with the country itself having a population of fewer than five million people. Hence, it involved the paradox that *New Zealand Idol* offered stardom to its winning contestant even while the New Zealand popular cultural marketplace could not underwrite the costs of celebrityhood. King sees a further compounding of this contradiction playing out in the sphere of public culture. There, a market fundamentalism criss-crosses a cultural and political biculturalism. Its cumulative effect in the case of the format adaptation was to promote musical authenticity by the emphatic promotion of Maori singing contestants.

Tanya Lewis, in Chapter 17, examines the circulation of another television genre now associated with the international movement of television formats, namely the makeover program. The latter has a long lineage in daytime programs in Australia and elsewhere, having to do with self and home improvement. However, this genre has been transformed through its incorporation of narrative structures and situations associated with reality television formats. Sketching this generic background is important to the chapter, which convincingly demonstrates that the encounter between formats and national cultures is also played out inside the television institution. This latter context has to do not only with the outlook and orientation of television sectors and networks, but also with generic preferences, programming philosophies and its perceived ties to an Australian 'national ordinary'. Lewis concludes with the caveat that this format speaks neither solely to the latter nor to a purely universalizing televisual culture of Western lifestyles, but rather to a television institution witnessing increasingly complex patterns of global and domestic concerns. Manuel Alvarado contributes a thoughtful and summative conclusion to the volume. In his Afterword, he points to the continuing significance of circulation as an area of vital interest and importance in film and television studies. The local/global nexus has a particular salience which he characterizes in terms of the Australian television service, which he first encountered more than three decades ago. As part of an Anglophone regional television system, Australia (along with Canada) has been an early warning system for a culturally complex 'conversation' with US and UK television (and, more recently, with Ireland, New Zealand and elsewhere). The features of this 'conversation' include importing, imitating, substituting and originating program content – features to which the authors in this volume return again and again.

References

Chalaby, J.K. (ed.) (2005), *Transnational Television Worldwide: Towards a New Media Order*, London: I.H. Tauris.

Cooper-Chen, A. (1994), *Games in the Global Village: A 50-Nation Study*, Bowling Green, OH: Bowling Green University Popular Press.

Dayan, Daniel and Katz, Elihu (1992), *Media Events: The Live Broadcasting of History*, Cambridge, MA: Harvard University Press.

Ellis, John (1982), *Visible Fictions*, London: Routledge and Kegan Paul.

Moran, Albert (1998), *Copycat Television: Globalisation, Program Formats and Cultural Identity*, Luton: University of Luton Press.

Moran, Albert and Malbon, Justin (2006), *Understanding the Global TV Format*, Bristol: Intellect.

Oren, Tasha G. and Shahaf, Sharon (2009), *Global Television Formats: Understanding Television Across Borders*, New York: Routledge.

O'Regan, Tom (1993), 'The Regional, the National and the Local: Hollywood's New and Declining Audiences', in E. Jacka (ed.), *Continental Shift: Culture and Globalisation*, Sydney: Local Consumption Publications, pp. 74–97.

Silj, A. (ed.) (1988), *East of Dallas: The European Challenge to American Television*, London: British Film Institute.

Skovmand, M. (1992), 'Barbarous TV International: Syndicated *Wheel of Fortune*', in M. Skovmand and K.C. Schroeder (eds), *Media Cultures: Reappraising Transnational Media*, London: Routledge, pp. 84–103.

Straubhaar, J.D. (1997), 'Distinguishing the Global, Regional and National Levels of World Television', in A. Sreberny-Mohammadi, D. Winseck, J. McKenna and O. Boyd-Barrett (eds), *Media in Global Context*, London: Edward Arnold, pp. 284–98.

Williams, Raymond (1974), *Television: Technology and Cultural Form*, London: Fontana.

PART II

Modelling and Theory-Building

Chapter 2

Rethinking the Local-Global Nexus Through Multiple Modernities: The Case of Arab Reality Television

Marwan M. Kraidy

'For many societies, modernity is an elsewhere,' wrote the Indian-American cultural anthropologist Arjun Appadurai (1996: 49–59). More often than not, this 'elsewhere' is the West which, after decades of colonialism and imperialism, plays an important role in the cultural, political and economic life of the rest of the world. However, in the wake of the decolonization movement and the cultural turn in the humanities and social sciences, the bond between the West and modernity is no longer iron clad, not the least because the notion of modernity itself has lost its conceptual unity. As the Mexican-Argentinean cultural critic Néstor García-Canclini (1994) wrote nearly two decades ago, 'there is not only one form of modernity but rather several unequal and sometimes contradictory ones' (1994: 182). If we are to agree with Garcia-Canclini that there are indeed several forms of modernity that are often at odds with each other, then understanding the dynamics of public life in nations around the world requires us to grasp the rival versions of modernity present in these societies. Debates over the meanings and implications of modernity tend to be heated in the non-West, where the trope of modernity conjures up, on the one hand, social progress, economic growth, the emancipation of the individual and sometimes cultural modernism, and on the other hand, cultural decline, the loss of authenticity, and political and economic dependency. There is disagreement in both camps as to whether the elsewhere of modernity is the West...or somewhere else.

In the Arab world, the proliferation of media forms over the last two decades has often animated debates about modernity and its discontents. In contradistinction to the early twentieth century, when newspapers in Ottoman cities like Aleppo witnessed an intense debate about modernity (Watenpaugh 2006), and the Saudi intellectual war over modernity from 1985 to 1995,[1] in the current debates television is not only a vehicle for debate but also an important catalyst of debates about modernity. Indeed, the Arab reality TV controversies which raged between 2003 and 2007 constitute a battleground in the debate over what it means to be Arab *and* modern. As I show in my book *Reality Television and Arab Politics: Contention in Public Life* (Kraidy 2009), though the debate took a distinct turn in the Arab world, reality TV was highly controversial in several countries, including France (see Schneidermann 2004). If modernity, as the Canadian philosopher Charles Taylor (1999: 168) has convincingly argued, involves 'the coming to be of new kinds of public space', then impassioned debates about reality TV constitute crucial moments of Arab engagement with *al-hadatha*. At a time when the 'war on terror' subjects Arab societies to contested suspicions and representations, reality TV contributes to 'the institutionalization of doubt' (Giddens 1990: 176) from within an Arab public space, opening a unique vista on the evolving shape of Arab modernities. The reality TV controversies should be seen less in terms of traditional forces lashing out at an encroaching modernity, and more as rival versions of modernity engaged in a drawn-out negotiation over the selective adoption of modernity. In fact, the Arab reality TV culture wars offer a stunningly interesting exemplar of how modernity, in the coinage of Leszek Kolakowski (1997), is on 'endless trial'. In that trial, modernity is never accepted as a given; rather, rival versions of modernity are advocated, attacked, scrutinized, negotiated, appropriated. As such, the reality TV controversies provide a glimpse of what multiple modernities may look like in a part of the non-West whose oil, religions, men and women are subjects of various Western fantasies.

Modernity is endlessly contested because the sources, paths and forms of modernity are multiple (see Hervieu-Léger 2003 for a discussion of the religious dimension of multiple modernities). As Taylor (1999) writes, 'instead of speaking of modernity in the singular, we should better speak of "alternative modernities"' (1999: 162). Taylor hastens to add that: '[A] viable theory of alternative modernities has to be able to relate both the pull to sameness and the forces making for difference' because 'there is undoubtedly *some* convergence involved in the triumphal march of modernity' (1999: 162). Taylor's advocacy of multiple modernities stems from his observation of differences in the ways in which various contexts negotiate socio-cultural and politico-economic change. He concludes that: 'The cultures that emerge in the world to carry the institutional changes turn out to differ in important ways from each other...What they are looking for is creative adaptation, drawing on the cultural resources of their tradition, that would enable them to take on the new practices successfully.' (1999: 163) As we shall see shortly, reality TV presents us with a particular case of creative adaptation, showing that the process (of adaptation) takes place at the social, institutional and individual levels. Taylor's reiteration that 'the point of the alternative modernities thesis is that these adaptations don't have to and generally won't be identical across civilizations' and that 'what is required by the wave of modernity is that one comes up not with identical institutions but with functionally equivalent ones' (1999: 164) will be illustrated as this chapter moves on to discuss how reality TV articulates cultural and political modernities.

Though there are multiple forms of modernity, the West – Appadurai's putative 'elsewhere' – occupies a privileged position *vis-à-vis* which other modernities are elaborated, in various degrees of compatibility and opposition. The term 'alternative', often used to describe non-Western modernities, reinscribes the West as a normative template. As a result, modernity nearly always involves a moving equilibrium, a creative tension between convergence and differentiation, mimicry and dismissal, with 'the West' looming large as an example to be emulated, scorned or appropriated. As a result, modernity systematically produces hybrid forms, which is true in several areas of social, economic and political life but perhaps most visible in the area of expressive culture (García-Canclini 1994; Gruzinski 1999; Toumson 1998). Reality TV is a case in point. The designation 'reality TV' refers to various game and talent shows that are largely unscripted, feature amateurs, and often require viewers to vote for contestants. Two European companies, Endemol in Holland and FremantleMedia in Britain, dominate this global trade. They develop 'formats', or program recipes stipulating creative, technical and dramatic components, which are then sold worldwide and adapted to language- and culture-specific audiences. For example, *Star Academy* is a knock-off of the British show *Fame Academy* and *Superstar* is the Arabic version of *American Idol*. Since adapting a format carries less business risk than creating a brand new program, Arab producers and directors have repeatedly told me that reality TV has changed the way they work. 'It used to be that we aimed to create the next great program; now we compete to adapt the next great format,' a director told me in Dubai, succinctly describing the shift. Clearly, the Arab modernity expressed in this quote is a variation on a theme – and a Western one at that, in this case reality TV formats.

Nonetheless, dismissing the television format adaptations as mere imitations of Western modernity glosses over the complexities and contradictions inherent in cultural translation that are better captured by the tropes of hybridity and *métissage* (Kraidy 2005). As local adaptations of global formats, Arab reality TV programs are 'hybrid texts' that mix foreign and local cultural sensibilities. Writing about Latin America, the cultural critic Néstor García-Canclini (1998: 2) observes that 'the uncertainty about the meaning and value of modernity derives not only from what separates nations, ethnic groups and classes, but also from the socio-cultural hybrids in which the traditional and the modern are mixed'. Arab literature and poetry are replete with cultural mixtures, but reality TV gives Arabs their most visible cultural hybrids. Arab reality TV is so intensely controversial, then, because it violates boundaries of identity and authenticity at a time when these boundaries have been hardened by 9/11 and its aftermath, widespread violence in the Middle East and various global controversies over Islam – Danish cartoons, papal comments, and so on – in addition to increased Western and Iranian interventions in Arab politics.

The intense and protracted controversies triggered by Arab reality TV shows are important for our understanding of modernity as the opening up of new public spaces because they articulate cultural mixture with political contestation, both processes of dealing with the Other. Controversies may polarize debates over issues, but they also increase the reach of these debates and broaden public exposure to them, in quantitative but also qualitative terms. In 2004, the Lebanese reality show *Star Academy* (the title is in English) captured record pan-Arab ratings, reaching up to 80 per cent of viewers in some countries (Kraidy 2006a). Unlike the predominantly adult and presumably male and Sunni Al-Jazeera audience, reality TV attracts youth, women and minorities. Reality shows have spurred heated controversies about the role of Islam in public life, Western cultural influence, gender relations and political participation, unfolding on television screens, in the living room or in the coffeehouse. Though Latin American *telenovelas*, Egyptian melodrama and televised Hindu epics have generated debate, pan-Arab reality TV is so polemical that it has triggered street riots in the case of *Al-Ra'is* (The Arabic version of *Big Brother* and *Loft Story*), compelled clerics to issue *fatwas* (in the case of *Star Academy* in Kuwait and Saudi Arabia) and fuelled transnational media wars (in the case of both *Superstar* and *Star Academy* in Lebanon and Syria).

A primary reason behind the controversy is that, unlike other entertainment television genres, reality TV claims to represent reality (for a sustained discussion of this issue, see Couldry 2003; Hill 2005; Le Guay 2005). Like news and documentary, reality TV's protagonists are not media professionals. Unlike news and documentary, reality TV relies on a continuous flow of television characterized by unpredictability. Despite its claims, we know that reality TV is not really real. As Damien Le Guay (2005) points out:

> The only reality in these programs is in their name. They are built, arranged, scripted... But this reality exists, even if it is arranged, controlled, monitored, spiced up by a variety of fabricated miscellaneous factoids, disposed by a small army of invisible hands moving back-stage...we are here in a false reality, an illusion of reality or rather an arranged reality. (2005: 20)

If, in the West, this manipulated reality is easily dismissed, with surveys showing most viewers to be sceptical of reality TV's claim to be real, in the Arab world clerics engage the claim ontologically with alarm. Because of this opposition, reality TV's claim to represent reality is paradoxically magnified.

The significance of reality TV in Arab public life resides in reality TV's articulation of the cultural and political dimensions of modernity always-already in the making. The cultural hybridity inherent in reality TV programs adapted to the Arab context from British or Dutch formats – with, in the case of LBC's *Star Academy*, France acting as a mediator – provokes contention in Arab Gulf countries like Saudi Arabia where a ritualized Islam provides the source of political power. Wahhabi Islam's insistence on cultural and religious purity is violated by culturally hybrid (and socially subversive) reality TV programs. Controversy ensues, leading to *political debate*. Even in less conservative Arab societies, *Star Academy* and *Superstar* have triggered heated controversies, one of the outcomes of which has been the linking of 'cultural' issues (i.e. hybridity) with 'political' themes (i.e. political contestation). The complex new relations between Arab popular culture and politics highlight the 'obliquity of symbolic circuits' which 'allows us to rethink the link between culture and power,' writes García-Canclini (1994: 261), because: 'The search for mediations and diagonal ways for managing conflict gives cultural relations a prominent place in political development.'

But the multiplicity of modernity is visible beyond the domain of culture. Reality TV's embroilment in Arab politics, narrowly defined – elections, diplomatic relations, parliamentary debates, ministerial performance – betrays various expressions of modernity, whether in terms of social differentiation or, in keeping with Bourdieu's criticism of differentiation theory, the emergence of multiple fields – or with the integration of diverse populations and identities under the aegis of the nation-state or the offering of new templates for the self. In Saudi Arabia and other conservative Gulf states – Bahrain, Saudi Arabia and Kuwait – reality TV programs ignited rhetorical firestorms about national political, economic and social issues. These public arguments, which focused on gender relations and deployed religious speech, have redefined key notions like national reputation, cultural authenticity and political participation, contributing to institutional and social pluralism typical of a modern sensibility.

The first episode in the reality TV wrangles followed the shutdown of *Al-Ra'is*, the Arabic version of *Big Brother*, in Bahrain in 2004. This touched off heated parliamentary debates between economic liberals and religious conservatives, giving rise to conflicting definitions of national reputation – as abidance to Islamic tenets *or* fitness for foreign investment (Kraidy 2006a). For various Islamists, *Al-Ra'is* violated Islamic values by putting unmarried young men and women in a confined physical space. The show's producer, Saudi-owned and Dubai-based MBC, had opted for Bahrain over Saudi Arabia to mitigate a potential controversy, and several MBC sources told me that all the women cast for the show were divorcées.[2] Yet, barely one week into the broadcast, an on-screen kiss triggered demonstrations, leading to a shutdown of the show. The parliamentary debate following the shutdown was fascinating. On one side, Islamists continued to argue that *Al-Ra'is* violated putative Islamic values, supporting the shutdown. On the other side, 'liberal' politicians warned that the shutdown sent a signal to foreign investors that Bahrain was a risky place to do business (Kraidy 2006a). The debate demonstrates the existence of several sources of public debate and policy claims, several fields of argument and authentication, a development which reflects a modern sensibility. As Kaya (2004) writes, 'the openness of modernity is due in one important way to the inability of modernity to unify irreconcilable perspectives, instead multiple "centres" of power, culture, rationality find home within modernity which turns modernity into an "endless trial"' (2004: 41).

The most contentious episode was sparked by *Star Academy*'s record ratings in Saudi Arabia. Incensed critics called it 'Satan academy' and 'moral terrorism', and the Higher Council of Ulamas issued a critical *fatwa*. *L'affaire Star Academy* in Saudi Arabia reflects social and political tensions in a context of Islamic prohibitions on gender mixing, a protracted struggle between Saudi conservatives and liberals, and Saudi censorship guidelines. At the heart of the controversy was the fact that, by fostering interaction between unmarried men and women (defined by Wahhabiyya as *ikhtilat*), and by celebrating cultural hybridity, reality TV's claim to represent reality and its participatory rituals subverted the Wahhabi view of Islamic authenticity (based on gender segregation and cultural purity), thus threatening the core of the Saudi social order.[3]

Another key feature of modernity is the integration of ethnically diverse and geographically fragmented populations into nation-states – a 'new' Arab nationalism because it is centred on reaffirming individual nation-states, in contrast to pan-Arab nationalism. In this process, communication technologies have historically played an important role in the Middle East (Gelvin 1999). The new Arab nationalism can be glimpsed in *Superstar*'s embroilment in the war of the airwaves between Lebanon and Syria, and the stunning reversal between 2003 – when a Lebanese contestant on *Superstar 1* was eliminated under full Syrian control of Lebanon – and 2006 – when a Syrian finalist in *Superstar 3* was ousted soon after Syrian troops withdrew from Lebanon. Broadcast from Beirut by the Hariri-owned channel Future TV, *Superstar* was usurped as a patriotic stage, with the Syrian finalist's father bursting on to the stage to wrap his daughter in a body-sized Syrian flag as others cheered on her Saudi competitor (author's analysis).

Though *Star Academy* also witnessed the expression of an anti-Syrian Lebanese nationalism after the assassination of Rafiq Al-Hariri in February 2005, that show's impact in Iraq is more remarkable. When, in 2007, a young Iraqi woman, Shada Hassoun, rose to the finals, more than seven million Iraqis voted for her, with both Sunnis and Shi'ites claiming her, leading insurgents to post online diatribes against *Star Academy* for showcasing a corrupt model for Iraqi women. Today, Shada Hassoun is a star featured incessantly on Al-Iraqiyya public service announcements propagating a peaceful and prosperous Iraq for the future. At a time when 'Sunni Triangle' and 'Shi'ite Crescent' echo assumptions of primeval identities, reality TV acts as an epideictic consolidator of nationalism in several Arab states. Ironically, at a time when Arab-nation states are no longer 'broadcasting states' (Guaybess 2003), reality TV becomes a force of national unity even as it stokes transnational discord.

More importantly, as we consider how Arab reality TV's opening of new social and political spaces articulates Arab modernities, we should understand the impact of reality TV's embroilment in 'street politics' as activists in Egypt, Kuwait and Lebanon adopted its alluring style and catchy slogans as an *idiom of contention* – a set of media-savvy tricks enlisted in political contests. Mobilization tactics, campaign slogans and voting rituals honed during reality TV shows (or inspired by them) are useful in street politics because 'popular culture's ability to produce and articulate feelings can become the basis of an identity, and that identity can be the source of political thought and action' (Street 1997: 10). One-word slogans reminiscent of *Star Academy* broadcasts capture political agendas: 'Now!' said Kuwaiti women agitating for political rights; 'The Truth!'[4] chanted Lebanese demonstrators after Hariri's assassination, as they 'nominated' reviled politicians to be 'voted off the island'; 'Enough!' clamored Egyptian activists protesting Mubarak's one-party rule (Kraidy 2006b). Even when not directly inspired by reality TV, these slogans clearly draw on a new semantic and iconographic sphere – to which Arab reality TV has greatly contributed. In all cases, the new lexicon makes political contestation noticeable in an age of attention scarcity.

Arab reality TV also contributes to the opening up of new spaces of expression by making Arab populations more aware of media convergence. To vote for their favorite contestants in *Superstar* or *Star Academy*, viewers conjoin mobile phones, email and television in fluid and interactive communication processes that elude censorship – what I have previously called *hypermedia space* (Kraidy 2006b). The popularity of reality TV causes a wide dissemination of these practices, which makes Arab publics aware of the potential social and political uses of media convergence. In that process, Arabs are aided by journalists who analyze the role of new media in Arab politics through the prism of the reality TV debates. Like *Star Academy* and *Superstar* enthusiasts, activists use text-messaging to mobilize supporters and glossy signs with witty slogans to attract media attention to their demonstrations – for example, in Beirut and Cairo. Reality TV has dramatized the role of media technologies in organizing, staging and publicizing political spectacles.

The emergence of hypermedia space is a result of the Arab 'media revolution' entering a phase of media convergence, not only at the technological level but also in terms of production and programming strategies focused on synergies. This is happening in the context of an explosion in print media, blogs and a proliferation of what the industry calls 'value added services': personalized ringtones, Multimedia Messaging Service and other mobile phone gizmos. In this vibrant media scene hungry for content, the reality TV culture wars are fuelled on talk-shows and opinion pages, which counterpose ultra-conservatives to neo-liberals, autocrats to democrats, clerics to feminists. In columns titled '*Star Academy*'s democracy' (Al-Bushr 2005) or 'The *Star Academy* of Arab Leaders' (Al-Baba 2005), journalists excoriate Arab politicians, mixing irony with an earnest desire for political change as they draw 'lessons in democracy' from reality TV shows. Driven by economic interests and its dramatic structure, reality TV sustains and feeds on the new hypermedia environment, opening up new avenues for public discourse.

Superstar's foray into the strained Syrian–Lebanese relationship foreshadows the momentous events of 2005 in Lebanon, coupling inter-Lebanese political struggles to regional and global turbulence involving the United States, France, Saudi Arabia and Iran. These events were a spectacular confirmation of the trends previously mentioned: the consolidation of nationalism as a belonging to one nation-state, in this case Lebanese nationalism (as opposed to Arab nationalism's pan-Arab project), the advent of new spaces of expression and new ways for citizens to address political leaders, and the importance of converging media technologies, especially mobile telephones and their simultaneous abilities to distribute text and images.

Most characteristic of modernity's 'endless trial' was the fact that social reality became the subject of a contest between rival political groups in Lebanon and even involved President Assad of Syria, auguring an era of multiple media epistemologies. When Assad chided some Lebanese television channels for exaggerating the number of anti-Syrian demonstrators and said that if they were to 'zoom out' the truth would show, demonstrators in Beirut replied with signs saying 'Syria, Zoom Out' and 'Zoom Out and Count'. Similarly, demonstrators used the language of reality TV to 'nominate' reviled politicians to go into retirement (President Lahoud) or jail (state prosecutor cum Justice Minister 'Adnan' Addoum). Many of the signs were in French and English, in addition to Arabic, indicating that the demonstrators were addressing multiple audiences at once, paradoxically internationalizing the Lebanese crisis – the United States, France and Saudi Arabia were already actively involved – at the same time as they were expressing a resurgent Lebanese nationalism in which the ubiquity of the national flag undermined symbols of sectarian identities and ideological affiliations (Kraidy 2007). In the battle to define social and political reality, these demonstrations were tailor-made for television, echoing Bourdieu's (1996) point that demonstrations are increasingly created for the main, if not unique, objective of ending up on television screens: 'More and more, one must produce demonstrations for television, meaning demonstrations susceptible of interesting those who work in television, taking into account their categories of perception, and once the demonstrations are relayed and amplified by television, they will reach their full efficacy.' (Bourdieu 1996: 22)[5] The ways in which reality TV was mixed up in political spectacles like the spring 2005 demonstrations in Beirut are also a harbinger of modernity in the way they articulate new uses of public space. Unlike officially staged media events, these demonstrations are *hypermedia events* made by media institutions and political groups, managing publics who, like reality TV fans, use a combination of mobile phones and television to fulfil a strategic goal: the victory of their candidate or the ousting of scorned politicians.[6]

In addition to spawning new kinds of televised spectacles, nationalistic battles or institutional differentiations, the reality TV controversies suggest various pathways to modernity through the remaking of individual and social identities. Reality TV's underlying premises focus on the subject – the exacerbation of desire and emotional conflict, the exaltation of individualism and the promotion of self-revealing behavior (Le Guay 2005). Le Guay explores how reality TV was variously used as a crime and terrorism-fighting tool in early post-Saddam Iraq (the equivalent of *Cops* in the United States), as a vehicle for Islamic values in Dubai, or as a reviled counter-example to the kind of personal piety promoted by Islamists from Algeria to Bahrain. Other, less controversial, reality shows, such as *Survivor*'s (*Expedition Robinson*) Darwinian premise, *Al-Wadi*'s (*Celebrity Farm/La Ferme Célebrités*) faux communitarian ethos, *Beauty Clinic*'s (*Extreme Makeover*) radical reshaping of Arab bodies – individual, through plastic surgery, and social – are expressions of conflicting ways of being Arab and modern.

Reality TV is contentious because it makes visible rival forces reshaping Arab identities and societies. In the United States and Europe, reality TV programs compel participants to unveil the most intimate personal-psychographic details, thus aiding in the creation of ideal consumers for niche marketing (see, for example, Andrejevic 2004; Couldry 2003). Likewise, Arab reality TV contributes to the creation of new selves, modern composite citizen-consumers. But, in contrast to the West, Arab reality TV provides a platform to reclaim things social and political. Several Arab reality shows reaffirm social norms, but with a twist: *Millionaire Poet* (Abu Dhabi TV) re-enacts traditional oral poetry contests in Arabian Gulf countries, and on *Green Light* (Dubai TV) contestants perform good deeds according to religious customs. This mutual pilfering between reality TV and social and religious customs re-enchants modernity – to use Weber's language – and demonstrates cultural acceptable forms of *métissage*.

In the Arab world and elsewhere in the non-West, television contributes to socio-cultural hybridization, the selective incorporation of foreign values and styles that I explored at length in my previous book (Kraidy 2005). By being culturally hybrid, by challenging regnant social and political norms and by compelling viewer participation, reality TV has pushed the boundaries of the permissible in public discourse. Throughout the Arab world, the reality TV culture wars have opened a space for suppressed desires, dissenting views and taboo topics, expanding the range of permissible speech, actions and identities, renewing public life and helping to elaborate what being modern means in the Arab world today. This elaboration is constantly in progress, because 'modernity is not only a space or a state one enters into or from which one emigrates…it is a situation of unending transit in which the uncertainty of what it means to be modern is never eliminated. To radicalize the project of modernity is to sharpen and renew this uncertainty, to create new possibilities to modernity always to be able to be something different and something more.' (García-Canclini 1994: 268) The multiple and variegated Arab experiences with modernity remind Arabs daily that the elsewhere of modernity is, in fact, one's own home.

Acknowledgement

Initially published as 'Reality TV and Multiple Modernities in the Arab World: A Theoretical Exploration' in the *Middle East Journal of Culture and Communication,* 1(1), pp. 49–59.

Notes

1. I will discuss the Saudi intellectual wars over modernity in the book project from which this chapter is drawn. Not much Saudi writing on modernity is available in English or French.
2. Three persons who worked on MBC's *Big Brother/Al-Ra'is* shared this information with me on the condition of anonymity.
3. For gender issues, see Doumato (1992); for discussions focuses on media, see Kraidy, (2006b, 2007).
4. 'Al-Haqiqa', Arabic for 'The Truth', *is* one word.
5. The French original is: 'il faut de plus en plus produire des manifestations pour la télévision, c'est-à-dire des manifestations qui soient de nature a intéresser les gens de télévision étant donné ce qui sont leurs catégories de perception, et qui, relayées, amplifiées par eux, recevront leur pleine efficacité' (author's translation).
6. Updating the framework proposed in Dayan and Katz (1992).

References

Al-Baba, Hakam (2005), 'The Camera Rules the World: Star Academy for Arab Leaders', *Al-Quds Al-'Arabi*, 6 April (Arabic).

Al-Bushr, Badreiah (2005), 'Star Academy's Democracy', *Asharq Al-Awsat*, 19 April (Arabic).

Andrejevic, M. (2004), *Reality TV: The Work of Being Watched*, Lanham, MD: Rowman & Littlefield.

Appadurai, A. (1996), *Modernity at Large: Cultural Dimensions of Globalization,* Minneapolis: University of Minnesota Press.

Bourdieu, Pierre (1996), *Sur la télévision*. Paris: Raisons d'Agir Éditions.

Couldry, Nick (2003), *Media Rituals*, London: Routledge.

Dayan, D. and Katz, E. (1992), *Media Events: The Live Broadcasting of History*, Cambridge, MA: Harvard University Press.

Doumato, E.A. (1992), 'Gender, Monarchy and National Identity in Saudi Arabia', *British Journal of Middle Eastern Studies,* 19(1), pp. 31–47.

García-Canclini, N. (1994), *Hybrid Cultures: Strategies for Entering and Leaving Modernity,* Minneapolis: University of Minnesota Press.

—— (1998), *Consumers and Citizens: Multicultural Conflicts in Globalization,* Minneapolis: University of Minnesota Press.

Gelvin, James (1999), 'Modernity *and* Its Discontents: On the Durability of Nationalism in the Arab Middle East', *Nations and Nationalisms*, 5(1), pp. 71–89.
Giddens, Anthony (1990), *The Consequences of Modernity*, Cambridge: Polity Press.
Gruzinski, S. (1999), *La pensée métisse*, Paris: Fayard.
Guaybess, Tourya (2003), 'De l'état émetteur a l'émetteur état dans le champ télévisuel Égyptien', in F. Mermier (ed.), *Mondialisation et nouveaux médias dans l'espace arabe*, Paris: Maisonneuve et Larose, pp. 103–23.
Hervieu-Léger, Danièle (2003), 'Pour une sociologie des "modernités religieuses multiples": une autre approche de la "religion invisible" des sociétés européennes', *Social Compass*, 50(3), pp. 287–95.
Hill, Annette (2005). *Reality TV: Audiences and Popular Factual Television*, London: Routledge.
Kaya, I. (2004), 'Modernity, Openness, Interpretation: A Perspective on Multiple Modernities', *Social Science Information*, 43(1), pp. 35–47.
Kolakowski, Leszek (1997), *Modernity on Endless Trial*, Chicago: University of Chicago Press.
Kraidy, M.M. (2005), *Hybridity, or the Cultural Logic of Globalization*, Philadelphia, PA: Temple University Press.
—— (2006a), 'Reality TV and Politics in the Arab World (Preliminary Observations)', *Transnational Broadcasting Studies* (peer-reviewed paper edition) 2(1), pp. 7–28; electronic version available, http://www.tbsjournal.com/Kraidy.html. Accessed 8 June 2009.
—— (2006b), 'Governance and Hypermedia in Saudi Arabia', *First Monday*, 11(9), available http://firstmonday.org/issues/ special11_9/kraidy/index.html. Accessed 8 June 2009.
—— (2007), 'Saudi Arabia, Lebanon, and the Changing Arab Information Order', *International Journal of Communication*, 1(1), pp. 139–56, available http://ijoc.org/ojs/index.php/ijoc/article/view/18/22. Accessed 9 June 2009.
—— (2009, forthcoming), *Reality Television and Arab Politics: Contention in Public Life*. Cambridge: Cambridge University Press.
Le Guay, Damien (2005), *L'empire de la télé-réalité, ou comment accroitre le 'temps de cerveau humain disponible'*, Paris: Presses de le Renaissance.
Schneidermann, Daniel (2004), *Le cauchemar médiatique*, Paris: Denoel/Folio documents.
Street, J. (1997). *Politics and Popular Culture*, Philadelphia, PA: Temple University Press.
Taylor, C. (1999), 'Two Theories of Modernity', *Public Culture*, 11(1), p. 168.
Toumson, R. (1998), *Mythologie du métissage*, Paris: Presses Universitaires de France.
Watenpaugh, Keith David (2006), *Being Modern in the Middle East: Revolution, Nationalism, Colonialism, and the Arab Middle Class*, Princeton, NJ: Princeton University Press.

Chapter 3

When TV Formats are Translated

Albert Moran

Introduction

For almost a century, radio and especially television broadcasting have been highly significant in shaping and renewing national bonds (Scannell 1996; Hilmes 2003). This has certainly been the case on the island continent of Australia, where television has addressed a predominantly white population in terms of assumed commonalities of language, culture, politics and history (Moran 2004). In short, television has been the means by which a nation has been able to communicate with itself about itself. Recent developments have unsettled and arguably reshaped this relationship. Globalization, for instance, is said to have led to the growing powerlessness of nation states (Lash and Urry 1987; Ohmae 1990; Julius 1990; Horsman & Marshall 1994). Others, however, counter the claim that governmental, financial and cultural authority have moved upwards to more supranational entities and downwards to local formations (Hirst and Thompson 1995; Weiss 1998; Price 2002), insisting on the continued relevance of the nation state as a political, cultural and economic actor. In any case, just how the recent world economic downturn and the emergence of national protectionist policies play out so far as the sovereignty sof nation states is concerned remains to be seen.

This dilemma strikes various contributors to this collection. Hence, for example, Chapter 12 by Gabriele Cosentino, Waddick Doyle and Dimitrina Todorova adopts this optic of the reconfiguration of the nation state and its institutions (including television) as a means of understanding the takeup of the television news parody genre show *Tearing Up the news.* On the other hand, a different scenario is implicit in Chapter 4 by Silvio Waisbord and Sonia Jalfin. These two authors affirm that television in Argentina continues to be understood by producers and audiences in terms of a national belonging and identity, no matter how exclusive and monolithic that cultural projection happens to be. Milly Buonanno (2009), in her recent book concerning television, has addressed the phenomenon of television in terms that throw light on this and other dilemmas yielded up by the technology and institution. According to Buonanno, television is not to be understood in exclusive dualistic terms – whether these be that of the private/public, the generalist/specialist or the national or global/local. These frictions are embodied partly in the phenomenon of finished and format programs themselves. The former category has, of course, to do with a program devised, produced and broadcast in one territory which is delivered elsewhere for transmission to other populations. When it plays in foreign-language territories, the imported program can be domesticated up to a point by dubbing or subtitling. Under the format program system, a program is devised, produced and broadcast in one territory. Subsequently, the program's format is distributed as a set of services or franchised knowledges, which allow the program to be remade for transmission in another market. As part of this adaptation, the program is customized in such a way as to seem local or indigenous in origin. As Tunstall (2008) has pointed out: 'Most people around the world prefer to be entertained by people who look the same, talk the same, joke the same, behave the same, play the same games, and have the same beliefs (and worldview) as themselves...they also overwhelmingly prefer their own national news, politics, weather, and football and other sports'. (2008: xiv)

In the emerging mix of broadcast and post-broadcast television, the national look and feel of many programs appear to be as important as ever. The institution strives to make its programs relevant for domestic audiences whether those programs are derived from elsewhere or produced locally. A key element is that local production as it applies to format franchising has to do with the decision-making process, involving a travelling consultant producer and local program production teams. This chapter explores this situation of choice-making, where formats are licensed, adapted and produced in national television production industries. It is based on interviews with consultant specialists attached to international TV format licensing companies, who have extensive experience with the startup of format adaptations in different national production industries.

The analysis uses general elements of literary translation theory to frame discussion. It is divided into five parts. The first suggests connections between the literary translator and the visiting production consultant. The next section examines the situation where a kind of literal translation arises thanks to a licensing company insisting that no customizing or indigenization of a format occurs. Usually, though, there is a recognition of the need for more creative local involvement in adapting a format to suit local taste. Accordingly, the third part of the chapter traces joint decision-making processes having to do with what might be called the 'linguistic code' level of format adaptation. This is followed by consideration of a broader level concerning 'intertextual codes' of format indigenizing. The next part focuses on negotiated format adaptation at a still broader level of 'cultural codes'. The conclusion summarizes the argument concerning localization, considers the significance of the analysis and suggests complementary lines of investigation that might be followed in any future inquiry.

The search for an adaptation model

Television program format remaking finds endless parallels and echoes across the humanities and social sciences. Elsewhere, with Michael Keane, I have edited a collection having to do with cultural adaptation across what might be called the culture industries or the creative industries (Moran and Keane 2009, 2010). Several writers in such areas as structuralist anthropology, semiotics, linguistics and philosophical theory have addressed the matter of cultural transformation, and have attempted to develop what I have called both categorical and relational models of adaptation. However, this level of model-building frequently runs the risk of abstraction and idealism. For the time being at least, it seems preferable to approach TV format remaking at a more concrete middle-range level in terms of using categories drawn from the self-understanding of some of those involved in the process of format adaptation. This chapter is, therefore, especially concerned with the figure of the producer consultant sent by a licensing company to assist the licensee company in another territory.

As part of their franchising operation, global copyright owners of formats typically provide the services of a 'travelling' specialist. Working with a local counterpart – whether in the shape of an individual or a team – this visitor will help fashion a national, customized version of the program package. Usually, the consultant has had a good deal of background in the startup of new versions of the format program, is experienced in common problems besetting the teething stage of production, and is concerned to help the new version of the format program repeat its success in other territories. Consultancy of this kind means carrying specific production know-how, valuable industrial experience, and a specialized awareness of production organization and routines to all corners of the world. The figure is an envoy from head office, mediating between the competing demands of maintaining the crucial elements of the program format while also customizing these for local audiences. This kind of television gatekeeping is relatively recent, although the general type of cultural decision-maker has a longer pedigree. In particular, this kind of adaptation has affinities with the activity of literary translation of cultural texts from one language to another (Venuti 1995). In the same way that those involved in the television production of a format adaptation must decide between adhering tightly to a format and varying it to suit local situations, so a translator must balance the need to respect the source with that of serving the reader of the translation (Biguemet and Schulte 1990). Thus, a more ancient translator can offer advice that is relevant to the decision-making of a modern television consultant producer:

> I do not always stick to the author's words, nor even to his thoughts. I keep the effect he wanted to produce in mind, and then I arrange the material after the fashion of our time. Different times do not just require different words, but also different thoughts, and ambassadors usually dress in the fashion of the country they are sent to, for fear of appearing ridiculous in the eyes of the people they try to please. (Perrot d'Ablancount, quoted in Lefevere 1993: 6)

However, television adaptation is more multi-tasked and labour intensive than is the frequently more solitary task of translating a written text. A visiting consultant needs to act collaboratively with local production personnel. Who, then, makes the key decisions regarding elements of an adaptation? Where is the final authority situated on these matters? How is a fidelity to source interwoven with a desire for audience accessibility? The general answer to the query of whether the licensing company or the licensor company has control of key decisions seems to be that both are usually important. The travelling consultant has extensive knowledge of the format and its inception in other places, the likely pitfalls and difficulties as well as potential triumphs and successes. National production personnel, whether in the form of individuals or teams, have a more intimate sense of the local audience culture, a greater intuitive sense of what will be suitable for viewers. Adapting and producing a TV format is usually an interactive process involving ongoing negotiation between the visiting consultant specialist and a local producer and production team.

Although the consultant producer is referred to in the singular as a sole ambassador or envoy who undertakes such consultation, several figures may fulfil this role. For example, with the Indian version of *Who Wants to Be a Millionaire?*, which was licensed from Celador in the United Kingdom and went to air on Star TV as *Kaun Banega Crorepati*, there was more interaction between more figures in the original setting up of the adaptation (Thomas and Kumar 2004). To maintain the success of the program, and to enhance the value of the brand and the franchise, Celador put a great deal of work into the collaborative activity of producing the Indian version of the program. Three staff were sent out from the London office to India to train the local production team. In turn, four Indians went to the United Kingdom for further training (Spencer 2006).

At the same time, however, the international adaptation of *Who Wants to Be a Millionaire?*, including its Indian incarnation as *Kaun Banega Crorepati*, involved an exceptional situation repeated with the international adaptation of only one other TV format, *The Weakest Link* (Jarvis 2006; Spenser 2006). In both cases, the licensed owners of the formats – Celador with *Who Wants to Be a Millionaire?* and the BBC with *The Weakest Link* – insisted that adaptations follow a highly standardized formula so far as the form and style of the shows were concerned. This kind of decision-making regarding different national adaptations, where local input and inflection are discounted entirely, is unique in the international TV format business – although cases have occurred elsewhere in the culture industries. Burston (2000, 2009), for example, has reported a parallel process of international reproduction of cultural lookalikes in the case of large-scale live musical theatre. One consultant producer explained the general situation of deliberate TV format program copycatting as follows:

> A fairly recent phenomenon…has been a stipulation that absolutely nothing is changed. If you watch [versions of] *The Weakest Link* from around the world they are absolutely identical. Under the format of the BBC they go to great lengths to insist that everything is exactly as the episode produced in the UK is. And the only place where they have had much variation on that is the USA. I suspect that is because the US producers have a lot more financial clout when faced with a situation of 'Either we change this or we change the show'. I can't see anybody standing up to that. In the show 'bible' it's specified down to the two-tone colours of the backdrops. (Cousins 2006)

However, these instances of lookalike adaptations, where a particular model is standardized and no allowance is made for local sensibility or sensitivity, are the exception rather than the rule. In fact, this course of action may be a strategy where matters of legal protection of the franchise property override local cultural considerations. The thinking appears to be that format owners are in a better legal position to challenge perceived infringement in different jurisdictions if their own adaptations adhere closely to the same formula (Cousins 2006; Spenser 2006).

In any case, it is clear how this particular practice of adaptation fits into the model being developed. With the *Who Wants to Be a Millionaire?* and *The Weakest Link* format adaptations, what is required in any particular remake in any territory is a repeat of the original version of the program. Head office has taken this crucial decision, and the consultant producer must follow this course of action – as must local production personnel. The objective is to produce an equivalent or literal translation of the original (Lotman 1990). With this kind of conversion or translation, each new adaptation of either program was intended to bear a close resemblance to the original version. A literal translation emphasizes a high degree of fidelity to an original, even if this new version makes little concession to the interests and taste of a new audience. In fact, in the case of *The Weakest Link* particularly, this insistence on closely following the UK original may have had fairly immediate and unwelcome consequences. Different versions of the program in different national territories, including the United States and Australia, saw spectacular beginnings so far as the early popularity of the program was concerned. This was, though, rapidly succeeded by an equally sudden drop-off in viewership, followed soon afterwards by the program's cancellation (Spenser 2006).

Elsewhere, I have labelled this kind of format program remaking situation a 'closed' adaptation (Moran 1998: 190–210). This situation of format adaptation is exceptional. Usually, a more 'open' adaptation is tolerated, or even welcomed. Consultants are given a good deal of autonomy in decision-making and there is likely to be far more equitable collaboration with local production personnel. To recall the words of the translator quoted above, TV format remakes are deliberately arranged to 'dress in the fashion of the country they are sent to, for fear of appearing ridiculous in the eyes of the people they try to please'. Frequently, in fact, the judgement and decision-making of local production personnel will increasingly be trusted over time. Stephen Freeman (1996), who has been a much-travelled consultant producer specialist on game shows for franchise owner King World, spoke about this respect and trust:

> In Australia and New Zealand, Grundy sublicensed *Wheel of Fortune* from us. Recently, when they changed the host, they cleared it with us. It's really just like a handshake and so long as the integrity of the format is unchanged and there's no legal problem as far as changing the game or the premise or format, we have no problem with that. In many cases the cultural side of it dictates minor changes and we have to agree that they know what they are doing in their own culture.

'Linguistic-code' translation

If translation theory helps delineate between the figure of the translator, the general process of translation and the translated work as the outcome of the activity, so others have sought to identify various levels in the translation process. Thus, Romy Heylen (1994) has suggested a tripartite scheme for understanding levels of activity in relation to a literary or written work (1994: 10–22). These are seen to range from the more elementary to the more complex levels of text, and involve linguistic codes, intertextual codes and cultural codes. This is a suggestive set of ideas that can help frame the discussion of the adaptation process relating to TV formats.

Of course, television programs do not operate with linguistic codes in the same way that literary texts do. Instead, the poetics of television are located in matters of form and style, with the latter consisting of staging, shooting or filming, editing and sound (Bordwell and Thompson 2004; Thompson 2004). These categories are complex, and involve numerous individual elements that can be manipulated. At this level, the adaptation of a program format will involve one or more of these television codes in a relatively simple operation of omission, inclusion, substitution or permutation. I have already quoted from consultant Stephen Freeman regarding Grundy's decision to change the figure of the host for the Australian version of *Wheel of Fortune*. Clearly, the action is one of substitution, wherein one element of the format is replaced by an equivalent element.

Colour is another component of television's *mise en scène* that is frequently deemed to be nationally sensitive in game shows and other format genres. Again, this matter may necessitate necessary cultural decision-making on the part of consultant producer and local production personnel in order to give a program a recognizable 'look' so far as domestic audiences are concerned. Referring to the production of different national versions of game shows, another adaptation specialist, Bob Cousins of FremantleMedia, explained:

> As a guy who goes around the world doing startup game shows, my view and our company's view is that shows need to look like they come from that country, and...there's also sensitivities of a cultural nature, mainly in colour. The show that you see in Sweden, if you take the same show to South Africa the colours have to be very different. If you look at episodes of *Family Feud* in Mexico and Venezuela, the number of hues is huge, the number and intensity. If you looked at *Sale of the Century* from Mexico, the number of colours is huge compared with a European production. We take the view that people in their own country know what they like best, that's why we have local production teams. (Cousins 2006)

However, localizing a format adaptation may require more than a stylistic alteration here and there, such as changing host or varying colours. Here, for example, is a description of an Italian version of what was originally a German game show, *Man O Man*. The outline clearly describes the stylistic and formal elaboration that the format underwent so as to 'Italianize' it:

> *Beato Tra Le Donne* is taped in summer in the Bandiera Gialla (Yellow Flag) discotheque in the fashionable Adriatic resort town of Rimini, and thus the program refers to a particular setting, time and mood. The setting is that of the beach and the sea, the time is the summer holiday season, and the mood is one of enjoyment, escape and carnival. Throughout this version, there is a consistent emphasis on the female body as a site of display and sexual attraction. The Italian title translates as (heavenly) happiness among women. In a country with a deep and complex Catholic heritage, the title conjures up a sense of the blissful and beatific completeness constituted by women, and this is confirmed in the program's imagery and action. The set is the largest of any version with a constant feeling of endless space and there is much exuberant camera work. The utopian plenitude suggested in the title is confirmed by the size of the studio audience, consisting of around 1,000 women. Some 200 of these form the program's jury – the largest, most physically attractive with the lowest-cut dresses of any of the juries. Similarly the hostesses, who double as dancers, are more numerous than their counterparts and their costumes and dance actions further emphasize their sexual attractiveness. The imagery invokes the aura of light entertainment and show business…and the succession of comedians, singers and dancers de-emphasizes the competitive elements of the format. But the imagery also invokes the sea as a site of pleasure and escape, a kind of secular utopia. *Beato* has a marked elongatory rhythm. The program is slow to eliminate its large number of contestants and thus is slow to allow males to become focii of attention. Instead, by limiting the number of male activities in each round, *Beato Tra Le Donne…*allows for a repeated number of sequences of jury women voting and hostesses dunking the unsuccessful males. The final round and the individual male victory receive relatively little attention in these two versions – indeed, *Beato* begins its final credits before the winner is acclaimed. (Moran 1998: 144)

Many other examples of variations in the television codes involved in a format adaptation might be cited. However, the kind of differentiation involved at this level is clear enough so that there is little need to offer further instances. Instead, it is worth ending this part of the analysis by noting that, with the exception of a handful of standardized formats, variation in television codes is almost constantly necessary as a means of helping to customize remakes. As Freeman (1996) notes above, the company in a particular territory knows what it is doing when it decides to modify elements of a universal format to suit the needs of a local audience. However, within the international television industry, there is recognition that this authorization to vary cannot become a blank cheque. As Graham Spenser (2006) points out: 'Too much cultural tinkering ends up with a very bland show which, because of that, will fail.'

'Intertextual-code' translation

The manipulation of intertextual elements in an adaptation is another matter entirely. These are not necessarily as discrete or self-contained as those discussed in the last section.

Intertextual elements appear to connect with specific bodies of knowledge held by particular communities. They are more varied in scope and more tangled in their relationships, so that their orchestration can set in train other necessary changes in and around a format adaptation. At least four different sets of intertextual elements can come into play so far as the customization of a TV format for a particular territory is concerned.

One set of intertextual codes has to do with television production industries themselves. TV formats carry the imprint of the institutions wherein they were first devised and developed. Frequently, the adaptation and production of a format will necessitate a significant readjustment in a national television production milieu. Organizational norms, routines and practices that have perhaps been traditional to a local television production industry may have to readjust to a different regime that is more international, 'modern' and mainstream. The consultant producer may be pivotal in effecting such a change. This point about having to readjust local production conditions to help facilitate the production of a format adaptation was raised repeatedly in interviews. It underlines the point that the licensing of a format from elsewhere may trigger a cross-cultural exchange that begins with the readjustment of ways of working in television, whether by camera operator, editor, writer or others.

Hence, Bob Cousins talked about visiting Uzbekistan to set up a production adaptation of *Family Feud* and discovering in the process that he needed to teach a camera operator how to frame master and other shots. By the same token, when Grundy World Wide (now merged into FremantleMedia) was producing a Spanish version of *Sale of the Century* by shooting in a television studio in Madrid, the visiting producer sent from Australia found it impossible to make the five episodes a day that were customary in Australia and elsewhere in the English-speaking world of television. Daytime temperatures at that time of the year in the studios under lights in Madrid were as high as 50 degrees Celsius. In such hot conditions, cameras simply ceased to function. Initially, Bill Mason, the visiting producer, was forced to make the program according to local practice – one episode at a time. However, as executive producer in charge of the production, he realized that temperatures cooled considerably at night. This enabled him to introduce a new production regime in line with the one with which he was familiar. Production was rescheduled for the late night and this enabled five episodes to be completed at a time. As Mason (1998) put it: 'If we take *Sale of the Century* to a new country, we are probably going to train people in that country in a new system of making TV. In the past they have made one or two episodes a day so the first leap is to make five in a day. It's important to have a role model so the set designers, electricians, camera operators, all the technical people have got a model to work from.'

A second type of intertextual codes, or factors that need to be addressed, arises in part as a result of technical necessities intermeshed with personal choices. Consultant Graham Spenser (2006) offered one such instance drawn from the experience of setting up national productions of particular game shows:

> Finding the right level of contestants is the next step. The computers' people have usually never seen this stuff before and we have to hold their hands, and also the electronics. The sets and hostess dresses are often chosen by the network, which has some favourite ideas and colours, but they have to agree with the skin tones.

A third branch of intertextual knowledge that can come into play has to do with the particular mode or genre of a format and the localizing disposition it might entail. For example, Graham Spenser (2006) believes that game shows and single-issue talk programs are more international than other genres. With talk shows, though, it is a matter of 'how far you let the audience go with the subject'. Even with a game show, a good deal of preparation is essential to ensure a necessary accommodation between format and local culture. Various cultural screenings come into play. He put it like this:

> As far as the cultural differences are concerned its important to realize that the questions are totally different from one culture to another. They are not just translated. Historical facts vary from country to country. So you have to quickly start to make a questions data bank which is accurate for that country, and have it verified and checked again. We use two or three sources to make sure we have the facts right. Then you audition the contestants using those questions because we want a new standard and some idea of what it will be. The writers will need some trial and error to find a level at which some questions are answered correctly but some not. The aim of the show is to get all the audience to get 50 per cent of the questions correct, so that the involvement factor is high. Finding the right level of contestants is the next step.

A further type of intertextual code can come into play because of the genre of the program being adapted for a particular territory. A drama series seems to offer greater latitude for cultural variation than does a game show (Moran 1998). For example, various local factors intervened between 1990 and 1995 to introduce new inflections into Dutch and German remakes of several drama serials which had originally been devised, developed and produced in Australia (Moran 1998). This was despite deliberate production decisions to adhere, with only minor variations, to the original Australian scripts translated into Dutch or German. Unavoidable shifts began to occur in the adaptations. Ray Kolle (1995), an experienced scriptwriter and devisor from Grundy's Australian office, explained the way that production casting could have a significant effect on drama serial adaptations:

> The show in Holland based on *The Restless Years*, for a long time they tried to hold it to just translating the original scripts. But they found that they couldn't after a period of time. Sometimes quite different characters rise to prominence. In Australia there may be a character who seems dominant due to casting. But you may not find such a strong actor in another culture...other characters, who were minor here, become more dynamic because of the casting, which changes the emphasis too. In the German version of *Sons*

> *and Daughters*, the twins are much more dynamic and Pat the Rat is just a minor character. Here [in Australia], it became the 'Pat the Rat' show but I don't think the German version will.

'Cultural-code' translation

The third level of elements affecting adaptation, and the localization or otherwise of a format, involves that combination of factors that make for communal and national difference. Broadly, these have to do with matters of language, ethnicity, history, religion, geography and culture. This combination of social factors is dealt with here under the collective name of 'cultural codes'. Irrespective of the genre involved, a format program will carry particular situations, figures, subject-matter and issues. The extent to which these will be recognizable and acceptable within particular cultural settings may vary considerably. Hence, Graeme Spenser saw no reason why *Survivor* would not work in Asia and the Middle East, even though no broadcaster in these regions had acquired the licence. After all, he pointed out, *Who Wants to Be a Millionaire?* did enormously well in India. Frequently, though, regional or local culture will deem specific subjects and situations to be taboo and will not entertain them on local television screens. One dramatic case in point was the Middle Eastern version of *Big Brother*, which was broadcast to several national territories in the region. In Lebanon, according to Spenser, the local French influence allowed for a more tolerant reception but in Saudi Arabia there was great anger and outcry:

> A Middle Eastern broadcasting company which was a [target for] outrage even after it tried to be as 'culturally sensitive' as possible by respecting the religious issues, having Islamic and Hindu. And there was no question of boys sleeping with girls. But even so, the result was that just the interaction in that hothouse atmosphere was somehow culturally wrong and the station was forced to pull it due to massive viewer outrage. (Spenser 2006)

Gender relations and public behaviours can be another area of cultural sensitivity so far as format adaptation is concerned. A case in point was the relative failure of *The Weakest Link* when the format was adapted in Asia. With its domineering female quiz compere, this format presented an insoluble dilemma for its adaptation for that region. On the one hand, both the format owner and its Asian licensees wanted to retain intact the central ingredient of the dominant woman compere. On the other hand, such a figure had no cultural resonance in that part of the world. As Spenser (2006) put it:

> There are formats…which are fashionable, and everyone wants them, but cannot work. For instance, *The Weakest Link*. It was big on the BBC so the Asian nations all wanted it. But the dominant woman was a problem in Asia, and the encouragement of the contestants

> to put each other down and vote each other off, cause each other to lose face, is an issue for the Asian nations. So after one season, it was usually taken off. You cannot change the loss of face element in *The Weakest Link*. You do away with that sort of dominatrix and subservience that is its central structure.

Reality programs and game shows are not the only kinds of format programs capable of affronting religious custom and tradition. Dramatic narratives and situations may also cause offence and generate controversy. In the early 1990s, Grundy World Wide had developed a telenovela for Chilean television based on a successful Australian format, *Sons and Daughters*. This was the Australian company's first venture into what was for it a foreign genre. Unlike *Big Brother*, the would-be adaptation did not go to air because its apparent cultural incompatibility with social mores operating in the territory had registered during an earlier phase of audience testing. As one of the storyliners put it:

> The Chilean drama fell through because they did a focus group on it and the audience reacted with great shock at the hint of romance between brother and sister, the basic *Sons and Daughters* story. The twins that had been separated [at birth] meet as adults and fall in love. The focus group felt that the audience in Chile [would] tend to react as the government think they should react, being a very Catholic country. And the channel withdrew it. (Kolle 1995)

In fact, at least one other cultural problem had arisen with the would-be adaptation, highlighting yet again the fact that localization must take critical account of the national culture that it seeks to enter:

> Another problem was one of the twins whisking the girl off on her wedding day, a la *The Graduate*. But it fell apart because in Chile…they get married legally a day or two before the big ceremony. And so he couldn't bundle her off in her wedding gown. Chile is surprisingly European but the attitude of men to women is still very chauvinist and this also affected the Pat the Rat character. (Kolle 1995)

This discussion of the third broad level of format translation has focused on cultural codes. These come into play when a program is being adapted for particular local audiences. What might be called translation failures are instances where sensitivity concerning the national culture might have suggested that no format adaptation should have occurred in the first place. However, these TV program adaptation mishaps are exceptional instances. More usually, successful localization does occur with formats. One example can be cited to round out this discussion. Attempting to explain the 1990s success of the Polish adaptation of the 1950s US television sitcom *The Honeymooners*, consultant specialist Bob Cousins tended to emphasize a set of temporal elements. On the one hand, he detected a kind of universally appealing situation that made the format seem timeless and eternally appealing to the female part of the general audience. At the same time, though, there were perhaps other elements in the program that gave it more contemporary resonance with the larger historical situation of post-communism Poland in the 1990s.

However, the success or otherwise of a localized format adaptation lies not so much in the efforts, sensitivities and actions of those involved in the remaking process – whether as visiting producers or as local production teams – but resides instead in the eyes of the national viewing public. It is the local audience that forms the most relevant yardstick so far as deciding about the degree of localization that a format has undergone. Cousins told a story wherein the localization of *The Honeymooners*' format seemed so complete as to persuade one of the members of the home audience that the Polish program was not an adaptation based on an overseas format import, but rather a program that was completely indigenous and homegrown to Polish culture:

> I was talking to a continuity girl and I said, 'Have you watched *The Honeymooners*?' And she said, 'Of course, it's very funny. I watch it every week. Why are you interested?' So I said that the company licensed out the scripts and she said, 'No, no, this is a Polish show.' This is the greatest accolade when they believe one of our shows is 'local'. (Cousins 2006)

Conclusion

The rapid growth in the worldwide flow of TV program formats highlights the onset of a new era in television broadcasting. Considered from a business point of view, this development suggests the increasing integration of national television industries into a global television system. Yet, more than ever, television viewers seek to watch programs that look and sound familiar and speak to them about the world they know. They insist on the continued relevance of the national, even if television producers and broadcasters fashion that imagining to their own ends. In fact, the practice of localizing TV formats addresses this need and signals that national cultures are as important as ever in television. This chapter has sought to interrogate the process of adaptation and production of format-based programs as a crucial site where global business rubs up against national cultural imaginings. Such a crossing of paths is symbolized in the interaction between a visiting consultant and local production personnel involved in remaking a format for a national audience. I have suggested that this process of transformation is usefully understood in terms of cultural translation. Such a metaphor helps clarify elements of the overall situation. One set of distinctions suggested by translation theory has to do with the demarcation between the translator, the translation process and the artefact that results from such an activity. The chapter has concentrated on the first and second of these elements, but clearly further analysis is necessary even on these.

In the case of television format adaptation and production, the translator is a composite figure. While the travelling consultant is important, so too are key national personnel who decide to license, adapt and produce a format program in the first place. Translation theory also talks of a set of possibilities so far as a translation is concerned, ranging from a closed, literal remaking to a more open, 'poetic' rendering. The chapter has investigated both types in a general way, but only within a range of sanctioned possibilities having to do with the licensing of a format for adaptation. Further inquiry into the even more open, poetic prospects made available (and even necessary) when the remaking has not been authorized deserves extended consideration.

Finally, drawing on other elements of translation theory, the chapter has attempted to distinguish three levels in the program adaptation process. This is very provisional and may ultimately be replaced by more empirical categories ranging from the less inclusive to the more inclusive. Overall, however, there is no doubting the fact that the micro situation of TV program format adaptation and production offers significant opportunity to explore just how the global comes together with the local in the domain of television format programming.

References

Biguemet, John and Schulte, Rainer (eds) (1990), *The Craft of Translation*, Chicago: University of Chicago Press.

Bordwell, David and Thompson, Kristin (2004), *Film Art: An Introduction*, New York: McGraw Hill.

Buonanno, Milly (2009), *The Age of Television*, Bristol: Intellect.

Burston, Jonathan (2000), 'Spectacle, Synergy and Megamusicals: The Global Industrialisation of Live Theatrical Production', in James Curran (ed.), *Media Organisation and Society*, New York: Oxford University Press, pp. 44–63.

Burston, Jonathan (2009), 'Recombinant Broadway, in A. Moran and M. Keane (eds), 'Cultural Adaptation', special issue of *Continuum: Journal of Media and Cultural Studies*, 23(3).

Cousins, Bob (2006), Interview with Albert Moran, FremantleMedia, London.

Freedman, Steven (1996), Interview with Albert Moran, King World, Los Angeles.

Heylen, Romy (1994), *Translation Poetics and the Stage: Six French Hamlets*, London: Routledge.

Hilmes, M. (2003), *The TV History Book*, London: BFI.

Hirst, P. and Thompson, G. (1995), *Globalisation in Question: The International Economy and the Possibilities of Governance*, Cambridge: Polity Press.

Horsman, M. and Marshall, A. (1994), *After the Nation State*, London: HarperCollins.

Jarvis, Colin (2006), Interview with Albert Moran, BBC Worldwide, London.

Julius, D. (1990), *Global Companies and Public Policy*, London: RIIA Printers.

Kolle, Ray (1995), Interview with Albert Moran, Grundy Television, Sydney.

Lefevere, Andre (1993), 'Introduction', in A. Lefevere (ed.), T*ranslation/History/Culture*, London: Routledge, pp. 1–25.

Lash, S. and Urry, J. 1987, *The End of Organised Capitalism*, Cambridge: Polity Press.

Lotman, Yuri (1990), *Universe of the Mind: A Semiotic Theory of Culture*, Bloomington, IN: Indiana University Press.

Mason, Bill (1998), Interview with Albert Moran, Grundy Television, London.

Moran, Albert (1998), *Copycat Television: Globalisation, Program Formats and Cultural Identity*, Luton: University of Luton Press.

—— (2004), 'Australia', in Horace Newcomb (ed.), *The Museum of Broadcasting Communications Encyclopedia of Television*, 2nd rev. ed., London: Taylor and Francis, pp. 173–80.

Moran, Albert and Keane, Michael (eds) (2009), 'Cultural Adaptation', special issue of *Continuum: Journal of Media and Cultural Studies*, 23(3).

—— (2010), *Cultural Adaptation*, New York: Routledge (Forthcoming).

Ohmae, K. (1990), *The Borderless World*, London: Collins.

Price, M.E. (2002), *Media and Sovereignty: The Global Information Revolution and Its Challenge to State Power*, Cambridge, MA: MIT Press.

Scannell, Paddy (1996), *Radio, Television and Everyday Life: A Phenomenological Approach*, Cambridge: Blackwell.

Spenser, Graham (2006), Interview with Albert Moran, London.

Thomas, A.O. and Kumar, K.J. (2004), 'Copied from Without and Cloned from Within: India in the Global Television Format Business', in A. Moran and M. Keane (eds), *Television Across Asia: Television Industries, Programme Formats and Globalization,* London: Taylor and Francis, pp. 122–37.

Thompson, Kristin (2004), *Storytelling in Film and Television*, Cambridge, MA: Harvard University Press.

Tunstall, Jeremy (2008), *The Media Were American: The US Mass Media in Decline*, Oxford: Oxford University Press.

Venuti, Lawrence (1995), *The Translator's Invisibility: A History of Translation*, London: Routledge.

Weiss, Linda (1998) *The Myth of the Powerless State*, Cambridge: Polity Press.

Chapter 4

Imagining the National: Television Gatekeepers and the Adaptation of Global Franchises in Argentina

Silvio Waisbord and Sonia Jalfin

The meanings of localization

For the past two decades, the concept of 'localization' has been central to analyses about media globalization (Hjarvard 2003). Like other concepts in the vast literature on globalization, localization eludes a straightforward definition. While anti-globalization writers refer to localization in terms of community self-reliance and movements to wrestle power away from global corporations (Hines 2003), media scholars have used localization in various ways. Localization alludes to the adaptation of global media content and formats to local factors as well as the persistence of 'local' cultures. It has been also used to describe the revitalization of local cultures and a commercial strategy to maximize profit in domestic media markets.

'Localization' has been central to criticisms of 'cultural imperialism' theories about the impact of media globalization, namely cultural homogenization and the dilution of local cultures. 'Localization' arguments suggest that the cultural consequences of globalization are complex, and cannot be predicted from cross-border movements of media capital and commodities. It is mistaken to predict that globalization inevitably results in the spread of unified media cultures worldwide and the loss of cultural uniqueness. Instead, global flows of media content and economics create more opportunities for interactions among local, national and supranational media and cultural processes. Many studies have demonstrated the persistence of 'the local' in the process of media and cultural creation and maintenance amidst globalization.

The literature on media globalization uses the concept of localization to discuss four distinct processes: glocalization, domestication, hybridization and local production.

First, localization has been absorbed in the neologism 'glocalization' (Robertson 1995), which is used to refer to 'the interpenetration of the global and the local, resulting in unique outcomes in different geographical areas' (Ritzer 2003: 193). It includes two processes: the flexibility of global media business to incorporate local factors, and the ability of local content to be expressed in global ideas and models. Several examples suggest how television producers adjust programming to meet local preferences and concerns to maximize audiences and profits (Chalaby 2005). Western media companies have adapted their programming and services to cultural themes promoted by the Chinese government to ensure smooth access to China's vast market (Fung 2008; Weber 2003).

Second, the term 'localization' has been used as synonymous with the 'domestication' or 'customization' of the international content. Media producers find ways to overcome the 'cultural discount' of international media content through strategies to make it less 'foreign' and thus closer to local audiences. Localization is expressed in various examples such as news coverage of 'global media events' focused on national and local angles and actors (Clausen 2004; Ruigrok and van Atteveldt 2007; van Leeuwen 2006), the adaptation of imported television programs and formats (Frau-Meigs 2006; Hetsroni 2005; Waisbord 2004a), the localization of video games (Mangiron and O'Hagan 2006) and consumer products and advertising (Jackson 2004; Prestholdt 2008).

Third, localization is central to the process of cultural hybridization: the blending of global and local cultural forms, the constant borrowing and meshing of styles and forms whose origins are geographically located in distant corners of the globe. Recent studies have stressed the significance of hybridization as a distinctive characteristic of contemporary cultural processes (Brah and Coombes 2000; García Canclini 1995). Cultural hybrids in the arts, architecture, cuisine, fashion and other cultural manifestations are certainly not new. For centuries, the synthesis of ideas and forms rooted in disparate cultures has been intrinsic to cross-border movements of goods and people. From religious syncretism to literary pastiches to architectonic mixtures, a various hybrids have resulted from global expansion, conquest, and migration. The recent wave of media globalization has accelerated cultural hybridization as it facilitates opportunities for vast numbers of people to encounter and incorporate media content produced outside their immediate communities. As expressed in a variety of cultural forms, hybridization is seemingly the dominant cultural form in today's globalized media cultures.

Fourth, localization also refers to the power of domestic media industries amidst the increasing complexity of media flows and economies. The presumed global juggernaut of Western companies neither eliminates local production nor simplifies global media flows. Rather, the affirmation of national industries and firms that produce substantial amount of audiovisual content and hold a leading position in national and geolinguistic markets demonstrates the strength of countervailing forces to global media behemoths (Banerjee 2002; Sinclair et al. 1996). The rise and consolidation of 'local champions' is a catalyst for the formation of multilayered media flows (Straubhaar 2007).

What drives localization? Several factors explain why localization has gained strength amidst media globalization. The search for profit leads global and domestic media companies to adjust business strategies and products to local interests and preferences. Protectionist policies push producers to adjust content to local considerations such as language and the utilization of domestic labour. Language, including accents and vernacular expressions, remains simultaneously a powerful unifier and divider that forces media producers to translate and adapt imported content. Hybridization reflects the dynamic nature of cultural production and the unpredictability of media consumption. Fuelled by political and identity-formation dynamics, localization represents both reactionary and progressive responses to reaffirm local uniqueness and pride against the onslaught of cultural globalization.

While we have reasonable explanations for why localization is central to contemporary media production and consumption and audience preferences (Straubhaar 2003), we still lack detailed analyses about how it happens. Plenty of anecdotes suggest that media producers 'localize' to make foreign content culturally resonant following vaguely defined 'rules of thumb'. Scholars have argued that 'cultural proximity' makes audiences more interested in media content that culturally resonates with their experiences. These insights, however, do not amount to grounded analysis about how media industries localize imported content, or theory-building about the significance of 'localization' in processes of cultural creation and renovation. How do foreign ideas metamorphose into domesticated cultural forms? What local references and sources are used to both erase foreignness and domesticate 'universal' content? What strategies are used to bridge the cultural distance between imported content and domestic audiences? What are the theoretical implications of localization as act of cultural (re)creation and maintenance of national identity and cultural belonging?

Our interest in this chapter is to discuss 'localization' as a set of industry practices during media production. In this sense, this study is positioned as a 'middle level' inquiry about the dynamics of global and local television (Moran and Keane 2006). As such, we aim to fill a gap in the literature about decision-making processes at the intersection of local and global media processes. The analysis deals with the domestication of imported programming formats in the Argentine television industry. As both importer and exporter of television program formats, the Argentine case offers plenty of experiences to examine the dynamics of localization. We focus on decisions made by television gatekeepers (including producers and writers) who are situated in a pre-eminent position as cultural mediators of the global traffic of television formats. Their decisions not only affect the viewing choices of audiences, but also outline national cultural boundaries.

In this chapter, our goal is to understand how television gatekeepers construct images of national audiences, and how those images inform decisions within the business constraints of the industry. Our argument is that television producers as 'cultural intermediaries' (Bourdieu 1984; Wright 2005) use a journalistic prism to localize content and make imported formats locally resonant. 'Journalistic prism' refers to a mode of sense-making of reality, a way of approaching television production informed by scanning news events as proxy for reality in order to assess audience interests and determine viable content. Like journalists, producers analyze local political, economic and cultural trends that may work as cultural markers in their shows. News and the analysis of current events are considered to localize content and define national audiences. The localization of television formats doesn't aim to be a form of journalism; instead, journalism offers a series of practices and procedures to interpret reality and make globalized programming relevant to domestic audiences.

Gatekeeping and localization in the television industry

We propose to approach television producers as 'gatekeepers' who transform imported content and formats into local productions. Originally used in media studies to describe the process through which information becomes news (Shoemaker and Reese 1991), the idea of 'gatekeeping' is appropriate to describe the organizational role of television producers in television industries.

As cultural gatekeepers between global flows and domestic audiences, they control the decision-making process that determines how foreign programs become 'localized' products.

A key question is how television producers select elements to locally anchor imported content. In principle, they have a broad cultural repertoire from which to draw ideas to domesticate program formats. National literature, historical narratives, folk arts, official heritage and symbols, and past media content offer possible references for localizing ideas. Localization is a nationalizing strategy in the sense that it aims to turn someone else's culture (e.g. programming formats) into a product that can be recognized as part of a specific national symbolic landscape. Put differently, the institutional reservoir of national culture offers ready-made references to bridge the gap between a foreign, decontextualized product and local audiences. Our analysis shows the use of a journalistic approach in the process of making imported programs locally relevant and contemporary.

Here we understand journalism as the reporting of news and information about contemporary happenings (Schudson 2003). We purposefully eschew normative definitions about journalism, whether in terms of its relationship with democracy and citizenship, or the quality and public relevance of its content. Instead, we embrace a minimalist definition focused on the unique tasks of journalism as a social institution that gathers and disseminates current news and information. Our interest is to emphasize the significance of journalism in building and maintaining a sense of cultural unification. Journalism essentially remains a local institution bounded by the concerns of local audiences, sources and advertisers. Thus, it maintains a close, immediate relation to specific localities, in the form of either the scope of coverage or the interests of audiences.

How does journalism build a sense of locality? Journalism constantly brings together a specific set of events and audiences within a given timeframe. It did so even before radio and television created mass 'media events' (Dayan and Katz 1992) that are simultaneously experienced by large, spatially scattered and culturally different audiences. The temporal dimension of news production and distribution is critical to the formation of publics who, despite a host of differences, share exposure to specific news and information. Journalism nurtures cultural commonness through regularly synchronizing content and publics. This idea is central to well-known arguments about the linkages between news and nationalism and democracy. It is found in Alexis de Tocqueville's idea that newspapers are key associations for democratic life because they 'put the same thought at the same time before a thousand readers' (1992: 489). It is also found in Benedict Anderson's (1983) argument about the role of news in creating 'unified fields of exchange' through simultaneously disseminating information to geographically dispersed readers.

Amidst the presumptive de-mediatization of contemporary societies and de-massification of media audiences, journalism retains the ability to select 'the issues of the day' and shape a sense of 'what's going on'. Television gatekeepers, we argue, resort to similar abilities. Like journalists, they analyze current events to determine their actuality and cultural relevance to local audiences. To fulfil their professional role, they scan reality to establish which current situations and concerns might be used to localize content.

Programming formats in a liberalized television industry

The process of localization of global program formats cannot be understood without addressing the remarkable changes in the Argentine television industry in less than two decades. As an industry strategy, localization is linked to broad business operations and the dynamics of importation and exportation in a growing industry.

In Argentina, television penetration is high: 96.6 per cent of the population owns at least one set. The national average number of television sets per household is 2.4, while viewing figures show an average exposure of 3.4 hours per day, making television the most prevalent medium in Argentines' cultural consumption. With a penetration of 58.5 per cent of TV households, cable television has by far the highest number of viewers in Latin America (Quevedo et al. 2005).

The Argentine television industry has changed dramatically over the last two decades. Two factors have chiefly been responsible for driving changes: the legal transformation of television ownership, and the ups and downs of economic cycles. Until 1990, Argentine TV was characterized by an oligopolistic structure of three major, commercially run networks under state control. The government directly controlled those networks, and the television market remained closed, under-funded and highly vulnerable to the changing winds of Argentine politics as sitting administrations exercised discretionary control over programming and funding (Galperín 2002). This structure changed in 1990 with the introduction of decree 578, which ordered the privatization of the Buenos Aires-based Channel 13 and Channel 11 (two state-controlled stations). That same year, the Congress overruled article 45 of the Broadcasting Law, which banned newspapers' ownership of broadcasting companies (Ulanovsky et al. 2006). In 1994, the complete opening of media markets to foreign investment put the final touches on a highly internationalized TV environment. As discussed below, liberalization had direct impact on both the importation and exportation of programming.

The seesaw evolution of the Argentine economy has also shaped the recent development of the television industry. The industry was severely affected by the unprecedented 2001 economic crisis. Just as it did across industrial sectors, the crisis caused a substantial contraction in investments in television production. Television executives shelved high-budget programs such as local versions of imported 'reality television' and game shows, many of which topped audience ratings in 2002. Instead, screens were filled with low-budget productions (Gorodischer 2002). As the domestic market suffered a drastic downturn, many local production companies turned their attention to international markets. The crisis thus brought an unexpected consequence: it forced companies to develop and market programs for regional and global export. This shift allowed them to establish a foothold, and eventually consolidate their position, in the international television business.

At present, the industry is characterized by fierce competition between the two major networks (Telefé and Artear), growing internationalization of both investments and programming, and a dynamic independent production sector. For the last two decades, national productions have dominated prime-time schedules, either original local programming or localized versions of imported shows and formats. In the past decades, domestic productions have dominated audience preferences as well as the overall content of the leading over-the-air networks and prime-time programming. In 2006, 39 of the 50 most highly watched programs were domestic shows; by 2007, that number had increased to 41.

What is remarkable is the presence of adapted foreign formats among the top-ranked shows in the past years. Both leading networks, Artear and Telefé, have relied on local versions of imported shows to lead audience preferences. In 2006, Telefe broadcast five adapted shows out of a total of 76 programs aired during that year. Four out those five adapted formats were among Telefe's top twenty shows. Likewise, Artear aired four adapted shows out of 74 programs scheduled for the season. All four shows were among the network's ten most popular programs. Of the 30 top shows during 2006, eight were local versions of imported programs. The two leading networks produced the majority of adapted shows aired that year.

A similar pattern was observed in 2007. The two most popular shows were local versions of foreign formats (*Big Brother* and the Mexican version of the British format *Dancing with the Stars*). Half of Telefe's twenty most successful shows were adapted versions of imported shows. Only one show, a local version of *Bewitched*, was considered a 'ratings failure'. For Artear, adapted shows were also largely successful: four adapted shows ranked among the top twenty shows. In total, Argentine networks broadcast 24 adapted shows, twenty of which were ranked among the 50 most popular programs in 2007. It is also important to note that none of the other networks (America, Channel 9 and Channel 7) which did not have any shows among the top 50 most-watched programs broadcast any adaptations of imported formats. This suggests that the adaptation of foreign formats is a successful business strategy that seemingly reinforces the position of the leading networks.

If we consider both 2006 and 2007, the figures unmistakably demonstrate the centrality of adapted formats in the contemporary Argentine television industry. Argentine networks broadcast 35 versions of foreign franchises,[1] with 28 of those shows ranking among the top 50 programs. In other words, 80 per cent of adapted shows ranked among the 50 most popular shows. These numbers suggest the popularity of adapted foreign formats as both programming strategy and amongst audiences. It is also noteworthy that the majority of the adaptations (94 per cent) were aired by the two leading networks that have been competing for audience ratings for several years. Adapting foreign formats has become a favorite programming strategy to win the battle for audiences and advertisers.

Simultaneously, both the number of production companies and the number of programming hours have substantially increased. While a few dozen production companies existed in the 1980s, it is estimated that approximately 300 companies are currently active, with a workforce of 25,000 employees (Artopoulos et al. 2007). Besides the increase of original domestic programming, the growth of the production sectors is linked to various processes, including the expansion of the format export business, the popularity of local versions of foreign imports, the provision of consulting and management services to regional and global companies, and the outsourcing of domestic labour (which is relatively cheap and well trained by international standards) and infrastructure for foreign productions.

A handful of companies have taken the lead in the production sector. According to Artopoulos et al. (2007):

> [T]here are currently at least four large and twenty small industry followers. Two of the large firms remain independent producers – Cuatro Cabezas and Endemol Argentina (currently P&P, following an acquisition) – while the other two are leading national broadcast corporations that have incorporated the production function – Telefé with its Telefé Contenidos division and Artear with two captive production companies (Pol-Ka and Ideas del Sur).

The integration of Pol-Ka and Ideas del Sur should not lead to the conclusion that there has been a process of increased concentration of production companies. Although a few companies produce the most popular shows in the two leading networks, the production sector continues to be characterized by fragmented ownership.

Since the late 1990s, the notable expansion in the export of original programming and formats has been one of the most remarkable transformations in the Argentine television industry. Amidst the overall growth of the international trade of programming formats, Argentine production companies have substantially increased their output and presence in global markets. Although 'official statistics for TV exports are difficult to find due to this variability and because the product is not processed through customs' (Artopoulos et al. 2007), current estimates suggest that approximately 45,000 hours were sold in 2005 for US$270 million.

Why localize?

As mentioned earlier, the boom in Argentine television exports is closely linked to the increase in the localization of TV imports. Not only do leading production companies maintain a key position in both the export of original programming and formats and the adaptation of imported programs, they have also used their position as both exporters and importers to consolidate their international presence. The companies that produced highly watched local versions of foreign programs are the same ones that successfully increased their global presence. One could argue that, as they became reliable partners for US, European and other Latin American firms in the domestication of formats, they also gained credibility as content exporters. Given their position as both exporters and importers, the largest production companies have refined the practice of localizing and globalizing content of various types of programming, including 'reality', 'makeover', fiction and game shows.

Here we propose to understand localization in two dimensions. First, localization is a conscious effort by program producers to tweak program content to make it culturally relevant to domestic audiences. It is about making programs 'real' and authentic, understanding reality as producers' particular understanding of a given local and national situation. Localization is implemented through a double, simultaneous movement: deleting foreign cultural markers that cause 'cultural discount' (Hoskins et al. 1998) of imported formats, and incorporating local elements that identify the show as a domestic product. Neither interest in national pride nor legal obligations to meet domestic production quotas animate localization in the Argentine television industry. Producers are chiefly concerned with the potential 'cultural discount' of foreign franchises rather than with using programs to present and promote public dialogue about national issues. The absence of quotas on domestic production releases them from having legal obligations to localize imported formats. Instead, economic calculations are the prime driver of localization. The logic of localization is linked to attracting large audiences and high ratings.

Second, localization also refers to the fact that the production of imported franchises cannot escape the unique political, economic and social context in which this process takes place. This refers not to deliberate strategies to make programs resonate with audiences, but rather to the need to adjust productions to unpredictable local and national events. Television programs are often subjected to unforeseen developments. From scheduling to casting decisions, unpredictable circumstances require producers to adjust their plans to respond to real events. Thus, localization is not only about revamping foreign programs to make them 'authentic', but also about how to adjust production when reality infiltrates television routine.

Localization as a deliberate effort to adjust content

When deciding about the appropriateness of imported television programs, producers weigh both economic and cultural factors. Economic factors are related to industrial dynamics and requirements such as initial investments, cost, scheduling and casting. For example, dubbed or local versions of daytime US soap operas are unsuitable for Latin American television because they are difficult to schedule. They contain too many episodes, the plots have endless twists and turns, and they feature a constant parade of actors and characters. Networks are typically interested in scheduling programming with clear beginnings and ends that can easily be continued or removed, depending on audience success. Also, new international shows may not be attractive for local programmers, even when they have been successful after one or two seasons. Because they are likely to have few episodes, local companies are unwilling to commit substantial resources to producing a show that may be discontinued in its original market. Instead, foreign shows with a substantial number of episodes produced over several seasons allow for the lowering of initial and fixed production costs. This is why, for example, Telefé decided to produce *The Nanny* out of dozens of sitcoms offered by Sony. Because the network wanted to air the sitcom on a daily basis, it selected a show with enough episodes to fit that programming strategy. Finally, some ideas might be simply too expensive to adapt. While preparing the first season of *Big Brother*, Argentine producers thought of including a series of fire games that had successfully been used in European versions. However, the high cost of the security measures discouraged producers from including those games in the show.

Cultural factors refer to whether 'distinct whole ways of life', to use Raymond Williams' (1958) definition of culture, are embedded in imported programs or formats. Producers disaggregate the components of television programs to assess what cultural aspects may be 'lost in translation' or deemed offensive to local sensibilities. What motivates the analysis of built-in components of foreign shows and formats is the interest in assessing the cultural resonance of imported programs among domestic audiences. Producers are interested in grounding programs in 'reality' and removing 'universal' issues or specific references to foreign cultures. Making programs culturally specific drives the localization of programs and formats, regardless of whether they purposefully represent 'reality' or are pure fiction.

Thus, localization needs to be understood as a series of efforts to make content 'real' through particular interpretations of local and national 'reality' at a specific time. It entails erasing cultural signs that establish cultural distance between programs and audiences, and instead developing markers that signal common belonging. Language and accents are obvious 'cultural markers' that immediately establish both cultural gaps and commonalities. Other markers such as humour and references to historical events and everyday places (e.g. streets, cities) are also used to develop cultural bonds between programs and audiences.

Localization consists of gatekeepers' decisions to define the nation by including cultural dimensions that evoke familiarity and 'reality' among domestic audiences. Our findings suggest that the television industry doesn't tap into state-sanctioned national culture to localize content and thus 'imagine' the nation. Producers typically eschew anchoring national cultures in history, myths, memory, symbols, territory and heritage. Nor do they resort to a relational model of national culture that defines 'us' as different and/or opposed to 'them'. Further, they don't embrace patriotism as collective mobilization and support for a given national identity. Rather, nationhood is defined as a collective culture shaped by a set of common and recent experiences. Localization entails sketching out 'the nation' at a particular moment in time. It is less about the past and more about the present. It is about everyday forms of shared experiences and concerns rather than official discourses about national culture. It is not about what makes a nation unique and/or different from others, but instead involves understanding prominent concerns and values in the population.

Focused on the present mood of national audiences, television producers use a journalistic sensitivity to outline the nation. 'Journalistic sensitivity' refers to the ability to have a pulse on 'reality', a reporter's eye for assessing current significant events as well as public sentiments and interests. It brings out the curiosity of the reporter about the immediate present that defines newsworthiness rather than the historian's long-term perspective of nation-building and renewal. It is about assessing the impact of concrete experiences rather than the legacy of past culture enshrined in the national canon.

The nation is understood as a community of shared experiences defined by current events. Current events are a key point of reference to determine the 'realness' of storylines, plots and characters. For example, political events and public perceptions were considered in the localization of the Spanish show *Aqui no hay quien viva* (*Nobody Can Live Here*), a fiction show broadcast in early 2008. The show focused on the lives of neighbours in a residential building. The building and the conflicts around its management were often portrayed as an allegory of Argentine contemporary politics. The building manager was characterized as someone who believes he had power but in fact didn't have it. In the eyes of the producers, the character was written to resemble popular opinions about former President Fernando de la Rua who, after two years in office, resigned amidst a financial crisis and raucous public protests in December 2001. The character of the manager was developed as de la Rua's doppelganger, an immediately recognizable character. Likewise, another character was developed as a corrupt and selfish 'nouveau riche', always looking for easy ways to make quick money but without a recognizable job. In the public mind, this type became associated with the giddy economic years of the Carlos Menem administration in the 1990s (just in case the audience missed the reference, the character's son, a soccer-obsessed and shallow youth, was deliberately named 'Carlitos').

The memory of recent politics also played a part in the adaptation of *Candid Camera* and *Big Brother*. Foreign versions of *Big Brother* featured a scene in which, at the beginning of the season, participants were kidnapped by a gang of hooded people who proceeded to rip their clothes before dropping them off in the house where the show took place. Such a beginning was unthinkable in the Argentine context. As the local producer says: 'One sees that and gets goosebumps. Given the history of dictatorships in our country, you cannot do that.' Likewise, the US version of *Candid Camera* featured a tank rolling over parked cars and actors dressed in military costumes chastising owners for supposed transgressions (the unsuspecting victims did not know that the event was a televised prank). The producers decided to replace the tank with a bulldozer to avoid images of a deadly military assault in the late 1980s. Still, images of threatening officers didn't sit well in a country that had recently suffered a cruel dictatorship. The supposed humorous aspects of the situation in the US version, such as the caricature of arrogant military officers, got completely lost in translation.

Taking economic reality into consideration has been central to the localization of game shows. The Argentine version of *The Price is Right* was broadcast in the aftermath of the economic crisis in the early 2000s. Based on audience feedback, the show eventually decided to offer a larger quantity of, but less expensive, prizes than in the US version. It added household items and appliances instead of cars and travel to make more people 'winners' of cheaper yet valuable items. A popular mindset shaped by the economic crisis also affected *Who Wants to Be a Millionaire?* The popular show was premised on the rule that participants could increase the amount of their take-home prize by betting all money earned in previous rounds of questions. However, amidst economic instability, participants frequently decided to stop competing after a few rounds, even if their earnings were a modest sum compared with the potential bigger prizes. Such decisions deprived the show of its signature moments, found in the gradual and suspenseful build-up towards big prizes.

The situation after the 2001 economic crisis also informed the adaptation of *Married with Children*. The family was portrayed as a former middle-class family that had suffered downward mobility after the crisis. The family (named 'Argento' to leave no doubt about its nationality) was purposefully set to represent the frustrated ambitions of the middle class. The father embodied the crashed dreams of a social group that once was convinced it could maintain a middle-class lifestyle, but found itself falling socially below its expectations after continuous political and economic turmoil. For the producers, this portrayal resonated with Argentina's historically large middle class, which saw its savings and jobs quickly disappear during the crisis.

The reality of massive impoverishment was also a point of reference in the localization of *Big Brother*. The Dutch version situated participants in a 'wealthy' house and sent weekly losers to a stable as the 'poor' house. This was not considered funny, fictional or exotic, but rather offensive in the Argentine context. Likewise, producers frowned upon the 'back to basics' concept in the original version of the program, which featured a house with amenities (e.g. swimming pool, garden, gourmet kitchen) considered typical of wealthy rather than 'average' people. In 2002, the harsh economic reality was the premise for the 'reality show' *Human Resources*, in which unemployed participants competed to get working-class jobs by demonstrating various skills.

Assessing social trends and lifestyles allows imported program scripts to be brought into local realities. For example, the libertine sexual mores of the lead character in *The Nanny* and the free-flowing, ironic remarks about the sexual life of the daughter in *Married with Children* were eliminated based on the belief that Argentine family conversations about sexuality are different. The character of the nanny mentioned frequent dates instead of double entendre jokes about regular sexual encounters. In *Married with Children*, the father never referred to the daughter's sexuality, and she was portrayed as frequently love-struck rather than promiscuous. Similarly, the idea that unemployed and on-and-off employed youth would shared a rented apartment together as in the show *Friends* is unconceivable in a country where, in all likelihood, they would still live with their parents.

As has been already argued (Gitlin 1983; Bielby and Bielby 1994), television producers rely on gut feelings and impressions to make decisions about localization. They speak about 'the ability to observe' and 'a hunger for information' to assess what cultural markers need to be removed or added. Many producers actually have worked as journalists in the past – an experience which, in their view, gave them skills to permanently scan ongoing events to determine public opinion and assess the suitability of foreign ideas. Although many regularly attend meetings organized by the US and European companies that own the franchises to share adaptation experiences, Argentine producers say that most ideas for localization are homegrown, based on the insights gained in the local and national contexts.

Localization as a reactive strategy to manage local reality

Localization is not only a conscious, deliberate effort to adapt content to make it culturally resonant; it is also a strategy to adapt the production of shows that explicitly engage with reality to unexpected local circumstances. Business logic requires the management of reality in order to deliver predictable products on a regular basis. While traditional shows that feature professional actors and are produced in studios are able to keep reality at a distance, the production of foreign formats of game shows and 'reality' shows faces different challenges posed by unpredictable events. Television production is situated in specific social and local contexts. Conventional shows manage to keep reality at bay. Shows that step out of the confines of studios need to control reality to meet industry expectations (e.g. content, schedules). This challenge is particularly noticeable in Argentina, given the constant and rapid changes that, by influencing program content and production, force gatekeepers to adapt.

Local reality seeps through in the process of casting average citizens for 'reality' and 'makeover' shows. 'Candid camera' producers reminisce about cases in which they encountered violent reactions from unsuspected protagonists who reacted in 'a typical Argentine way' against the show's premise. Producers also contend that reality inevitably seeps into the casting of 'reality shows'. Casting sessions dip into reality, and encounter 'average folks' experiencing a variety of unique circumstances in the country's history. Contestants typically embody life stories and personalities that symbolize ongoing public trends and opinions, which tend to be expressed in storylines and improvised dialogues of 'reality shows'. So, while participants expressed the optimistic times of the 1990s, they revealed widespread suffering in the aftermath of the 2001 economic crisis.

Also, shows that are shot outside the predictable environment of television studios are bound to encounter local reality. One unnamed television producer offers a glimpse into the challenges of making programs that incorporate real people and settings:

> We are currently making [a domestic version of] *Got Talent*, and we suddenly realized that we cannot escape Argentina. We wanted to cast people from around the country amidst the 'farm revolt'[2]...So, in [the province of] Mendoza, we were stuck due to an airline strike. We planned to shoot the first episode in [the city of] Rosario on May 25 [the day when farmers held a large rally]. At first, we though about cancelling, then we decided to move on...[Also], it took us five days to shoot in a theatre in Tucuman because our trucks had to pass through fourteen roadblocks [between Buenos Aires and the Northern city amidst massive country-wide protests].

Likewise, the producers of *Operación Triunfo* had to adapt to the growing massive popularity of the show. Although they originally planned a live broadcast from participants' houses to assess reactions to studio performances, they never expected the contestants to become so popular. In some cases, they had to coordinate with governors, mayors and the police for the broadcast of mass events organized in support of local heroes. In their assessment, the show had unexpectedly touched a nerve among local citizens who felt represented by their home participants. Given that networks, production studios and creative personnel have been based in the capital since the beginning of the industry, television content was historically centred in Buenos Aires. A program that aimed to showcase participants and settings from different corners of the country had to deal with unprecedented logistical and production challenges.

Conclusion

In this chapter, we have argued that localization is a two-pronged business strategy to adapt imported content and adjust productions to local circumstances. Localization suggests 'industrial flexibility' with two goals: minimizing cultural obstacles to maximize audience, and managing unpredictable events to ensure a smooth, time-bound industrial process.

The force of localization should not be interpreted romantically as the triumph of local pluralism against the cultural steamroller of globalization. It would be hard to argue that domestic television programs consistently mirror local and national cultural diversity, a question that goes beyond the scope of this chapter. Suffice to say that local adaptations express gatekeepers' particular selection of themes and issues driven by profit-making concerns. Localization is less about television serving as an egalitarian platform for cultural diversity. Instead, it evidences the awareness of television gatekeepers that cultural premises embedded in program formats often do not transcend their original settings. It indicates the need to 'domesticate' foreign content, both in the sense of making it 'at home' (*domus*), and turning it into controllable products (as in the domestication of animals or plants).

To suggest that the strength of localization in the television industry attests to the centrality of 'the local' amidst media globalization is important yet insufficient. As previously indicated, many studies have already indicated this point. The localization of television content confirms what we already know about the persistence of 'the national,' even as domestic industries have been subjected to the intensification of trans-border flows of capital, technology and programming in the past decades (Schlesinger 1991; Waisbord 2004b).

We propose to draw three theoretical implications from the Argentine case for the study of media and globalization: the role of television in shaping and maintaining national cultures; the position of television gatekeepers as nation-builders with a journalistic sensibility; and the dynamics of 'cultural flexibilization' in the global television industry.

First, localization suggests the persistent role of television in shaping and renewing national bonds. The globalization of the television industry does not undermine the role of the medium as a force in maintaining national boundaries. This role is facilitated by the specific characteristics of television markets such as Argentina's, which has a sizable audience advertising investments coupled with a growing domestic production sector. When such conditions exist, then, television programs offer opportunities for nation-building and maintenance.

The localization of foreign formats suggests that 'the nation' is constructed as an imagined, dynamic collective actor with shared social, economic and political experiences that determine specific cultural characteristics. Everyday television renews the nation through programs that ostensibly are designed to speak about issues that resonate with domestic audiences. Localization signals the role of television as a form of 'banal nationalism' (Billig 1991) which is a social institution that provides daily, invisible reminders of national bonds and shared experiences. Such invisibility is precisely the goal of strategies aimed to turn the foreign into real and authentic products, almost undistinguishable from programs and other cultural manifestations originated locally. Localization represents the erasure of foreign, abstract components and their replacement with specific markers of national belonging.

This process leads to a second conclusion with important theoretical dimensions: television producers occupy a privileged position to document aspirations and problems of national audiences at a given time. If nations persist and the media – specifically television – play a significant role in affirming a sense of 'the national' amidst globalization, it is worth understanding the role of media producers in that process. Prime-time shows command large numbers of viewers, are endlessly profiled in other shows, and become woven into vernacular cultures. Given the centrality of television in public life and cultural renewal, producers hold a dominant position in shaping cultural taste, as Bourdieu (1994) observed, and outlining 'the nation'. They act as arbiters of national cultures through the use of a journalistic sensibility to determine what contemporary experiences shape 'the nation'. Whether it is producing fictional programming or 'reality television', they are sensitive to assessing 'national reality' to judge the authenticity and believability of programs.

A question that awaits further research concerns the implications of the increasingly important role of television gatekeepers in outlining national culture. Given the dominant business concerns of the industry, they are hardly motivated to provide nuanced, wide-ranging portrayals of national experiences. Localization is instrumentally linked to the intention of ensuring that content does not smack of foreignness among mass audiences. It is not about democratic efforts to portray and nurture cultural diversity, but rather the attempt to minimize 'cultural discount' in search of mass audiences. The point is not to suggest that television producers have eclipsed traditional nation-building institutions such as the state, armies and schools, or individuals such as politicians, policy-makers and intellectuals who historically articulated notions of nationhood. Rather, we want to call attention to the need to study the role of television gatekeepers in forming and reinforcing popular conceptions about the nation. If we approach nations as cultural formations in permanent process (rather than 'dead' or completed once and for all), then we need to address the role of media institutions and gatekeepers in efforts of national renewal and redefinition.

Third, the Argentine case demonstrates new dynamics in the global television industry. Although the Argentine production sector is not a major player by global standards, it demonstrates the process of 'cultural flexibilization' in the production and trade of television programs in the international market. 'Cultural flexibilization' refers to the twin procedures of incorporation and removal of cultural markers that denote specific national belonging.

Just as producers localize foreign franchises to make content culturally familiar, they also extricate elements that may attach program formats to specific cultural contexts. Interested in producing content that easily crosses national boundaries, they unburden versions 'for export' from specific connotations. As Argentine production has become increasingly export oriented, concerns about global markets become, if not paramount (given that the local market remains the main source of revenue), then certainly more prominent.

Television programs become composites of different parts that can easily be removed and replaced according to the demands of specific national markets. As Artopoulos et al. (2007: 51) write:

> The adoption of the export business model implies a change not only in the characteristics of end products experienced by viewers but also in the nature of the process that leads to the final product. To develop formats, producers must create TV content with a strong plot structure or framework yet allow for variation in production procedures, requiring a more flexible, professional and organized staff. The minimal requirement to export a format is for a TV program to be purged of local content and licensed to other firms that keep the main structure and characteristics of the program but adapt specific components to local tastes.

Thus, television programs need be conceived as 'culturally flexible' commodities that are boiled down to minimal contents not specific to any locality, yet easily 'localizable' according to the unique considerations of the gatekeepers of national television.

The Argentine case suggests that stripping and inserting elements associated with local and national cultures are central processes in the globalization and localization of television programming. Global business increasingly requires content that, if not absolutely neutral, does easily lend itself to be adjusted ('localization'). By the same token, business considerations also demand content that can quickly be adapted. The global trade of programming requires culturally eviscerated, boiler-plate formulas that can be localized according to gatekeepers' assessment of local idiosyncrasies. Given the main themes of this book, this chapter has focused on localization as one side of 'cultural flexibilization'. The flipside of this process – that is, the removal of local elements to make programs accessible to global markets ('delocalization') – has not been explored here.

Our analysis suggests that 'local/national culture' is an important but fragile component of program design and production. While it is significant to convey familiarity and tap into current trends, it is easily disposable to ensure that programs are able to 'jump over' cultural barriers. Localization indicates the process of 'cultural flexibilization' at work, and suggests the complex linkages between culture and economics in media globalization. It should not be comprehended as either the capitulation of cultural distinctiveness to global forces or the manifestation of absolute cultural pluralism. Rather, it demonstrates the persistence of cultural uniqueness rooted in specific socio-political and economic processes within the national boundaries of television, and the conviction among television gatekeepers of the need to be sensitive to and flexible about at least some aspects of local realities.

Notes

1. This includes different shows that are part of the same format, such as *Big Brother*, which features debates and special performances at various times.
2. The 'farm revolt' refers to massive, nationwide protests, including roadblocks and demonstrations, staged by farmers against the decision of President Cristina Fernandez de Kirchner to propose a tax increase on agricultural exports during the first half of 2008.

References

Anderson, Benedict (1983), *Imagined Communities: Reflections on the Origin and Spread of Nationalism*, London: Verso.

Artopoulos A., Friel, D. and Hallak, J.C. (2007), 'Challenges of Exporting Differentiated Products to Developed Countries: The Case of SME-dominated Sectors in a Semi-Industrialized Country', typescript prepared for the Inter-American Development Bank.

Banerjee, Indrajit (2002), 'The Locals Strike Back? Media Globalization and Localization in the New Asian Television Landscape', *Gazette: International Journal for Communication Studies*, 64(6), pp. 517–35.

Bielby William T. and Bielby, Denise D. (1994), '"All Hits are Flukes": Institutionalized Decision Making and the Rhetoric of Network Prime-time Program Development', *American Journal of Sociology*, 99(5), pp. 1287–1313.

Billig, Michael (1995), *Banal Nationalism*, London: Sage.

Bourdieu, Pierre (1984), *Distinction: A Social Critique of the Judgment of Taste*, London: Routledge.

Brah, A. and Coombes, Annie E. (2000), *Hybridity and Its Discontents: Politics, Science, Culture*, London: Routledge.

Chalaby, Jean (2005), 'Deconstructing the Transnational: A Typology of Cross-border Television Channels in Europe', *New Media & Society*, 7(2), pp. 155–75.

Clausen, Lisbeth (2004), 'Localizing the global: "Domestication" Processes in International News Production', *Media, Culture & Society*, 26(1), pp. 25–44.

Dayan, Daniel and Katz, Elihu (1992), *Media Events: The Live Broadcast of History*, New York: Oxford University Press.

Frau-Meigs, Divina (2006), '*Big Brother* and Reality TV in Europe', *European Journal of Communication*, 21(1), pp. 33–56.

Fung, Anthony (2008), *Global Capital, Local Culture: Localization of Transnational Media Corporations in China*, New York: Peter Lang.

Galperín, Hernán (2002), 'Transforming Television in Argentina', in Silvio Waisbord and Elizabeth Fox (eds), *Latin Politics, Global Media*, Austin, TX: University of Texas Press.

García Canclini, Néstor (1995), *Hybrid Cultures: Strategies for Entering and Leaving Modernity*, Minneapolis, MN: University of Minnesota Press.

Gitlin, T. (1983), *Inside Television*, New York: Pantheon.

Gorodischer Julián (2002), 'Después de la gloria, regresa el cartón pintado', *Página 12*, 23 July.

Hetsroni, Amir (2005), 'Rule Britannia! Britannia Rules the Waves: A Cross-cultural Study of Five English-speaking Versions of a British Quiz Show Format', *Communications*, 30(2), pp. 129–53.

Hines, Colin (2003), 'Time to Replace Globalization with Localization', *Global Environmental Politics*, 3, pp. 1–7.

Hjarvard, Stig (ed.) (2003), *Media in a Globalized Society*, Copenhagen: Museum Tusculanum Press.
Hoskins, Colin, McFadyen, Stuart and Finn, Adam (1996), *Global Television and Film: An Introduction to the Economics of the Business*, New York: Oxford University Press.
Jackson, Peter (2004), 'Local Consumption Cultures in a Globalizing World', *Transactions of the Institute of British Geographers*, 29(2), pp. 165–78.
Mangiron, Carmen and O' Hagan, Minako (2006), 'Game Localisation: Unleashing Imagination with "Restricted" Translation', *The Journal of Specialised Translation*, 14, pp. 306–17.
Moran, Albert and Keane, Michael (2006), 'Cultural Power in International TV Format Markets', *Continuum: Journal of Media & Cultural Studies*, 20(1), pp. 71–86.
Prestholdt, Jeremy (2008), *Domesticating the World: African Consumerism and the Genealogies of Globalization*, Berkeley, CA: University of California Press.
Quevedo, Luis Alberto, Barman, R. and Mármora, Lelio (2005), 'Informe sobre el Sistema Nacional de Consumos Culturales, Secretaría de Medios de Comunicación', Jefatura de Gabinete de Ministros, Presidencia de la Nación, Argentina.
Ranganathan, Maya and Lobo, Bernadette (2008), 'Localizing the Global: Analysis of Nationalist Ideologies in MNC Advertisements in Indian TV', *Nationalism & Ethnic Politics*, 14(1), pp. 117–42.
Ritzer, George (2003), 'Rethinking Globalization: Glocalization/Globalization and Something/Nothing', *Sociological Theory*, 21(3), pp. 193–209.
Robertson, Roland (1995), 'Globalization: Time-Space and Homogeneity-Heterogeneity', in Mike Featherstone, Scott Lash and Roland Robertson (eds), *Global Modernities*, Thousand Oaks, CA: Sage, pp. 25–44.
Ruigrok Nel and van Atteveldt, Wouter (2007), 'Global Angling with a Local Angle: How US, British, and Dutch Newspapers Frame Global and Local Terrorist Attacks', *Harvard International Journal of Press/Politics,* 12(1), pp. 68–90.
Schlesinger, Philip (1991), *Media, State and Nation: Political Violence and Collective Identities*, London: Sage.
Schudson, Michael (2003), *The Sociology of News*, New York: W.W. Norton.
Shoemaker, Pamela and Reese, Stephen (1991), *Mediating the Message: Theories of Influences on Mass Media Content,* New York: Longman.
Sinclair, John, Jacka, Elizabeth and Cunningham, Stuart (eds) (1996), *New Patterns in Global Television: Peripheral Visions*, New York: Oxford University Press.
Straubhaar, Joseph (2003), 'Choosing National TV: Cultural Capital, Language, and Cultural Proximity in Brazil', in M.G. Elasmar (ed.), *The Impact of International Television: A Paradigm Shift*, Mahwah, NJ: Lawrence Erlbaum, pp. 77–110.
—— (2007), *Global Television*, Thousand Oaks, CA: Sage.
Ulanovsky, Carlos, Itkin, S. and Sirvén, Pablo (2006), *Estamos en el aire. Historia de los medios de comunicación en la Argentina,* Buenos Aires: Emecé.
van Leeuwen, Theo (2006), 'Translation, Adaptation, Globalization: The Vietnam News', *Journalism*, 7(2), pp. 217–37.
Varela, Mirta (2005), *La Televisión Criolla, desde sus inicios hasta la llegada del hombre a la luna, 1951–1969,* Buenos Aires: Edhasa.
Waisbord, Silvio (2004a), 'McTV: Understanding the Global Popularity of Television Formats', *Television & New Media*, 5(4), pp. 359–83.
—— (2004b), 'Media and the Reinvention of the Nation', in John Downing, Dennis McQuail, Philip Schlesinger and Ellen Wartella (eds), *The Sage Handbook of Media Studies*, Thousand Oaks, CA: Sage, pp. 375–92.

Wang, Georgette and Yeh, Emilie (20050, 'Globalization and Hybridization in Cultural Products: The Cases of *Mulan* and *Crouching Tiger, Hidden Dragon*', *International Journal of Cultural Studies*, 8(2), pp. 175–93.
Weber, Ian (2003), 'Localizing the Global', *Gazette: International Journal for Communication Studies*, 65(3), pp. 273–91.
Williams, Raymond (1958) *Culture and Society 1780–1950*, New York: Columbia University Press.
Wright, David (2005), 'Mediating Production and Consumption: Cultural Capital and Cultural Workers', *British Journal of Sociology*, 56(1), pp. 101–21.

Part III

Institutional Approaches

Chapter 5

Trading in TV Entertainment: An Analysis

Katja Lantzsch, Klaus-Dieter Altmeppen and Andreas Will

Global TV format trade belongs to the field of worldwide acquisition and production of entertainment programs in TV. Hence its analysis provides information about the acquisition and production structures in the field of TV entertainment. Additionally, it answers a question regarding the mechanisms used by the media in presenting entertainment to society.

Initially, the object of format trade is the agreement between licensor and licensee on an international level. But, strictly speaking, format trade is a combined form of acquisition (licensing) and production of entertainment formats, where licensor and licensee sell and buy formats to create a remake of an already existing program in another country. A global communication process in the form of a comprehensive know-how transfer is associated with the format licence, enabling the licensee to produce a remake in consideration of national and cultural particularities respectively. But how is this global communication process organized?

Despite a worldwide market volume of TV format trade in the thirteen most important TV markets worth approximately €2.4 billion (Schmitt 2005; Schmitt et al. 2005), a considerable lack of knowledge still exists about the mechanisms in the field of entertainment acquisition and production in general and the international format trade in particular.

This chapter looks first into the black box of format trade and answers the question of how the global communication process within the TV format trade is organized. In order to find answers to the research question, the organization's specifics are elaborated. An empirical survey (interviews with managers) about organizational analysis is the basis, while priority is given to the actors, their characteristics and the organizational forms of TV format trade. As inter-organizational networks are the relevant organizational form, this chapter concentrates on the global communication process that occurs inside the network of licensees and licensors in order to adapt program formats.

Consequently, the remainder of this chapter is organized as follows. First, the TV format trade and the term 'TV format' are described and analyzed, as well as differentiated from other forms of acquisition and production. Then we give a brief overview of research in TV entertainment, especially format trade, followed by a short description of the methodology. We continue by summing up theoretical approaches to entertainment acquisition and production, highlighting network theory. Based on the results from an empirical study, we introduce the concept of inter-organizational networks as an appropriate model to describe and better understand the international TV format trade. Some concluding remarks can be found in the last part of this chapter.

Formats and TV format trade

What is a format? To date, there is no commonly accepted agreement about what a format is. One definition is provided by Meckel (1997: 478): 'A format is a multipart program concept, which is in its content, in its internal structure and its way of presentation concentrated on a specific audience and a certain program slot.' Another, oft-cited definition is given by Lausen (1998: 15), who says a TV format is 'the totality of all characteristics of a broadcasting program or a production run [which] is coming back in each episode.' However, both definitions refer to national market formats only. Lausen's definition is rather unspecific, whereas Meckel points out the focus on specific target groups and the audience flow. Both definitions neglect the fact that formats are tradable products bought and sold on international markets. In contrast, the following definitions by authors from the United Kingdom are more appropriate: 'A television format is a program or program concept, with distinct elements that can be exported and licensed to production companies or broadcasters outside its country of origin for local adaptation.' (Schmitt 2005) Or, even clearer: 'A format sale is a product sale. The product in this instance is a recipe for reproducing a successful television program, in another territory, as a local program.' (Bodycombe 2005) By the way, all experts interviewed in our study agreed with the latter definition, and especially with the term 'recipe'. Thus we can describe formats within the format trade as a package resulting from a finished program that consists of an idea, a paper concept, materials and know-how. A formats is a combination of trading goods and related services that is tradable on the global content market (Lantzsch 2008).

International format trade can be defined as selling and purchasing licences for TV formats between an exporting licensor and an importing licensee. The licensee is thus granted the opportunity to adapt the format to the needs of the domestic TV market and to achieve a balance between cost-efficient standardization and cultural differentiation. Format trade can be classified as a combination of self-commissioned production and program imports. Self-production is realized by the broadcasters or in collaboration with production companies (commissioned production). Another possibility for procuring entertainment content is to import programs (i.e. finished made-for-TV programs) – for example, Hollywood blockbusters. Format trading is mainly concentrated on mass-attracting, serialized, non-fiction formats such as game and quiz shows, reality TV or even chat shows, while daily soaps/telenovelas are predominant in the fiction area. The formats themselves are characterized by relatively low production costs and their suitability to be distributed broadly (Hallenberger 2003; O'Donnell, 1999; Hoskins et al. 1997; Magder 2004).

Obviously, the essence of format trade lies in the devolution of rights from the licensor to the licensee, yet the success of a format is just as much determined by the access to production and marketing know-how made available to the licensee (Lang 2001). Having obtained the rights to produce a highly standardized TV program, the licensee is able to adjust various elements of the respective programs to the needs of the domestic market (Windeler 2004; Bignell 2004).

Due to the fact that formats have usually been tested in advance on the market of the exporting country, the licensee acquires a number of strategic advantages: the higher probability of success (risk reduction) based on the assumption that success in one market is an indicator for success in a foreign market; the lower cost compared with finished made-for-TV programs; the additional sources of income (merchandising, call-in revenues); a partly domestic program; and the fulfilling of national program quotas (Television Research Partnership, Colwell and Price 2005). The core advantage is the higher probability of success, based on the preference of audiences for 'national' programs. One of the experts interviewed describes this as follows:

> People like to see themselves, they like to see their own lives, and I think particularly in these formats which are very often to do with ordinary people succeeding, earning money, becoming a pop star, becoming a dancer, getting a job in business – you don't want to see an American getting a job in business, you want to see a German getting a job in business. (Interview 15)

The licensor has the opportunity to maximize his profits. Another expert interviewed summarizes:

> The whole thing is attracting money and the second thing is to kind of keep it on as long as possible. (Interview 12)

It is important to note that research on the acquisition and production of TV entertainment is still in its developing stage, especially in Germany. So far it has largely concentrated on the content, use and effects of entertainment. Existing work can be found either in the form of analyses on market structures and performance (Pätzold and Röper 2003; Seufert 2002; Kauschke and Klugius 2000; Moran 1998; Hachmeister and Anschlag 2003; Hallenberger 2002) or in the form of organizational studies on the various processes of production (for an overview, see Sydow and Windeler 2004). In addition, studies specifically focusing on the European market have been published by the European Audiovisual Observatory (2000) and by various consulting companies (e.g. Andersen Consulting 2002). Finally, the initiatives of the producers' association and the regulatory authorities in Great Britain, the world market leader in format export, have also produced a number of studies (e.g. Television Research Partnership, Colwell and Price 2005; Price 2002).

Markets for formats

The number of broadcast format-based TV hours increased by about 22 per cent from 2002 to 2004. Dominant players are transnational production companies like Endemol and FremantleMedia. Endemol, as the largest originator, producer and distributor of formats in the world, dominates the format industry. In terms of production value, reality programs are the most important genre, while game shows represent 50 per cent of global format airtime (Schmitt et al. 2005).

In terms of production value, the United States is the most important format market. Germany is the world's largest format importer, with the highest expenses for buying formats: 5.092 program hours between 2002 and 2004. In contrast, the United Kingdom is the largest exporter. More than 12.543 program hours of British formats were distributed within the thirteen most important TV markets during the same period (Schmitt et al. 2005; Schmitt 2005).

Even though format trade seems to be a success story at first glance, there are a number of profound problems. One is that 'only a small proportion will actually sell, and of these few will become genuine international hits, and of these fewer still become "evergreens", able to sustain their success across many years' (Television Research Partnership, Colwell and Price, 2005: 27). A second problem is that the costs of producing instead of buying are much higher. This problem corresponds with another pressing issue within the format trade: the vague and ill-defined legal framework (Hallenberger 2003; Waisbord 2004). Format theft is a well-known phenomenon in the TV industry. In 2000, the Format Recognition and Protection Association (FRAPA) was founded to protect format theft, enforce legally binding norms and apply enforceable sanctions against format theft. Numerous format owners, producers and broadcasters are affiliated to FRAPA.

In spite of these problems, the size of the format trade market is steadily increasing. Mainly driven by digital distribution technologies and the deregulation of TV markets, it has resulted in the creation of numerous new TV channels. A further reason can be found in the risk commercial broadcasters face: given the uncertain chances of success in the entertainment industry, the use of well-tried formats may reduce the risk of failure compared with the production of entirely new programs. Finally, the networks of national TV markets brought about by globalization and the increasingly significant role of the big transnational media companies have induced a remarkable acceleration in the growth of the global format trade. The congruent aims of the broadcasters (and even the audience) are realized by means of homogeneous content (more of the same) and related strategies of acquisition, marketing and customer retention (Hallenberger 2003).

Methodology

Based on the observation that format trade is more than licensing, the starting point for the research presented in this chapter is the following questions: Who are the organizations involved? What kind of structures are representative of international format trade? And how is the process of global communication within television format trade organized? As research on international TV format trade is in its earliest stage, we wanted to understand how the international TV format trade is organized generally, and who are the actors involved. More precisely, we wanted to uncover the global communication processes of TV format trade.

To answer these questions, we analyzed the actors and their characteristics, the processes and organizational patterns of TV format trade. Theoretical backgrounds were provided by Anthony Giddens, (1984) theory of structuration (here associated with media organizations), the resource dependence approach, the resource-based view and the core competence approach, recent approaches of strategic management and the cognitions of organizational science, especially concerning inter-organizational networks.

To gain further insight into the field of international TV format trade, an empirical study funded by German. Research Foundation (DFG) was set up, based on a theoretical framework drawn from the theory of structuration and from organization and management theories. To answer the research questions, we decided to conduct semi-structured in-person interviews with managers from broadcasting stations, production companies and rights traders, complemented by interviews with related experts. A questionnaire was constructed, including six main question blocks concerning the definition of formats and format trade, the involved actors, their goals, strategies, the relevant rules and resources, and finally the organizational patterns and processes.

To recruit the participants, we decided initially to concentrate on the German TV market (export and import). Then, four formats were pre-selected (i.e. *Ladykracher*, *Strictly Come Dancing*, *I'm a Celebrity – Get Me Out of Here* and *Schillerstraße*). The formats were selected on the basis of the following criteria: global format trade, no children's formats, export and import produced formats (not only options), success of the format, timeliness of the formats, a mix of dependent and independent producers, and attendance of rights traders. In a further step, the participants were selected from the management of the organizations involved in the development/production, adaptation, broadcasting and trade of the four formats. Our sample of respondents was complemented by experts such as lawyers and managers from broadcasting unions or industry associations. Based on the questionnaire sketched above, a total of sixteen in-person interviews were conducted between May and October 2006. The interviews took place at the offices of the respondents in Germany, the United Kingdom, Belgium and Switzerland.

In the next section, we sum up the main results of our study, thereby focusing on the organizational patterns by introducing the concept of inter-organizational networks as the predominant organizational form in global TV format trade. The general findings are illustrated by the example of the British TV format *Strictly Come Dancing*. A broader overview, including all analyzed formats and further aspects of the acquisition and production of TV entertainment, can be found in Lantzsch (2008).

Theoretical approaches

It is possible to draw from a broad variety of approaches to analyze format trade. They range from economic (transaction cost theory) to organizational ones (organizational theory, cooperations, network theory). In the following we briefly outline these approaches to give a basic overview.

The most significant aspect of the format trade is cooperations. These are characterized by a common processing of assignments while maintaining the economic autonomy of the companies involved (Schumann and Hess 2002). In cooperations, the companies work together on a voluntary basis, conclude contractual agreements, and jointly coordinate their activities (Rautenstrauch et al. 2003; Picot et al. 2001). They are therefore an effective means to reduce the costs of transactions – for example, costs of seeking and checking products or services as well as costs of negotiation and contracting. In terms of structure, cooperations are a hybrid organizational pattern between market and hierarchy. Most of the acquisition and production patterns in the entertainment sector are arranged on a continuum of market and hierarchy – for example, commissioned productions (Sydow and Windeler 2004).

Networks, in turn, are specific forms of cooperations aiming at realizing competitive advantages. Organizational networks assume a polycentric form of organization, often strategically conducted by one of the companies involved. The relations between the legally autonomous, but economically often interdependent, companies are relatively stable and of a cooperative rather than competitive nature (Sydow 1992).

On the basis of this definition, several network typologies can be subsumed under the generic term. Strategic networks are networks managed by one or more focal companies – for example, in the automotive industry. Regional networks are restricted to a certain geographical area and often determined by informal rules and emergent strategies, such as Silicon Valley. Project networks are temporarily limited, focused on specific projects and the predominant form of network in the TV production industry.

Researchers in Germany have adopted a specific and unique view of networks in an effort to overcome the dualism of action and structure, based on Giddens' (1984) structuration theory. In this sense, networks are a particular type of social system, produced by competent actors under circumstances of reciprocity of acting and structure (Windeler 2005). According to this view, the structures of international format trade are both enabling and restricting the actors' scope of action, while at the same time the actors produce these structures by means of their action. This reciprocal process facilitates the emergence of inter-organizational networks which consist of more than two independent organizations and are generally determined by a complex web of social relations and interactions coordinated between the organizations involved (Windeler 2001).

The theory of structuration provides several benefits for analyzing format trade. Most important is the definition of structure as the combination of the basic elements, rules and resources. From this perspective, format trade is a process comprising various rules (e.g. coordination in networks), including codified rules (e.g. contracts). Even more crucial, format trade is a process of dealing with resources, which makes it possible to integrate and adapt both the resource-dependence view and the resource-based view. Taking resource theories into consideration, it is possible to analyze the extent to which formats are structure generating (resource-based view) or causing dependence (resource-dependence theory). The resource-dependence approach addresses the attempts of companies to reduce insecurity by establishing long-term binding relationships. This is a strategy frequently applied by media companies when installing networks or cooperations in the format trade. In contrast, the resource-based view focuses on the core resources of companies and interprets the success of a company as a result of the appropriate use of these resources (thus relying on the resources–conduct–performance paradigm rather than the market structure–conduct–performance perspective). The combination of both resource paradigms is a very appropriate way to analyze the impact of resources on organizational patterns. A network itself, for example, might become a crucial resource when, as in the case of format trade, the competences of several firms are essential for the production process, especially when there are low barriers to imitation of the product's specifics.

In sum, structuration theory, combined with the resource approaches, is well suited to analyzing entertainment acquisition and production in general, and the format trade in particular.

Empirical findings on international TV format trade

Our empirical results led us to our first conclusion: that all formats pass through a number of different stages during the development process. The starting point is an idea, which in a second step is outlined as a so-called paper format describing the basic idea, the genre, the patterns of presentation and the targeted audience. In the ideal case, a pilot already exists at this stage.

The third stage consists of the TV format package. This essentially is a know-how package, enabling autonomous production and encompassing the concept, production rules and elements required for reproduction, such as consulting, the production 'bible', graphic design, demo tapes, music and set-drafts. By and large, this stage in the process is regarded as the most crucial and fundamental. The final stage is the TV program format, which encompasses the complete produced program. Our primary interest is in format packages, the dominating object of format trade. These are usually the precondition for global format trade, since clients generally request formats which have already been tested on a market so that findings about the market success are included in the package.

In sum, the international format trade is an iterative process comprising the stages of development, distribution (selling and purchasing), producing and reproducing (adaptation) respectively, and broadcasting entertainment programs. In international markets format trade can be described as a cycle (see Figure 5.1).

Figure 5.2 illustrates the value chain of a format on international TV markets (with emphasis on the plural 'markets' since a successful format will regularly be exported to a multitude of foreign markets). There are four distinguishable levels on the national market: the level of developing ideas and conceptions; the level of acquisition and distribution; the level of production; and finally the level of broadcasting. With the exception of development, the international extension displays the correlating elements of the national value chain: international acquisition/distribution, reproduction, adaptation and re-broadcasting.

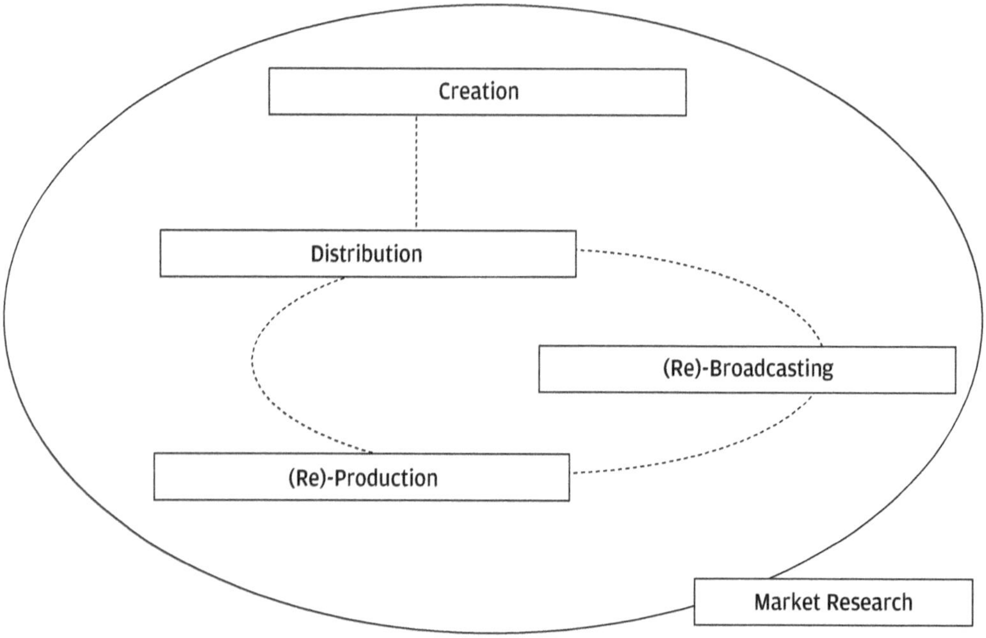

Figure 5.1: Cycle of format trade.

Following a successful broadcast on the domestic market, the format is offered to international markets by the licensor and bought by a licensee.

With the exception of the broadcasting level, each level is characterized by a set of different actors and organizations. Originators of formats may be format developers as well as producers or broadcasters, while format traders as well as producers or broadcasters can handle format distribution. The production level is usually handled by one organization only – producers in case of a commissioned production and broadcasters in case of a self-production. Hence, the actors involved have multifunctional roles, depending on their resources. Broadcasters act as publishers and have competencies and resources in the packaging and broadcasting of TV programs. They are able to demand the attention of the audience. The most relevant rule is a high quota. Broadcasters seldom produce their own programs, because they often do not have sufficient resources in developing and producing TV entertainment. Production companies build up the production know-how and distributors build up the know-how of the sales market.

In summary, two phenomena are crucial in this regard. The first is the obvious plurality of organizations involved in the format trade. The continuum ranges from only one actor (in which case the format trade is arranged within a media group) to a variety of different actors (in which case the functions of creation, distribution and production are conferred on several distinct organizations).

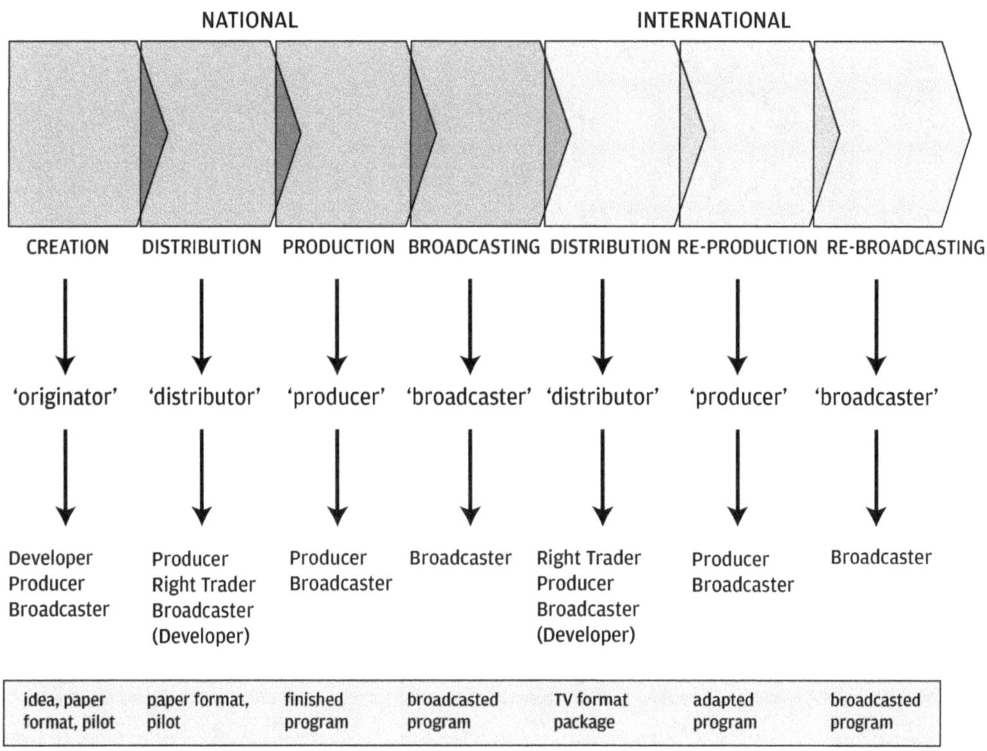

Figure 5.2: Value chain of formats in international TV markets.

The second crucial fact is the changing nature of formats in the trading process, from an idea – via a paper concept – to a finished program to a know-how package, and again to a finished and broadcast program. This course of the changing nature of formats is related to the organization of the value chain: the organizations involved can assume multifunctional roles, depending on the respective stage and their specific resources. Regarding this, it is important to recognize that only the broadcaster possesses the resources to act as a publisher of the finished program, which in turn is a necessary prerequisite for the international distribution of TV formats.

We illustrate these findings with *Strictly Come Dancing*, a British format that was sold to Germany, among other countries (see Figure 5.3). The licensor is BBC Worldwide, a commercial distribution and production company of the BBC with a specific business model: BBC Worldwide is financially engaged in the development process – also within the BBC – to get the property rights for the programs. BBC Worldwide undertakes the international licensing. Licensees buy single or multiple broadcasting rights from BBC Worldwide, depending on the specific contract.

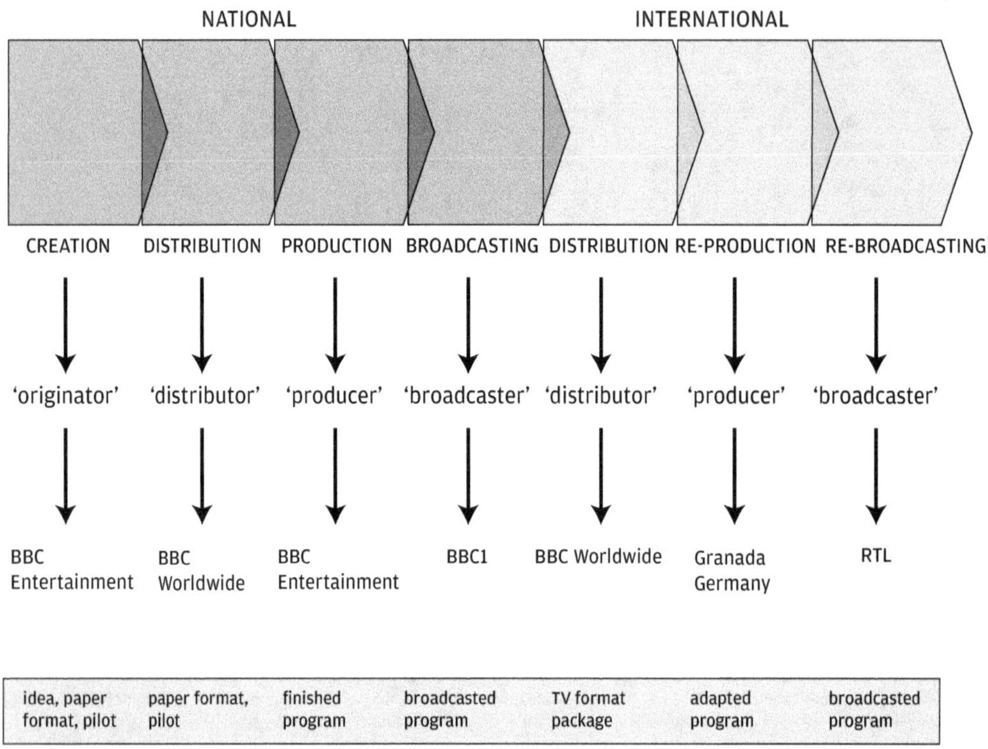

Figure 5.3: *Strictly Come Dancing/Let's Dance* (UK and Germany).

BBC Entertainment created the format on the base of another former BBC format (*Come Dancing*). The broadcast channel in the United Kingdom was BBC1. In the further value chain, BBC Worldwide performs the functions of distribution. The licensee in Germany is the biggest private broadcaster, RTL, which acquired the license for the German market from BBC Worldwide. Granada Germany produced the format for RTL.

Figure 5.2 and the example of *Strictly Come Dancing* in Figure 5.3 refer to the potential plurality of the organizations involved and the various possible constellations of rights ownership in terms of dependence on the available resources. The concrete constellation of organizations dealing with format trade depends on exactly who is the licensor and who is the licensee, and on the form of the traded rights (paper format, TV format package). These preconditions, in turn, are crucial for the choice of organizational patterns. Thus the ownership of formats determines the rules of organizational patterns.

The over-arching forum of format trade ties up all actors and organizations involved – that is, broadcasters, developers, producers and format traders. Their functions in the process of format trade are constantly and rapidly changing. The licensor who supplies a format may be a developer, a producer, a broadcaster or a format trader, while all of these actors may also be licensees. The constellation depends on the specific resources of the actors involved. Besides these actors, several other organizations are engaged in format trade with the task of providing certain endorsed services. They may be market research agencies, advocates, observers (e.g. scholars) or operators of program fairs.

Coordination and cooperation within and between these stages is a complex and challenging question of organizing media. If only suppliers and clients are engaged in the format trade, this usually leads to market operations or near-market patterns of coordination. In general, the trade goods concerned are the format package; in exceptional cases, it may be the paper format only. The producer in the foreign country purchases the right for their specific broadcast area (Karstens and Schütte 1999). The type of coordination typically is a simple transaction.

In most cases, however, format trade cannot be reduced to a simple transaction. To understand global format trade, it is necessary to incorporate into the analysis the preceding national value chain and the following levels of adaptation and re-broadcasting on the international markets. The core process of format trade consists of three stages: the development and production stage in the country of origin (the production stage); the takeover of a (successful) format (the acquisition stage); and the adaptation stage, where the format is reproduced and tailored to national or cultural requirements (the reproduction stage). Together, these stages make up the process of format acquisition and (re)production. Organizations operating on all stages (e.g. as developer, producer, distributor) inevitably gain high market power because of their broad control over the resource 'format' and the related know-how. Accordingly, exclusive rights traders are seldom found on the format market, as they can only influence the trade sector. Nonetheless, it remains difficult to gain control over the complete process of format acquisition and production, which also explains the existence of organizing patterns beyond hierarchy and market.

Even if the empirical study revealed certain particular differences in the organizational forms of the formats observed, we found a general organizational concept in the form of different inter-organizational networks, which together build the global network of format trade. This concept is composed of several different patterns of organizing the process of TV format acquisition and production. In the following, we scrutinize the various levels of this process.

Figure 5.4 shows a number of different networks. While the stages of creation and distribution/acquisition have not been analyzed in depth by our study, a first network of interest can be identified in the stage of production for the domestic market (Sydow and Windeler 2004). Besides producers and broadcasters, several actors – such as technical service providers and freelancers – participate in this network. It is characterized by latent network relations and tends to be more hierarchical than market driven, while exhibiting a strong dominance by the broadcasters due to their role as financiers and the related financial resources. This network can be seen as the starting point of format trade.

When a program is produced and successfully broadcast on the domestic market, the licensor will generally sell the format on the international market. The trade stage, with its

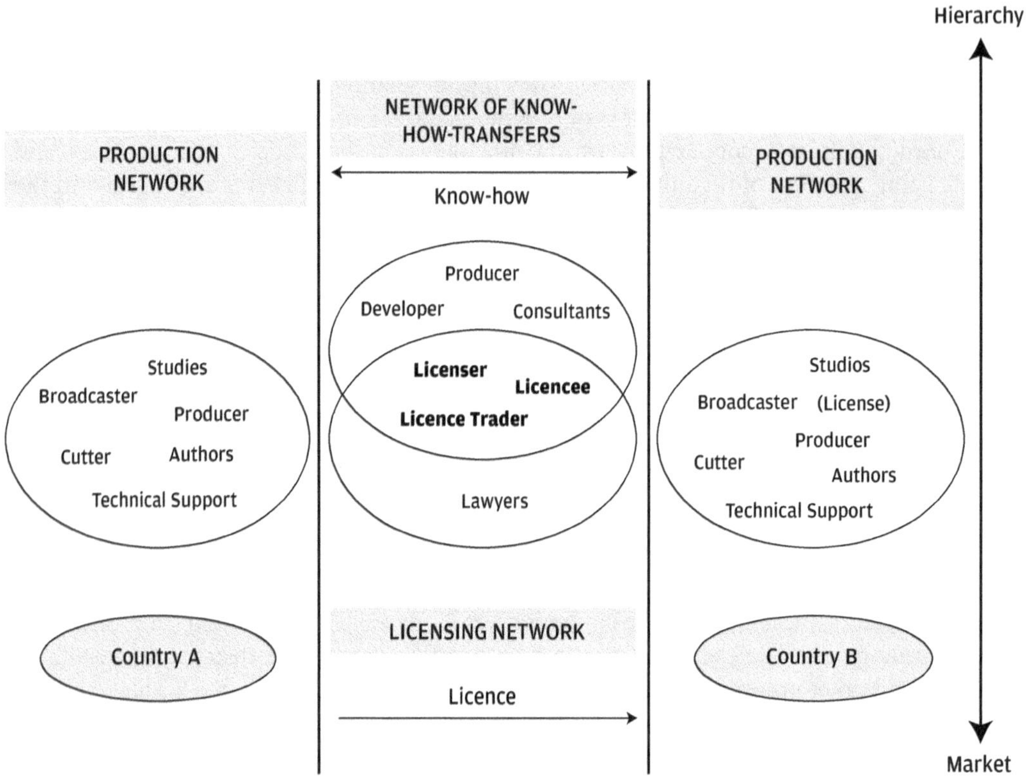

Figure 5.4: Entertainment acquisition and production – inter-organizational networks in the global format trade.

contractual conditions, is a near-market cooperation in the case of only two partners, or a near-market network where more than two partners are involved (broadcaster, producer and rights trader). Upon completion of the trade contract, the adaptation stage begins with the reproduction network.

Thus the organizational structure of the format trade process changes from a production-oriented network to a contracting-oriented form of organization and back again to a production-oriented network – each affected by its own organizational patterns and the related rules answering to, and at the same time creating, the respective requirements to manage the process.

Underlying the format trade process is another network of know-how transfer. Within the scope of the contractual conditions, the licensee purchases the right to adapt and broadcast a format for a specified area. This right is for the most part accompanied by further obligations and production rules. On the one hand, the licensor reserves the right to maintain control of the contract conditions, because they are trying to protect their resource 'format'. On the other hand, the licensee purchases format-related know-how. This know-how usually consists of consulting in the form of a production 'bible' or specialized consultants (e.g. competent and experienced staff supporting the production on the foreign market). We call this organizational pattern project-related knowledge networks between licensor and licensee. Such project-related knowledge networks embrace both the production networks on the domestic and the foreign market and exert considerable influence on the format trade due to the fact that consulting is part of the trade contracts.

For communication within the networks, the usual possibilities are used: phone and email are the preferred means. Additionally, personal contacts are common:

> Usually we go over for two days at the beginning of the production, meet everybody... and then it's on the phone and the email. (Interview 14)

In sum, global format trade is a sequence of different organizational patterns between market and hierarchy. The actual format trade as bilateral or multilateral cooperation (between two or more companies) is located between production networks on the one hand and networks

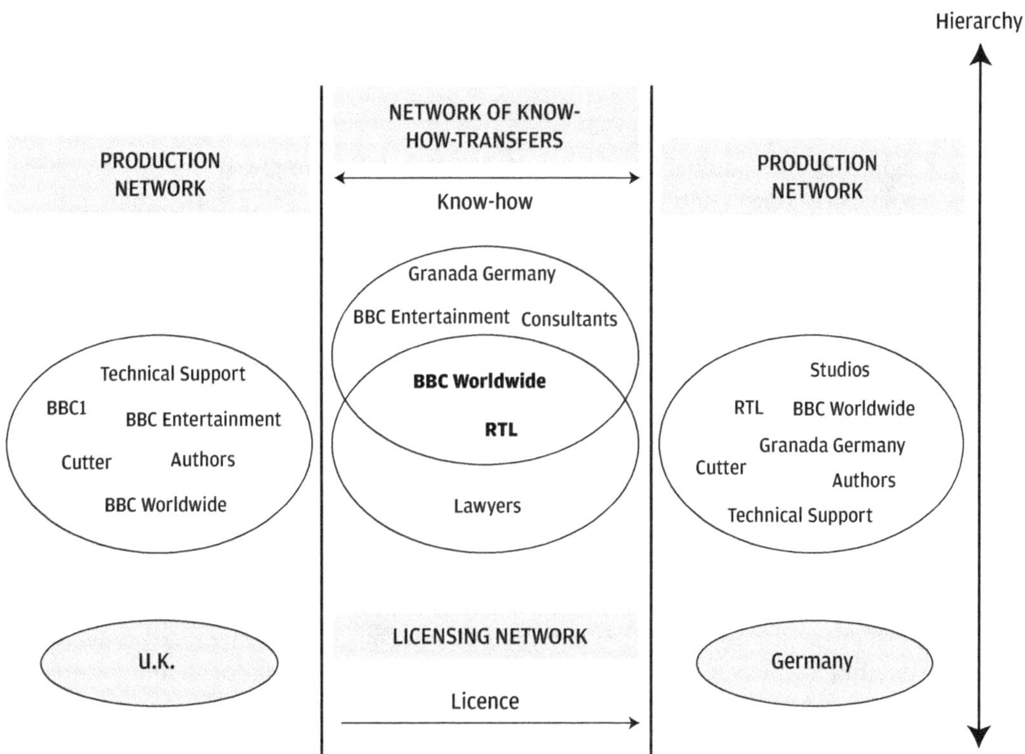

Figure 5.5: Inter-organizational networks involved in the format *Strictly Come Dancing*.

of know-how transfer on the other. For communication within the networks several ways of communication are used.

Again, we illustrate our findings by the example of *Strictly Come Dancing*. On the British domestic market, the network of format trade consists of BBC Entertainment and BBC1 as the main actors. Further actors involved are authors, studios, editors and technical supporters, who all work under the leading organization BBC Entertainment (see Figure 5.5). BBC Worldwide and RTL together build a near-market cooperation (only two actors). In the German TV market, the network of reproduction especially consists of Granada Germany and RTL. In the network of know-how transfer, BBC Worldwide, BBC Entertainment, Granada Media and RTL work together to adapt the British version of the format to the German market.

The format *Strictly Come Dancing* has the possibility of being sold internationally when it can be offered as a successful domestic format. Therefore, the networks of production on the national market are very important. Two strong cooperating actors, the production company and the broadcaster, dominate the production network within the domestic market. At the same time, these two actors are competitors in the struggle to sell successful formats to international markets.

Conclusion

At first sight, the international TV format trade seems to be simple. It can be described as '[a] producer in one country licensing the rights to produce an existing program to a producer in another country' (Television-Research-Partnership, Colwell and Price 2005). Our research has shown that, around this core process of contracting, the format trade is organized in complex patterns. The theory of structuration complemented by management and organization theories, especially the resource-oriented paradigm, serves to describe and help us to better understand these complex patterns by revealing the interlinkages of structures and the acting of the organizations.

A TV format passes through a number of different stages, ranging from creating to broadcasting on the national level, followed by the international stages of acquisition, reproduction, and broadcasting. Networks are well suited to communicating globally, and to managing the different challenges arising at the various stages. Networks as an organizational pattern become a resource by themselves, used by managers to procure and produce TV content. In the format trade, we distinguish between at least four networks: the network of the licence trade, the networks of content production and reproduction, and the interlinking network of know-how transfer. Only the interplay of all four networks constitutes a successful format trade.

The reason for the existence of different inter-organization networks, which together build the network of global format trade, is the several actors involved in the format trade, ranging from developers to producers, broadcasters and right traders, both on the national and international levels. These actors generally adopt different functions and roles along the value chain. The constellation depends on the resources of the involved actors. On the other hand, the character of the format varies from an idea, via a paper concept and a finished program, to a know-how package and then to a finished and broadcast program, depending on the stage of the format trade.

In conclusion, TV entertainment is acquired and produced by different actors, who communicate globally and choose different organizational forms, depending on their operation conditions, with different inter-organizational networks typical. Thus, society is entertained by actors adapting to the conditions of their actions, always orientating on the specific situation and in turn influencing these conditions by their strategic actions the sense of a recursive interaction. As one of the interviewed managers stated: 'Well, there is no one and only way – it's a very dynamic process.' (Interview 1)

The business of entertaining provokes management to operate in rapidly changing environments. In the small but highly competitive entertainment business, management skills needed to build stable business relations strongly focus on personal relationships and the ability to communicate globally rather than on formal contractual rules. Further research should focus on the entire management process and the skills needed in media organizations concerning the entertainment industry. It will then be possible to gain a deeper insight into the mechanisms of how TV content is produced, distributed and reproduced worldwide.

References

Andersen Consulting (2002), 'Outlook of the Development of Technologies and Markets for the European Audio-visual Sector up to 2010', http://europa.eu.int/comm/avpolicy/stat/tvoutlook/tvoutlook_finalreport.pdf. Accessed 30 April 2005.

Bignell, J. (2004), *An Introduction to Television Studies*, London: Routledge.

Bodycombe, D. (2005), 'What is a Format? FAQ'. http://www.tvformats.com/formatsexplained.htm. Retrieved 26 April 2005.

European Audiovisual Observatory (2000), *Economic Analysis of European TV Fiction. An INA Study in Order by the European Audiovisual Observatory and the CNC*, Straßbourg, France: Centre national de la cinématographie (CNC), Institut national de l'audiovisuel (INA).

Giddens, A. (1984), *The Constitution of Society: Outline of the Theory of Structuration*, Cambridge: Polity Press.

Hachmeister, L. and Anschlag, D. (eds) (2003), *Die Fernsehproduzenten. Rolle und Selbstverständnis [TV Producers. Role and self-image]*, Konstanz, Germany: UVK.

Hallenberger, G. (2002), 'Eurofiction 2001: Stabiles Angebot an fiktionaler Eigenproduktion. Erstausgestrahlte einheimische fiktionale Fernsehproduktionen in Deutschland' [Eurofiction 2001: Stable supply of fictional self-production. First-time broadcasted indigenous fictional television productions in Germany], *Media Perspektiven*, 10, pp. 501–11.

—— (2003), 'Fernsehformate und internationaler Formathandel' [Television formats and international television format trade], in Hans-Bredow-Institut (ed.), *Internationales Handbuch Medien 2004/2005 [International media handbook 2004/2005]*, Baden-Baden, Germany: Nomos, pp. 159–67.

Hoskins, C., McFadyen, S. and Finn, A. (1997), *Global Television and Film: An Introduction to the Economics of the Business*, Oxford: Oxford University Press.

Karstens, E. and Schütte, J. (1999), *Firma Fernsehen. Wie TV-Sender arbeiten. Alles über Politik, Recht, Organization, Markt, Werbung, Programm und Produktion [The television company. How TV broadcasters work. All about politics, law, organization, market, advertising, program and production]*, Reinbek, Germany: Rowohlt.

Kauschke, A. and Klugius, U. (2000), *Zwischen Meterware und Maßarbeit. Markt- und Betriebss trukturen der TV-Produktion in Deutschland [Between yardware and bespoke work. Market and business structures of TV production in Germany]*. Gerlingen, Germany: Bleicher.

Lang, S. (2001), 'Effekte von *Big Brother* auf den deutschen Programm- und Produktionsmarkt' [Effects of *Big Brother* on the German market of programming and production], in K. Böhme-Dürr and T. Sudholt (eds), *Hundert Tage Aufmerksamkeit. Das Zusammenspiel von Medien, Menschen und Märkten bei 'Big Brother' [One hundred days of attention. The interaction of media, people and markets at 'Big Brother']*, Konstanz, Germany: UVK, pp. 253–65.

Lantzsch, K. (2008), *Der internationale Fernsehformathandel. Akteure, Strategien, Strukturen, Organizationsformen [The International TV Format Trade. Actors, Strategies, Structures, Organizational Forms]*, Wiesbaden, Germany: VS Verlag für Sozialwissenschaften.

Lausen, M. (1998), *Der Rechtsschutz von Sendeformaten [The legal protection of broadcasting formats]*, Baden-Baden, Germany: Nomos.

Magder, T. (2004), 'The End of TV 101: Reality Programs, Formats, and the New Business of Television', in S. Murray and L. Ouellette (eds), *Reality TV: Remaking Television Culture*, New York: New York University Press, pp. 137–56.

Meckel, M. (1997), *Die neue Übersichtlichkeit. Zur Entwicklung des Format-Fernsehens in Deutschland [The new clarity. About the development of format television in Germany]*, Vienna: Rundfunk und Fernsehen, pp. 475–85.

Moran, A. (1998), *Copycat TV: Globalisation, Program Formats and Cultural Identity*, Luton: University of Luton Press.

O'Donnell, H. (1999), *Good Times, Bad Times: Soap Operas and Society in Western Europe*, London: Leicester University Press.

Pätzold, U. and Röper, H. (2003), 'Fernsehproduktionsvolumen 1998 bis 2000. Fortschreibung der Formatt-Studie über Konzentration und regionale Schwerpunkte der Auftragsproduktion' [The volume of television production from 1998 to 2000. Extrapolation of the format study about concentration and local key aspects of order production], *Media Perspektiven*, 1, pp. 24–34.

Picot, A., Reichwald, R. and Wigand, R.T. (2001), *Die grenzenlose Unternehmung. Information, Organization und Management. Lehrbuch zur Unternehmensführung im Informationszeitalter [The boundless firm. Information, organization and management. Textbook about corporate governance in the information age]*, 4th ed., Wiesbaden, Germany: Gabler.

Price, D. (2002), 'Der Porgrammrechtemarkt im digitalen Zeitalter. Analyse am Fallbeispiel Großbritannien' [The program rights market in the digital age: Analysis of the case of Great Britain], *Media Perspektiven*, 7, pp. 319–33.

Rautenstrauch, T., Generotzky, L. and Bigalke, T. (2003), *Kooperationen und Netzwerke. Grundlage und empirische Ergebnisse [Cooperations and networks. Basics and empirical results]*, Lohmar, Germany: Eul.

Schmitt, D. (2005), 'Quantifying the Global Trade in Television Formats', lecture presented on 10 June as part of the workshop 'International Television Format Trade' by the Erich-Pommer-Institute, Palma de Mallorca, Spain.

Schmitt, D., Bisson, G. and Fey, C. (2005), *The Global Trade in Television Formats*, London: Screen Digest.
Schumann, M. and Hess, T. (2002), *Grundfragen der Medienwirtschaft [Fundamentals of Media Economics]*, 2nd ed., Berlin, Germany: Springer.
Seufert, W. (2002), *Film- und Fernsehwirtschaft in Deutschland 2000/2001. Beschäftigte, wirtschaftliche Lage und Struktur der Produktionsunternehmen. Studie im Auftrag der Direktorenkonferenz der Landesmedienanstalten [Film and television business in Germany 2000/2001. Employees, economic situation and structure of production companies. Study by order of the directors' conference of the state media authorities]*, Berlin, Germany: Vistas.
Sydow, J. (1992), *Strategische Netzwerke. Evolution und Organization [Strategic networks. evolution and organization]*, Wiesbaden, Germany: Gabler.
Sydow, J. and Windeler, A. (eds) (2004), *Organization der Content-Produktion. [Organization of content production]*, Wiesbaden, Germany: VS Verlag für Sozialwissenschaften/GWV Fachverlage.
Television-Research-Partnership, Colwell, T. and Price, D. (2005), *Rights of Passage: British Television in the Global Market*, Commissioned by British Television Distributors' Association and UK Trade & Investment, London: UK Trade & Investment.
Waisbord, S. (2004), 'McTV: Understanding the Global Popularity of Television Formats', *Television New Media*, 5(4), pp. 359–83.
Windeler, A. (2001), *Unternehmensnetzwerke. Konstitution und Strukturation [Company networks. Constitution and structuration]*, Wiesbaden, Germany: Westdeutscher Verlag.
—— (2004), 'Organization der TV-Produktion in Projektnetzwerken. Zur Bedeutung von Produkt- und Industriespezifika' [Organization of TV-production in project networks. About the importance of specifics in products and industry], in J. Sydow and A. Windeler (eds), *Organization der Content-Produktion [Organization of content production] Wiesbaden*, Germany: VS Verlag für Sozialwissenschaften/GVW Fachverlage (pp. 55–76).
—— (2005), 'Netzwerktheorien. Vor einer relationalen Wende?' [Network Theories. Before a relational turn?], in J. Zentes, B. Swoboda and D. Morschett (eds), *Kooperationen, Allianzen und Netzwerke. Grundlagen, Ansätze, Perspektiven* [Cooperations, alliances and networks. Basics, approaches, prospects], 2nd ed., Wiesbaden, Germany: Gabler, pp. 211–33.

Chapter 6

The Rise of the Business Entertainment Format on British Television

Raymond Boyle

For most of its half-century of media dominance, TV has not had much truck with business programming.

– Virginia Matthews, Business Writer, *Management Today*, February 2006

It's easy to forget that before Harvey-Jones there was no room on popular TV for business.

– *Management Today*, September 2006

This chapter examines the rise of what has been called by television executives the 'business entertainment' format on British television over the last decade. As the traditional boundaries between news and current affairs, drama and documentary have blurred, British television has responded to these shifts by engaging with the world of business through differing forms and formats.

This research traces the development of the business entertainment format through programs such as *The Apprentice* and *Dragons' Den*. It develops work that has specifically examined the changing representation of business on factual television in the United Kingdom (Boyle 2008; Boyle and Magor 2008). While both formats originate from outside of the UK television market, the British versions are distinctly shaped by the wider public service culture that runs through large sections of the industry, and the BBC in particular.

The first section examines the broader changes that have taken place with regard to media business coverage with a particular focus on the role played by the BBC. Attention is then turned to television and the documentary tradition of business programming across British television channels before examining the rise of the 'business entertainment model' that has dominated the last few years. What do these formats tell us about the changing ecology of broadcasting in the United Kingdom?

Of particular interest here is the extent to which wider shifts in society and the related media ecology have helped shape a new and different interpretation of the role played by business and finance in the individual and collective lives of the United Kingdom. To what extent has television simply responded to wider social and economic change in society, or has the medium itself, through a particular focus on international television formats framed by drama, entertainment and performance, played a key role in redefining how we frame our engagement with issues related to business and finance?

Changing formats, changing times: The BBC and business

There are two strands that run through the evolution of the business entertainment format and its relationship with the BBC. The first is the engagement of the corporation through the years with business and financial journalism and its relative absence from the core of the BBC's journalistic remit until the appointment of Greg Dyke as Director-General in 2000. The second centres around the evolution of factual television formats through the BBC's documentary traditions, the development of the docu-soap in the 1990s and the evolution of this format into the ubiquitous reality television format of the last decade (Boyle 2008). In both strands, the ways in which the BBC engaged with business and financial issues has been crucial in shaping the culture that has allowed particular international formats to be recalibrated for a UK audience. In this process, it has also facilitated the BBC's legitimation of these forms as examples of what the delivery of public service content should look like in the increasingly competitive digital world of multi-platform delivery. Initially, let us examine the first of these strands: the BBC and its treatment of business and financial journalism.

The BBC, money and its audience

In 1966 the BBC launched *The Money Programme* (1966–), which would go on to become one of the longest running shows on British television. The BBC had been slow to appreciate that there might be any public appetite for investigations into the business world. According to the show's current editor, Clive Edwards, the initial drive within the BBC to create a program looking at the international world of business was less than enthusiastic:

> The idea for *The Money Programme*, according to its first editor, Terry Hughes, was handed down in a grand memo from the BBC Secretary Harman Grisewood: 'Now is the time we should be doing something about the economy for the people.' Behind the scenes, the suggestion was not welcomed. It was said that executives in the BBC felt 'money was boring'. (Edwards 2006)

Even television producers at the BBC were far from convinced that an audience existed for a program looking at business and the world of money.

Perhaps if they had looked more closely at how financial print journalism had developed in the 1960s they might have sensed a changing perception and attitude to matters of finance among sections of the public. Porter (2003) has documented the long tradition of popular financial journalism that has existed in the newspaper industry, more or less from its inception as a mass medium, while Sandbrook (2006: 15) argues that the long growth of the consumer society stretches back decades in British society, well before the 1960s, by which time newspapers such as the *Daily Mail* were devoting more and more space to personal finance issues.

The pace of social and economic change over the last few decades has been considerable, and a number of key issues have helped shape the changing relationship between the media more generally and their engagement with business in particular. As James Harding, then Business and City Editor of *The Times* and now its Editor, argues:

> Since the string of privatizations in the UK in the late 1980s and early 1990s there has been a spread in share ownership, and that means you have a volume of readers who have a stake in the business pages that you did not have a generation ago. At the same time you have had an enormous growth in the types of financial products available. So while you have more people interested in stocks and shares, that is only a part of the story. You have to understand that institutional shareholders are just a fraction of your readership now. (Interview with author, 15 March 2007)

These massive shifts in the economic structure of the British economy during the 1980s and 1990s saw the manufacturing sector being usurped by the services and financial sector, which in turn was facilitated by the opening up of the City to global influence. Sampson notes that:

> Over forty years the media has devoted more space and broadcasting time to business news, but it was normally segregated in separate sections from political and foreign news, and judged by different yardsticks of success, based on profits and bottom lines, with little reference to the political and social implications. Business journalists were slow to investigate shady companies and exaggerated claims or to risk expansive libels. (Sampson 2005: 244)

Doyle (2006) has demonstrated the extent to which financial journalism is often too close to those organizations it scrutinizes, and often lacks the will to apply journalistic rigour to this aspect of economic life.

The print media have reflected this economic shift, as well as legitimizing and endorsing the associated cultural changes in attitudes to business and finance. Labour correspondents on newspapers have all but disappeared, to be replaced by consumer affairs journalists, and there has been an explosion in the space devoted to personal finance in the print media. From housing to mortgages, pensions and investment portfolios, and Child Trust Funds, personal finance journalism has grown dramatically.

Jeff Randall has been a business journalist across both the print and broadcast media for over 25 years. Before becoming Editor-at-Large of the *Daily Telegraph*, he was for five years the first Business Editor at the BBC (he would also be directly involved in recruiting Sir Alan Sugar for the BBC version of *The Apprentice*). He argues:

> I think there has been a cultural shift in attitudes to business, and in many ways television was slow to catch on to this shift. In the 1970s profit was a bad word. If you made a profit

you exploited people. I think this was how the media classes wanted to see business. It changes in the 1980s when the Thatcherite revolution made business acceptable and desirable, and business moved from the business pages to the front pages. I think newspapers were quicker to pick up on this than television. Growth in personal finance issues across *The Sunday Times*, the *Sunday Telegraph* and the *Sun* has meant they have had a business editor for years. (Interview with author, 11 January 2007)

Shaped by, and in turn helping to reinforce, a broad political consensus that business was a central part of the wealth-creating process and that it benefited consumers, home owners and pension fund holders, media coverage of business changed.

The 2007–08 global financial crisis that originated in the sub-prime mortgage markets of the United States has, of course, catapulted business and financial news up the mainstream news agenda. In the United Kingdom, Robert Peston, who succeeded Jeff Randall as the BBC's Business Editor, has become one of the most high-profile television journalists in the country, responsible for breaking a number of major stories for the BBC around the banking crisis. Peston notes the emerging sea change at the BBC and its journalistic attitude to business:

When I arrived at the BBC I didn't think it gave enough weight to stories that were pretty important and it was harder to get stuff on air. This was the time the BBC thought it was ticking the business boxes with *Dragons' Den* and *The Apprentice.* But now the instinctive reaction of the BBC on a quiet news day is to turn to the business and economics department for a lead in a way that would have been unthinkable two or three years ago. (Quoted in *The Guardian*, 8 September 2008)

The origins of the two iconic BBC programs mentioned by Peston lie in the evolution of the BBC's migration from documentary engagement with the world of business to the construction of the business entertainment format.

The factual television formats for business content

The defining moment in the birth of the distinctive British version of the modern-day business entertainment format was the BAFTA award-winning *Troubleshooter* series, which aired on the BBC in the early 1990s and ran for two series and had two specials, the last in 2000. The BBC producer Robert Thirkell was the one of the key figures who, initially through his work with the BBC and its Business Unit and more recently as an independent producer, helped define and shape factual television's engagement with the world of business and work. The impact of the *Troubleshooter* series has been discussed elsewhere (Boyle 2008). However, its format – which had industrialist Sir John Harvey-Jones visiting ailing businesses offering advice – has been reformatted on a number of occasions over the last two decades. The most recent popular reincarnation (with more swearing, for example!) of this format can be seen in a program such as *Ramsay's Kitchen Nightmares* (Channel 4, 2004–), in which chef and restaurant owner Gordon Ramsay attempts to help failing restaurant businesses.

When Sir John Harvey-Jones died in 2008, the BBC broadcast an episode from the original 1990 series. It was introduced by Evan Davis, the presenter of *Dragons' Den* and a former BBC Economics Editor. It was striking to draw comparisons between the original forerunner of the business entertainment format and the present version. Looking at the *Troubleshooter* series now, one is struck by a number of factors: how fixated it was with the manufacturing economy (little examined today); how dated the factories and sites of British manufacturing look almost twenty years on (an indicator of their impending decline); and how much the program, while dominated by the larger than life Harvey-Jones, really is focused on offering a serious business analysis of the problems and challenges being faced by the various companies he visits. Of course, the engagement for the viewer is partly in the centrality of personalities and the role of communication (or lack of it) in contributing to the problems in the respective businesses. The program mobilizes a fly-on-the-wall documentary form and links it with a recognizable format (business guru visits failing business to see if he can help turn it around) that helps manage audience expectations.

While the documentary form had been used to look at the world of work and business, the arrival of the synergized docu-soap format in the mid-1990s allowed this area to be revisited by factual television, with the emphasis on character and entertainment. As Hill (2005: 78) has argued, 'The twin issues of performance and authenticity are significant to our understanding of popular factual television.'

Alan Yentob, Controller of BBC1 during the 1990s, recalls commissioning a number of relatively cheap docu-soaps for the channel to air during a quiet summer lull in the schedules in the mid-1990s, and being taken aback by the popularity and ratings achieved by programs such as *Driving School* and *Airport*.[1]

This decade become one characterized by both public and private sector businesses seemingly keen to raise their media profiles, and seeing television exposure as both potentially positive for the business and, in the case of the Royal Opera House for example, as a means of countering the negative publicity they had received in the print media. *The House* (BBC2, 1996) gave a behind-the-scenes insight into the business of running a major arts institution. Through clever editing, selection and the rejection of anything that was not seen as interesting, the series represented the Royal Opera House as a shambolic operation. Even with his vast television documentary experience, Sir Jeremy Isaacs, the Director of the Royal Opera House, failed to understand until too late that the series the BBC wanted to make about the organization was not a 'fly-on-the-wall' documentary, but rather a docu-soap. Isaacs (2000: 287) notes how 'everything these films sought to capture was exceptional; there was nothing of routine', and how the show's highly selective representations damaged the Royal Opera House's reputation.

Other programs worked better for the businesses involved. Perhaps the most significant and long running of these docu-soaps was first broadcast by ITV in 1999. *Airline* focused on easyJet, one of the pioneers of the then-emerging 'no-frills', low-cost airlines that restructured the aviation industry in the United Kingdom during the 1990s. There had been previous examples of airlines being involved with television documentary makers. Travel writer Simon Calder notes how:

> ITV dusted off the name of a documentary series made in the '70s about the daily life of British Airways...There are plenty of casualties of these 'warts and all' programmes in the travel industry. The country's biggest charter airline, Britannia (now Thomsonfly), did not emerge well from its flirtation with the cameras, while depictions of the excesses of some of Unijet's overseas reps reinforced the image of debauchery in Mediterranean resorts. (Calder 2008: 131)

Yet, for Stelios Haji-loannou, the founder of easyJet, allowing the cameras access to the business was part of a strategy to raise the profile of the company and emphasize its honesty as an employer. For Stelios, the program helped make easyJet a household name so it was a risk worth taking and an example of a business preparing to be open and honest with television documentary makers. Not all excursions into the genre of the docu-soap were successful for the businesses involved. Matthews (2006) notes how environmental health officers at London's Haringey Council claimed that the BBC series *Life of Grime* (2001), which focused on the council's Environmental Services division, 'wrecked recruitment' for three years (2006: 40).

By the start of the new century, the key ingredient that had been added to the docu-soap mix was that of jeopardy and risk, together with the arrival of 'reality television'. As Crisell (2006) argues:

> Reality TV is a prime example of the way that in which television endlessly combines and recombines older genres, for its antecedents are many, some of them time-worn... In recent times, television viewers have enjoyed the milder pleasure of watching people being humiliated when competing on game shows, but reality TV incorporates certain elements, and offers certain gratifications, that are recognisable from other generic forebears. (Crisell 2006: 89)

In the United States, an exemplar of this was a format devised by a former British paratrooper called Mark Burnett that would soon by exported across the globe. Burnett had developed a highly successful career in developing reality television formats in the United States. His idea to develop what was to become *The Apprentice* rested with securing the participation of Donald Trump and building an extended job interview around a series of weekly business tasks. The tasks would be undertaken by teams, with the losing team having one of its members fired. Burnett notes how originally he wanted to pitch the two teams as one of college graduates against non-college graduates, but difficulty in the casting process meant that, for the first series, they reverted to men versus women (Burnett 2006: 226).

The Apprentice: Business as entertainment

> Intelligent reality is back with a gripping insight into the machinations of the business world.
>
> – Roly Keating, Controller of BBC2, Press Release, 7 February 2006

> This is not a game. There is no phone-in here. There is no 'text-a-number'. There is no panel of judges that's gonna make the decision.
>
> – Sir Alan Sugar, *The Apprentice*, BBC Television

The commercial drive for television to create content for evolving formats that connected with a changing society and ostensibly brought something new to the audience has intensified in the last number of years. As these increasingly international formats merged with more traditional genres such as the game show, it would be the business arena that would offer the possibility of reimaging the world of commerce and the entrepreneur. It was estimated in 2007 that, in the thirteen most important television markets, entertainment acquisition and production were worth £1.87 billion (Altmeppen et al. 2007: 94).

What was significant about the US version of *The Apprentice* was that the program itself became an exemplar of the extent to which television formats were being both shaped by, and embedded in, the wider commercial broadcasting environment. As the New York-based company Hitwise (www.Hitwise.com), which analyzes commercial internet traffic and provides marketing intelligence to a range of industries, suggests:

> With an increasing number of consumers skipping commercials due to the popularity of TiVo and other digital video recorders, the reality-television revolution has provided marketers with a critical new generation of product placement. (http://www.hitwise.com, posted 25 April 2005)

Marketing analyst Rebecca Lieb is executive editor of the ClickZ Network (http://www.clickz.com). She notes how *The Apprentice* offered a unique opportunity for explicit product placement television, allied with a multi-platform format that drove television viewers to commercial internet sites. For the public service BBC version of the program, however, such an overtly commercial structure would need to be modified.

For the BBC, this format allowed it to make claims about its evolving public service remit in an increasingly competitive multi-platform digital age. It also reflected the wider cultural shift taking place across its journalism, and its attitude to business and enterprise discussed at the beginning of this chapter (Boyle 2008). Writing in *The Times* about *The Apprentice*, Tim Teeman argued that:

> As a reality show that majors on business rather than bed-hopping, it has a figleaf of Reithian propriety about it. A colleague's children watch it and apparently learn something

> about buying and selling. A friend who works in Whitehall reports that it is discussed at departmental meetings. (*The Times*, 10 May 2006)

What was beyond doubt was that it offered a very different image of the world of business than had been explored decades earlier in *Troubleshooter*. For example, the first episode of series two (broadcast in February 2006 on BBC 2) intercuts between the fourteen contestants all arriving by rail, road and tube to the metropolitan centre, framed against a backdrop of communications and data babble, iconic London cityscapes and the incessant movement of people. It's brash, exciting and monied, and represents what business supposedly means in twenty-first century Britain; it's about getting ahead and competing, and indicates that the only success that matters is the bottom line. It is the 1980s cinematic image of Thatcher's Britain, given a stylistic makeover for television and suggesting that making money and the centrality of business and entrepreneurship in British society are by the 2000s viewed as the norm. The underlying message of *The Apprentice* is that an ideological battle (that making money is good) has been won.

There is also a debate about the educational merit of these programs. In the United States, where *The Apprentice* with Donald Trump was first broadcast in 2004 on NBC and was securing an audience of nineteen million viewers, numerous college and university business courses were using it as a 'career advice tool' (Kinnick and Parton 2005: 430). Indeed, both the show's creator Mark Burnett and its US star Donald Trump felt that the educational dimension was part of its audience appeal (Burnett 2006: 215). Elsewhere, academics were divided over the relative educational merits of the show, with some thinking it offered insight into business leadership and management issues (Simon 2004), while others considered that it presented a partial, distorted view of the world of business and the skills needed to succeed (Cadden 2004). In the United Kingdom, business broadcaster and journalist Jeff Randall suggests:

> Does [*The Apprentice*] really tell people about business? Well not in a new way. It has been a success because Alan Sugar is such a ghastly character in such an attractive way and the structure of the show is episodic, building to a climax and you get to know the characters in the way like a soap opera. *The Apprentice* works because he is Alan Sugar. (Interview with author, 11 January 2007)

Interestingly, the third BBC series of *The Apprentice* (2007) involved recruiting Michele Kurland as Executive Producer. Kurland, whose background at the BBC had been in the Business Unit, came with a strong business journalism background. She was recruited by the show's makers Thames Talkback to strengthen the business dimension of the program, which some felt was becoming diluted, with too much focus on the human-interest dimension of the characters. However, as Kinnick and Parton (2005) argue with regard to the US version of the show:

> The legacy of this television show for educators is that it is driving home the need for effective communication skills in vivid and memorable ways that business schools have failed to provide. If audience members get the message, whether the show is realistic is probably beside the point. (2005: 448)

The same argument may also be applicable to the BBC version, despite criticism from organizations such as the Confederation of British Industry (CBI) that such shows are unrealistic (Budd 2007).

The Apprentice uses the full range of BBC platforms from television (including a spinoff show) across to a dedicated site on the Internet (which includes extensive video clips of both past and forthcoming episodes). This is an example of what the BBC calls '360 degree programming', which means that program content should be available across media platforms from television to mobile phones in a coherent manner (*The Apprentice* BBC website received four million requests for content downloads between February and May 2006). Thus, for the BBC, the 'business entertainment' format has been of significant importance in both raising its profile and presenting an organization that is innovative in terms of new formats.

In one of the quirks of what Raymond Williams (1974) famously called television's flow, the second series of *The Apprentice* on BBC2 was followed by a stylistically different docu-soap called *The Armstrongs* (2006). In this, we followed the husband and wife team of John and Ann Armstrong as they ran U-Fit, 'the third largest double glazing firm in Coventry'. Visually influenced by the BBC comedy *The Office* (2001–03), and underscored by a laconic Bill Nighy voiceover, the series allowed the viewer into the esoteric, chaotic, idiosyncratic and comedic world of business according to the Armstrongs. For example, the episode in which they go France in order to expand their business has a number of set-piece comedy moments, as does the one involving Zimbabwean motivational coach Basil Mienie's attempts to increase productivity among the lack-lustre workforce.

Here were juxtaposed two differing visions of doing business in twenty-first century Britain, viewed through differing television formats that shaped the material, defined the narratives and set the program structure to suit a particular genre and the audience at which it was aimed. In fact, the Armstrongs had first appeared in a one off BBC2 documentary in 2003, and their business had been considered as a possible case study for an episode of the Gerry Robinson BBC series (2003–) *I'll Show Them Who's Boss*, but it was felt they were not suitable.

Enter the Dragon...

One of the other business entertainment formats that has proven to be successful, particularly in its UK version, has been *Dragons' Den* (2005–). This format originated in Japan, and a show called *Money no Tora* (meaning *Money Tiger*) that was created by Sony and broadcast on Nippon television in 2001. At the core of the BBC program – which is the longest running of any of the versions of the format that have been sold to Australia, New Zealand, Israel, Canada, Finland and the Netherlands – is the idea of business investors having ideas pitched at them by a range of inventors and/or entrepreneurs. The investors (dragons) put up their own money, and those seeking investment in their idea/product/business must secure the full investment or leave with nothing. In so doing, they echo the practice of business 'angels' type investment, where venture capitalists take various forms of risk by investing in new startup ventures.

The pitches take place in a rather rundown warehouse location and, while the dragons have changed over the six series of the program, two have remained throughout the series. Indeed, both Duncan Bannatyne and Peter Jones have used the media profile that the program has offered them to develop and enhance their own broader media and business profile (most of the dragons will produce autobiographies and business self-help books). Jones has himself moved into television production and extended his media portfolio into creating new television formats, including co-creating *American Inventor* (which ran for two seasons on ABC Television from 2006) and *Tycoon*, which his production company also produced for ITV in the United Kingdom in 2007.

In the United Kingdom, the *Dragons' Den* version has aired on BBC2 and been fronted by Evan Davis, who was then the BBC's Economics Editor and has since become one of the key presenters on BBC radio's flagship morning news *Today* program. Davis is clear that the format comes out of BBC Entertainment; however, that does not mean it has no other merits beyond being a simple entertainment mode of address to the audience – not least in having an educational element regarding the world of business. He argues:

> It's good fortune is that it has had both of these elements. I think it can be educational, and there are words used on the *Dragons' Den* that would not get on a news program. For example, you would tend to use the word 'shares' rather than 'equity' on a news program. On *Dragons' Den*, the word is used all the time. I do think that TV can create a climate of opinion, but that is not necessarily the intention. I wouldn't want you to think there is any mission here. There is no mission here other than to entertain. By good fortune, the entertainment requires a bit of educational fibre and those of us who like the public to get exposed to those sorts of things are quite happy to join in with it as we know this is a pretty good way to give people a sense of what goes on. I think programs such as *Dragons' Den* have brought ideas about enterprise to a wider audience. I base that on the reaction from the public, and particularly younger people, to the show. Among, say, fourteen to twenty-two-year-olds, they are interested in the program and TV has helped shape that climate of opinion. (Interview with author, 12 January 2007)

In late 2008, Mark Burnett, the United States-based creator of *The Apprentice*, had secured a pilot slot from ABC television for his version of *Dragons' Den*, called *The Shark Tank*. In the world of business entertainment formats, it seems that what goes around certain television markets comes around, although all these programs are specifically tailored for their particular institution location and the particular television market and audiences at which they are aimed.

Conclusion

> *The Apprentice* has as much to do with business as bullfighting has to do with animal husbandry.
>
> – Television producer Peter Bazalgette, interview, 2008

In part, what is being argued here is that, in an age of international formats, not only do the particularities of national television audiences still matter, but also the institutional histories and memory that shape organizations such as the BBC are important. The social, cultural and political context within which television content gets consumed remains crucial in defining popularity and meaning among the audience. This, of course, does not mean that significant change is shaping that experience and interaction between consumers, citizens and media.

There is also a key role played by certain individuals in shaping and driving formats. In the United States, Mark Burnett has been a key instigator of a number of reality television format successes including *The Apprentice*, while in the United Kingdom over the years – first at the BBC and later as an independent producer – Robert Thirkell has been a key innovator in thinking about how television might engage with the world of business and work.

Thirkell would leave the BBC in 2003 to set up as an independent producer and work on programs such as *Jamie's School Dinners* for Channel 4, which mixed aspects of celebrity recognition with campaigning and agenda-setting television. Although not about business *per se*, a raft of programs could be found in the schedules relating to some aspect of business and entrepreneurial culture, often grouped under the rubric of lifestyle television. At the core of many of these programs were aspirational notions of walking away from a mundane job, as well as stories of people who had decided to change their lives through some risk-taking decision.

A more market-orientated television industry has seen British public service broadcasters such as the BBC and Channel 4 increasingly embrace – at least rhetorically – the centrality of enterprise and aspiration in British society. However, over 40 years on from the launch of *The Money Programme*, the challenge for public service broadcasters such as the BBC is to find ways to engage with the deeper structures and processes that are driving and shaping the impact of business in a globalizing economy on society and its citizens. As broadcasting becomes increasingly commercially orientated, concerned with delivering entertainment content to specific audience demographics and stopping advertising revenues leaking to other media such as the Internet, there remains a need for PSB television to offer a range of representations about what it is like to live and work in modern Britain. Leaving that task solely to the domain of news and current affairs limits the ability of television to play a role in any national conversation.

In the midst of the global economic downturn of the late 2000s, the extent to which the media really address the complex and multifaceted ways in which people's lives are shaped and influenced by business issues has become increasingly important. In his overview of the political, economic and cultural changes that have shaped modern Britain, Anthony Sampson (2005) argues that, despite more media coverage being devoted to the worlds of business and finance, these areas remain under-reported. He suggests:

> During the past four decades big corporations, financiers and banks have hugely extended their influence over the lives of ordinary people who have become more dependent on them for shopping, their leisure or their credit. Government itself has cooperated much more closely with the private sector, as the Treasury has delegated more and more projects to commercial consortia. And...lawyers, academics and journalists who have a record of proud independence, have all become more interlocked with the interests of big business. (2005: 244)

The related issue is also whether the formatted television mode of address is best suited to redressing this imbalance. As Stella Bruzzi (2000) has argued:

> The characteristics that have come to represent the docusoap subgenre of observational documentary are its emphasis on the entertainment as opposed to serious or instructive value of documentary, the importance of personalities who enjoy performing for the camera, soap like fast editing, a prominent, guiding voice-over, a focus on everyday lives rather than underlying social issues. (2000: 76)

As we enter an era that will see the web and television grow ever more interconnected, there is a need to map out innovative ways of drawing in an audience through formats that, for example, may offer them a stake in shaping the narratives and stories being told. Commercial television is more likely to tweak already successful formats and focus on the entertainment angle. Public service broadcasters should be mobilizing a range of journalistically driven factual entertainment formats and genres that offer differing representations and insights into the ongoing ways in which business and the world of work are changing, and in turn being changed by, contemporary society. Before his death in 2008, the original troubleshooter Sir John Harvey-Jones criticized the style of business management being celebrated on UK television. He insisted that the ethos behind his shows was always one of constructive guidance, arguing: 'It is not your job to exploit your position of power. It's easy [to do that]. My experience of life is that you get the best out of people by encouraging their self-belief.' (Quoted in *Birmingham Post*, 1 January 2008)

In terms of television's engagement with the world of business, one could argue that the picture of a workforce characterized as bored, frustrated, disillusioned and harbouring blighted ambition portrayed in the hit BBC television comedy *The Office* (2001–03) or the BBC docu-soap *The Armstrongs* (2006) is at least as accurate in articulating the cultural context of the British worker in the twenty-first century as the reality business entertainment formats which purport to reflect the dynamic business environment of contemporary Britain. Yet, given the massive displacement that the current economic crisis is likely to have across all sectors of economic and social life, a substantive revisiting of the world of work and business will likely occur. While this will no doubt focus on the human impact of the financial meltdown, the challenge in the United Kingdom will be to develop appropriate television formats that can capture, illuminate and explain this process while also entertaining an increasingly distracted audience.

Note

1. Alan Yentob was speaking in an interview in the Channel 4 documentary *Who Killed the British Sitcom?* broadcast on 2 January 2006.

References

Altmeppen, K.D, Lantzsch, K. and Will, A. (2007), 'Flowing Networks in the Entertainment Business: Organizing TV Format Trade', *International Journal of Media Management*, 9(3), pp. 94–104.

Boyle, R. (2008), 'From *Troubleshooter* to *The Apprentice*: The Changing Face of Business on British Television', *Media, Culture and Society*, 30(3), pp. 415–24.

Boyle, R. and Magor, M. (2008), 'A Nation of Entrepreneurs? Television, Social Change and the Rise of the Entrepreneur', *International Journal of Media and Cultural Politics*, 4(2), pp. 125–44.

Bruzzi, Stella (2000), *New Documentary: A Critical Introduction*, London: Routledge.

Budd, A. (2007). *Report of the Independent Panel for the BBC Trust in impartiality of BBC Business Coverage*, London: BBC.

Burnett, M. (2006), *Jump In!* New York: Ballantine Books.

Cadden, David (2004), 'You're Fired!' *BizEd*, July/August, pp. 42–49, http://www.aacsb.edu/publications/archives/JulyAug04/p42-49.pdf. Accessed 11 June 2009.

Calder, S. (2008), *No-Frills: The Truth Behind the Low Cost Revolution in the Skies*, London: Virgin Books.

Corner, J. (2004), 'Afterword: Framing the New', in S. Holmes and D. Jermyn (eds), *Understanding Reality Television*, London: Routledge.

Crisell, A. (2006), *A Study of Modern Television: Thinking Inside the Box*, Basingstoke: Palgrave.

Davis, E. (2005), *Dragons' Den: Your Idea Can Make You Rich*, London: Vermilion.

Doyle, G. (2006), 'Financial News Journalism: A Post-Enron Analysis of Approaches Towards Economic and Financial News Production in the UK', *Journalism*, 7(4), pp. 433–52.

Edwards, C. (2006), 'Forty Years of *The Money Programme*', http://www.bbc.co.ukgo/pr/fr/-/hi/business/4772275.stm. Accessed 11 June 2009.

Elliott, L. and Atkinson, D. (2007), *Fantasy Island: Waking Up to the Incredible Economic, Political and Social Illusions of the Blair Legacy,* London: Constable.
Hesmondhalgh, D. (2007), *The Cultural Industries*, 2nd ed., London: Sage.
Hill, A. (2005), *Reality TV: Audiences and Popular Factual Television,* London: Routledge.
Isaacs, J. (2000), *Never Mind the Moon: My Time at the Royal Opera House,* London: Bantam Books.
Keating, R. (2005), *The Rebirth of Business Television*, speech given at Enterprise Britain Summit, 14 November.
Kilborn, R., Hibberd, M. and Boyle, R. (2001), 'The Rise of the Docusoap: The Case of *Vets in Practice*', *Screen,* 42(4), pp. 382–95.
Kinnick, K.N. and Parton, S.R. (2005), 'Workplace Communication: What *The Apprentice* Teaches About Communication Skills', *Business Communication Quarterly*, 68(4), pp. 429–56.
Lambert, R. (2006), 'Business is the Beating Heart of Society', speech to the Social Market Foundation, London, 5 September.
Matthews, V. (2006), 'Docu-soap Can Get in Your Eyes', *Management Today,* February.
Moran, A. and Malbon, J. (2006), *Understanding the Global TV Format*, Bristol: Intellect.
Porter, D. (2003), 'City Slickers in Perspective': The *Daily Mirror*, Its Readers and Their Money, 1960–2000', *Media History*, 9(2), pp. 137–52.
Sandbrook, D. (2006), *White Heat: A History of Britain in the Swinging Sixties,* London: Little Brown.
Sampson, A. (2005), *Who Runs This Place? The Anatomy of Britain in the 21st Century*, London: John Murray.
Schlesinger, P. (2006), 'Creativity: From Discourse to Doctrine?' *e-compos*, 7, http://www.compos.org.br/e-compos, Accessed 2 December 2008.

Chapter 7

Collaborative Reproduction of Attraction and Performance: The Case of the Reality Show *Idol*

Yngver Njus

Since 2002, *American Idol* has been produced annually, regularly attracting more than 30 million Americans to their television screens, which is practically unheard of in the current multi-channel system. Rival channels call it the 'death star', and the same program format has enjoyed equally overwhelming success in Norway since the first production in 2003, although some seasons have shown signs of weakness.

This chapter explores the work that goes into reproducing and maintaining the format's initial success. This work is particularly significant today in light of the range of television channels emerging in global and national markets over recent decades, which has also coincided with a drastic rise of online and mobile media (Deuze 2007). In this context of intensified competition for audiences' attention, television companies have decreasing margins of failure and increasing imperatives for maximizing and defending their most popular output. Here I am concerned with evolving efforts and techniques for preserving audiences' attention, and in this regard I present an analysis of the licensed talent contest *Idol*, which has been reproduced in more than 40 territories around the world.[1]

My interests here locate this chapter under the heading of media production studies, as I attempt to relate media structures and institutional practices to program output. The relatively few existing format studies primarily deal with industry mega-structures, and arise from an interest in global trade and media culture (e.g. see Moran 1998; Waisbord 2004; Steemers 2007; Jensen 2007). The studies respond appropriately to the need for analyses of the effects of globalization on cultural industries that is called for by Scott (2006), among others: 'In general, far too little research addresses phenomena at this level even though scholars are well aware that among the most significant developments of our time are the rise of trans-societal associations and organizations.' (2006: 306) Scott argues that such studies are particularly important in periods of rapid change, and they ought to range from the most macro to the most micro levels of analysis. I concur, and in this chapter intend to direct attention to a problem area that remains rarely touched upon: the work behind reproducing program success in different contexts (see also Kjus 2007). I consider the following questions: (1) How do media producers collaborate across organizational and geographical borders? (2) How do formats reproduce popular content, and using what tools and routines? (3) How do people handle the particular challenges of reproducing or maintaining attraction in reality game shows, including the participation of so-called everyday people? I hope to come up with a description of program production and program output that best reflects the evolving strategies, practices and collaborative forms of central actors in the television industry.[2]

Variations of 'reality' and 'game show' programs dominate the global format trade (Schmitt et al. 2005), and are of particular interest to television industry analysis. This study focuses on the Norwegian version of *Idol* produced by the hybrid broadcaster TV2 (a commercial enterprise with certain public service obligations). Since its first season in 2001 (for ITV), *Idol* has been one of the most successful programs in the entire television industry, and has inspired format developers and producers worldwide. Before I begin this specific discussion, I will place reality game shows in a historical and industrial context in order to emphasize their strategic importance and some of their core production dilemmas. A particular challenge in the genre involves handling the participation of so-called ordinary people, and making their stories intriguing. I evaluate how *Idol* deals with this, in particular analyzing the importance of key format scripts, such as set design and running order, and reviewing the ways in which production know-how is circulated. I argue that format scripts of this kind are key discursive entities for the stability and innovation of a format, and that they are negotiated on a managerial level as well as a concrete production level.

Reality game show attractions

Game shows have had a prominent position in broadcasting almost from the start, utilizing the basic structures of human involvement and engagement that are incumbent to game play (Hoerschelmann 2006). They were among the very first television programs to be patented and licensed for reproduction, and different variations on the same formats or themes turned out to have massive appeal. Particularly (in)famous is the national frenzy over *The $64,000 Question* and *Twenty-One* on US networks in the late 1950s, as well as the subsequent fraud scandal and drop in popularity (Anderson 1978). The genre's prestige has risen and fallen over the years, while inviting considerable hybridization, producing daytime and evening shows as well as innovative variations such as *Have I Got News for You* and *The Lyrics Board* in the 1990s, which were fuelled by the appeal of current events and talented singers, respectively.

At the end of the 1990s, the game show genre took another dramatic turn with programs such as *Survivor*, *Big Brother*, *Idol* and *So You Think You Can Dance*, all of which introduced an essential twist: docu-soap elements. Docu-soaps portray real biographical people using narrative techniques from both documentaries and soap operas. In reality game shows, these techniques intensify the drama of ordinary people stepping into the limelight of the media, performing, and in this way possibly becoming something extraordinary (Jerslev 2004).[3] The impact of this program trend is highly visible on US television, where only those game shows with human-interest stories are able to compete in prime-time slots. In Norway, with the aid of the international reality game shows *The Farm*, *Idol*, *Dancing with the Stars* and *Norway's Got Talent*, TV2 has even been able to challenge the traditional weekend prime-time fortress of the market leader NRK. The day-to-day unfolding of the dramas in these contests has a prodigious ability to attract audiences and media coverage, thereby counteracting both intensified competition in the timeslots and viewer fragmentation. However, in order to achieve this, program producers need to present ordinary people doing something extraordinary, and master the contradictory work of controlling people's performances while preserving their authenticity.

Attraction and deception

Game shows build drama in different ways and present different temptations to producers. For instance, the big money quizzes of the 1950s created great tension around the moments of truth when answers were given and participants' fortunes were made (or not). Many participants rocketed to national fame; however, in order to guarantee success (and assert their control over it), producers began to provide them with the questions in advance (Anderson 1978). When the cheating was revealed, the genre imploded in America. Interestingly, 50 years later, in the summer of 2006, the BBC experienced a similar scandal, a 'black Wednesday' for public service broadcasting in the United Kingdom. It was discovered that numerous phone-in competition programs had been faked, including flagship charity appeal programs such as *Children in Need*, *Comic Relief* and *Sport Relief* (e.g. see Gibson 2007). The transgressions included production staff passing themselves off as members of the public as well as the announcement of fictitious winners. The excuses mostly involved technical difficulties with the programs' massive telephone response, but to viewers the treachery still resembled the 1950s scandal.[4]

In general, then, when the basic premises of a game show are challenged or otherwise stressed, the whole program, and even the entire genre, can be endangered. Syvertsen (2001) found the same sort of problem in a Norwegian dating game in the 1990s: actual romance between participants waned as the producers became more concerned with instructing them to appear romantic on screen. In trying to make the most of the show, in effect, the producers risked its essential authenticity. Syvertsen argues that the producers' efforts to generate intimate drama resemble the effort spent on securing the 'money shot' of daytime talk shows, which Grindstaff (1997: 168) describes as 'the moment of raw emotion, from angry denunciation to tearful confession'. Grindstaff describes in detail the work of making the participants – so-called ordinary people – express their private emotions in public, which is a principal aim of reality game show producers as well. However, in the wake of reality formats designed to evoke these displays, participants have become aware of how to play along, and audiences have in turn become sceptical, and begun to hunt for those moments that cannot possibly be faked (Hill 2005).

The production techniques of recent reality shows should be seen in this light. In a study of *Big Brother*, Ytreberg (2006) shows how this social experiment is premeditated and 'indirectly directed' by scripts that aim for an 'unscripted feel'. One central script in his analysis is the set design which, through the arrangement of bedrooms, bathrooms and living rooms (and the corresponding camera placement), frames and then captures the desired interactions. In what follows, I will extend this approach to *Idol* as well (and thus to formats that stage distinctly different events), demonstrating how the scripts of the national talent contest generate engaging performances while preserving the authenticity (and drama) of the song competition. Scripts are the documents that are used to organize production on the concrete level of staging interactions and coordinating their recording. I argue that, in *Idol*, a set of key scripts is essential for successful reproduction, and my analysis focuses on game rules, set design and running order.[5] The game rules define the over-arching structure of the program; the set design defines the space and social architecture; and the running order governs the temporality and the eventual editing (and knitting together) of the program. These are all elements specified in the 'bible', which is the collection of production documents that comes when a format licence is purchased. However, format scripts are not fixed, but rather developed and negotiated in ways I will examine below.

Approaching reproduction structures

There are several challenges associated with studying the reproduction process of formats, and first among them is the magnitude of the work carried out across time and space. In terms of research capacity, it is impossible to track the reproduction history of *Idol*, beginning in 2001 and ranging across 40 countries to date. Moreover, reproduction involves a host of collaborations across media organizations, and the entirety of their work is inaccessible in practical terms. Therefore, I have had to make strategic selections concerning material and perspective, and what I find here may not be valid for other *Idol* realizations, let alone the many other formats and actors in the business. However, *Idol* is managed and licensed (and sometimes produced) by the global production company FremantleMedia, which became the largest and most experienced trader of game show formats when it acquired Grundy Television in the 1990s (Moran 1998). It is therefore as good a place as any to start to chart practices. (*Idol* was originally developed by, and is still owned by, the global media entertainment company 19.) My window into the life of *Idol* is its reproduction in Norway, where I can study the collaborative work of reproducing success while providing comparative material for other format studies as well.

My main research methods include interviews with core producers, observations during a handful of episode productions between 2005 and 2007, and a qualitative analysis of the program output.[6] These methods allow me to relate issues of organization to program effects, and thereby elucidate central processes and sites for the development and exchange of production competence. These processes and sites result in a program format that transcends the format 'bible', and include the follow-up work of the format-holder which, through its 'travelling producers' and format consultants, seeks to maintain the value of its format brand across territories. This effort involves regular contact with, and occasional visits to, local producers – not only to control but also to coordinate and guide them. An important aspect of this work is to transfer production competence from one realization to another, which is also accomplished by having producers from different countries visit one another, particularly in the start-up and innovation phases. Perhaps the most explicit sites for format development are annual industry conferences such as MIPCOM in Cannes, where *Idol* producers from all over the world can exchange experiences and tips.

The agents so far mentioned also engage in a range of informal correspondence (typically via phone and email) among themselves, comprising a network that interacts in a variety of ways in the work of reproduction. These interactions are unfortunately not available to me firsthand, and a full ethnographic study of these collaborations would be invaluable to the study of formats. However, my methods and sources also provide access to key practices and rationales of format exchange.

Game rules and framework

The concept behind *Idol* is to host a national singing contest in order to create a successful pop artist. It is therefore important for FremantleMedia to prioritize the largest television companies in each territory – those with the greatest reach and resources (Jensen 2007). In order for the contest to appear to be an extensive and exceptional event, the process behind *Idol* involves auditions in cities all over the country, where everyone within a given age limit is given the opportunity to perform. Importantly, viewers themselves decide the outcome of the contest via telephone voting. These over-arching game rules define the 'magic' framework of *Idol*, where dreams can come true, and they are crucial to the format's ability to engage the audience. Johan Huizinga (2000) has shown how gameplay, and especially the acceptance of extraordinary rules within given time/space limits, has deep roots across cultural traditions. The universal familiarity of gameplay thus helps with the transfer of *Idol* and similar formats across different countries and television systems.

As we evaluate the work of recreating *Idol*, we must distinguish between the motives of the global licence-holders and those of the local television producers. The former are generally more interested in retaining the long-term value of their format brands, whereas the latter prioritize immediate success and ratings. As one of *Idol*'s travelling producers from FremantleMedia puts it: 'Ultimately, it's our show. For [television companies] it's like heroin.' (Lieberman 2005) A key expression of this latter compulsion is the tendency of local producers to identify contestants whom they believe will catch the attention of the audience, and to present them more favourably.[7] *Idol* thereby violates a basic game rule – that of equal chances and treatment – and should this be revealed, it might harm not only the local realizations of the show but also the global brand. That is why the game rules of *Idol* are strongly emphasized in the 'bible' as well as by format consultants, particularly with regard to the equal treatment of all contestants.[8]

Idol's set of rules constitutes a script that all local producers must follow – any variations (for instance, due to local transmission schedules) must be checked with the format-holders. On a more detailed level, the game rules prescribe every stage in the contest, down to how many songs the participants must memorize to audition, whether they can bring musical instruments, where they need to walk and perform, and so on. They also prescribe how many contestants proceed to the semi-finals (between 24 and 50) and the finals (between eight and twelve), and how the finalists are trained and tested until a winner emerges.

The basic contest sequence, repeated throughout *Idol*, consists of the performance of a contestant followed by an evaluation by a board of judges. The board is made up of pop music professionals, and they continue to pass judgement in the semi-finals and finals, although the power to decide the fates of contestants shifts to the viewers after the auditions. An essential mission of this sequence of events is to depict the encounter of everyday amateurs with the music industry, and to condense the drama as their dreams meet reality. The game rules of *Idol* ensure that everyday people, with no experience with professional media production, can function in highly professionalized television production suited for prime-time schedules. They only need a minimum of instructions to perform their roles as song contestants, thereby preserving the spontaneity and authenticity of their emotional reactions. Moreover, the pop songs structure the participants' performance in suitable temporal units (and provide them with verbatim scripts), and the familiarity of the songs provides the viewers with a basis for recognition and evaluation. The 'money shot' of *Idol* arrives when participants are evaluated – criticized or embraced, rejected or accepted – and they deliver their often-emotional response. These moments have three levels of intensity: after each song performance; at the end of each episode when someone is voted off (in the semi-finals and finals); and in the final episode when the new 'Idol' is elected.

The rules of the contest create a structure for both audience involvement and the recurring emotional displays of the contestants, and they have accommodated effective reproductions of the format in numerous countries. However, the *Idol* project leader in the Norwegian television company insists that a program must not only adapt to local conditions, but also continually reinvent itself: 'Otherwise it will die, and that is something everyone in the business knows.' Correspondingly, within the basic framework described in the show's 'bible', FremantleMedia not only allows for variation, but actually encourages it. In Norway, the most drastic of such measures was taken after the fourth season. For three seasons, the show's popularity had grown, but in the fourth season it fell markedly – there were complaints that the contestants were boring and that the winners did not succeed as pop musicians. According to the project leader, the format needed a makeover, and staffers drew inspiration from the production network described in the previous section. In the United States, the Fox television network was enjoying incredible success with the format, and central personnel from TV2 flew over to study *American Idol* and talk to its producers. Subsequently, several game rules were copied. The age limit was extended from 28 to 25 years, allowing for a greater range of talent and more focus on singing skills than on the attractiveness of teenagers. Contest episodes were also structured around established pop artists (such as Elton John in the United States and Morten Harket (from A-ha) in Norway), who trained the participants. Apart from the added attraction of seeing these celebrities, this twist also added to the credibility of the program as a music industry contest.

FremantleMedia immediately accepted most of these measures. The format consultant responsible for European territories also visited TV2, promoting the adjustments that had been made in other parts of the world. Another change decided on by TV2 was inspired by the Australian version of the show, in which contestants were allowed to bring a musical instrument to the auditions. The large production network of *Idol* facilitated this kind of format renewal. The new rules not only reinforced the credibility of the program but also became attractions in their own right. They redrew the 'world' set up by the game rules and re-posed the question 'What will happen now?' Changing the rules also generated broad media coverage for TV2 and introduced a new sense of the possible and the unpredictable to *Idol*. The effort certainly contributed to the renewed popularity of *Idol* in its fifth season, which found it back on the top of the charts.

Set design and social drama

Whereas the rules script determines the overall structure of the game, the way it is staged and captured on camera depends on other scripts, such as the set design. The essential drama of *Idol* is the encounter of hopeful amateurs with the brutal realities of the music industry. A set design script defines the space of the studio and the general positioning of cameras, thus anticipating the movement of performers within it. It creates, in effect, a social architecture that emphasizes the emotional tension and release of performing on stage. A dramaturgical motor of reality TV in general is to move back and forth between front-stage social interaction and back-stage intimate disclosure.[9] In *Idol*, these spaces encourage the sought-after contestant behaviour particularly well, because the front-stage is an actual stage for the artists' performances. The adjacent rooms are carefully designed as a back-stage that emphasizes the drama of entering and exiting the stage. It is therefore divided into two spaces, called the waiting room and 'death row' by the producers, and contestants are led in

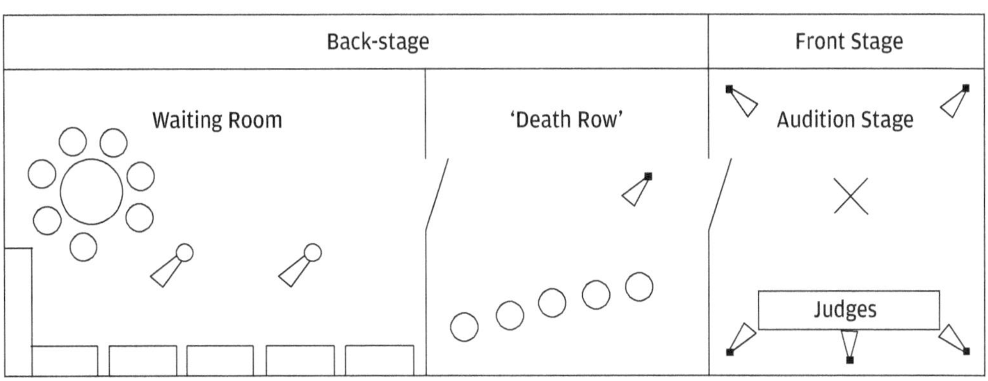

Figure 7.1: The general set design for the auditions.

groups of five from a relaxed lounge area into a small room with a line of chairs leading up to the door behind which the judges wait. Figure 7.1 provides a sketch of the standard set design.

As contestants move from one room to the next, their nerves tighten and different camera crews follow and interview them along the way. The emotional intensity is underscored by décor, lighting and camera positions, which are also standardized in the set design. As the participants are led from lounge sofas to the chairs of 'death row' and on to the x-mark of the audition stage, the cameras used to capture the drama go from handheld and impulsive to stationary and fixed. Consequently, emotional build-up and disclosure are generated with a minimum of direct instruction and intervention.

Set variations and their effects

The auditions hardly diverge from the described set script, but in the semi-finals and finals producers often change things from season to season. First, the decoration of the main stage is always tweaked in order to give each season a sense of novelty. Moreover, by making alterations to the social spaces of the set, the producers often attempt to refine the viewing experience. The set design of the semi-finals in 2005 therefore tried to maintain a sense of a dramaturgical back-stage, despite the fact that these episodes were produced before a live studio audience. The Norwegian producers decided to put up a screen behind which the contestants would sit before and after each performance, and where they were interviewed about their expectations and feelings (see Figure 7.2).

This simulated back-stage was supposed to make the amateur participants express themselves spontaneously despite the pressure of a large live studio production. However, the producers were somewhat disappointed by the contestants' expressiveness in the back-stage sequences, and in the 2006 season the screen was removed. The talk with the contestants was

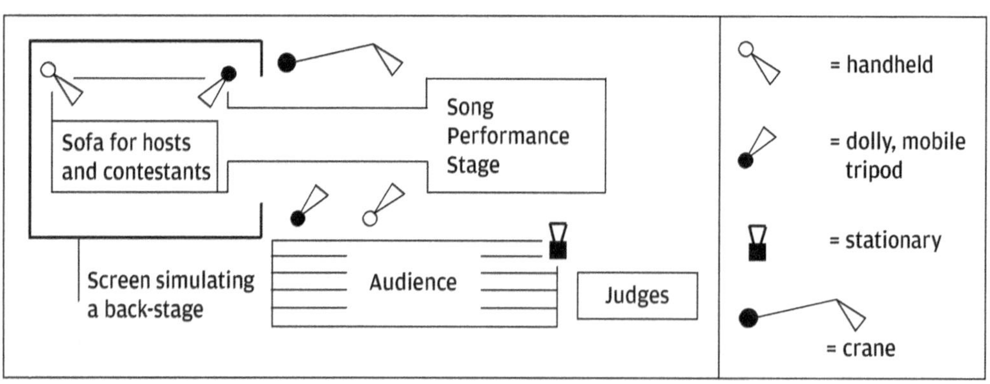

Figure 7.2: The set design in the semi-finals in *Norwegian Idol* 2005.

therefore reduced and, in order to emphasize the concert experience, the size of the studio audience was also increased. These variations to the set design were sent to FremantleMedia for advance approval. It turned out, however, that the ratings in 2006 were poorer than those in 2005, especially in the semi-finals, and in 2007 the producers reinstated a partial back-stage and placed the contestants on a sofa halfway behind the studio audience.

Encouraged by successful peer productions abroad, producers made further efforts to enhance back-stage and front-stage drama in 2007. Throughout the auditions, a 'confession booth' was included in the back-stage area, where rejected participants were encouraged to express their heartfelt opinions about the judges in private. Moreover, the areas where the judges retired and socialized between takes were turned into a back-stage as well, with a small camera crew following them around. This twist was inspired by the American and French versions, where a stronger focus existed on the judges and their involvement in the contest.[10] Inspired by another FremantleMedia format called *Got Talent*, the contestants in the finals were now interviewed individually behind the stage just before entering it. This feature was intended to emphasize the excitement of stepping up to perform and to encourage the contestants to express themselves more spontaneously.

This brief analysis indicates how, by working with the existing studio spaces, program producers build up drama and intensify emotional disclosures. The basic set design distributed in the format 'bible' is derived from the very first run of *Idol* in 2001, but local producers have been allowed to experiment within the main framework. The format-holder is strict primarily in terms of key visual and auditory signatures, including the presentation of the *Idol* logo, but otherwise FremantleMedia consultants are most concerned with 'keeping the brand fresh'.[11] Therefore, format experiments are followed very closely, and when they are successful, they are in turn promoted to other producers. The primary method of circulating such innovations is via tapes, because local producers need to see the show in action in order to visualize the changes and adapt them to local conditions, studio facilities and budgets.

Running order and momentous moments

The running order refers to the plan for the sequential coordination and editing together of a program, and it is particularly important in live-to-air broadcasts, of which *Idol* primarily consists. It is coordinated with the other production scripts and defines, for instance, how long the program hosts are supposed to stand and chat with contestants back-stage before they enter the music stage. Whereas the set design stages the drama via spatial structuring, the running order coordinates it temporally and synchronizes everyone in the production crew, from moment to moment, as the contest unfolds.

Distributed in the format 'bible' is the original running order from *Idol* in 2001; this basic template is in turn adapted to local transmission schedules, length of shows, and so on. For instance, countries like the United States and Canada span several time zones, and therefore the outcome of a given night's voting is announced the next day. The format consultants allow such adjustments 'in order to make the structure of the show work as effectively as possible'. Local producers are also permitted to make several types of changes on their own, without pre-approval, in order to intensify their influence on audiences. Key sequences in that regard are the front-stage evaluations, and the most important moments in *Idol*, with the highest ratings, are the 'eviction rituals' at the end of each episode, when the audience votes are counted (Kjus 2006). One practice in *Norwegian Idol* was to replay highlights from the evictee's appearances in *Idol* after the results were announced. Splitting the screen in two, one part showed memorable moments while the other showed a live close-up of the contestant who was about to leave the show and go back to ordinary life. *American Idol*, however, completed the voting ritual with the contestant performing his or her song for the last time, and amazing ratings testified to the appeal of this ending. In 2007, *Norwegian Idol* included this feature and combined it with a split-screen showing the highlights.

It is not unusual for contestants to cry during the voting ritual, and an event in 2006 provided a telling example of how reality game show formats generate such displays. A girl who had come second in the final in the 2005 *Idol* participated in *Dancing with the Stars* in 2006 (also on TV2), where she came third. In *Idol* she had kept her cool during the voting, but in 2006 she began to cry and could not stop. The emotional outburst attracted much interest in the tabloid press, and she explained to one journalist: 'When I lost the final in *Idol* I was never shown the video with highlights from my time in the contest. But it was shown here, and that is what got to me. I didn't cry a tear for the second place in *Idol*, but now everything got so intense.' (Hagen 2006) In the final, the production apparatus focuses on the winner and his or her emotional response, but in the other episodes it focuses on the evictee. This interview provides an interesting view from within the show's machinery.

The voting ritual has actually been a routine 'money shot' of reality game shows since the seminal reality format *Survivor* in 1997. The above analysis demonstrates how the television industry and *Idol* continuously develop this crucial element. Important to this work are the format consultants who, according to one, 'share ideas that have worked in other *Idol* productions', the best of which are in time included in the format 'bible'.[12] FremantleMedia is far less strict about these conceptual features than it is with logos and other brand signatures, partly because the former are harder to copyright. The owners of *Survivor* encountered this precise problem in 2004, losing a lawsuit against the owners of *Big Brother* over their copying of content elements (Tall 2006). Central actors in the television industry are in fact relieved at the general unwillingness of courts to recognize copyright over program concepts and elements, as it would strongly limit their own opportunities and creativity within formats (Malkani 2004).

Conclusion

The centrality of formats in television indicates that they serve and protect various industry interests, and I have studied their functions not in legal terms as the word 'protection' might imply, but in terms of production. I explored the work of maintaining, refining and developing audience attraction, which is obviously essential to the durability of a particular format, and I have focused on the work of recreating engaging dramatic moments. The persuasiveness of *Idol*, as with reality game shows in general, arises from the authenticity of ordinary people and their non-professional, unguided interactions, which are generated indirectly via a handful of format scripts – the key to the reproduction of *Idol*'s success. These format scripts are tools of global collaboration and the circulation of know-how, and television companies all over the world, in addition to the format-holder, have an interest in recreating the show's success. However, the format-holder will be particularly concerned about preservation, as bad ratings or scandals in one territory can potentially harm the entire brand in a globalized media world. In this context, format maintenance is becoming an increasingly important niche of media production.

At first glance, it may seem strange that format licensing in fact flourishes, since buying a licence is more costly than producing a program on your own. Courts generally do not even recognize copyrights in formats (Moran and Malbon 2006), and unlicensed spinoffs often multiply in the wake of successful formats. The *Idol* owner actually planned a lawsuit against its most successful makeover, *The X-Factor*, but it was (typically) settled out of court in 2005, actually through a collaboration agreement. Courts generally apply copyright law to concrete works, not concepts, which covers logos and visual/auditory format signatures rather than the heart of the format itself. This explains why FremantleMedia maintains strict control of the script that details these elements. To deal with concept-related infractions, established format actors are developing their own practices. The industry guild FRAPA, founded in 2000, is 'based on a series of gentlemen's agreements' (Malkani 2004), and can sanction offenders by exclusion from the association. The survival of FremantleMedia is largely based on this type of producer network dependency, where national television companies that 'play by the rules' are offered long-term gains. Because of FremantleMedia's global reach, it can offer the best assistance with regard to successful program reproduction, as well as access to a range of other formats. In practice, then, FremantleMedia's most important asset is the success of its local realizations, confirming its attractiveness as a partner. This is reflected in its contact with local producers, which usually consists of '80 per cent assisting and 20 per cent restricting', according to *Idol*'s format consultant.

For long-established international format actors like FremantleMedia, transferring innovations and variations from one country to another is not new but in fact decades old, particularly with game shows such as *The Price is Right*. Still, the practice has developed rapidly alongside globalization and increased competition. Particularly after the turn of the millennium, with the rapid increase in new media, new actors and new audience attractions, established television companies around the world have sought any and all means for safeguarding market shares and revenues. The most important formats in this crackling atmosphere of collaboration are what FremantleMedia calls 'the big classics', which can be reproduced successfully everywhere in the world, and which almost invariably create a strong sense of eventfulness and 'must see'. These are mainly reality game shows

(FremantleMedia's include *Idol*, *The X-Factor*, *Got Talent* and *The Farmer Wants a Wife*), and they have also proven particularly effective in engaging audiences via online and mobile media platforms (e.g. see Jenkins 2006) – a promising and strategically important area of format enterprise. The work of maintaining and developing formats must balance conservation and innovation, as is reflected in the relationship between the scripts and the bible. The most successful local script variations are gradually incorporated in the bible, which functions as a centre of gravity for the format. These entities and the interplay they facilitate are vital to more and more television production work, and to the fact the 'the very idea of production has been redefined in such a way as to suggest a more elongated series of steps' (Keane and Moran 2008: 165). This chapter has, using one case study, pointed to some key aspects of how production occurs across traditional boundaries of time, space and organizations by focusing on the intermediary role of the format-holder. But more research is needed to chart the collaborative practices, as well as the content they generate, on old as well as new media in this large and developing field.

Notes

1. If we count the individual nations participating in transnational versions such as the African and Arab *Idol* shows, the number of countries involved exceeds 70. The global name of the format brand is *Idol*, but it is often adapted to national cultures or languages with titles such as *American Idol*, *Pop Idol* or just *Idol*.
2. The study is part of the research project TIDE at Lillehammer University College, which is funded by the Research Council of Norway. Thanks go to Paddy Scannell, Arnt Maasø and Roel Puijk for their invaluable contributions.
3. 'Reality game show' is an analytical term primarily used in academia rather than the industry itself, where 'reality', 'game show' and 'docu-soap' are normally separated, and where formats like *Idol* and *Dancing with the Stars* are often referred to as 'light entertainment' or 'talent shows'.
4. Demonstrating the importance of being true to the audience, the public regulator Ofcom fined the BBC for the first time, and all BBC competition programs on television, radio and the web were temporarily suspended.
5. These scripts are not available to me in their original form as producers are contract bound not to expose the format 'bible' externally. However, local variations to the running order circulate freely during production, and other scripts, such as the game rules, are easily recreated by watching the program.
6. The interviewees include FremantleMedia executive producer and format consultant Sheldon Bailey, TV2 project leader Rolf Wenell, Monstermedia production leader Hege Andreassen and the Monstermedia executive producers responsible for the different *Idol* seasons: Trond Kvernstrøm, Ingvild Daae and Ole Peder Olsrud.
7. Favouritism takes the form of more screen time on screen and better positions in the succession of performances in the episodes (preferably the beginning or the end). Producers in the Norwegian version, who wish to remain anonymous, have confirmed this tendency.
8. The production leader of the Norwegian version, Hege Andreassen, interviewed 22 August 2005.

9. See Jerslev (2004) for an in-depth discussion of how the terminology of back-stage and front-stage, inspired by the sociologist Erving Goffman, illuminates the construction of authenticity in reality TV.
10. Producer Jon Peder Olrud, interviewed during production observation on 14 June 2007.
11. Format consultant Sheldon Bailey, interviewed on 26 March 2008.
12. Sheldon Bailey, interviewed on 26 March 2008.

References

Anderson, Kent (1978), *Television Fraud: The History and Implications of the Quiz Show Scandals*, Santa Barbara, CA: Greenwood Press.

Deuze, Mark (2007), *Media Work*, Cambridge: Polity Press.

Owen Gibson (2007), '*Comic Relief* Among Shows that Deceived BBC Viewers', *The Guardian*, 19 July, http://www.guardian.co.uk/media/2007/jul/19/bbc.broadcasting. Accessed 15 March 2008.

Grindstaff, Laura (1997), 'Producing Trash, Class, and the Money Shot', in J. Lull and S. Hinerman (eds), *Media Scandals: Morality and Desire in the Popular Culture Marketplace*, New York: Columbia University Press, pp. 164–202.

Hagen, Gunnar Sohlberg (2006), 'Skræva for mye', *Dagbladet*, 18 November.

Hill, Annette (2005), *Reality TV: Television Audiences and Popular Factual Entertainment*, London: Routledge.

Hoerschelmann, Olaf (2006), *Rules of the Game: Quiz Shows and American Culture*, Albany: State University of New York Press.

Huizinga, Johan (2000), *Homo Ludens: A Study of Play-Element in Culture*, London: Routledge.

Jenkins, Henry (2006), *Convergence Culture: Where Old and New Media Collide*, New York: New York University Press.

Jensen, Pia Majbritt (2007), Television Format Adaptation in a Trans-National Perspective: An Australian and Danish Case Study, PhD dissertation, Aarhus University.

Jerslev, Anne (2004), *Vi ses på tv: Medier og intimitet*, Copenhagen: Gyldendal.

Keane, Michael and Moran, Albert (2008), 'Television's New Engines', *Television and New Media*, 9(2), pp. 155–69.

Kjus, Yngvar (2006), 'Når publikum blir produsenter. Publikumsdeltakelse i det kommersielle underholdningsformatet *Idol*', *Norsk Medietidsskrift*, 13(3), pp. 220–41.

—— (2007), 'Ideals and Complications in Audience Participation for Public Service Media: Open Up or Hold Back?' in G.F. Lowe and J. Bardoel (eds), *From Public Service Broadcasting to Public Service Media*, Göteborg: Nordicom, pp. 135–50.

Lieberman, David (2005), '*American Idol* Zooms from Hit Show to Massive Business', *USA Today*, 29 March, http://www.usatoday.com/money/media/2005-03-29-media-usat_x.htm. Accessed 15 March 2008.

Malkani, Gautam (2004), 'Haven't We Seen That Programme Somewhere Before?', http://www.friends.ca/News/Friends_News/archives/articles09200401.asp. Accessed 15 March 2008.

Moran, Albert (1998), *Copycat Television: Globalisation, Program Formats and Cultural Identity*, Luton: Luton University Press.

Moran, Albert and Malbon, Justin (2006), *Understanding the Global TV Format*, Bristol: Intellect.

Schmitt, Daniel, Bisson, Guy and Fey, Cristoph (2005), *The Global Trade in Television Formats*, London: Screen Digest.

Scott, W. Richard (2006), 'Promising and Neglected Types of Studies on Cultural Industries', in J. Lampel, J. Shamsie and T.K. Lant (eds), *The Business of Culture: Strategic Perspectives on Entertainment and Media*, Mahwah, NJ: Lawrence Erlbaum, pp. 305–09.

Steemers, Jeanette (2007), 'Europe: Television in Transition', in Lee Artz and Yahya R. Kamalipour (eds), *The Media Globe: Trends in International Mass Media*, Lanham, MD: Rowman and Littlefield, pp. 57–78.

Syvertsen, Trine (2001), 'Ordinary People in Extraordinary Circumstances: A Study of Participants in Television Dating Games', *Media, Culture and Society*, 23(3), pp. 319–37.

Tall, Nicholas (2006), 'Copy *Idol*?' *Solicitors Journal*, http://www.solicitorsjournal.com/story.asp?storyCode=7285. Accessed 15 March 2008.

Waisbord, Silvio (2004), 'McTV: Understanding the Global Popularity of Television Formats', *Television and New Media*, 5(4), pp. 359–83.

Ytreberg, Espen (2006), 'Premeditations of Performance in Recent Live Television: A Scripting Approach to Media Production Studies', *European Journal of Cultural Studies*, 9(4), pp. 421–40.

Chapter 8

Auditioning for *Idol*: The Audience Dimension of Format Franchising

Doris Baltruschat

Are audiences active or passive consumers of media? This question has traditionally determined one of the fault-lines between culturist approaches and political economy perspectives. With the advent of interactive television, audiences undeniably engage with media texts. At the same time, active audiences redefine the value chain of content production through contributing their labour, and thus enhancing the overall program structure. In this new 'circuit' of media production, audiences tend to be not only active participants but are, in many instances, collaborators and co-creators in content development as well.

With the convergence of television and the Internet, audience engagement with program content is twofold. On the one hand, interactivities allow viewers to participate in discussions around programs and, as Andrejevic (2008) comments, make suggestions as to how story structures could be enhanced. On the other hand, producers are aware of audience contributions and tap into their creative output as a new revenue stream for participation TV. As a result, producers and broadcasters increasingly target peer-to-peer (P2P) networks, which generate a wealth of information and knowledge exchanges (Benkler 2006). The interest of conglomerates such as Time Warner and Google in sites like YouTube, which began as a P2P site for sharing video clips, is an indication of the growing infiltration of commercial interests in domains based on a digital commons principle.

In this new context of 'participation TV', viewer engagement results in value-added programming and enhanced narratives. For example, incorporating short message services (SMS) and multimedia messaging services (MMS) as part of a program structure allows producers to extract economic capital and surplus value from viewers. This is evidenced by the Italian reality TV program *Isola dei Famosi* (Ventura 2007, a version of *Celebrity Survivor*), which invites viewers to send text messages directly to contestants, as well as text messages in response to questions posed on game shows such as *Who Wants to Be a Millionaire?* (Van Dusseldorp 2005). Media participation and interactivity thus take place within pre-established frameworks determined by producers and website developers. Consequently, this limits the degree of audience engagement to a determined spectrum of choices. As Murray (1997) rightly points out: 'there is a distinction between playing an active role within an authored environment and having authorship of the environment itself' (1997: 152). Questions about audience interactivity therefore have to consider production contexts, which enhance as well as delimit opportunities by defining degrees of participation.

Another form of interactivity with reality formats is facilitated through the staging of media events, such as national auditions, to recruit contestants for a new television cycle. As discussed in the audience study below, these events are publicized across different media and create the desired 'buzz' around a show. At the same time, they highlight a new trend in the global media economy, namely the recruitment of semi-professional performers for television as a cost-effective measure. Reality formats therefore involve 'virtual' communities as well as 'actual' communities, thus amplifying and extending audience engagement with media texts.

The *Idol* franchise

The story of *Canadian Idol* is inevitably linked to the development of *American Idol* (Fuller 2002),[1] which is based on the original UK *Pop Idol* format (Fuller 2001). The *Idol* format is a reality TV contest with the aim to find a 'pop idol' and recording artist through staging nationwide auditions. The more 'interesting' moments in these auditions are broadcast to showcase 'broken dreams and shattered egos' (Schmitt et al. 2005: 147). Each week, the public and a group of four judges (or three, in the case of *American Idol*) vote off one contestant – out of the final ten – until the winner is made the 'Idol' for a particular television cycle.

The *Idol* format involves elements of universal appeal. It is a family-oriented program that is reminiscent of earlier televised talent contests during the era of 'broadcasting', such as Pat Boone's *Star Search* and *The Original Amateur Hour* (Graham 1948). However, global franchising and format interactivity have made *Idol* a 'business changer for all of network television' (Carter 2006: 194), since it exemplifies how to 'maximize ancillary exploitation of a format in order to generate maximum revenue' (Schmitt et al. 2005: 147).

The original concept was developed by Simon Fuller from 19 Entertainment in the United Kingdom and Simon Cowell; the pair then collaborated with FremantleMedia to establish the format as a brand for markets around the world. *Pop Idol* aired on Britain's ITV for the first time in the autumn of 2001 (Schmitt et al. 2005: 148). By 2007, the *Idol* format had been licensed to over 35 countries, such as Belgium, Germany, South Africa, Norway, countries of the Arab World, Australia, Russia, Croatia, Serbia and Montenegro, the United States, West Africa (with its first season in 2007), Kazakhstan and Canada (FremantleMedia 2006; '*Idol* series' 2006). As with all format sales, 19 Entertainment and FremantleMedia maintain control over the show's adaptation in local markets. 19 Entertainment also manages the careers of the show's winners and takes a cut of their profits generated through concerts and record sales (Hearn 2004). The *Idol* program has generated high audience ratings in England, the United States and Australia, where it became the country's highest rated show of 2004, excluding the Rugby World Cup (FremantleMedia 2004). In Canada, the format earned one of the highest ratings in Canada's television history, with almost 3.6 million viewers for the closing section and winner announcement on *Canadian Idol* in 2003 (Edwards 2003: 17).

The producers of *Pop Idol* had tried to break into the lucrative US market as early as 2001, but received little interest from networks, which were reluctant to commit to the format due to the failure of previous music shows such as *Fame Academy* (Hardcastle 2002) and *Popstars* (Geddes 2003). However, *Pop Idol* (Fuller 2001), which Cowell pitched to network executives as representing the 'American Dream' (as cited in Carter 2006: 177), received a major breakthrough from Fuller's connection with Hollywood's talent agency CAA (Creative Artist Agency). Two British formats, *Who Wants to Be a Millionaire?* (Gentile 1999) and *Survivor* (Burnett 2000), had become hits in the United States, and CAA's strategy was 'to pitch *Pop Idol* as a perfect new reality programming vehicle for the summer of 2002. It was light, entertaining, and not very expensive to produce.' (Carter 2006: 191) Also, since *Pop Idol* had aired in the United Kingdom, the producers were able to submit fully executed weekly editions on tape, which served as the template for the American version. After negotiations with Fox, network executives agreed to license the format if it were fully sponsored. Consequently, CAA approached one of its clients, Coca-Cola, which was interested in sponsoring the family-oriented show (Carter 2006: 181–83).

Yet another key connection for the producers and CAA was Elizabeth Murdoch, daughter of Rupert Murdoch, who worked for her father's News Corp's TV operation in the United Kingdom and had experienced the success of *Pop Idol* (Fuller 2001) at first hand. She had met CAA executives at MIPCOM in France and, when CAA contacted her about *American Idol* (Fuller 2002), she telephoned her father and recommended the show for his Fox network in the United States. According to Carter (2006), Rupert Murdoch demanded that Fox license the program and keep the original framework: 'You don't change a thing…This show works in England. And you're going to make the same show they made in England.' (2006: 188) Consequently, *Pop Idol* served as a template for *American Idol*, and also provided the blueprint for the Canadian show.

Canadian Television (CTV) licensed the format for Canada and hired Insight Production in Toronto for development. Pre-production for *Canadian Idol* began in November 2002, when John Brunton and Mark Lysakowski, producers for Insight, went to Los Angeles to attend *American Idol* auditions. Even though *Canadian Idol* was a hybrid of *Pop Idol* and *American Idol*, its fundamental structure and content always followed the original *Idol* format. According to Lysakowski (personal communication, 29 April 2004), the program therefore adhered to the format 'bible'[2] as closely as possible:

> The whole philosophy of a single person coming through a door to audition for a show to the ultimate winner chosen by the public. It's the journey that the person takes to become the next *Idol*, an American, British or whatever – that's the underlying theme of the show. The basic structure of the series remains the same.

In some instances, the Canadian producers found the UK show to be closer to Canadian sensibilities, while at other times they utilized elements from the value-added American adaptation. In order to successfully 'glocalize' *Idol*, the producers emphasized certain 'Canadianisms', which were reflected in stories about contestants. From the young teacher from Saskatchewan who was voted most popular by her high school students to the best friends from the Maritimes heading for Toronto, local aspects of culture were intertwined with *Idol* to create viewer identification with the program's characters.

When adapting the Canadian franchise, producers were aware that Canadian audiences were familiar with *American Idol*, which was produced with a bigger budget. According to *Canadian Idol* host Ben Mulroney (personal communication, 29 April 2004):

> It's not as easy as taking a successful show, changing the accent and selling it to the public. You have to know your public and you have to give them something they can identify with. And this is especially difficult in Canada, because we are working with smaller budgets.

Still, as data from the audience study revealed, *Canadian Idol* audiences were aware of differing production values and consequently commented on the 'cheaper' look of the Canadian franchise.

Another aspect for which Canadian producers were responsible was the localization of the format through staging media events, including national auditions. These auditions were held in major Canadian cities where contestants were selected for televised elimination rounds. Since *Canadian Idol* aired during the summer months, auditions coincided with the final episodes of *American Idol*, resulting in extensive cross-promotion for the shows. *Canadian Idol* was produced on a seasonal basis and its success, based on audience ratings and advertising rates, determined future production and employment for local producers and crews (Lysakowski, personal communication, 29 April 2004).

Overall, *Canadian Idol* closely resembled the UK version but with juxtaposed Canadian stories and overtones from the American copy. The localization of this global format was achieved through extensive cross-promotion and insertion of local stories, and by skilfully embedding it into local communities through media events and auditions. Moreover, through tapping into the symbolic matrix of national and cultural familiarities, *Idol* achieved a proximity to viewers that heightened the potential for interactive engagement.

Auditioning for *Idol*

Starting in 2003, Toronto's Insight Production produced *Canadian Idol* for CTV's summer season. The format 'bible' and program guidelines stipulated that contestants had to attend two auditions before they could advance to the 'celebrity' judges comprised of music industry producers and pop singers – a 'golden ticket' served as the entry pass for the celebrity round. The whole process created excitement and anticipation amongst the 16–28-year-old demographic, who attended the auditions for various reasons such as possible advancement in the entertainment industry, as a personal challenge, or simply for a 'fun time' with friends and family. Most of the attendees were students or worked in lower-income professions such as the food industry and sales. The majority were young women who had an interest in music and the arts (see below for a detailed breakdown of survey results). Overall, attendance numbers ranged from 9,000 to 16,000.

Canadian Idol producers selected a variety of public and commercial venues across the country for the auditions. In 2006, the auditions were staged in the Vancouver Centre for the Performing Arts. Many of the attendees were dressed in colourful stage outfits and carried guitars 'to look the part'. To entertain the crowd, a video screen played scenes from former *Idol* shows, especially the 'revealing moments' of previously crowned winners. Occasionally, the waiting and watching were punctuated by contestants who ran in front of the screen and waved their 'golden ticket', signalling their advancement to the next audition round. Overall, the staging, music and excitement, as well as the crowd and their visual display of pop, rock and hippie folklore, combined with the occasional surprise winner waving their golden ticket, produced a peculiar ambience of one-part Woodstock and two-parts *Willy Wonka*.

Idol auditions were filled with excitement, which was generated by producers animating the crowd, contestants' 'jitters' before their audition, the giant video screen playing '*Idol* moments' and *Idol* host Ben Mulroney appearing on stage before he circulated through the venue with a camera crew in tow to interview attendees for the CTV evening news and the entertainment program *eTalk*. The lively atmosphere was amplified by contestants' socializing with friends, meeting other contestants, practising songs for the audition, or completing several tasks associated with the event such as filling out the competitor's release form with its stringent guidelines that restricted semi-professional performers' copyright, moral rights, integrity rights as well as personality and privacy rights because 'the interests of the Program shall override those of any Competitor' (for a more detailed analysis of this aspect of reality TV formats, see Baltruschat 2008).

Researching *Idol* audiences

The audience study targeted a particular group of viewers, as its intention was to investigate the degree of engagement with a reality TV program through attendance at media events, auditioning, voting behaviours, voting technologies and comprehension of the 'competitor's release' form. The study was designed to measure qualitative as well as quantitative data in order to gain insights into who is drawn to auditions with regard to age, gender and professional background. The survey also explored viewers' perceptions of a format franchise in regard to its market – US or Canadian – and differences between adaptations. The study therefore assessed how successful *Idol* producers were in inscribing the format's narrative for local audiences as well as the degree of 'transparency' and awareness viewers possessed of format glocalization processes.

Profile and demographics

The audience survey was conducted during the *Canadian Idol* auditions in Vancouver, BC in 2004 and 2006. It generated 200 valid responses for the study, which yielded a total of 1,043 comments, reflections and opinions. Most attendees were women, 71 per cent in 2004 and 77 per cent in 2006. Age groups were fairly evenly represented in three groups, 16–18-year-olds, 19–22-year-olds and 22–28-year-olds, with an increase in the 16–18-year-old group in 2006.

The study revealed that the motivations for attending an audition for a reality format are manifold – from social aspects to mastering a personal challenge to pure curiosity. Many of the attendees were accompanied by friends and family (67 per cent in 2004, 76 per cent in 2006), highlighting the 'social aspect' of the event. Nearly 50 per cent of the attendees were students for both years. The other half of the participants worked in low-paying, entry-level jobs, which included 'Food Service Industry Workers' (11 per cent in 2004, 12 per cent in 2006), 'Clerical' (9 per cent in 2004, 6 per cent in 2006) and 'Sales' (8 per cent in 2004, 5 per cent in 2006), as well as 'Artists' (5 per cent in 2004, 3 per cent in 2006), 'Professionals' (6 per cent in 2004; 10 per cent in 2006) and 'Unemployed' (8 per cent in 2004, 6 per cent in 2006).

Employment backgrounds highlighted a link between 'star transformation stories' and the evocation of fame, a connection which underpins many reality TV contests. In the case of *Canadian Idol*, the transformation narrative was clearly linked to the celebrity cult, which has grown in recent years due to extensive cross-referencing in tabloid-style magazines and on TV programs. Holmes (2004a: 156) states that 'the emphasis on the ordinariness of the contestants contributes to the deliberate blurring between contestant and viewer and, as a result, a potential invocation of the audience's own aspirations (or fantasies) of success and stardom'. As a result, reality formats such as *Canadian Idol* tap into the 'success myth' which, as part of the 'American dream', creates the illusion that, in spite of social stratification, anyone can rise above their rank (Dyer 1998: 42). These programs, in particular, are paradigmatic of the success myth through their predominant focus on the 'innate' talent of contestants and their personal transformation through dedication and professionalism (Holmes 2004b: 119–20). Furthermore, they epitomize the construction of 'celebrity' to maintain control over a program franchise, and to manage financial risks through manufacturing multiple celebrities as promotional vehicles (Turner 2004).

Motivations and reasons for attending auditions

The survey investigated the motivations for attending an event that sources semi-professional performers for a reality format. Questions about why audience members participated in these events yielded a spectrum of answers, of which the majority of responses fell into the 'Personal Challenge' category for both years (see Figure 8.1). Comments such as 'To see what I'm made of' and 'I want to achieve my dream' were frequent, as were statements like 'For the experience' and 'To see if I'm any good'. These responses highlight an aspect of reality TV which, according to Hill (2005), is linked to perceived educational elements in these programs. According to Hill's study, viewers believe that they can learn valuable aspects related to daily life, from cooking tips to pet care. Viewer feedback also reflected a persistent attitude towards the television medium itself, with its dual purpose of entertaining as well as educating.

Responses in the 'Career Advancement' category included: 'To see my chances in the music industry' and 'To gain more experience as a singer and gain a recording contract'. Other comments highlighted the importance of the 'Social' and 'Fun' aspects of *Idol* events. This was reflected in the number of people who were accompanied by friends and family in 2004 and 2006, as well as statements such as 'It's fun to meet new people', and 'I'm here to support my girlfriend'.

One significant difference between 2004 and 2006 was the doubling of responses in the 'Fame/To Win' category. This was the result of successfully transmitting the 'success myth' of the franchise, in addition to a growing emphasis on celebrities in tabloid-style TV programming and newsprint. Statements such as 'Fame and fortune' and 'Because I love to sing and my dream is to become famous' in 2004 were similar, but amplified in 2006 with 'To be the next Canadian Idol. Fame, fame, fame', 'To have fun and maybe get my fifteen minutes of fame', 'To get rich and famous' and 'To possibly get discovered' – all of which revealed the

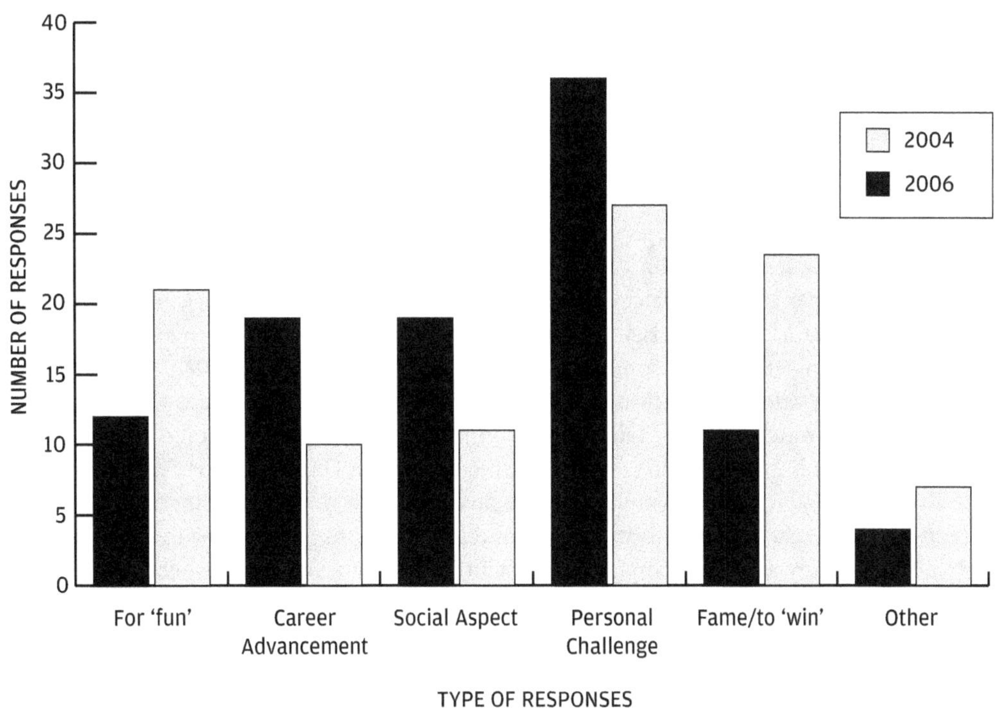

Figure 8.1: Motivations and reasons for attending auditions.

attraction of the program and the desire to gain access to the music/entertainment business in order to attain celebrity status. These responses highlighted the successful transmission of the 'American Dream' and star transformation narrative that accompanies *Idol*.[3]

However, Hibberd and colleagues' (2000) study about public participation in TV programs reveals that, even though producers generally seek informed consent from participants, '[production] pressures will almost inevitably result in some producers behaving less honourably than they should with contributors' (2000: 67). The authors therefore recommend stringent guidelines for contracting 'semi-professional' on-air personalities, and propose that informed consent should be based on participants' understanding and knowledge of a program's format, objectives and aims. This is especially important considering the age group *Idol* targets for recruitment. Questions about ethics are also relevant in light of recent revelations that participants in programs such as *Paradise Hotel* (Ringbakk 2003), *The Real World* (Murray and Bunim 1992) and *Joe Millionaire* (Cowan and Michenaud 2003) are frequently provided with free alcohol to manipulate the story plot for comedic effect (Fletcher 2006).

The *Idol* glocalization process

Watching *Canadian Idol* and *American Idol*

The unique Canadian geography, with many of its urban centres located along the Canada–United States border, exposed Canadian audiences to two adaptations of *Pop Idol*. In 2004, most of the respondents were familiar with *American Idol*, while just over 50 per cent had seen *Canadian Idol*. The discrepancy can be explained by the fact that *Canadian Idol* had launched only its second season that year, in contrast to *American Idol*'s third season. In comparison, 83 per cent had watched *Canadian Idol* and 85 per cent *American Idol* in 2006, an indication that *Idol*'s popularity had increased over the two years due to extensive inter-textual referencing and cross-promotion.

In comparing categories within and across formats, it became evident that Canadian viewers enjoyed watching 'local' talent, thus confirming that, if given a choice, most viewers preferred to watch programming with domestic references (Juneau 1993). This sentiment was also expressed in the following response favouring the glocalized franchise: '[I enjoy] everything, now that the talent is in Canada and allows you to get to know the contestants.'

Not surprisingly, the 'Auditions' and 'Host-Judges' were a favourite aspect of the show (see Figure 8.2). Inscribed into the program's 'bible' as a key element for staging comical and entertaining scenarios, often intentionally accompanied by humiliating contestants on air, respondents commented on this aspect of the show with 'I like to see how good (or bad) people are at singing. I mostly just watch the auditions.' However, in the Canadian franchise, *Idol* judges tended to have a softer approach in comparison to their American counterparts.

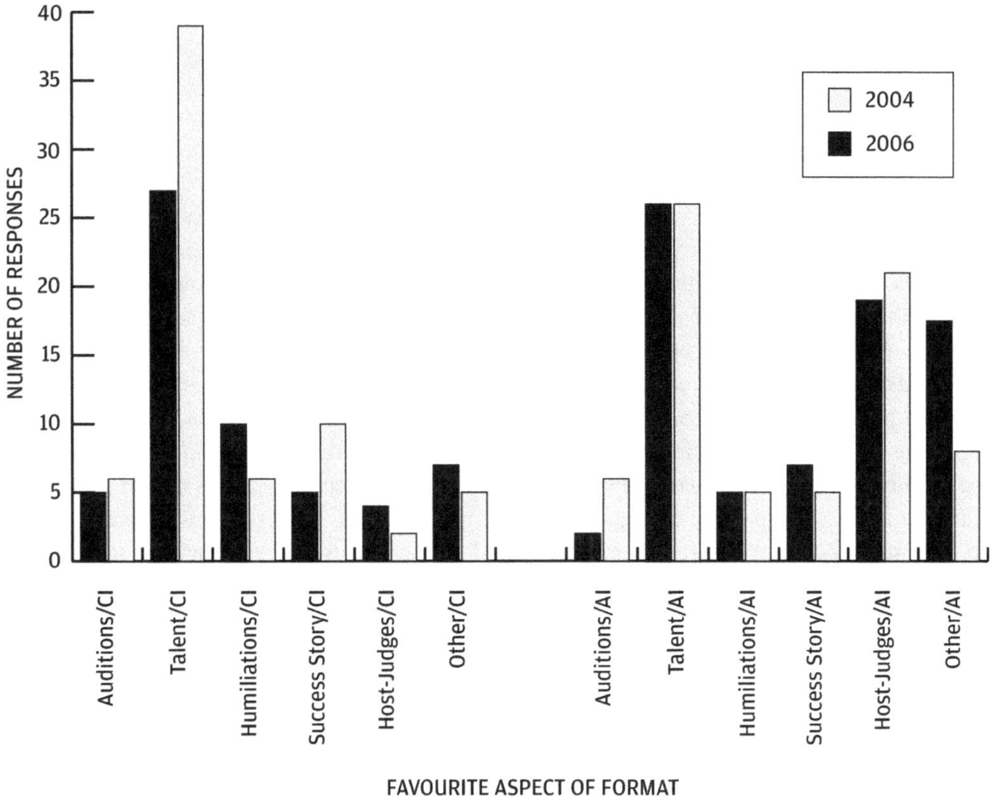

Figure 8.2: Figure 8.2: Favourite aspects of *Idol* format.

Insight producer Lysakowski (personal communication, 29 April 2004) confirmed that the Canadian franchise was friendlier because this is 'the Canadian way'.

Significantly, in 2006 the popularity of 'Success Story' and 'Talent' increased for the Canadian franchise, pointing again towards the successful transmission of the 'transformation' narrative and its closely linked evocation of stardom. This was also reflected in comments that showed a preference for 'Seeing all the rising stars', and '[It] gives people a chance to fulfill the dream'.

Perceived differences between *Canadian Idol* and *American Idol*

In response to the question: 'Do you think there is a difference between *Canadian Idol* and *American Idol*?' 74 per cent answered 'yes' in 2004, while 26 per cent thought the franchises were the same. This contrasted with figures from 2006, when 35 per cent declared the formats to be similar.

Comments about format differences revealed the extent to which viewers possessed 'surface' knowledge of television production processes. The Canadian format, with its lower budget, was perceived as being less 'glamorous', whereas the American show was seen as better promoted and therefore better known. The majority of responses highlighted the promotion of the formats, underscored by comments such as 'Bigger ratings for *American Idol*' and 'The American budget is bigger and the judges have more status and character'.

Attendees also remarked on the differences in talent featured on the shows, with comments like '*American Idol* is better, better host, better talent, better judges' in contrast to '*Canadian Idol* lacks charisma'. Again, these comments pointed towards the recognition of production values and budgetary restrictions, which inevitably impact on the 'look' and 'feel' of a show as a result of technical aspects, sponsorship, crew and staging. These statements also reflected discrepancies between Canadian/US television markets in general, which translate into production processes and audiences numbers.

At the same time, respondents commented favourably on *Canadian Idol* because of its local characteristics. This was expressed in statements like '*American Idol* is too "Hollywood". *Canadian Idol* is more talent than looks', and 'Canada has more diversity, less "candy"'. These statements indicated a preference for the Canadian format, as well as a loyalty to Canadian talent and its cultural context. They also pointed towards the successful glocalization of the format.

Major differences between the formats became evident in responses to '*Idol* Career Advancement'. For both years, respondents stated that *Canadian Idol* contestants had less of a chance to advance their music career than their American counterparts. Statements like '*American Idol* guarantees fame for the top participants. *Canadian Idol* requires more effort to make oneself known. Americans also seem much more ready to make "ordinary" people into stars' and 'Yes, the American contestants get way more publicity' confirmed that viewers possessed a good understanding of industry differences between Canada and the United States.

Format interactivity

Format interactivity through cell phone voting and online purchases of program-related merchandise correlated with the increase of mobile technology use in Canada. The relatively late introduction of program interactivities in the Canadian market – due to incompatibilities between mobile service providers – was reflected in the high usage of landline phones versus cell phones. At the same time, 80 per cent of the respondents had used the Internet to find out more about the program, a figure that increased to 85 per cent in the 2006 survey.[4] Finally, in answering the question about 'who viewers had voted for', the Canadian format had received most of their attention, with 81 per cent in 2004 and 91 per cent in 2006.

Comprehension levels for 'competitor's release form'

In 2004, 60 per cent had signed the competitor's release form for *Canadian Idol*, while 40 per cent had not. Of the respondents who had signed the form, the majority stated that they understood the form 'very well' (42 per cent) and 'well' (39 per cent). In contrast, in 2006 a total of 84 per cent had signed the competitor's release form, which 41 per cent understood very well and 52 per cent understood 'well'. This result had to be placed within the context of the release form being the 'entry ticket' for the auditions. The fact that contestant could not advance without signing the form probably influenced results. This was also reflected in verbal responses from several attendees, who raised concerns about participating in the study in case it might jeopardize their chances to audition for *Insight* producers and casting agents. More specifically, four respondents inquired whether 'they would get into trouble' for participating in the survey and two refused to sign the questionnaire on the same grounds.

Discussion and conclusions

The *Canadian Idol* audience study yielded a plethora of perceptions, impressions, reflections and opinions on the North American franchises. More than just comments about the programs, the results provided insight into the effectiveness of the 'format mosaic'[5] and its translation into active audience engagement and interactivity. Moreover, results highlighted the extent to which creative interpretations of the format translated into a learning opportunity for some attendees while others appropriated the events as a social experience. At the same time, the format's 'bible' informed comments about auditions, *Idol* judges, talent and their on-air representation. Finally, the study revealed a surface knowledge of television production processes as they relate to the Canadian and US markets, as well as the correlation between budgetary restrictions and production values.

The study emphasized that audition experiences were as diverse and individual as interpretations of the format narrative itself. Many attendees sought out auditions as a personal challenge and a learning experience, which confirmed that viewers gain valuable insights from engaging with reality TV programming (Hill 2005). Moreover, it verified that viewers associated the television medium with entertainment and education, especially for programs rooted in the documentary genres. Not surprisingly, *Idol* auditions unleashed unbridled creativity, resulting from the active engagement of attendees, who appropriated diverse aspects of the events and transformed them into a 'fun' experience for themselves and their friends. As described, the social aspect of auditions was as important as being part of the taped event, meeting the *Idol* host and participating in a much-talked about TV program.

However, participants also contributed to the 'buzz' around the show by taking part in auditions; they therefore actually 'became' the event. Within the parameters of format glocalization, audience participation therefore enhances and deepens the *Idol* mosaic while adding value to the franchise for adaptations in other markets. In other words, producers are able to mine contestants' creativity, engagement and social capital for ratings and further format trade.

Accordingly, media events around reality TV programs continue to spurn unorthodox job recruitments, characterized by thousands of people attending auditions and casting calls for programs like *Idol* and *The Apprentice* (Burnett 2004). Yet a lack of guidelines and harsh contractual obligations tend to result in highly exploitative conditions for semi-professional performers, which are amplified by a lack of awareness of TV production practices and work environments. Concomitantly, a growing emphasis on celebrity culture adds to the lure of participating in reality formats. The doubling of responses in the 'Fame/To Win' category of the study thus highlighted an amplifier effect, produced by the programs themselves as well as their inter-textual references. The path to 'celebrity status' appeared like a shortcut to advancement in life – circumventing the traditional routes of finding a career – while highlighting the pervasiveness of a value system tied to capitalist notions of wealth accumulation and a high degree of individualism.

The promulgation of the success myth – the core of the transformation narrative in the program – also drew viewers to the shows to watch the talent and their progression played out in weekly episodes until the season's finale. Statements in the 'Talent' and 'Success Story' categories were punctuated with key words such as 'change', 'success', 'fame' and 'making it' for both franchises. Yet *Idol* programs also deliver entertainment through musical performances that appeal to a wide range of viewers and demographics. The study therefore highlighted the complexities and variations that underscore audience engagement and interactivity with formatted texts. Consequently, the results emphasized the creative interpretations and active engagement by audiences *as well* as the successful translation of formatted narratives about competition, stardom and success.

With regard to format differences, the study produced interesting results about viewers' knowledge of production processes and formatted content. As noted above, Canadian audiences offer a unique study sample since they are familiar with both US and Canadian reality formats. Comments about the programs revealed insight into production processes and highlighted the extent to which producers were able to successfully transmit formatted elements, especially in relation to *Idol* judges. For example, low expectations in the 'Humiliation' category for auditions indicated a correlation with the 'softer' portrayal of judges and their treatment of contestants in the Canadian franchise.

The main differences between the formats were noted with regard to production values. Key words in statements by respondents included 'bigger ratings', 'bigger deal', 'better promoted and advertised', 'more financial support', 'larger scale', 'more publicized', 'better quality' and 'more popular' for *American Idol*, which were juxtaposed with comments such as 'more real', 'less pretense', 'more diverse', 'more down to earth', 'more about the whole package', 'less superficial', 'more diversity' and 'less candy' for *Canadian Idol*. Comments clearly indicated knowledge about market differences in the United States and Canada, and the correlation between production budgets and production values. Statements also revealed preferences for a local style as well as loyalty to a familiar cultural context, which highlighted the successful glocalization of the format for domestic audiences. Within the broader context of format adaptation, this underscored the importance of consultations between licensor and licensee to create a locally recognizable program.

Additional statements about differences between adaptations related to the inscription of the success story and possible career advancement of contestants. These also reflected knowledge of market differences and broader ramifications of the Canadian and US entertainment industries. The following response from an attendee at the 2004 audition, '*American Idol* guarantees fame for the top participants. *Canadian Idol* requires more effort to make oneself known. Americans also seem much more ready to make "ordinary" people into stars', also pointed to differences with regard to celebrity culture and the centrality of the success myth in the two markets. However, the growing emphasis in the 'Fame/To win' category in 2006 indicated a change in perception of the Canadian franchise while marking a shift in motivation to participate in auditions in order to gain access to the entertainment industry and attain celebrity status. The doubling of responses in this category also pointed towards an amplifier effect, resulting from the program's popularity, the promulgation of the success myth associated with celebrity culture as well as extensive inter-textual references across media and platforms in the United States and now also in Canada.

Not surprisingly, respondents commented on greater similarities between the two franchises in 2006. In noting common elements between the *Idol* programs, a respondent pointed towards the glocalization process itself by emphasizing the 'copycat' nature of the shows. Within the context of proliferating reality formats on US and Canadian television, perceived similarities between programs also reflected the increasing 'sameness' across TV program offerings, which were marked by a dramatic increase in the number of reality TV shows in both countries.

Increased use of online access portals to the *Idol* mosaic was evidenced by 2006 responses, in which more viewers voted for the format than in 2004. The high usage of landlines in the voting technology section pointed towards a more conservative use of mobile technologies than anticipated. Yet, considering the age group, avoidance of cell phone and text-messaging charges is understandable. Nonetheless, an increase in both cell phone use and text messaging was evidenced in the 2006 survey, which indicated the growing popularity of these technologies for interactive engagement.

Finally, responses regarding the competitor's release form indicated that attendees understood the form 'well' to 'very well'. However, results for this section of the survey had to be placed within the context and purpose of signing the form. Since contestants were not able to audition without signing the form, responses were likely more positive than truly reflective of overall comprehension of a contract that entails complex legal language and terminology. This is disconcerting since contestants, through signing the form, 'irrevocably' waive their 'entire copyright and all other rights of whatsoever nature' to the producers – including their 'moral rights' – and write off the receipt of 'fees, royalties, residuals' or any form of payment for their performance with regard to broadcast, rebroadcast, retransmission or use in any type of media ('Competitor's Regional Auditions', 2006: 2–3).

The *Canadian Idol* study highlighted the complexities of engaging with a format's mosaic through active modes of participation, creative interpretation and appropriation as well as individualized interactivity. At the same time, the survey emphasized that successful format adaptations are closely linked to inscribing narrative elements with culturally specific connotations that appeal to local audiences. Yet, even though participation in auditions offered different, individualized experiences, they were firmly embedded in the format's mosaic, which defined the parameters of engaging with media events while allowing producers to take advantage of the sentiment around notions of 'stardom' promulgated by the shows and their inter-textual references.

Notes

1. *American Idol's* worth as a television franchise is estimated at US$2.5 billion. It generates US$500 million in TV advertising revenues alone, in addition to US$30–50 million in sponsorship deals (International Format Lawyers Association 2007).
2. A 'format bible' stipulates structure, content and production value for a franchise, such as script, casting, logo, music and interactive elements. It consequently serves as a guide for all new format adaptations.
3. This success myth also underscores other reality TV shows, and has led to the recruitment of semi-professional performers across North America. In 2007, over 50 casting calls could be accessed on Internet sites such as jobsearch.about.com, which provided recommendations on 'how to audition' for reality TV shows on all major networks, including NBC, CBS, FOX, ABC and MTV, as well as smaller ones such as CW, BRAVO, SciFi, TLC, VH1, HGTV and the Food Network (Reality TV World 2007).
4. In 2007, *Canadian Idol's* online chat forum included 15,463 members, who had posted 721,425 messages for that year (CTV 2007b).
5. Janet Murray (1997) borrows the notion of the 'mosaic' from Marshall McLuhan to describe multiple entry points into stories, as well as news media and films, which are instantaneously recognizable by users of multiple media (1997: 156). For instance, a reader of newspapers has learned to process multiple types of information in one quick 'snapshot' of the front page. Also see Baltruschat (2007) concerning the '*Idol* mosaic'.

References

Andrejevic, M. (2008), 'Watching Television Without Pity: The Productivity of Online Fans', *Television & New Media*, 9(1), pp. 24–46.

Baltruschat, D. (2007), 'The New Media Geography of Global and Local Production Networks', *Media International Australia*, 124, pp. 134–44.

—— (2008), 'Film and Television Formats: The Cross-Border Adaptation of Interactive Media Productions', in J. Wasko and M. Erickson (eds), *Cross-Border Cultural Production*, Youngstown, NY: Cambria Press, pp. 299–332.

Benkler, Y. (2006), *The Wealth of Networks: How Social Production Transforms Markets and Freedom*, New Haven, CT: Yale University Press.

Burnett, M. (Executive Producer) (2000), *Survivor* [Television series], Los Angeles: CBS Television.

Burnett, M. (Creator) (2004), *The Apprentice* [Television series], New York: National Broadcasting Company (NBC).

CTV (2007a), '*Canadian Idol* by the Numbers: 2.75 Million Watch on CTV as Brian Melo Crowned 2007 Champion', 12 September, http://www.ctvmedia.ca/idol07/releases/release_print.asp?id=9739. Accessed 15 October 2007.

—— (2007b). *Canadian Idol* forum, http://ctvforum.insinc.com/forums. Accessed 15 October 2007.

Carter, B. (2006), *Desperate Networks*, New York: Doubleday.

Competitors regional auditions – 2006, Competitor's release form (2006). http://www.ctv.ca/idol/gen/Home.html. Accessed 18 March 2006.

Cowan, C. and Michenaud, J.M. (Executive Producers) (2003), *Joe Millionaire* [Television series], Beverly Hills, CA: Fox Broadcasting Company.

Dyer, R. (1998), *Stars*, 2nd ed., London: BFI Publishing.

Edwards, I. (2003), 'A Year to Remember…or Maybe Forget', *Playback Magazine*, 24 November, p. 17.

Fletcher, H. (2006), 'Drink Up: It's Not Like You Have Lines to Learn', *New York Times*, 29 October, p. AR32.

FremantleMedia (2004), 'Programmes: Entertainment, Factual, Idols', http://www.fremantlemedia.com. Accessed 18 July 2004.

—— (2006), 'Global Hit Formats: Idols', http://www.fremantlemedia.com/our-programmes/view/Global+Hit+Formats/viewprogramme/Idols. Accessed 16 September 2006.

Fuller, S. (Creator) (2001), *Pop Idol* [Television series]. London: FremantleMedia.

—— (Creator) (2002). *American Idol: The Search for a Superstar* [Television series], London: FremantleMedia.

Geddes, M. (Executive Producer) (2003), *Pop stars* [Television series], Winnipeg, MB: Canwest.

Gentile, D. (Director) (1999). *Who Wants to Be a Millionaire?* [Television series], Burbank, CA: American Broadcasting Company (ABC).

Graham, L. (Executive Producer) (1948), *The Original Amateur Hour* [Television series], New York: National Broadcasting Company (NBC).

Hardcastle, A. (Series Producer) (2002), *Fame Academy* [Television series], London: BBC.

Hearn, A. (2004), '*Idol* Thoughts', *Toronto Star*, 19 April, http://thestar.com. Accessed 18 July 2004.

Hibberd, M., Kilborn, R., McNair, B., Marriot, S. and Schlesinger, P. (2000), *Consenting Adults?* London: Broadcasting Standards Commission.

Hill, A. (2005), *Reality TV: Audiences and Popular Factual Television*, London: Routledge.

Holmes, S. (2004a), '"Reality Goes Pop!" Reality TV, Popular Music, and Narratives of Stardom in "Pop Idol"', *Television & New Media*, 5(2), pp. 147–72.

—— (2004b), 'All You've Got to Worry About is the Task, Having a Cup of Tea, and Doing a Bit of Sunbathing': Approaching Celebrity in *Big Brother*', in S. Holmes and D. Jermyn (eds), *Understanding Reality Television*, London: Routledge, pp. 111–35.

'*Idol* Series' (2006), *Wikipedia*, http://en.wikipedia.org/wiki/Idol_series. Accessed 19 November 2006.

International Format Lawyers Association (IFLA) (2007), *Value of Television Formats Continues to Grow Despite Legal Uncertainty*, http://www.ifla.tv/format.html. Accessed 19 June 2007.

Juneau, P. (1993), 'Overview of Issues in Culture and National Identity', in R. de la Garde, W. Gilsdorf and I. Wechselmann (eds), *Small Nations, Big Neighbour: Denmark and Quebec/Canada Compare Notes on American Popular Culture*, London: John Libbey & Company, pp. 15–21.

Murray, J.H. (1997), *Hamlet on the Holodeck: The Future of Narrative in Cyberspace*, Cambridge, MA: MIT Press.

Murray, J. and Bunim, M.B. (Executive Producers) (1992), *Real World* [Television series], New York: MTV Networks.

Reality TV World (2007). 'Recent Show Application News', http://jobsearch.about.com. Accessed 1 November 2007.

Ringbakk, R. (Supervising Producer) (2003), *Paradise Hotel* [Television series], Beverly Hills, CA: Fox Network.

Rojek, C. (2001), *Celebrity*, London: Reaktion Books.

Salerno, C. (Executive Producer) (2004), '*Urban Rush* on Location with *Canadian Idol*' [Television series episode], in C. Salerno (Executive Producer), *Urban Rush*, Vancouver, BC: Shaw Cable Community Programming.

Schmitt, D., Bisson, G. and Fey, C. (2005), *The Global Trade in Television Formats*, London: Screen Digest Ltd and FRAPA with the support of the German Federal State of North Rhine-Westphalia.

Turner, G. (2004), *Understanding Celebrity*, London: Sage.

Van Dusseldorp, M. (2005), 'Participation TV Trends', *Mobile Messaging Forum*, http://www.mmf.ie. Accessed 9 August 2006.

Ventura, S. (2007), *Ilsola dei famosi* [Television series], Rome, Italy: Rai Due.

Part IV

Comparative Cross-Border Studies

Chapter 9

Adapting Global Television to Regional Realities: Traversing the Middle East Experience

Amos Owen Thomas

In less than a decade and a half, television in the Middle East has moved out of the strictures of domestic state-owned terrestrial public stations, with satellite and cable technology allowing viewers to watch broadcasts from throughout the region and beyond. This period has also seen the growth of deliberately regional and transnational channels broadcasting in Arabic and other languages.

Is adaptation of global program formats just a natural means to cope with the increased broadcast hours to be filled? On the one hand, management on many channels in the larger Middle East region tends to consist of expatriate staff originally from more culturally liberal nations of the Levant sub-region, such as Lebanon, Syria, Jordan and Egypt, and often the programming has been sourced from those countries. On the other hand, network ownership and consumer buying power come largely from the more culturally conservative countries in the oil-rich Gulf sub-region, comprising Kuwait, Bahrain, the United Arab Emirates, Qatar, Oman, Saudi Arabia and Yemen – hence the importance of viewer acceptance of television programming there. Can and does cultural contextualization of program formats take account of various regional sensibilities? Is global format adaptation merely an antidote to the relative lack of expertise in quality program production in the Gulf sub-region that this chapter explores?

Previewing regional television

Surveying the historical development of media in the region, particularly consumer access to television and the Internet, Gher and Amin (1999) share the concern of moderate governments that the influx of Western cultural products has fostered an Islamic fundamentalist reaction that could destabilize societies unless governments act to censor media content. While this may fly in the face of Western notions of press freedom, Gher and Amin acknowledge that such censorship is well tolerated – even expected – by most citizens of the Arab world. Deploring the Third World levels of development in parts of the Middle East, Gher and Amin somewhat idealistically believe that the communications revolution holds great promise for not just economic growth, but political, social and cultural development as well, though they do not elaborate on the latter. In documenting the consequences of satellite television and video piracy of limited local programming for Iranians, Mowlana (1997) asks how traditional notions of Islamic culture might be reconciled to a contemporary medium such as television. But Khiabany (2003) questions Mowlana's

Orientalist-style assumption of uniformity within the Islamic world in his own argument for an alternative model of communication to the dominant Western ones.

Any legimitization of a medium by its use, even in a highly regulated fashion, leads inexorably to its gaining a foothold and eventual undermining of traditional cultures. Hence Khalil (2004) focuses on three forms of global exchange in television programming that have been prevalent in the Middle East. The first of these is the widespread program plagiarism that existed on Lebanese television, facilitated by the regulatory void due to its civil war – which nonetheless did not prevent the programs being seen regionally via satellite. Second, he contends that some of the most popular programs were those that the producer-director had culturally reformulated for the format so they were imperceptible to the undiscerning viewer. Third, as well as turning to lesser-known European channels for 'inspiration' and specific programs to clone, Middle Eastern broadcasters increasingly resorted to licensed format adaptations. Chaker (2003) acknowledges that the establishment of Dubai's Media City to protect and promote the Arabic and Islamic culture of the Gulf was at the same time the Emirates' further integration into the global media marketplace and cultural industry. Yet he maintains that, with careful formulation of public policy, media production there could be economically successful while upholding the cultural values of the region. Evidently this was the rationale for the inauguration by the governments of Egypt and Jordan of rival 'media cities', albeit with different resources, structures and chances of success, given their tentative commitment to freedom of expression (Quinn et al. 2004).

There has been extraordinary growth in the television of the Arab world over the last decade or more as a result of the introduction of satellite and digital technologies (see Table 9.1). Chronicling the consequent competition for audiences through programming by transnational commercial broadcasters, Ayish (2000) found that this had raised

Table 9.1: Leading channels by penetration across the Gulf sub-region (%).

Channel	Saudi Arabia	UAE	Kuwait	Oman	Bahrain	Qatar
MBC	63.0	27.0	73.0	36.1	50.8	26.5
LBC	45.0	28.6	51.0	32.6	2.6	1.3
FTV	42.0	25.9	46.0	26.4	1.6	6.9
ESC	36.0	22.3	61.0	24.1	38.0	20.9
Saudi TV 1	41.9					
Dubai Satellite		46.0				
Kuwait Sat			41.7			
Oman TV				60.0		
Bahrain Arabic					59.0	
Qatar Arabic						52.0
Al-Jazeera	47.8		57.3			

Source: Bates Pan-Gulf (2004).

more questions than answers in relation to the role of television in Arab society. Some governments resented yielding to commercial imperatives within public broadcasting but were then constrained due to funding from sourcing development of socially relevant programming. Commercial broadcasters might have excelled at reproducing entertainment programs with popular appeal throughout the region, yet they were faced with declining advertising and subscription revenues amidst rising competition both from within and from outside. One explanation was the failure within the region to incorporate contemporary concepts in business and technology, which Fakhreddine (2000) decries, demonstrating the lack of development in Arab language dictionaries from the formal or 'classical'. Another consequence was the persistence, even growth, of colloquial dialects that has caused difficulties for business communications across the region. Needless to say, this impediment has also plagued television broadcasters and program broadcasters seeking to cater to contemporary audiences across the Middle East.

The satellite broadcasting industry in the Middle East may have catered well to Arabs deterritorialized within the region or beyond, by labour migration and ethnic upheaval or by seeking to overcome repression within the confines of their country of origin. Still, Sakr (1999) argues that the political elites within the Middle East – namely individuals and groups in Saudi Arabia and Egypt – have utilized this transnational medium to promote their conservative religious views and the political status quo. Even the commercial broadcasters coming out of generally liberal Lebanon have been subject to political influence over their news coverage, both from inside the country and outside. A notable exception has been Al-Jazeera, broadcasting out of Qatar, which has endeared itself to region-wide audiences with its liberal approach to news and current affairs. Yet, for all its cosmopolitan pan-Arab credentials, even Al-Jazeera has faced constraints in tackling controversial social topics believed to alienate Middle Eastern audiences (Salamandra 2003). For it is noteworthy that, in documenting the media usage and preferences in Morocco, Tessler (2000) found that there was only limited difference between generations. Education and gender were more significant moderators of cultural attitudes, implying that, even in middle-of-the-road Middle Eastern countries, any media-led social change would have to be incremental and in the context of wider cultural continuity.

Multi-faceted study

The present research might even qualify as ethnography, as explicated by Miriampolski (2006), seeking as it does to bridge insider (consumers' and producers') and outsider (this and other researchers') perspectives on the phenomenon of television program format adaptations. Most interviews in the present research were in-depth, face-to-face and one-on-one encounters, which allowed for the establishment of rapport with the interviewees and therefore a conducive atmosphere to discuss even sensitive issues. The disadvantages of interviews include the fact that not all respondents are articulate or knowledgeable, and the information provided may not be objective but filtered through the perceptions of the respondents. These drawbacks were overcome in the present research by the fact that all respondents had been commended for their expertise on the phenomenon by other practitioners in the industry. Evidence was also triangulated via the use of industry secondary data, newspaper clippings and broadcaster websites. Furthermore, the researcher observed hours of prime-time television in the Gulf sub-region during fieldwork there, and monitored websites relating to the leading reality programs on his return home. Unfortunately, there was little opportunity to interact with the contributors to programs' web pages as these were accessed some time after the end of their broadcast season, and were thus rather more a documentary record of interactions among viewers, somewhat resembling a transcript of a focus group discussion.

Derived originally from social and cultural anthropology, such qualitative research sees reality as constructed by social actors; therefore, the research is conducted in a participative, even collaborative, manner with the informants with whom the researcher empathizes or may even identify. Such research acknowledges that reality is value laden, and the researcher declares his or her bias in the process of arriving inductively at concepts and variables from the analysis of data from the informants (Creswell 1994). Among the methods utilized in qualitative research are in-depth interviews, focus groups, case studies and ethnographies, and they tend to be utilized where theory is weak, variables unknown, the context relevant and the research exploratory. As Strauss and Corbin (1990) have long contended, the criteria for deeming such research 'scientific' need to be redefined to suit the qualitative approach of analyzing complex social phenomena such as media production and consumption in depth. In recent years, qualitative research methods have gained ground even in previously resistant fields like business that this research traverses, and so need less justification of choice (Woolcott 2001). However, pursuing such an approach to knowledge discovery is no licence for aimless meandering, so the preceding literature review will be utilized to structure analysis of the findings in this exploratory investigation.

Producers' perspectives

In the early to mid-2000s, there were a number of notable program adaptations of global formats in the Middle East, enjoying varying degrees of success, which provided the impetus for this study. About half a dozen executives from the media, market research and advertising industries in the constituent states of the United Arab Emirates were interviewed on the practice of program format adaptations within the Gulf sub-region. Their opinions on its prevalence, success factors and rationale were sought and synthesized to provide an intra-regional, intra-industry perspective on documenting a business history of the phenomenon in the Gulf and wider Middle East region. Contact with and referrals via the interviewees also resulted in the researcher being granted access to secondary data to which the interviewees were privy. In addition, the method allowed the researcher considerable control of the direction of the inquiry through the asking of appropriate questions in an iterative fashion.

Motivations for adaptation

The leading regional broadcaster, MBC, was reported to have done extensive format adaptation because it could afford the licence fees, arguing that these were practically 'ready-made' programs and thus less risky. Lebanese television stations and production houses were also said to pay their own staff comparatively lower rates, and so were able to afford the format licences, while other Middle Eastern stations outside the affluent Gulf sub-region found the fees prohibitive (Interview Glf04). The fact that Arab culture is deemed largely oral might explain the preponderance of talk-shows on air. Many of these bore close resemblance to similar programs on global or foreign television, but were considered examples of a programming genre rather than format adaptations. On the other hand, one interviewee considered that it was not suitable to translate the local folklore and traditional music from the stage to television simply by filming them unimaginatively with fixed cameras. He believed that the youth generation, particularly in the Gulf region, appreciated sophistication in visual communications and would not be impressed by such low-cost productions (Interview Glf05). Thus the high cost of production may also help explain why there were scarcely any Arabic adaptations of dramatic program formats from abroad.

The question then arises as to why the Arab world has not come up with more original television ideas, instead of simply adapting foreign formats. The conventional wisdom expressed was that formats were preferred by producers and channels who claimed they had been market-tested and proven abroad (Interview Glf03). Another view was that, with television being a 'Western' innovation, the various program genres necessarily had foreign roots that Arab stations duly had to imitate. Having been under the British and French mandates after Turkish imperialism, there might even be the legacy of a post-colonial mentality of looking 'West'-ward (Interview Glf05). Nonetheless, some producers recognized there was a possibility of developing original Arabic genres and formats. Since values are often universal, it was thought that television programs would only need to touch on these to succeed equally with people of different cultures. One radical idea mooted was for an original Middle Eastern format that would be a reality television documentary on middle-class families – one Arab, another Arab-American and yet another Israeli (Interview Glf03). However, such comments might have been meant as an industry public relations exercise directed at foreign stakeholders, rather than any serious plans by the broadcaster for the near future.

Talk shows were observably common in prime-time programming in the region, explained as being due to their commanding high ratings (Interview Glf06). Apart from a cultural predilection for discussion and debate, this phenomenon might reflect the limited scope for socio-political expression on the national level, where support for representative democracy, civil society activism and press freedoms might be fickle. A different view was that stations in the Middle East simply used a lot of talk-shows to fill the programming hours inexpensively, and that these were more like 'radio programs with pictures', and not television in the strictest sense (Interview Glf04). Mexican soaps dubbed into Arabic were noticeably prevalent, but notably not as much as local clones of the US soap *The Bold and the Beautiful* (Interview Glf06), betraying a cultural aspirational bias. Unlike other regions in the developing world, most program format adaptations in the Middle East were claimed to be licensed. The licence fees are not an insurmountable economic issue, particularly for the television industry of the oil-rich Gulf sub-region. Arguably, it was also essential for local channels to respect copyright in order to build credibility with global television producers whose program formats were much sought after (Interview Glf03). The resulting licensed regional adaptations were then capable of being marketed successfully at a programming market held annually in Bahrain for the television industry throughout the whole of the Middle East (Interview Glf02).

Successes and failures

Industry executives interviewed attributed the secret of LBC, MBC, ESC and FTV being the leading channels in the region largely to their programming strategies, including their successful adaptations of foreign formats (see Table 9.2). Notably, the first major quiz show in the region was *Who Wants to Be a Millionaire?*, adapted in the early 2000s, which led to considerable financial reward for MBC (Interview Glf06). Nonetheless, this MBC adaptation was actually made in London for the entire Arabic world, and was said to be successful because it chose the 'right sort' of presenter. Evidence cited for this was that an unlicensed clone of it on the rival channel LBC failed virtually from the outset, which was attributed primarily to the presenter proving rather unpopular with audiences (Interview Glf01). Later, *Star Academy* was LBC's response to the anticipated *Big Brother* regional adaptation aired by its competitor MBC (Interview Glf01). Among some industry executives, *Star Academy* was perceived as practically another clone of *Big Brother*, but with a local cultural twist (Interview Glf06). In reality, these were two separate global program formats, even if both

Table 9.2: Format adaptations observed in the Gulf sub-region.

Original format	Originator	Adaptation	Broadcaster
Millionaire	Celador	Licensed	MBC
The Chair	Touchdown	Licensed	Abu Dhabi TV
Star Academy	Endemol	Licensed	LBC
Big Brother	Endemol	Licensed	MBC
Hard Talk	BBC	Unlicensed	Al-Arabiya
Hard Talk	BBC	Unlicensed	Al-Jazeera
News on the Hour	CNN	Unlicensed	Al-Arabiya

Source: Bates Pan-Gulf (2004).

were licensed from the same Dutch-based producer, Endemol, and both utilized the same idea of a shared residence under surveillance.

Prior to *Who Wants to Be a Millionaire?*, quiz shows were reportedly never on prime time in the Middle East, and LBC had ambitiously attempted two or three quiz-show creations of its own but they failed for unknown reasons (Interview Glf06). Another quiz program, *The Weakest Link*, did not work in the Middle East and failed after just a few months. Made by Future TV of Lebanon and broadcast regionally via satellite, it was considered culturally offensive by Middle East viewers, especially because the contestants had to scheme to win (Interview Glf01). While Egyptian and Lebanese television stations tended to adapt television dramas from elsewhere within the region and beyond for the mass market, it was pointed out that Syrian stations as a general rule did not but aimed instead to excel at the niche market for classical Arab cultural programs (Interview Glf02). Among the Gulf-based channels, Abu Dhabi TV franchised a quiz show called *The Chair*, in which contestants had their stress levels raised artificially through the studio environment. Contestants succeeded only if their heart rate managed to remain within a certain range while answering questions. Though adapted under licence, it failed – in large part due to Abu Dhabi TV not being a highly rated channel within the Gulf region in the first place, much less in the wider Middle East (Interview Glf07). This outcome proved that it was not simply the quality of the adaptation of the program format itself that mattered, but its programming milieu and the audience targeted by the television network.

Inter-media observations

Format adaptations in the Middle East would arguably not have been possible without a unique conjunction of media commercialization and new communications technology at the turn of the twenty-first century, both enabled by the oil wealth of station owners and relative affluence of audiences in the Gulf sub-region. Based on monitoring of television programming content and audience-response websites, as well as informal interactions with the citizenry, a number of observations may be made about the researched context. While not claiming to be definitive, some conclusions might well be extrapolated from these sources that relate to the phenomenon of television program adaptations in the Middle East.

Cross-cultural ambivalence

If socio-political commentary in other media – including the internet and print – is any guide, there appears to be a love–hate relationship in the Middle East as a whole towards the media culture of the West. To a hardened minority, foreign programming or format adaptations would seem further confirmation of the decadence of the US and European cultures, and their detrimental effects on traditional culture in the Middle East. Yet there have been aspirations towards the affluence of the developed world, as evidenced by migration there as well as consumption of its products at home. Thus, through exposure to progressive programming from elsewhere within the region as well as beyond, available via satellite and cable, the wider majority of audiences could gradually be acculturated to a Arabic culture hybridized out of local, regional and foreign elements, the latter being not necessarily 'Western' in origin.

Anonymity of views

On balance, more respondents at audience feedback websites on television tended to be in favour of the programming innovations that resulted through format adaptations than against. The general consensus among the more liberal views expressed on sites like 'Mahmood's Den' (Al-Yousif 2004) was that a small but politically influential minority was seeking to hold back modernization of Arabic culture. That the vast majority of respondents chose to use the pseudonym 'Anonymous' perhaps reflects the current cultural and political dynamics in the Middle East. The fact that this pseudonym was preferred by both liberal and the conservative commentators alike suggests also that the latter were not necessarily confident about the acceptability of their views – especially among the more educated and affluent population with greater access to the Internet. However, this new electronic medium that is far less regulated or capable of being regulated has become a forum for far weightier issues of Arabic cultural identity and Middle East politics than television programming, despite occasional judicial setbacks faced by the participants identified.

Media ownership

By and large, ownership of television networks in the Middle East remains in the hands of the region's political and economic elites, whose cultural agendas can be quite varied – even changeable. Some of the more liberal transnational or regional networks are owned in part or whole by ruling families, which also oversee quite conservative national networks in their home countries. Furthermore, given their substantial wealth from other sources – primarily oil in the Gulf region – these elites are in a position to take financially costly measures such as cancelling highly popular programs that might still offend a conservative but influential minority. Until such time as media ownership in the region is more diversified and diffused, its media management more professionalized and its revenue more dependent on streams that are market driven and audience focused, the rate of progress for program adaptation of global television formats could be slow, if somewhat unpredictable.

Ratings and revenue

For the present, audience ratings are limited to parts of the Middle East. Even where available, there is a dearth of data on what motivates the viewership (Fakhreddine 2000b). Furthermore, advertising expenditure figures are generally deemed inaccurate due to widespread discounting, and play only a partial role in programming decisions. Yet the available figures do confirm the economic dominance of the oil-rich Gulf sub-region within the Middle East advertising market (see Table 9.3). Over time, ratings and revenue might act as significant catalysts in the programming innovation and press freedoms of commercial broadcasters (possibly including some new entrants). For the present, the cultural conservatism of the owners of many established broadcasters at the behest of their religious support base has proven a dampener. Much depends on which becomes the more significant segment of the audience mass market, though one might reasonably speculate that the more liberal and much larger younger population segment will grow and predominate in the future. Eventually, the larger – albeit for now mostly less affluent – populations of many Middle Eastern countries beyond the Gulf sub-region might become a more significant factor in audience demand for regional programming in a more economically progressive future.

Critical commentary

Understandably, the increasingly practice of program format adaptations has had a chequered history in a context of varying religious conservatism, political freedoms and economic affluence within the Gulf sub-region. Viewer responses across the wider Middle East to television websites suggest that format adaptation may also be a trigger for both political assertion by progressives as well as resurgent authority by conservatives in contesting Arab

Table 9.3: Advertising expenditure in the Gulf and Levant sub-regions.

Market	Expenditure (US$ million)	% contribution
Pan Arab Media	1,022	32
Saudi Arabia	472	15
United Arab Emirates	344	11
Kuwait	280	9
Other Gulf countries	158	5
Lebanon	220	7
Egypt	524	17
Other Levant countries	126	4
Total	*3,146*	*100*

Source: Bates Pan-Gulf (2004).

cultural identity. As Varan (1998) has argued, the transcultural impact of television might not be simply negative cultural deflation but positive cultural cross-fertilization involving local cooption of the medium to counteract undiluted foreign influences abroad. More recently, Moorti (2004) has demonstrated how, in the context of linguistically different southern India, adaptations of television formats blur the global–local boundary and reinvent chauvinistic sub-national cultures into a cosmopolitan complement to the contemporary global cultural economy. As Moran and Keane (2004) argue, the essence of effective cultural production for global markets remains a 'pie-and-crust' model where the culturally appealing local content is effectively set within a globally proven vehicle. But this characteristic 'difference within repetition' in program format adaptation can work towards either the stimulation or the stifling of domestic television production, depending on how the cultural technology transfer is managed. Therefore, it is incumbent on format originators, program adaptors, broadcast networks and advertising agencies to understand and work creatively within those regional paradoxes, even as they seek patiently to introduce incremental cultural change. The present research suggests the distinct possibility that the existing multi-channel television environment might allow audience segments across the Gulf sub-region to select the level of modernity with which they are comfortable at present, without being concerned about accessing other programming that causes undue cultural offence.

References

Al-Yousif, Mahmood (2004), 'Big Brothers Stop Big Brother Arabia', Mahmood's Den blog, http:// mahmood.tv/ 2004/03/01/ big-brothers-stop-big-brother-arabia. Accessed 25 November 2008.

Ayish, Mohammad I. (2000), 'Arab World Television in Transition: Current Trends and Future Prospects', *Orient: German Journal for Politics and Economics of the Middle East*, 41(3), pp. 415–34.

Chaker, Mohammad Naim (2003), 'The Impact of Globalization on Cultural Industries in the United Arab Emirates', *Journal of American Academy of Business*, 3(1–2), pp. 237–52.

Creswell, John W. (1994), *Research Design: Qualitative and Quantitative Approaches*, Thousand Oaks, CA: Sage.

Fakhreddine, Jihad (2000), 'Singing the Arab Market Economy's Notes', in Leo A. Gher and Hussein Y. Amin (eds), *Civic Discourse and Digital Age: Communications in the Middle East,* Stamford, CN: Ablex, pp. 159–66.

Gher, Leo A. and Amin, Hussein Y. (1999), 'New and Old Media Access and Ownership in the Arab World', *Gazette*, 6(1), pp. 59–88.

Khalil, Joe (2004), 'Blending In: Arab Television and the Search for Programming Ideas', *Transnational Broadcasting Studies*, 13, http://www.tbsjournal.com. Accessed 25 November 2008.

Khiabany, Gholam (2003), 'De-westernizing Media Theory or Reverse Orientalism: "Islamic Communication" as Cited by Hamid Mowlana', *Media, Culture & Society*, 25, pp. 415–22.

Miriampolski, Hy (2006), *Ethnography for Marketers: A Guide to Consumer Immersion,* Thousand Oaks, CA: Sage.

Moorti, Sujata (2004), 'Fashioning a Cosmopolitan Tamil Identity: Game Shows, Commodities and Cultural Identity', *Media, Culture & Society*, 26(4), pp. 549–67.

Moran, Albert and Keane, Michael (2004), 'Joining the Circle', in Albert Moran and Michael Keane (eds), *Television Across Asia: Television Industries, Program Formats and Globalization*, London: RoutledgeCurzon, pp. 200–03.

Mowlana, Hamid (1997), 'Islamicizing the Media in a Global Era: The State–Community Perspective in Iranian Broadcasting', in Kevin Robins (ed.), *Programming for People: From Cultural Rights to Cultural Responsibilities*, New York: United Nations Television Forum.

Quinn, Stephen, Walters, Tim and Whiteoak, John (2004), 'A Tale of Three (Media) Cities', *Global Media Journal*, 3(5), pp. 129–49.

Sakr, Naomi (1999), 'Frontiers of Freedom: Diverse Responses to Satellite Television in the Middle East and North Africa', *The Public*, 6(1), pp. 93–106.

Salamandra, Christa (2003), 'London's Arab Media and the Construction of Arabness', *Transnational Broadcasting Studies,* 10, http://www.tbsjournal.com/ salamandra.html. Accessed 25 November 2008.

Strauss, A. and Corbin, J. (1990), *Basics of Qualitative Research: Grounded Theory Procedures and Techniques*, Thousand Oaks, CA: Sage.

Tessler, Mark (2000), 'Changing Media Habits and Entertainment Preferences in Morocco: An Inter-generational Analysis', paper delivered at the Conference on Diffusion of New Information Technology in the Middle East, Tucson, Arizona, 14–16 April.

Varan, Duane (1998), 'The Transcultural Erosion Metaphor and the Transcultural Impact of Media Systems', *Journal of Communication*, Spring, pp. 58–85.

Woolcott, Harry (2001), *Writing Up Qualitative Research*, Thousand Oaks, CA: Sage, pp. 27–28.

Respondents

Interview Glf01, media researcher
Interview Glf02, academic researcher
Interview Glf03, regional broadcaster
Interview Glf04, domestic broadcaster
Interview Glf05, media researcher
Interview Glf06, advertising executive
Interview Glf07, regional broadcaster

Chapter 10

How National Media Systems Shape the Localization of Formats: A Transnational Case Study of *The Block* and *Nerds FC* in Australia and Denmark

Pia Majbrit Jensen

Television programs are increasingly traded internationally as program *formats*, which are subsequently adapted locally to meet national market conditions outside their country of origin, and hence form a new, different and highly internationalized business and production model. However, despite being a result of the increasing internationalization and even globalization of world media, the formats demonstrate tremendous trans-national elasticity, and the same format is often produced very differently from country to country according to the media systemic and sociocultural conditions of specific local markets. In fact, even when the same format is produced similarly in different national markets, the local adaptations more often than not contain subtle but nonetheless important variations. Often the explanation for such variations has been sought in general sociocultural variations between countries, and variations have been viewed as representative of specific local cultures.

Nevertheless, it is this chapter's main argument that an investigation of the specific *media systemic conditions* (such as media policies, funding, market competition and broadcasting history) that shape local production gives a much more detailed and comprehensive explanation and understanding of even the subtler transnational variations. Consequently, the chapter argues that national sociocultural particularities offer only a small part of the explanation for differences between local adaptations.

Methodology

By comparatively analyzing the Australian and Danish versions of *The Block* (known in Denmark as *Huset*) and *Nerds FC*, the elasticity of the two formats is examined, and possible contributing factors – be they sociocultural or media systemic – in similarities and dissimilarities are put forward. The choice of precisely these two formats builds on the fact that, on one hand, both are factual entertainment programs despite each representing one distinct sub-genre of factual entertainment: *The Block* is essentially a lifestyle program; *Nerds FC* is a reality program. Also, one format – *The Block* – is adapted radically differently in the two countries, whereas *Nerds FC* is adapted similarly. Lastly, *The Block* originates in Australia and *Nerds FC* in Denmark. All of this should combine to avoid comparing apples with oranges, and at the same time it should secure a certain analytical case variation.

The same can be said about the choice of Denmark and Australia. On one hand, the two share a number of similarities, the two most important being that they both belong to the

Western geolinguistic region (Cunningham et al. 1998; Sinclair et al. 1996). On the other hand, with Australia's predominantly Anglophone cultural heritage and liberal media system, and Denmark's Northern European heritage and historically more public service-oriented media system, they also display important sociocultural and media systemic differences. According to Hallin and Mancini (2004), the Northern European countries, including Denmark, constitute one prototypical media systemic model – the democratic-corporatist model – whereas the Anglophone countries constitute another, and in many aspects quite different, model – the liberal model. As for television broadcasting, these differences come to the fore in the fact that television is more commercialized and liberalized in the Anglophone countries, whereas commercialization and liberalization are less dominant in Northern Europe – where, for example, public service broadcasting continues to play a prominent role (see also Jensen 2007).

As for Danish and Australian television specifically, their television systems are essentially quite different. The Danish system has always been, and still is, dominated by the public service sector despite a recent and turbulent transition into a mixed public and private system. From the very beginning, the Australian system has been, and still is, dominated by the private free-to-air sector, with the public broadcasters being regarded as merely an alternative to the private broadcasters. The public sector domination in Denmark is reflected in the audience ratings – Danes spend almost 70 per cent of their television viewing time watching channels with a public service remit – as well as in the media regulations, which have traditionally favoured the public sector. The complete opposite is the case in Australia. Australians generally prefer the private sector and spend 64 per cent of their television viewing watching the private broadcasters. In addition, the three free-to-air private broadcasters have enjoyed a fair amount of political and legislative goodwill, which until recently has protected them from competition from other sectors, including the public and the subscription sectors. Also, in the Australian system continuities in the institutional organization have been stronger than forces for change. This in turn has led to conservatism in the system, the structure of which remains largely as it was in the 1960s. Meanwhile, the last two decades have seen the Danish system undergo a turbulent transition from a public service monopoly with only one broadcaster (and only one channel) to a fully fledged mixed multi-channel system with no less than twelve Danish-language channels in addition to many foreign and transnational channels.

In addition, it is important to note that the specific broadcasters, both between and within the two countries, exhibit large dissimilarities. Some broadcasters, such as Danish TV2 (which adapted *The Block*) and Australian SBS (which adapted *Nerds FC*), operate under a public service remit and are therefore much more regulated compared with commercial and privately owned broadcasters such as Channel Nine and TV2/Zulu (the original developers of *The Block* and *Nerds FC*, respectively). Additionally, some channels, such as TV2/Zulu and SBS, cater primarily for niche audiences as opposed to TV2 and Channel Nine, which are providers of full-scale services.

The Block and *Nerds FC* introduced

In *The Block*, four couples are each chosen to renovate an apartment in the same block – hence the show's original title. The couples have a limited period of time and set budget to do this and, to put further pressure on the couples, everybody must maintain their daytime jobs during the renovation. Furthermore, the apartments are in a fairly bad condition, which means that the work includes a number of expensive, difficult and time-consuming tasks, such as full bathroom and kitchen renovations. The competitors' overriding goal during the series is to complete the best, most popular renovation. In the Australian series, 'best and most popular' means the apartment that in the last episode sells for the highest price at an auction. In the Danish series, it means the apartment the viewers like the best. The Australian couples all get to keep any profits they may make at the final auction, but the couple that gets the highest price will receive double their profit as a prize. The Danish couples compete for a cash prize of DKK500,000.[1] On the whole, the format contains equal shares of reality and lifestyle elements, and therefore abundant possibilities to combine and play with the two genres, both of which will be explained and compared below. Both countries have aired two series of the format, and for the analysis carried out here I have chosen episode one of the second series in both countries, as this is where the narrative and competitive plot is struck and the competing couples are introduced. As such, first episodes are easier to compare than later episodes, where the Danish and Australian narratives take different directions.

Nerds FC is called *FC Zulu* in its original Danish version. The first series of *FC Zulu* was broadcast in 2004 on TV2's youth-skewed supplementary channel, TV2/Zulu (hence the title), where it quickly became a cult hit with audiences following above-average ratings for the small channel. It is important to note that TV2/Zulu is a 100 per cent commercially funded channel and does not operate under a public service remit. The format's basic idea and humour-laden plot are to turn a group of 'nerds' into (sports)men by teaching them how to play football and then ultimately have them play against a team of A-league professionals. As such, the show falls within the reality genre. For the analysis carried out below, I have chosen episode four of both adaptations, which sees the nerds take on a team of hardened prisoners. However, as is the case with the analysis of *The Block*, other episodes will be referred to when they shed further light on the argument.

Factual entertainment: Lifestyle and reality

Factual entertainment consists of two primary genres: lifestyle and reality. The two have a lot in common, the most important being the fact that they both have ordinary people in their private sphere as their dramaturgical pivotal point. However, the two also demonstrate many differences, which may be summed up by classifying lifestyle as harmless small-talk TV with a focus on ordinary everyday experiences such as interior decorating and gardening, and reality as a kind of 'peak realism' (Jerslev 2005: 28, my translation from the Danish 'højdepunktsrealisme') exclusively focusing on the *extraordinary* events of ordinary people. Lifestyle television deals with ordinary people's everyday lives.

The lifestyle genre includes programs on interior design and home improvement, personal makeover, food and, more recently, personal coaching on issues such as cleaning. The programs revolve around everyday life and the surfaces, routines and behaviour of our private sphere, in particular its *physical* organization. Programs within the lifestyle genre are most often didactical at their core and give practical advice and inspiration on food, fashion, body, garden and house – all of which are phenomena through which we express and develop our identities.

The reality genre, on the other hand, deals with ordinary people experiencing an emotional breakup of the everyday, and happens when the everyday breaks out of its routine and becomes dangerous and exciting. Programs within the genre are more often than not centred around contestants competing against each other (Jerslev 2005). As such, the genre contains a built-in guarantee of crisis and often involves contestants' loss of face – for example, when contestants on *Survivor* must live off a bowl of rice a day and form strategic but callous allegiances, or when *The X Factor* contestants give it all they have on stage but still receive harsh criticism from the judges. Thus, reality nearly always involves the exposure of less flattering aspects of human behaviour and emotions. On the other hand, a lifestyle program rarely involves participants' loss of face, although participants publicly expose private feelings (especially in the 'reveal'). In lifestyle shows, we never get too close. Everybody has a good time and the façade remains intact.[2]

In summary, lifestyle programs are games of *inclusion* in which everybody participates on equal terms, and where there are no obvious winners and losers. Reality shows, on the other hand, are games of *exclusion*, with real winners and losers, and emphasize an exclusive individuality in their contestants. As Bruun (2005) has pointed out, these differences make up two very distinct types of entertainment, where lifestyle is *egalitarian* and inclusive and reality *elitist* and exclusive. However, we shall return to this in more detail in the analytical comparisons of the two formats.

The Block and *Huset* compared

The Block and *Huset* are, as mentioned, radically different and this has a lot to do with how the two versions choose to combine the two genres and ultimately shows the great elasticity of the lifestyle genre. The Australian version makes maximum use of the reality elements contained in the format, with large emphasis on conflicts, scandal, emotional drama and competitiveness, and relatively little emphasis on the lifestyle elements – all of which essentially makes it highly *melodramatic*. The Danish version, on the other hand, is less reality skewed and seems to play down conflicts and the built-in competitive elements. As a consequence, *Huset* puts its emphasis on the 'fun' of renovating and on the creation of a communal feeling among the competing couples. Having said this, *Huset* still contains many reality elements and actually only a few lifestyle elements. It may therefore be classified as 'reality light' meets 'lifestyle light', and ultimately comes across as much more documentaristic. Also, the two adaptations have very different narrative guiding principles in the sense that *Huset* has an overriding narrative focus on egalitarian principles such as 'ordinariness', 'plainness' and viewer recognition ('I could achieve that look'), whereas *The Block* has its narrative focus on elitist principles such as 'extraordinariness', 'abnormality' and 'oddness'. All of this will be elaborated below by comparing a number of key constituents of the format, including program introductions and finales, the state of the apartments and casting. These are all vital areas in which the two adaptations differ considerably, and we look at how they differ with regard to viewer contact and appeal, the use of competitive elements, the use of DIY and other informative elements, and the use of the reality genre.

Casting: Australian extraordinariness versus Danish ordinariness

There are considerable differences between the Australian and the Danish couples in four areas: age, looks, sexual orientation and competitiveness. The couples on *The Block* are all gorgeous and glamorous people in their twenties and thirties, most of them with well-paid jobs and big city lives lived in the fast lane. They are certainly not your average Australians, and would no doubt all look spectacular scantily clad on the cover of a magazine – which, of course, is where they wound up as a result of the publishing deal with an Australian weekly magazine. Besides this, one of the couples is gay, which is just another example of what one might call the 'casting of the extraordinary' strategy that has clearly been employed by the producers. In addition, all four couples are very competitive and emphasize that they are on *The Block* to win. Contrary to the Australians, the Danish contestants on *Huset* are fairly average in terms of jobs, looks, sexual orientation and age. In the first episode, none of the couples so much as mentions the competition and the possibility of winning half a million DKK. Instead, they talk about the challenges that lie ahead for them as couples. Another characteristic of this 'casting of the ordinary' strategy is the large variety of ages – the youngest contestant is 26 years old, the oldest 62 – in contrast to the Australian version's exclusive focus on the young.

If we quite reasonably assume that the average Australian viewer is not nearly as gorgeous, glamorous and successful as the couples on *The Block*, but rather your typical Australian with a normal job and a standard, run-of-the-mill partner, the casting is likely to have a high *fascination* potential with viewers. The fascinating lifestyles, personalities and looks of the couples are likely to provoke dreams and envy, and perhaps even disgust and antipathy, as the viewers either wish they were like the contestants or dislike them for being so competitive, glamorous and gorgeous, and so different from themselves. This becomes particularly evident in the decision to cast the gay couple, which has the potential to cause some sort of controversy, scandal, amusement and/or offence with the average viewer. The Danish couples in *Huset* are much closer to the average viewer than is the case with the

Australians. It is likely that Danish viewers will find some sort of *identification* with one or more of the contestants when it comes to occupation, age, geographical origin, vernacular, relationship or looks. So, even though the couples are actually fairly different, they are different in an ordinary, average way, and each couple thus personifies one standard Danish lifestyle among other standard lifestyles.

Conflict versus team-building

Both the Australian and Danish first episodes take the viewers through the first day on *The Block* and *Huset*. That is, the plot and the four couples are introduced, the couples see the apartments and meet each other for the first time, get their first assignment, and start work on the renovation. Nonetheless, the first day progresses very differently in the two versions. The first day on *The Block* is filled with drama, scandal, emotion and interpersonal conflict, whereas the first day on *Huset* focuses on the fun of renovating, team-building and interpersonal bonding. Again, the differences between the two adaptations centre very much on Australian extraordinariness versus the Danish ordinariness when it comes to the state of the apartments, the competitive elements and the different use of reality and lifestyle elements in the two adaptations.

State of the apartments

There are obvious differences in the state of the apartments. The Australian apartments are in very bad shape. They are extremely dirty and have no floors or walls intact. There are too many room dividers and no plaster on the walls or ceilings. In addition, the floors have big holes through to the apartment downstairs, some of the toilets do not flush, and the sewerage pipes are exposed. This means that Dani and Monique can hear Steven and Richard going to the toilet and Kirsten and Jason can hear Matt and Jane talking privately. This naturally enhances the potential for conflict. For example, dust falls from the ceiling in Dani and Monique's apartment when Richard and Steven clean, and Kirsten and Jason can hear when Matt and Jane talk about the other couples – including Kirsten and Jason – behind their backs. The glamorous and sophisticated couples are literally trapped in the dirt! That the apartments are in such a bad state exposes the high social status and glamour of the Australian couples even more, and their extraordinariness becomes even more obvious. In this sense, the viewers are given an opportunity to laugh at the contestants and perhaps gloat a little over the fact that these chic and classy people are caught in a very unsophisticated situation.

The Danish apartments are in bad shape as well, although they are nowhere near the poor condition of the Australian apartments. Cords are hanging from the ceiling, taps are dripping, and everywhere is filthy but the walls, ceiling and floors are fairly intact and the rooms are already laid out. Even though the Danish couples are initially a bit horrified by the state of the apartments, they all manage to stay quite positive throughout the episode. Unlike in *The Block*, in the first episode of *Huset* there is no emphasis put on the conflict that may arise from the bad state of the apartments. Instead, the similarities of the apartments – and thus fairness of the competition – are emphasized. The host makes a point of informing the viewers that, even though the apartments differ a little, the four apartments have the same size and are in 'equally bad shape'. Hence, the ordinariness can also be found in the apartments. Their state is not too bad; they just need to be redecorated with some tender loving care. Additionally, and in contrast to the Australian version, the Danish couples do not have to clean the apartments on the first day. Instead, their first assignment is to build a communal workshop in collaboration with the other couples.

Competitive elements

This brings us to the competitive elements of the two adaptations. The communal workshop assignment mentioned above is a good example of how the Danish adaptation focuses on 'lighter' or 'softer' competitive elements that do not necessarily augment conflict between and within the couples, but rather enhance the interpersonal bonding among the contestants. The couples have six hours to build a communal workshop. Everybody has changed into similar work clothes: grey pants and white t-shirts. The women have a little disagreement over the wall colour, and Christian cannot work out how to assemble one of the power tools. However, the women quickly reach a civilised agreement, and Jørn helps Christian. As such, the workshop is generally built in a feel-good atmosphere. After the conclusion of this first assignment, the couples are even treated to a communal barbecue as a reward after a hard day's work. Additionally, another feel-good surprise awaits the couples when they go to bed: the producers have had the couples' private beds transported to *Huset* complete with duvets, pillows and bedspreads.

In stark contrast to the downplaying of the competitive elements on *Huset*, from the beginning *The Block* places a large emphasis on the competition between the couples. Before even entering the apartments, the four Australian couples have to compete against each other to decide which couple gets which apartment. The host tells them to rush to four differently coloured Toyota four-wheel-drives. Inside each car is a key with number 1, 2, 3 or 4, and this number decides who gets the first, second, third and fourth pick of the apartments. The four apartments differ considerably from one another. Two of them have gardens, and another has an extra room. In the Danish version, the allocation of the apartments takes place by the couples simply drawing lots. Furthermore, the Australian audience can enter a 'people's choice awards' competition, where they have to vote for the most popular couple. At the end of the series, the most popular couple will be announced, and among the people who voted for that couple there is a draw to win a car similar to the one the couples have just received. Furthermore, the competition adds to the general feeling of conflict in the Australian series.

It is basically a popularity contest that asks the viewers to take an active stance regarding the conflicts brewing on *The Block*.

The Danish viewers of *Huset* are also asked to vote for their favourites. Actually, it is the viewers who, by SMS or telephone, almost exclusively decide which couple wins both the main competition and the sub-competitions. However, unlike the Australian audience, the Danish audience members are asked to pick their favourite *renovation* and not their favourite couple. Even though one's favourite renovation may very well belong to one's favourite couple, it still focuses attention on the actual renovation and not on the personalities of the contestants. The Danish viewers are not asked to judge the personalities of the contestants, but rather the contestants' DIY skills and creativity.

Melodrama versus docudrama

Reality elements

The two adaptations also differ when it comes to the use of elements from the reality sub-genres. *The Block* has a melodramatic narrative resembling that of the fictional soap genre and of the reality sub-genres, whereas *Huset*'s narrative is much more docu-dramatic, realistic and hence ordinary. Reality focuses precisely on the extraordinary situations and events in 'ordinary' people's lives, and often employs a melodramatic narrative (Jensen 2007; Jerslev 2005; Turner 2005), which again fits well with the analytical findings discussed so far. This means that *The Block* creates its narrative progress using elements from fiction, whereas *Huset* plays on elements from the documentary genre and plays down the potential melodrama. This is best exemplified in the two first episode finales.

The Australian version's first episode finale consists of a teaser about what will happen within the next two weeks on *The Block*. The teaser hints that there will be lots of future conflicts in the form of contestants clashing with each other, and creates a fantastic cliff-hanger that is sure to make the audience curious and titillated. The teaser hints at a growing conflict between Jason and Kirsten and the other couples. At the end of the teaser, a new and even more scandalous conflict is hinted at: the press has got wind of the fact that one contestant has been in jail. The contestant, Dani, is being interviewed saying that he has served his punishment already and that he only took the blame for somebody else. To make things worse, Dani's partner Monique's grandfather dies the day after the reveal. There are lots of tears and emotion, and you see Monique packing a suitcase and wonder whether they will be leaving the show. This last segment, centred on the revelation of Dani's criminal past in the press, shows how *The Block* explicitly involves the contestants' personal lives in creating a melodramatic narrative very similar to that of a fictional soap. His past catches up with him. His loving family façade cracks. And we are there to watch as it all happens.

The episode finale of *Huset* employs a different tactic, focusing on the creation of a feel-good atmosphere among the contestants. In a classic documentary-like approach, all four couples are interviewed to camera, stating that they have had a great, fun-filled day, and everybody likes everybody. Everybody also seems quite hopeful about the renovation task ahead. After this, the host gives them their first renovation assignment. The bedroom must be finished within a week. The couples subsequently go to their apartments, where their own beds await them and lights are turned off in the apartments. However, at 3.00 a.m. Christian and Ulla still cannot sleep and decide to do something about the cooker hood above the stove instead, which results in them short-circuiting the electricity of the entire apartment. There is not a trace of conflict in sight, only plenty of feel-good vibes through and through with a funny and silly 'gag' at the very end. In contrast to the first Australian episode, there are no melodramatic cliffhangers hinting at conflicts galore and revealing what will happen next.

As it turns out, there is a pragmatic explanation for the absence of cliffhangers about what will happen next in the Danish version. Due to the viewers deciding the outcome of the competitions, *Huset* was broadcast 'quasi live', meaning that production was done very close to broadcast and consequently the renovation happened as the series was broadcast. The producers therefore had no idea what would happen the next week or the week after, and hence could not make a cliffhanger similar to the Australian one (Nikolajsen 2006). This also meant that a comparatively large part of each episode had to be dedicated to the SMS competition, and therefore left less time to develop the main storylines around the relationships of the couples (Nikolajsen 2006).[3]

DIY elements

Neither the Danish nor the Australian first episode contains a lot of DIY or other informative elements. As already mentioned, the focus in both episodes is on the plot, the contestants and their initial reactions. Nevertheless, while the informative elements on *The Block* are practically absent, they play a slightly larger role on *Huset*. This becomes most evident in the Danish couples' first communal assignment, the building of the workshop. Also, the informative elements' relative absence in the first episode of *Huset* is clearly made up for in its sister program *Huset Direkte*, which follows directly after the main program. As is evident from the title, it is a studio-based program broadcast live immediately after the conclusion of episode one. It contains various informative segments on renovating in general and on episode one specifically. The show starts off with a story on shoddy construction work and gives advice to viewers on what precautions to take to avoid shoddy tradespeople. There is also a story about the Danes' relationship with the 'workshop' seen from a historical and sociological perspective. Also, an historian explains the history of the apartment block, and finally an interior designer gives advice on how to decorate a bedroom. As the lifestyle genre (as opposed to the contentious reality genre) is generally acknowledged as being acceptable within public service circles and actually forms part of a long public service tradition of useful programming (Carlsen and Frandsen 2005), *Huset Direkte* obviously serves a dual purpose. By giving the viewers lots of information, it also serves as a political 'public service justification'. Because *Huset* has very little DIY and other informative elements, *Huset Direkte* is more or less the only reason the executive producer of *Huset* can call it lifestyle – or 'everyday documentary' – rather than reality (Rømer 2006). Also, it is yet another way of 'normalizing' what happens in *Huset* and making it relevant to the ordinary viewer.

Elitist versus egalitarian entertainment

In essence, and to use a single comparison, the Australians renovate in Armani jeans and high heels and every couple gets their own tools; the Danes renovate wearing similar and practical work clothes and they have to share the tools provided in the communal workshop. Here, there is a clear parallel to Bruun (2005) and her theories on egalitarian and elitist TV entertainment. Aided by its melodramatic style, the Australian adaptation clearly has an elitist bias, focusing on the narrative principles of extraordinariness, abnormality and oddness, whereas *Huset*'s documentaristic style supports an egalitarian bias with narrative principles such as ordinariness, plainness and viewer recognizability at its core. Consequently, the Australian version is exclusive and elitist at its core, exemplified in the casting and conflicting competitiveness, whereas the Danish version is much more inclusive and egalitarian, exemplified in the downplaying of conflict and episode one's construction of a general feel-good ambience.

Australian commercial versus Danish public service TV

Many of the reasons for the exclusive focus on the normal and the ordinary in the Danish TV2 adaptation – as opposed to the original Channel Nine version's extraordinariness – are likely to be found in the two broadcasters' positions in the Danish and Australian TV system, respectively. It is likely that, even though *The Block* most probably had a larger budget than *Huset* – and therefore better financial opportunities to create a more spectacular and extraordinary narrative – a large part of the explanation relates to the fact that *Huset* is adapted by a broadcaster with a public service remit, while privately owned commercial broadcaster Channel Nine did the original version. This is substantiated by the fact that similar analytical differences are at play in the Australian and Danish versions of the format *Ground Force* (*Hokus Krokus* in Danish), which were also adapted by a privately owned Australian broadcaster (Channel Seven) and a Danish public service broadcaster (DR1) (see Jensen 2005, 2007 for a detailed comparison of the two).

In fact, according to format developer David Barbour (2006), *The Block* was originally envisaged as a soap opera dealing with the human drama that inevitably arises during renovation work. Barbour wanted to take the focus away from the DIY aspect of the lifestyle shows and instead focus exclusively on the hardships involved in getting tradesmen to turn up on time, organizing a DIY renovation around one's work schedule, and so on. This notion corresponds perfectly with the prior analysis of *The Block* and also illustrates my point about public service versus commercial broadcasting. A Danish public service broadcaster could never say that they wanted to take DIY out of a lifestyle program and make it into a reality show or soap! This would go against everything that is considered acceptable in the Danish public service tradition for lifestyle programming, the primary justification for which is that it contains information relevant to viewers (Carlsen and Frandsen 2005). On the other hand, the quote is perfectly legitimate for a privately owned commercial broadcaster in Australia, whose primary responsibility is to attract (the right kind and number of) viewers.

It is precisely the more public service-oriented programming policy and basic programming values that TV2's commissioning editor points to as the reason why the Danish adaptation looks different from its Australian predecessor. She characterizes TV2's core values as 'inspirational' and 'aspirational' and she prefers to call *Huset* 'lifestyle or everyday documentary' rather than reality (Rømer 2006). The reason why she is opposed to the term 'reality' is that the producers do not actively plant or cultivate conflict. Instead, they often play down conflicts, as the analysis has shown. Rømer believes that TV2 viewers would be opposed to this harder, conflict-ridden approach. As TV2 is commercially funded, despite its public service remit, the playing down of conflict in turn reflects the channel's competition with its closest commercial competitor, TV3, in which TV2 endeavours to ensure it does not look like TV3, whose programming profile is dominated by precisely the harder, conflict-ridden reality shows such as *Survivor*. Hence, internal conflicts regarding renovation issues are acceptable, whereas conflicts between neighbours are not because these would bear too much similarity to TV3's profile (Rømer 2006).

Danish cultural distaste for conflict and competition

Rømer (2006) also briefly touches upon what she calls 'Danish culture' as an explanation for why the Danish adaptation is less competitive, conflict-ridden and sensationalistic. She believes that Danes are less competitive than Australians, whom she sees as 'highly competitive'. Rømer sees the Danes and thus Danish media as having less taste for sensation and scandal. According to her, these cultural differences come to the fore in the way TV2 contestants are cast, avoiding people with the 'slightest hint of mental imbalance'.

However, contrary to what she suggests, this less extraordinary casting could also be related to the Danish public service tradition rather than to inherent traits in the Danish national character, especially because other, privately owned Danish broadcasters such as TV3 are certainly not shy when it comes to conflict and harder reality type shows. Public service TV – or at least Rømer's and thus TV2's interpretation of it – may not offend viewers. It must gather the nation, not divide it, as might have been the case if TV2 had cast people with a 'mental imbalance' or extraordinarily gorgeous, glamorous and competitive people.

The executive producer of *Huset* indirectly points to this as well when he talks about why *Huset* was different to the Australian original (Nikolajsen 2006). While his team deliberately chose 'relations over renovations', and therefore had to employ 'a few reality tricks along the way', the reality elements had to be 'cosy and positive' and in line with TV2's programming policy and values, as opposed to 'nasty' and conflict-ridden (Nikolajsen 2006). An example of a positive reality trick is making the contestants believe they have to sleep on uncomfortable sofa-beds, after which the producers have their private beds brought to *Huset*.

In this respect, it is interesting that the other Danish public service broadcaster, DR, recently adapted British talent show *The X Factor*, with an overwhelming ratings success as a result, despite the fact that this format – including DR's adaptation of it – is widely seen as an example of precisely this type of nastier, conflict-ridden and reality-skewed entertainment program. This consequently suggests that Danes, contrary to what Rømer believes, do not oppose a more elitist and exclusive type of programming. Rather, it suggests that other explanations are most likely at play here, and it is this chapter's argument that these explanations are found within the media system itself and the people acting in it, and that they have to do with conditions such as national broadcasting history, pervasive industry ideologies and changing competitive situations. This argument is elaborated later in a final discussion, and in comparison with previous academic works on the subject of transnational differences in TV usage and content. But let us first turn to a comparison of the *Nerds FC* format.

FC Zulu and *Nerds FC* compared

> What will happen when you take 14 nerds, who have never touched a football in their lives; coach them for three months…and then let them play a professional team in front of 25,000 people? We'll find out when we turn boys into men, mice into lions, nerds into athletes and proudly present the football team, Nerds FC.

This quote is the Australian program introduction that starts every episode of the series. It is an almost exact translation of the Danish program's introduction, and the words accurately describe the main plot of the format. For three months, the nerds must endure hard physical and mental training in order to become capable of playing football to a tolerable standard. Additionally, each episode has its own mini-storyline or storylines, with a smaller challenge such as recording a theme song or, as it is the case with the episode being analyzed in this chapter, playing a match against a team of prison inmates. Thus the format clearly falls within the reality genre: a group of contestants is put in a staged and unfamiliar reality in which contestants must face a number of physical, social and mental challenges. However, it is important to note that it also differs from other reality game shows such as *Big Brother*, *Survivor* and *Idol* in three important ways.

First, it is a light-hearted, irony-packed and actually very funny format that stands ready to poke fun not only at the participants but also the constructed reality of the format itself.

It is not a serious reality show due to the fact that the main challenge in itself is essentially impossible. It *is* possible to get the nerds to play football in front of 25,000 people – just not well – and the nerds, and the viewers with them, realise that they will never become highly skilled football players who can match professional athletes. Most of them simply do not have the basic motor skills required of a top athlete, and this makes the series funny to watch. In other reality formats, the contestants usually have certain skills – like singing talent on *The X Factor* and mental and physical endurance skills on *Survivor* – that make them and the viewers believe they can rise to the challenge and win the competition. Second, it is a positive reality format in the sense that we, the viewers, laugh *with* the nerds when they try the impossible. We do not laugh *at* them. The format does not humiliate the nerds by putting them in compromising situations. This is something that other reality formats thrive on by encouraging different types of less flattering human behaviour such as backstabbing, elbowing and slyness among the contestants. However, this is not the case with *Nerds FC*. It seems that the nerds enjoy the challenge and laugh at themselves as much as the viewers do. Third, there is no prize to win, which means that the nerds are there for the 'fun' of going through a different experience and therefore are probably not willing to humiliate themselves too much. This air of positivism, humour and light-heartedness recurs in both *FC Zulu* and *Nerds FC*, and the two versions are generally 'radically similar', especially when it comes to dramaturgy, editing, production value, casting and narrative 'feel-goodness'. However there are also subtle but important differences between the two, which make *Nerds FC* slightly more serious, competitive and melodramatic than *FC Zulu*, which in turn is more comical, satirical and ironic.

Similarities between *FC Zulu* and *Nerds FC*

The similarities between the Australian adaptation and its Danish original cover most areas from the program introductions, to editing style and production value, to the overall progression and general humoristic feel-good nature of the series. As such, the two adaptations both evolve around rather universal themes such as personal development and manhood (or what it means to be a 'real' man). Below are some examples of these similarities and themes divided into three main categories.

Dramaturgy

The eight episodes of the series progress in exactly the same way in the two adaptations. That the two adaptations have similar storyline structures, both in the overall course of the series and within each episode, makes the over-arching narrative plot exactly the same in the two versions. Each episode, as well as the entire series, demonstrates a classical, fairytale 'home-away-from-home' dramaturgy, in which the nerds conquer a challenge they did not think they were able to overcome. In the process, they are enriched and end up better and stronger people than when they took off on their journey to – in the case of episode four – the match against the prisoners. In prison, the nerds' challenge is to face their worst fear as they battle it out against a team of hardened criminals. In other episodes, there are different challenges – such as singing and dancing for their theme song – but the dramaturgy stays the same. The 'home-away-from-home' dramaturgy – with a valuable lesson learnt – adds to both narrative progress and the general positive feeling of both adaptations and very much thematizes positive personal development.

Editing style and production value

The two adaptations have chosen very similar editing styles, which in turn have an effect on the production value. Two examples will be mentioned here: the program introductions, as we have already mentioned briefly, and the presentation of the prisoners. Nevertheless, there are a lot of similar examples throughout this specific episode as well as throughout the other seven episodes. As for the program introductions, the wording of the Australian introduction is, as mentioned, an almost word-by-word translation of the Danish introduction. However, this is not the only similarity in the introductions. Generally, the two introductions have almost identical editing styles. During the introduction, we see funny clips of the nerds trying in vain to control the football – one shot shows a nerd getting hit in the groin by the ball, another nerd gets the ball straight in the face, and so on – while there are cross-cuts to funny and ironic statements from both coaches and nerds. For instance, one of the Australian nerds, who is slightly overweight, says that his 'exercise regime usually consists in walking to and from the car', after which we see him fumble with the football. And the coach says that he has never before come across people with 'such a basic lack of general motor skills', while we see some of the 'motor skills challenged' nerds trying in vain to kick and intercept the ball. In this way, the introductions create an ironic and humorous narrative tone from the very beginning. Another example of the radical similarity in editing styles is the way the prison inmates are presented before the match against the nerds in order to make them as scary and as different from the nerds as possible. We see the prisoners working out in the gym – with the visual focus on their big muscles – and some of the prisoners are later presented by first name, criminal offence and how many years they are serving. Again, this creates a strong ironic and humorous contrast to the more 'delicate', less muscular and certainly less physical nerds, with a particular emphasis on their nervous reactions of having to play the criminals. These similarities in the editing process seem to make the production values – that is, the overall quality and look of the two versions – appear similar as well. Also, both versions employ a documentary-like, semi-professional and on-the-spot reporting style, and neither adaptation looks more expensive or well-produced than the other, as was the case with the more visually appealing and expensive looking Australian version of *The Block*.[4]

Casting and conflict

The Danish and Australian nerds are also similar, except for the fact that the Australian nerds – like Australian society in general – are ethnically more diverse than the Danish nerds, of whom only one seems to be of another ethnic origin than Danish. They are *not* nerdy in the sense that you feel sorry for them or laugh at them because they, for instance, do not have any social skills, are unsophisticated, or say embarrassing things. They are funny, self-ironic young men with above-average intelligence and weird interests such as stargazing or inventing a new language. In this sense, all of them are academic achievers and very passionate and knowledgeable about their particular fields of interest. Because they are intelligent young men, they also do not kid themselves that they can actually become top athletes in three months, and they therefore stay at a self-ironic arm's length from the main challenge during the entire ordeal. One example of this is when one of the Australian nerds comments on the fact that he is inside a prison: 'I'm in a hostile environment with a bunch of people who want to kick my arse – it's just like being back in primary school.' The nerds may not win even one game, but at least they try, and they enjoy themselves doing it. In addition, we never see any negative and malicious sides to the nerds, and conflicts are always of a positive nature. For example, the nerds may feel extremely frightened and threatened by the prison environment but they rise to the occasion and play a decent match and in the end impress their coaches and even the prisoners. Another reality show may have had a completely different set-up, in which the nerds were psychologically traumatised unnecessarily and the prisoners played even rougher. In reality shows such as *Big Brother* and *Survivor*, and even *The Biggest Loser*, the plot thrives on negative conflicts and the contestants submitting to the pressure and showing less flattering personality traits. This is not the case with either *FC Zulu* or *Nerds FC*. The casting and positive conflicts combined make the viewers laugh *with* the nerds and not at them, which again adds to the strong feel-good quality of the two adaptations.

Despite the great similarities between the two adaptations, there are also a number of subtle but rather important differences. Together, these differences make *Nerds FC* slightly more serious and competitive than *FC Zulu*, which in turn is more comical, satirical and 'meta-ironic'. In addition, and as a consequence of this, *Nerds FC* has a broader, more melodramatic and more universalistic appeal than *FC Zulu*, which seems to target a narrower and culturally 'initiated' audience with its use of irony and inter-cultural references.

Danish inter-cultural references and ironic comedy

The Danish episode four has two inter-cultural references that are both of significant importance for an understanding of the humour and irony of *FC Zulu*. First, there is an inter-textual and inter-cultural reference to the Danish *Olsen Banden* (translates as *The Olsen Gang*) comedy movies when the nerds leave the prison and their coach is outside to greet them waving Danish paper flags. This is an inter-textual and highly ironic take on a famous and recurring scene in the *Olsen Banden* movies, and on the fact that the Danish national team is actually called *Olsen Banden* in the press because the coach's surname is Olsen. Even the music played during the scene is the famous soundtrack from the movies. However, this is only funny in the local Danish context where these movies are part of most Danes' cultural heritage. For outsiders, the scene does not make any sense and therefore is not particularly funny.

Second, and even more importantly, a large part of the humour and irony of not only episode four but the entire Danish series is derived from the fact that the Danish nerds have absolutely no knowledge of the game of football. One example is the nerds' look of bewilderment when they are introduced to their famous assistant coach from one of the Danish A-league clubs, FCM. They obviously have no idea who he is, let alone what 'FCM' means. Another example is when two of the nerds use a completely wrong terminology to describe the 'wing' and 'centre-forward' positions, leaving the assistant coach in a state of shock and bafflement. Having no knowledge of basic rules, field positions, or famous Danish players and coaches is highly unusual in Denmark, where football is the national sport – especially among the male sector of the population. For a Danish (male) audience, it is therefore funny, and a true sign of 'nerdiness', whereas a lack of football knowledge is rather normal in Australia, where Australian Rules football, Rugby League and Rugby Union are the primary winter sports, and football – or soccer – is a developing code. Despite a recent popularity surge following the Australian participation in the 2006 World Cup, football remains a minor sport compared with the national sports listed above. As hinted above, and especially because the male part of the Danish population is generally very interested in football, the inter-textual humour contrived from the nerds' lack of football knowledge is particularly targeted towards Danish boys and men. Danish women would most likely be a little less football savvy, and as such miss part of the humour and irony, making the Danish version more narrow and exclusive – also within the Danish cultural context.

Another subtle yet important difference between the two adaptations is that *FC Zulu* seems slightly more comical, silly and ironic than *Nerds FC*. One example from episode four is the bouncing sounds that accompany one of the nerds as he jumps up and down to warm up before entering the field. The bouncing sounds put even more focus on his lack of basic motor skills, and add a rather silly and cartoon-like touch to the humour. The same is the case when the assistant coach's bewildered facial expression to the nerd's unfamiliarity with basic field positions is replayed in slow motion. This comical silliness serves to ramp up the ironic volume of *FC Zulu* by saying 'do not take this seriously – we are taking the mickey out of other reality shows', and thereby emphasizes what could be considered the 'meta-ironic' layer of *FC Zulu*, which is practically non-existent in *Nerds FC*. This layer represents an ironic comment and perhaps even a criticism of the reality genre as such. In this respect, *Nerds FC* seems to take the reality genre more seriously, which will be elaborated below.

Australian melodrama and 'serious' fun

Another noteworthy difference between the two adaptations is the Australian ending of episode four, which adds a melodramatic and rather serious layer to the episode. Contrary to the Danish ending, in which the nerds leave the prison immediately after the game, the Australian nerds stay for lunch and a chat with the inmates. The nerds and the prisoners obviously enjoy each other's company and the experience leaves the nerds contemplative. As one nerd says after the meeting (accompanied by a melodramatic music score):

> After the match, and after we sat down and started to have lunch together, I got more contemplative. Because here were these really young men – probably some of them our age – they're animated, they can talk, and some of them were well informed. I just began to reconsider the whole concept of 'bad guy'–'good guy'. So it was a really amazing and mind-bending experience.

The episode clearly has a moral. The meeting with the prisoners has taught the nerds an ethical and politically correct lesson about the many grey areas between good and bad, and – together with the rather histrionic soundtrack – this sequence contributes in part to the more serious and melodramatic appeal of *Nerds FC*. This ending is completely absent in the Danish version. The Danish nerds do not even speak about the prisoners, but only talk about the lessons they have learnt as a team. Another contributing factor to the melodrama and seriousness of the Australian ending is the speech made by the Australian coach after the match, again accompanied by an (over-)emotional soundtrack:

> Congratulations to you all. You've made it inside the jail and happily you've made it outside the jail. You've mixed it with guys that have really pushed life's envelope to the very edge, and you stood your ground. You conducted yourself with real aplomb and with real grace and in a number of cases with real athleticism. I cannot believe I've said it but there you go. Congratulations!

The Danish coach also says he is 'proud' of his players, but he does not give an emotional speech directly to the players like the Australian coach does. Instead, he says it to the camera in an interview, in which he also mentions the many things that still need to be corrected. His statement is therefore nowhere near as overwrought, serious and melodramatic as the Australian coach's speech cited above. Generally, the Australian adaptation seems to take the challenge more seriously and thus is slightly more focused on the competitive elements than its Danish counterpart. This is, for instance, reflected in the Australian coach's more serious attitude and in the fact that *Nerds FC* does not have the same comical appeal, as *FC Zulu*. It seems that there is a much larger focus on getting the nerds to actually achieve something athletically. The Australian adaptation thereby treats the reality genre more seriously. Although *Nerds FC* is indeed very funny and humorous, it is 'serious' fun as opposed to the ironic comedy of *FC Zulu*.

Elitist ironic comedy versus egalitarian 'serious' fun

FC Zulu and *Nerds FC* are in many ways radically similar, and both have a positive, humorous and 'feel-good' narrative plot about personal development. The adaptations are examples of an inclusive, warm, humorous and optimistic reality that does not thrive on negative conflicts and off-putting human behaviour, and therefore differs from other nastier reality formats. Nevertheless, there are also a few subtle but important differences. First, the Danish original has more inter-cultural and inter-textual references. This basically means that only people initiated in Danish culture will fully understand the humour in *FC Zulu*. Also, the Danish version is sillier, more comical and ironic in its humour, which ads a meta-ironic layer that comments on – and partly makes fun of – the reality genre as such. On the other hand, the Australian adaptation is more melodramatic and moralizing – especially towards the end of episode four – and seems to take the competitive elements, and thereby the reality genre, more seriously than its Danish equivalent. In this respect, *Nerds FC* is serious fun. *FC Zulu* is ironic comedy.

These differences, combined with the fact that a large part of the ironic humour of *FC Zulu* is rather masculine and derived from the fact that the Danish nerds have absolutely no knowledge of the game of football (as opposed to 'real' Danish men), make the Danish original not only youth-skewed but also targeted towards young *males* specifically. *FC Zulu* may therefore be characterized as a rather elitist program in the sense that it excludes a fair amount of the Danish population, including the older demographic and maybe even a large proportion of Danish women as well. This fits well with the fact that the format was originally developed for TV2/Zulu's much narrower, perhaps more male-oriented and indeed younger audience segment. In contrast to this, *Nerds FC* seems more egalitarian in the sense that the humour, together with a larger emphasis on the nerds' personal development, is more widely appealing and most likely reflects the broadcaster's demographically more dispersed target audience.

Again, the same differences between elitist and egalitarian values are in play, as was the case in the Australian and Danish adaptations of *The Block*. Nevertheless, in contrast to *The Block*, it is the Danish adaptation that is more elitist and the Australian that is more egalitarian. This fits well with Bruun's (2005) main thesis that elitist values are more predominant in public service programming (in this case, on SBS) than commercial programming (in this case, on TV2/Zulu). However, it also shows that reality is not necessarily elitist entertainment, as Bruun suggests. Reality can be produced with a fairly egalitarian mode of address as well.[5]

Multicultural universalism versus national and demographic parochialism

The end result is that *Nerds FC* has a somewhat wider, more universal audience appeal than *FC Zulu*. Everybody, regardless of age, gender, nationality or ethnic origin, would most likely understand the humour and the plot of *Nerds FC*. Melodrama and big emotions are more universal, and therefore translate more easily than *FC Zulu*'s cliquish inter-cultural references and irony. The Australian adaptation in this sense is more 'transparent' than the Danish original, which in turn is more 'opaque' (Olson 1999). This is very likely to be a reflection of the Australian broadcaster's multicultural charter on the one hand, and Australia's multicultural reality (and general national football ignorance) on the other. SBS specifically, and Australian broadcasters generally, must appeal to a heterogeneous audience, and therefore probably often choose a universalistic and less constricted audience approach. That SBS's multicultural charter affected the production of the format is partly confirmed in the interview with *Nerds FC* executive producer Paul Waterhouse, who also confirms that it was a deliberate strategy to tone down the irony of the Danish original and instead opt for melodramatic ingredients – or what he calls 'the emotional roller coaster' in order for the audience to 'bond to the nerds and the program better'. As for the increased focus on the format's competitive elements, commissioning editor Margaret Murphy states that part of the attraction of the show was to see how high achievers in the field of academia would do in another discipline – that of sports. Here she indirectly points to the importance of the competition.

Danish broadcasters, on the other hand, communicate to a homogenous audience and can therefore make more frequent use of inter-cultural references and a cliquish kind of humour. In addition, *FC Zulu* was first made for and broadcast on TV2's supplementary channel TV2/Zulu, which is not operated under a public service charter, and whose programs are targeted towards young people and often exhibit a great deal of youthful and cliquish irony. This means that the differences between *FC Zulu* and *Nerds FC* are actually best explained using a combination of media systemic explanations to do with target groups and channel charters on one hand, and less tangible cultural explanations to do with Australia's *multiculture* as opposed to Denmark's *monoculture* on the other.

Conclusions and perspectives

A significant number of media scholars have worked with cross-cultural differences in media content and usage, and in the process have often explained differences in content by referring to differences in national culture. Following are four examples of such academic contributions, two of which deal with general differences in the employment of a certain genre, with the remaining two dealing specifically with format adaptations. In a study on how TV viewers around the world respond to news programs, Bruhn Jensen (1998: 164ff) identifies two types of 'correlated cultures' – 'cultures of crisis' and 'cultures of stability' – within which viewers share similar responses to news. Consequently, the similarities within the correlated cultures are explained by the fact that they share similar 'cultural and national-political contexts'. When it comes to another highly internationalized genre, the game show, Cooper-Chen (2005, 1994) points out four 'cultural continents' (the Western, East Asian, Latin and Equatorial) by examining game shows in 50 countries. Within these regions, local TV tastes seem to converge, and only a few game show formats have crossed into another region. If we look more specifically at concrete format adaptation studies, Skovmand (1992:

98–99) also views the differences between the local Danish, American, German and pan-Scandinavian versions of *Wheel of Fortune* as representative of the four local cultures, as does Moran (1998: 74ff) in his comparative analyses of Dutch, German and Australian versions of the same scripted fiction formats. National culture undoubtedly plays a part. Nonetheless, my argument is that looking into specific media systemic conditions of the local adapting broadcasters provides us with more detailed and comprehensive explanations for similarities and differences in local adaptations of the same formats.

Sociocultural 'mores' or pervasive industry ideologies?

Let me explain by delving into two of the main dichotomies that seem to be at play between the Danish and Australian adaptations – the Australian preference for melodrama and the Danish preference for meta-irony which, according to my previous research (Jensen 2007, 2005), actually seem to be a general dichotomy between Australian and Danish adaptations of other lifestyle and reality formats such as *Ground Force* and *Idol*.

A melodramatic taste apparently transcends both Australian public service and commercial broadcasters, and would thus indicate an Australian national cultural preference for melodrama as opposed to a more matter-of-fact documentary-style Danish preference. However, if we look into Australian broadcasting history, which has always been dominated by commercial networks, we find a long-running tradition of soap opera, a genre characterized by melodrama and emotional over-dramatization. Hence, employing a melodramatic narrative to a lifestyle program would probably be second nature to producers. In Denmark, the soap genre has never been an intrinsic part of schedules, and the reason for this can most likely be found in the historical and present dominance of public service broadcasting. In contrast to soap opera, with its roots in lowbrow cultural phenomena such as romance novels, Danish TV's drama production has its roots in highbrow classical theatre and literature, and this may very well still be reflected in today's Danish schedules and production practices. Despite the fact that Danish PSBs have indeed, and with great international acclaim and success, embraced *televisual* fiction genres, it has mainly happened within higher-end genres such as crime and historical drama. As romance novels and the like are as popular in Denmark as anywhere else, I see no reason why Danes should have a general cultural distaste for melodrama and prefer a documentaristic and more 'sober' approach. On the contrary, it is most likely a reflection of a pervasive Danish public service interpretation of what viewers want, which in turn has been formed by a media policy that has historically and maybe even presently favoured a kind of public service broadcasting which is still essentially *patriarchal* at its core (see Jensen 2007: 147ff). As a consequence, Danish public service broadcasters and producers – perhaps often unknowingly – continue to make programs with an apparent ethical stance on what is 'best' for viewers. Nevertheless, with the recent success of DR's *The X Factor* adaptation in mind, this interpretation of public service may be changing.

As for the meta-ironic layer of *FC Zulu*, it could very well be traced back to a particular Danish tradition of media-critical and ironic children's and youth television originating in the 1980s (Christensen 2006). Danish television has a long tradition of children's and youth programs made at eye-level with young viewers, without any educational purposes and in opposition to the world of adults. During the 1980s, this tradition took a meta-ironic turn and started to challenge young viewers' ability to undertake 'media-critical reflection' (Christensen 2006: 85, my translation from Danish). This media-critical and ironic approach set a fashion for the decades to come, and this may very well be what is reflected in *FC Zulu*. However, this still does not explain why the media-critical and meta-ironic form appeared specifically in *Danish* television, and why it does not seem to be present to the same extent, for example, in Australia. Again, a significant part of the explanation may be found in less tangible, and possibly specifically Danish, sociocultural perceptions of children and young people, which is also pointed to by Christensen (2006). Nevertheless, having pointed to possible sociocultural explanations *outside* the media system, the Danish presence of meta-ironic media reflection may also – as was the case with the relative absence of melodrama – have a lot to do with a pervasive public service ideology *within* the Danish television industry rather than be merely a reflection of the Danes' cultural taste and sociocultural mentality. With the history of Danish public service television in mind, it makes sense that Danish youth television has contained media-critical reflections, as television according to this ideology is considered essentially 'bad' and of no use if it is not controlled by the public service system. As a result, young people must learn to be critically astute when it comes to media.

Notes

1. In Denmark, houses and apartments are not sold at auctions. Despite this, the first series of *Huset* tried the auction model – but failed miserably. No bidders attended the auction, which was telecast live, and the company which had originally sold the apartments to TV2 had to buy the apartments back without any competition from others. The result was a complete anti-climax and the auction model was subsequently abandoned in the second series (Nikolajsen 2006).
2. See Jensen (2007: 75ff) for a more detailed comparison of the two genres.
3. Nikolajsen (2006) also points to a smaller budget as an important explanation for the differences between *Huset* and *The Block*. Metronome may not have had the option of hiring as many staff as would have been required to obtain a level of detail similar to the Australian original. However, as none of the executive producers involved in either adaptation wanted to disclose exact budgets, this cannot be verified.
4. This probably also has something to do with the size of the budgets. TV2/Zulu spent between two and three million DKK ($450,000–$650,000AUD) (Reinicke 2006). Neither the Australian broadcaster nor the producer wanted to disclose the exact budget of *Nerds FC*, which unfortunately means we cannot make a comparison. However, it is probably safe to say that, as a small public broadcaster, SBS's budget would be considerably smaller than, for instance, a similar budget for one of the commercial broadcasters, and therefore closer to the Danish budget.
5. That this is the case is also confirmed in an analysis of another reality format, *Idol*, that I have undertaken elsewhere (Jensen 2007). The *Idol* format demonstrates similar differences in its Australian and Danish adaptations, with the Danish *Idols* being elitist and excluding while *Australian Idol* is rather egalitarian and inclusive.

References

Barbour, D. (2006), Interview with David Barbour, Channel Nine, Sydney.
Bruhn Jensen, K. (ed.) (1997), *Dansk Mediehistorie 1960–1995*, Copenhagen: Samleren.
—— (ed.) (1998), *News of the World*, London: Routledge.
—— (2003), *Dansk Mediehistorie 1995–2003*, Copenhagen: Samfundslitteratur.
Brunsdon, C., Johnson, C., Moseley, R. and Wheatley, H. (2001), 'Factual Entertainment on British Television', *European Journal of Cultural Studies*, 4, pp. 29–62.
Bruun, H. (2005), 'Public Service and Entertainment: A Case Study of Danish Television 1951–2003', in G.F. Lowe and P. Jauert (eds), *Cultural Dilemmas in Public Service Broadcasting*, Gothenburg: Nordicom.
Carlsen, J. and Frandsen, K. (2005), *Nytte-og livsstils-programmer på Dansk TV* (working paper), Aarhus: Center for Kulturforskning.
Christensen, C.L. (2006), 'Børne og ungdoms-tv', in S. Hjarvard (ed.), *Dansk TV's Historie*, Copenhagen: Samfundslitteratur.
Cooper-Chen, A. (1994), *Games in the Global Village*, Bowling Green, OH: Popular Press.
—— (ed.) (2005), *Global Entertainment Media: Contents, Audiences, Issues*, Mahwah, NJ: Lawrence Erlbaum.
Cunningham, S., Jacka, E. and Sinclair, J. (1998), 'Global and Regional Dynamics of International Television Flows', in D.K. Thussu (ed.), *Electronic Empires - Global Media and Local Resistance*, London: Arnold.
Hallin, D.C. and Mancini, P. (2004), *Comparing Media Systems: Three Models of Media and Politics*, Cambridge: Cambridge University Press.
Jensen, P.M. (2005), 'Formatversionering – et overblik', *Mediekultur*, 35. n.p.
—— (2007), Television Format Adaptation in a Trans-national Perspective – an Australian and Danish Case Study (PhD thesis), Aarhus: Department of Information and Media Studies.
Jerslev, A. (2005). *Vi ses på tv: Medier og intimitet*, Copenhagen: Gyldendal.
Moran, A. (1998), *Copycat TV: Globalisation, Program Formats and Cultural Identity*, Luton: University of Luton Press.
Nikolajsen, K. (2006), Interview with Kent Nikolajsen, Metronome Production, Copenhagen.
Olson, S.R. (1999), *Hollywood Planet: Global Media and the Competitive Advantage of Narrative Transparency*, Mahwah, NJ: Lawrence Erlbaum.
Rømer, A. (2006), Interview with Anette Rømer, TV 2/Denmark, Odense.
Schmitt, D., Bisson, G. and Fey, C. (2005), *The Global Trade in Television Formats*, London: Screen Digest.
Sinclair, J., Jacka, E. and Cunningham, S. (1996), *New Patterns in Global Television*, Oxford: Oxford University Press.
Skovmand, M. (1992), 'Barbarous TV International – Syndicated Wheels of Fortune', in M. Skovmand and K.C. Schrøder (eds), *Media Cultures: Reappraising Transnational Media*, London: Routledge.
Søndergaard, H. (2006), 'TV som institution', in S. Hjarvard (ed.), *Dansk TV's Historie*, Copenhagen: Samfundslitteratur.
Turner, G. (2005), 'Cultural Identity, Soap Narrative and Reality TV', *Television & New Media*, 6(4), pp. 415–22.

Chapter 11

Transcultural Localization Strategies of Global TV Formats: *The Office* and *Stromberg*

Edward Larkey

This chapter compares the pilot shows of the US version of *The Office* with the German version of the same program, called *Stromberg*, both of which are currently being shown on television networks in each country. They are based on the original British program called *The Office*. I will assume with Moran (1998: 23) that *The Office* is a format – that is, 'a cultural technology which governs the flow of program ideas across time and space'. Comparing *The Office* with *Stromberg* illustrates how the 'adaptation…for a particular territory…involves considerable amounts of skill and experience in adapting, varying, amending, improvising, creating, and so on using the initial format as a source' (Moran 1998: 22). I compare the plot and storylines, as well as the character development, focusing on the main characters, Bernd Stromberg (played by actor Christoph-Maria Herbst) and Michael Scott (played by comedian Steve Carrell). I also examine the settings (a fictitious insurance company – Capitol Versicherung – in the German city of Cologne and the also fictitious Dunder-Mifflin paper company in Scranton, Pennsylvania. I discuss culturally specific aspects of each series as it has been adapted to its respective national audience.

Both programs employ similar structural elements in their narratives, particularly the use of documentary-type interviews with the characters to expose duplicitous and other types of behaviours characteristic of deleterious office relationships at the heart of the comedic intent of each program. Both are the same approximate length: 23 and a half minutes. While *Stromberg* was first released on the TV channel ProSieben on 11 October 2004, the US version of *The Office* premiered on NBC on 4 March 2005. Contrary to many assumptions about the international format trade based on contractual agreements (Moran and Keane 2008: 156), the production of *Stromberg* was not contractually negotiated prior to its broadcast, but was the object of a lawsuit threat for plagiarism after it was produced and broadcast (http://www.rickygervais.com/notwqanda.php). According to Keane and Moran (2008: 157), the format arises when a program developed in one country:

> can be reformatted in different territories and the local producer and broadcaster can access a template that has already withstood two rounds of R&D – first, to survive development and trialing before broadcasting executives; and secondly, further testing before viewing audiences.

Each of these two iterations of the British-created program represents a case of localization strategies, which are 'language-block-by-language block or country-by-country approach to deal with differences within a region' and involve 'broadcasting in local languages via dubbing or subtitling, rescheduling or repackaging programs to suit local viewing preferences, buying materials from local studios, and producing local programming through co-production or forming joint ventures with local sectors' (Chang 2003: 4). The propensity for local programming adaptations is prompted by what Straubhaar (2007: 26) calls the 'cultural proximity' principle, whereby audiences are attracted to cultural products 'that are close in cultural content and style to the audience's own culture(s)', since 'most audiences seem to prefer television programs that are as close to them as possible in language, ethnic appearance, dress, style, humor, historical reference, and shared topical knowledge'.

The setting of *Stromberg* and *The Office*

A few short detailed shots of Scranton figure prominently in the opening credits to precisely locate the staging of *The Office*. The sequence of opening shots – taken in the winter when there are no green trees and the scenery looks desolate – moves quickly from urban street scenes to the external building of the loading dock of Dunder Mifflin before a longer sequence of short segments inside the office building. In these, the main locations and persons featured in the story are depicted: the main figure, Michael Scott, a fax machine, a desktop calculator, one of the office workers, Dwight Schrute (played by Rainn Wilson), shredding a magnetic card, a close-up of someone using white-out, an overflowing copying machine, sales rep Jim Halpert (John Krasinski) on the telephone, working on papers, Pam Beesly (Jenna Fischer), the receptionist, and a water dispenser. The last shot of the opening credits features the name of the show in white on a black background before Michael Scott introduces 'his' office, turning first to his receptionist, Pam.

While opening credits in the US version of *The Office* initiate the show, in *Stromberg* the show starts off with a documentary-style interview with the main character, Bernd Stromberg, sitting in his office facing the camera (at first located outside his separate office through venetian blinds, but with a later cut to a shot from inside the office) while a computer technician attends to his computer. The actual credits introducing the program come a little more than a 90 seconds into the program. In the credit lead-in sequence, the first thing to be seen is a pedestrian bridge over a multi-lane road shot from approximately 10 metres above the bridge, first with nothing and no one on it. After several seconds, pedestrians appear on the bridge and cars drive on the street below. The next sequence frames a spiral walkway at the end of the bridge, after which the camera focuses on a bus stop with passengers disembarking the bus, all filmed from behind the shelter, followed by a revolving door scene in which the camera is pointed to the floor so that one can see only people's legs and feet. In the next sequence, the camera is directed to a grey and nondescript 1970s-era office building from below, looking up at a corner of the building. The final scenes are from inside the office building in the elevator lobby, with the camera facing the elevators as the office workers pile into them. The last one into the elevator before the door closes is Bernd Stromberg himself, who yawns just as the elevator door closes before the camera. In the next scene,

Stromberg enters 'his' office, and introduces the two office rivals, Ulf and Ernie. There is no explicit reference to the particular city in the opening credits, which allows the audience to generalize about its urban setting and make the program less regionally specific, perhaps because strong regional identities in Germany might indicate a kind of provincialism that would restrict the program's appeal. One can only infer through knowledge of the German insurance industry that *Stromberg* is probably based in the insurance capital of the country – Cologne. It is in the western part of the country sometimes referred to as the 'old' Federal Republic, which was severely damaged during World War II. It is now home to the largest of the German regional public broadcasting services, the Westdeutscher Rundfunk (WDR), as well as a number of other media companies (including RTL). Also, the German Ford Motor company has its headquarters in Cologne, but the city has attempted to refashion and re-brand itself as a centre for electronic media production. It is located close to the former capital of Bonn.

Scranton, Pennsylvania is a backwater rustbelt industrial/mining town in the eastern part of the state, and symbolizes the consequences of deindustrialization and economic deterioration of many East Coast and Mid-Western industrial cities over the last 40 years. While Dunder Mifflin is a paper distributor, Capitol-Versicherung does business with even less tangible products. Both kinds of companies were subject to considerable downsizing in the last several decades. The manufacturing sector of the United States has outsourced thousands of jobs, while the insurance sector in Germany has been the object of intense computerization that has seen drastic job losses.

The two television shows also employ their documentary-style interviews differently in the narrative. In *The Office*, there are explicit references to statements made by other office workers to the documentary film people on camera, which indicates that they have actively injected themselves into the diegesis of the program, effecting a lack of the objectivist role normally attributed to documentary-type films. In *Stromberg*, however, there are no explicit references made by the interviewees to statements made by others, and there is also more initial reticence by the office workers to reveal intimate details of their lives in front of the camera, which is more in keeping with the objectivist role of the documentary filmmaker located outside of the intimate in-group.

Main figures

One expects a television program named after its main character to focus on the foibles of that character, while the rest of the cast plays a merely supporting role. This is only partly the case in *Stromberg*, with Stromberg himself ensnarled in a web of relationships with his superior, Frau Berkel (whom he calls Tuberkel ['tuberculosis'], a play on words), two antagonists Ulf and Ernie, the office workers Tanja and Erika, and Stromberg's nemesis, Mr Turculu, a department manager like himself who is from the ethnic minority of Turks in Germany, but equal in status at the company. In contrast to Turculu's quiet competency and reserve, Stromberg is the embodiment of managerial incompetence, duplicity, deviousness, insensitivity and egotistical impetuousness, as well as being racist and sexist. Stromberg shares with Michael Scott the incompetence and the declaration that he treats the people working in his department as part of his 'family', where everyone gets along. However, whereas Michael Scott would like to have everyone 'like' him, Stromberg is too wrapped up in trying to look good to be deeply concerned about being liked.

Storylines and plot development

The first episode of *Stromberg* is devoted not only to the primary storyline of merging the two departments of Mr Turculu and Stromberg, but also has two sub-plots as well: the magic marker drawing of a naked Tanja on the women's room wall with her name written underneath, and Stromberg's wish to have a higher status parking space – one with a roof over it – for himself, since other underlings with less status than him have these. This illustrates his intense awareness of status hierarchies in the office in the very beginning of the episode.

The pilot episode of *The Office*, appropriately entitled 'Pilot', revolves primarily around the problem and discussion of downsizing, and does not develop sub-plots around a new temporary worker. The first episode of *Stromberg* is named after the parking lot storyline. During the opening scene with the computer technician, Stromberg learns that, as a mid-level manager, his parking space is further away from the office building than those of many of his underlings, and that Herr Hilpers, an asthmatic office worker, has recently been put in charge of distributing the parking spaces. Stromberg invites Hilpers – who is not allowed to smoke any more due to his asthmatic lungs (nicknamed 'Röchel-Hilpers') – to smoke a cigar with him as a means of enticing him into obtaining a better parking space. The next day, Hilpers' wife comes to Stromberg to ask whether he knows anything about Hilpers smoking, since it has landed him in hospital. Stromberg denies any knowledge of it, and proceeds to flirt with Frau Hilpers. Eventually, Stromberg gets his parking space right next to Frau Hilpers, but while pulling into the parking space he smashes into her car, causing some damage, which he initially fails to report.

This storyline is connected with the second one, that of the drawing in the women's room. Ernie – who never tires of mentioning to the camera that his real name is actually Berthold Heisterkamp, and who is the equivalent of Dwight Schrute in *The Office* – is obsessed with finding the perpetrator. He proceeds to investigate the case – much to the increasing consternation and disgust of Tanja, whom he is trying to impress. He has everyone in the office draw a naked woman on the office flip-chart and then write the name 'Tanja' underneath. Near the end of the episode, when Stromberg is already in serious trouble for denying that he was the one who smashed up Frau Hilpers' car – even after being confronted with incontrovertible videotape evidence proving his guilt – Stromberg inadvertently reveals himself to be the author of the Tanja drawing by making an organizational diagram on the office flip-chart. In doing so, he is induced to write Tanja's name, which shows that his writing is the same as that under the drawing in the women's room. The presence of Frau Berkel during this scene only heightens the sense of deceit, and shows Stromberg up as a devious, duplicitous and sexist incompetent.

These two sub-plots play out against the background of the poor performance of Stromberg's department (Damage Control M–Z) in the face of plans to merge it with Turculu's (A–L); as part of the merge, Stromberg could potentially lose his position.

Both Michael Scott and Bernd Stromberg are told in meetings with their young female superiors about the possible mergers and downsizing. This is the main storyline in both episodes ad the pivotal scene in both shows. The scenes come at different times within the narrative. While this scene occurs in the thirteenth minute of *Stromberg*, and plays out for a little over one minute (13.28–14.34), in *The Office* the scene takes place much earlier in the episode (at approximately five minutes into the screenplay) and plays out for almost two minutes, with a short interview interruption of several seconds. Michael Scott sees his carefully crafted, self-delusional role as jocular comedian and the equal of those in the office put in jeopardy by possible downsizing, which he would be responsible for carrying out, whereby the Stamford, Connecticut office and the Scranton office are to be merged. The decision about *who* gets merged and downsized *where* is a question that will be solved by the performance of the respective departments in each show. Each of the main protagonists has a different reaction. In his helplessness, Stromberg lashes out against Turculu with a condescending remark ('I am all for integrating foreigners, so I would voluntarily say, the Turkish guy should do it, but first of all I have been here longer, and secondly…').[1]

In *Stromberg*, the downsizing is only mentioned explicitly in the announcement scene with Berkel and Stromberg, and in a shorter scene in which Stromberg flies off the handle with Erika and Tanja over the mention of sexual harassment. Implicitly, the downsizing is the underlying cause of tension and anxiety in the major scene in which Stromberg is caught lying about hitting Frau Hilpers' car in the parking lot, even after examining the video footage proving his culpability. The second implicit reference to the downsizing is Stromberg's appearance in front of the flip-chart in the last scene of the episode, in which he states that 'we' – that is, the whole department – are being observed. The downsizing narrative in the *Stromberg* episode thus includes punishment for Stromberg's incompetent management of the department, whereby Berkel has him under her special 'observation'. The viewer is therefore called upon to make the explicit connection between the 'observation' and the 'downsizing' played out in other scenes of the film narrative.

The topic of downsizing is thus structured in *The Office* as a part of an explicit narrative in three major scenes, as well as in two lesser scenes. The announcement of the downsizing is staged for the first time in the scene with Jan Levinson-Gould, Pam and Michael Scott. The second time comes with the staff meeting in which Michael Scott tries to deflect any rumours and anxiety about the downsizing by denying that his department will be downsized. The third major scene in which downsizing plays a role is the one in which Michael plays the practical 'joke' that Pam will be fired. In the first of the two lesser scenes immediately after the meeting between the abovementioned three, several employees are sitting around a table discussing how to react to the merger and downsizing. The second one is an interview with Dwight, in which he claims that he always advocated downsizing, mentioning it in his job interview and states 'Bring it on!'

Michael Scott attempts to deflect any unpleasantness from the whole procedure in a discussion with his employees, a ploy that Stromberg does not embrace. Stromberg himself uses the merger talk as an instrument to discipline his staff and create uncertainty about their job security. Instead of focusing on sub-plots, *The Office* develops the major relationships in the series: between Jim and Dwight, between Jim and Pam, and between Scott and his office staff – primarily Pam. Stromberg also develops the relationships among the office workers, primarily between Ulf and Ernie, but also the rivalry of both of them for Tanja's affection.

One of the most telling scenes in *The Office* comes when Scott is sitting with Ryan Howard, the new office temp, whom he lets in on the 'joke'; he then calls in Pam and proceeds to announce to her that she will be let go with the downsizing, but then tells her it was just a practical joke. She leaves the office upset and angry at the humiliation, in spite of an earlier interview in front of the camera where she claims that if she were to be let go, she would turn to drawing for her occupation.

Both main protagonists display impolite and insensitive behaviour not only in discussions with their office staff, but also in those with their superiors. While the downsizing plans are being revealed to him, Michael Scott takes a phone call – on speakerphone – from one of his best sales reps, who then proceeds to disparage Jan Levinson-Gould for all to hear. This comes after Scott must reveal that he threw away the agenda to that very meeting, which was faxed to him earlier. This was staged in the opening scene of Scott in the office in front of Pam. She reminds him of this during the meeting with Levinson-Gould, which creates an embarrassed silence between them.

While Frau Berkel is explaining the merger plans to him, Stromberg tries to cover up his tension and nervousness by playing with a piece of candy wrapper, throwing it into the garbage from in front of Berkel's desk. After the wrapper misses the trash can, he gets up and goes over to the trash can and puts it in while she is in the middle of her explanation.

Power distance and culturally specific adaptation

I will now discuss the culturally specific adaptations of the television programs on the basis of two different dimensions of cultural variables: the depiction of power distance relationships, and that of masculinity and femininity. The cultural variable of power distance is one of the mainstays of intercultural communication analysis. According to Gudykunst and Kim (2003: 77), power distance 'is useful in understanding strangers' behavior in role relationships'. According to these authors, people from high power distance cultures 'do not question their superior's orders' but expect to follow them, whereas in low power distance cultures people 'do not necessarily accept superiors' orders at face value', but instead 'want to know why they should follow them'. For the purposes of my analysis, the concept of power distance is not used in an essentializing manner to characterize the cultural communication of one society or the other, but rather to discuss the different depictions of behaviour of the main characters and their interactions with their subordinates and superiors. I argue that much of the dramatic tension and comical value arises out of the clash of expectations generated by different approaches to power distance in the relationship between the respective bosses (Michael Scott and Bernd Stromberg) and their subordinates.

On the basis of his own statements, Michael Scott wishes for a more equal, non-hierarchical relationship with the employees of his office, claiming to be part of one big family in the interviews, cracking bad jokes (for instance, an inappropriate 'wazzup' exclamation in the first scene with Dwight and Jim), and making inappropriate sexist remarks to Pam in the opening encounter. While the employees expect both greater power distance and respect from their boss, he continually violates this expectation in various scenes. The most conspicuous is the long scene where the 'joke' is played on Pam that she will be fired. On the other hand, when Dwight attempts to elevate his position in the staff meeting by stating that he is the 'assistant manager', Michael Scott immediately and forcefully corrects him by stating that he is merely 'assistant *to the* manager', refusing to provide him privileged information about the impending merger and downsizing.

Power distance expectations are also violated in the scene in which Levinson-Gould meets with Michael Scott and asks for the agenda she has faxed to him just hours before. After Scott attempts to place the blame on Pam for not providing him with the fax, Pam reveals to Levinson-Gould that Scott was the one who threw it in the trash can, something that the audience witnessed in the corresponding scene early in the episode. While a hierarchically organized vertical office structure would have prevented Pam from revealing this embarrassing information about her boss in order to preserve his face, she defends her own actions in front of both Levinson-Gould and Scott. Furthermore, when queried later by Scott at the staff meeting about the merger and downsizing plans, she reveals to her colleagues that, contrary to the false assertions by Scott, their branch might be closed and not Stamford.

Additionally, the camera position in the pivotal downsizing announcement scenes in both episodes reinforces the two kinds of power distance relationships in each. The scene in *The Office* has the three characters representing different positions in the vertical hierarchy (supervisor, manager, receptionist) sitting next to each other (literally) horizontally in the conference room, with the camera at eye level or lower, zooming in on each of women when Michael Scott does something that embarrasses them. In *Stromberg*, on the other hand, the Berkel–Stromberg downsizing scene starts with the camera at eye level from the point of view of Stromberg, who is sitting behind the desk being talked to. The camera pulls away to a panorama shot of both Stromberg and Berkel who, while continuing to explain the restructuring, has to witness how Stromberg unsuccessfully tosses the candy wrapper into the trash. When he gets up to retrieve the wrapper, indicating that he is either not concentrating on the content of her message or is too nervous to keep still, he violates the expectation of politeness accorded to superiors when they are speaking to their staff. The camera initially follows Stromberg going to the trash can several feet away from the desk, then pulls back to focus on Stromberg at his eye level while he is standing, but outside Berkel's frame. Then the camera pulls back further to reveal Stromberg talking down to Berkel, who has remained sitting throughout his reply to the downsizing plans. Finally, the camera cuts to Stromberg while he explains that there are more important things than economic results at the office, like 'atmosphere'. Berkel's answer to that is to announce that Stromberg and his department are being especially closely watched for their performance. The camera cuts back to Berkel at eye level while she is explaining this, but she is looking away from the camera to her right to where Stromberg is standing. Thus, the viewer witnesses the violation of the office hierarchy perpetrated by Stromberg's activity, and this violation is reinforced by the camera position which takes Stromberg's point of view, even when he is violating these norms.

Language use

In *Stromberg*, the more hierarchically organized office structure is indicated in the formal speech accorded to 'Herr Stromberg' by both his subordinates and his supervisors, while he employs the less formal use of first names, demonstrated by the introduction of 'Ulf' and 'Ernie' while he is introducing his office space and staff to the viewer. In *The Office*, Michael Scott calls his superior 'Jan' by her first name, indicating a more horizontally organized office structure in comparison to the more vertical structure in the German office. Stromberg also attempts to undercut the formal office hierarchy by calling his staff 'one big family', maintaining that everyone is working in the common interest. This is undercut by his attempts to garner a better parking space more in keeping with his managerial status, after he determines that many of his subordinates have better spaces. Instead of just merely requesting a better parking space, Stromberg uses the devious method of the bribe of the cigar with Hilpers to attain his goal, which immediately jeopardizes Hilpers' life and provokes the ire of his wife. Another indication of trouble between the employees and Stromberg is the scene in which the drawing of Tanja in the women's room is discovered. In the same scene, a drawing of Stromberg is also found in one of the booths, along with the epithet 'Wichser' ('wanker', figuratively 'idiot') written underneath.

In addition, when questioning the office staff about who did the Tanja drawing, Ernie uses the formal 'Sie' address, indicating higher power distance in a situation in which the 'Du' familiar form would have been customary among employees, indicating horizontally equal power relationships. This violation of expectations is generated by Ernie's wish for a higher position of authority in the office hierarchy, just as Dwight tries to make himself 'assistant manager' and not 'assistant to the manager'. The use of the formal 'Sie' prompts an astonished query from the puzzled colleague as to why he is being addressed in the formal polite form and not the customary 'Du'. Ernie ultimately switches back to the familiar form.

Stromberg always uses the formal 'Sie' when addressing his office staff, in spite of using their first names to address them.

Even before Stromberg's first meeting with Berkel, in which she reveals the merger of the two departments and downsizing, his incompetence has firmly been established – not only because he has failed to deliver the quarterly report on time, but also because his department's performance lags far behind that of his competitor, Turculu. His inappropriate behaviour with both Hilpers and Hilpers' wife with regard to the parking space, as well as the revelation of his authorship of the women's room drawing of Tanja, signifies that the office hierarchies inherent in the Germany company have largely been violated by Stromberg himself, in spite of the formal hierarchical organization of the office. Stromberg, however, is not averse to wielding his manager status and power to discipline employees with threats, demonstrated in the only scene in which the downsizing plans are mentioned to anyone on the office staff. When he brusquely cuts off Erika's wish for 'a little sexual harassment' as a complimentary form of attention, he tells her to stop making fun of it, replying that when there are plans for 'restructuring', everyone should be 'pulling on the same rope' ('an einen Strang ziehen'). This figure of speech is open to various types of sexual interpretation, prompting laughter from Erika. Her laughter is quickly extinguished when Stromberg retorts that he hopes she is still laughing when she has her pink slip in her hands because of the restructuring. Seventeen minutes into the program, this is the first time that anyone in the office hears about the plans.

Michael Scott violates the power distance norms with embarrassing openness, indicating that he is an adherent of a less hierarchically organized office. Bernd Stromberg's deviousness and duplicity in violating the norms of power distance illustrate that they constrict and determine his thinking to a greater extent. Instead of trying to ignore them, he attempts to consciously circumvent them if possible.

Depictions of masculinity and femininity

Closely related to the issue of power distance are the depictions of masculinity and femininity in both programs. According to Gudykunst and Kim (2003: 77), high masculinity is indicated by 'high value placed on things, power, and assertiveness', in addition to 'performance and ambition', while low masculinity and high femininity focus on 'people, quality of life, and nurturance'. In both shows, women in positions of power have displaced the men who have traditionally held these roles. As incompetents, the men are not in a legitimate position to challenge the power and authority of their female supervisors. However, the men have not relinquished their sexist attitudes, while at the same time needing to acquire qualities typically reserved for the feminine gender roles like the cultivation of relationships. This not only collides with their sexist attitudes, but also leads to gender confusion, manifesting itself in *The Office* as the loss of power distance towards the office staff and the inability on the part of Michael Scott to competently negotiate the loss of control and authority to the female boss and reconcile his true role in the office hierarchy with traditional notions of male power and privilege. This results in the messy and inappropriate outbursts with Pam, the baby talk with his boss, the inability to police the Dwight–Jim relationship, and the assertion of power in front of the office staff – power he does not ultimately possess – to prevent downsizing-related job loss.

While neither Michael Scott nor Bernd Stromberg excels in the performance and ambition realms, the two men differ in their manner of pursing power and assertiveness. Certainly, Stromberg is more aware of power hierarchies in the office, and it is characteristic that the threat induced by the restructuring of both offices is staged differently. Whereas Bernd Stromberg's competitor, Turculu, works in the same building and for the same division, Michael Scott's nemesis, Josh, is located in the more distant Stamford, Connecticut office and is not physically present in the first episode. Stromberg encounters, and competes with, Turculu almost on a daily basis, but Michael Scott has no daily competitor or rival. At times, Michael Scott seems oblivious to the power differential inherent in his position and its effect on his office staff. In the face of Jim's practical joke (encasing Dwight's stapler in jell-o), he goes along with the joke until Dwight calls on him to reprimand Jim, one of the few times that Michael Scott's 'official' managerial role is staged. His 'joke' on Pam can be interpreted as a blatant misogynist exercise in humiliation and power exhibition for the benefit of temp worker Ryan.

Stromberg, on the other hand, never openly confronts Berkel, though the camera positioning in the downsizing conversation scene plays with the tension inherent in the Stromberg–Berkel relationship. In taking Stromberg's point of view and following him outside of the frame occupied by Berkel, the camera attempts to subvert Berkel's authority. It maintains Stromberg's eye level in a close-up, and then looks down on Berkel while she is explaining the downsizing plans. However, at the end of her explanation, the camera comes back to her at eye level. During her explanation, she continues to sit behind her desk in a position of authority, even while talking to Stromberg standing several feet away looking down at her, but outside of her frame.

Stromberg is quite conscious of his power over his employees, and does not hesitate to invoke it when he feels threatened. His assertiveness is not as open as, but is more egotistical than, that of Michael Scott, as can be seen in his obsession with obtaining the covered parking space. In spite of this assertiveness, the viewer never witnesses the decision by anyone except Ernie to find out who is the author of the Tanja drawing. This leads the viewer to assume, as Ernie claims, that his efforts have been authorized by those 'higher up' ('*von ganz oben*'). However, Stromberg seems almost uninterested in the exercise, and Ernie has to explain the activity to the oblivious Berkel in the last scene of the program. Moreover, Stromberg's managerial incompetence in motivating Ulf to work in the beginning of the episode shows that he has not mastered the art of exerting his authority adequately.

Stromberg must show deference to his boss, Frau Berkel, when she explains that she is observing his behaviour as a part of her decision about who will be retained as manager after the restructuring. However, he still attempts to avoid admitting his culpability for the damage to Frau Hilpers' car in the company parking space, even when confronted with video evidence implicating him beyond any doubt. He uses the derogatory name for her, Tuberkel, in situations with both his own employees as well as with his competitor, Turculu, indicating a lack of respect for her. In addition, his drawing of Tanja on the women's room wall indicates an almost adolescent sexism, replicated by Michael Scott's opening remark about how good Pam looked years ago when she started to work for Dunder Mifflin. Michael Scott also calls Jan 'Hillary Rodham Clinton' to disparage his boss, but not to her face.

Stromberg provides several examples of his sexist attitudes during the show. In one interview, he states that sensitivity is important, 'especially in dealing with employees of different genders, for instance, women'. At the end of that scene, Stromberg declares that he 'looks every once in a while at a women's magazine like *Brigitte* or others, only to see how they tick, the females (*die Weiber*)', using the derogatory slang term. In another scene following the one in which he hits on Frau Hilpers, Stromberg explains that 'sexual harassment and charm are two different hats' and says that he is automatically charming with an attractive women, something that 'he can't avoid'. He closes his remarks just before he is ordered into Berkel's office to explain his behaviour regarding the damage to Frau Hilpers' car by stating that 'you can't hold out a bone to an old hunting dog and then complain when he salivates'.

Since women are in a position of power and authority in both of the shows, they have displaced the usual privileged positions of a patriarchal society in which males are dominant. Because of the portrayal of both main figures as complete incompetents, they are not in a position to openly subvert the power of their supervisors. However, they have not abandoned their sexist positions, which are exposed to the viewer in very explicit fashion. In *The Office*, Michael Scott even employs a baby language when confronted with the authority of Jan Levinson-Gould, both when he must tell her that he does not have the agenda and when he reacts to the information about the downsizing. This is further evidence that Scott has not coped well with the power displacement. Stromberg does not embark on the same infantilization strategy. Instead, as his denial of culpability in the Hilpers accident demonstrates, he attempts to weasel out of responsibility.

The Office, *Stromberg* and the new digital economies

One way of analyzing both television programs as cultural adaptation strategies is in the context of what Eric Louw (2001) has called the growth of the new networked elites during the post-Fordist capitalist phase that has emerged since the 1990s, which he calls 'global network capitalism' (2001: 57). During this phase, a new elite has emerged which he terms the 'global networkers'; these people are competing with, and replacing, the old managerial elites, who themselves replaced the original owners of the means of production. According to Louw, these new elites, who are connected with the new digital media, advertising and other cultural industries, promote discourses of 'networking, teams, outsourcing, change management, e-commerce, e-communication, e-service delivery and de-regulation and re-regulation discourses of downsizing managerialist infrastructures' (2001: 58). They work with greater creative autonomy, are globally networked, and achieve greater flexibility in their organizational structure. Instead of the command-style, top-down hierarchies of the previous managerial elites, the global networkers 'allow each unit to organize itself in ways deemed appropriate by those in situ' (2001: 63). Keane and Moran (2008) indicate that even the creative process in the development of new formats can be attributed at least in part to the organizing creativity of the new global networkers (2008: 166). In their quest to achieve hegemony over the managerial elites, they continuously 'colonize new organizational spaces' (Louw 2001: 63), displacing the power of the professional managers of the old elite to professional networkers.

I would argue that this development is underlying the conceptual basis of both *The Office* and *Stromberg*, in which incompetence and inability to navigate the insecure hierarchies of the corporate world can be seen as more than merely an individual subjective problem. I would further argue that the deconstruction of the managerial profession in both shows is driven by the younger generation – depicted in the roles of the two female supervisors, Jan and Frau Berkel, who represent the interests of the new global networked elite. They have acquired their positions through meritocratic means – that is, educational qualifications – and are in a position of power over those managers like Stromberg and Michael Scott who have moved up through the ranks and have not acquired the cultural or educational capital to compete successfully. Their racist and sexist defense postures belie their inability to navigate and negotiate the changing corporate environment successfully. Neither is able to establish control over the organizational structures determining their conditions at each of the companies. While Stromberg attempts – unsuccessfully – to circumvent and subvert these structures, Michael Scott tries – also unsuccessfully – to defy or pre-empt them.

Hallenberger (2001: 124) argues that the concept of 'Eurofiction' includes programs 'predominantly set in the 1990s and urban areas, as leads there are usually mixed-gender groups of characters, not single protagonists'. He points out that in, the countries of France, Great Britain, Italy and Spain, 'the preferred genres are those which use topics close to everyday life (like relationships, health, etc.).' However, he asserts that the final products of programs involved in format transfer (like that of *The Office*) vary greatly from country to country due to the fact that 'characters dress, talk and behave differently in each country, their homes look different and they use differing means of transportation'.

Hallenberger (2001) believes that even the shooting and editing styles are specific to each country, such that 'viewers have few problems identifying a program as typically "French" or "German"'. Hallenberger disputes the cultural imperialism hypothesis with regard to the export of US programs to other parts in the world, and calls these an aspect of globalization because US television has 'developed in all genres of global relevance a particular style of "universal stereotypes" intended to appeal to different segments of the American audience', an audience he considers heterogeneous such that success on the US market ensures success in others (2001: 126). He proposes that many US television fiction narratives are inherently transcultural, such that their commercial success abroad is guaranteed but is still 'inferior to domestic TV fiction' due to the fact that domestic programs 'are usually closer to the everyday life of the viewers, reflecting social, political or cultural situations in their country, presenting actors from the respective country and more accurate images of everyday life' which provide a competitive advantage over the US programs (2001: 129). This relationship can be seen with the adaptation of *Stromberg* and the US version of the British format *The Office*. Steve Carrell is a well-known comedian who has been on several successful television shows, including *The Daily Show*, and in recent films. Christoph-Maria Herbst is also a well-known comedian who worked with Anke Engelke in various comedy shows (e.g. *Ladykracher*) on German television prior to his *Stromberg* role.

Note

1. 'Tja, ich bin ja für Ausländerintegration, insofern würde ich freiwillig sagen: Der Türke soll es machen…nur, erstens bin ich länger dabei und zweitens', pp. 26–27, Originalbücher.

References

Chang Y.-L. (2003), '"Glocalization" of Television: Programming Strategies of Global Television Broadcasters in Asia', *Asian Journal of Communication*, 13(1), pp. 1–36.

Gudykunst, W.B. and Kim, Y.Y. (2003), *Communicating with Strangers: An Approach to Intercultural Communication*, 4th ed., Boston: McGraw-Hill.

Hallenberger, G. (2001), 'Aesthetic Conventions in European Media Cultures', in *Emergences*, 11(1), pp. 117–31.

Keane, M. and Moran, A. (2008), 'Television's New Engines', *Television & New Media*, 9(2), pp. 155–69.

Louw, Eric (2001), *The Media and Cultural Production*, Thousand Oaks, CA: Sage.

Moran, A. (1998), *Copycat TV: Globalisation, Program Formats and Cultural Identity*, Luton: University of Luton Press.

Straubhaar, J. (2007), *World Television: From Global to Local*, Thousand Oaks, CA: Sage.

Straubhaar, J., Fuentes-Bautista, M., Abram, D., McCormick, P., Campbell, C. and Inagaki, N. (2003), 'National and Regional TV Markets and TV Program Flows', paper presented at the International Communication Association Conference, San Diego, CA, pp. 1–34.

Chapter 12

Tearing Up Television News Across Borders: Format Transfer of News Parody Shows Between Italy and Bulgaria

Gabriele Cosentino, Waddick Doyle and Dimitrina Todorova

As this book makes clear, format adaptation is a phenomenon whose growth is evident around the world, and we are seeing many local adaptations of global formats in franchise remakes in different regions. Program format transfer involves local adaptations of a global format. However, Tunstall (2008) argues that news and political journalism remain resolutely national and local. This chapter considers the format transfer not of traditional news, but of news parody – a genre that has become increasingly politicized – from Italy to Bulgaria. One of the first news parodies in the world was *Striscia la notizia* in 1988 in Italy, the format of which was exported to Bulgaria in 2000. This is an unusual example of format transfer because news and news parody are rarely formatted and transferred. Here, we explore the reasons why this transfer took place and the impact the program in question has had on the two nations and on their media.

News programs in the first decades of television were linked to the rise of national television networks where the key moment in the evening's viewing was the television news, which acted as the 'lead-in' to the evening's entertainment (Attalah 1986). This was a near-universal phenomenon in television systems across the world, enabling the news bulletins to do their key work in establishing imagined communities of national citizenry while also defining national audiences and establishing access to national advertising markets. News was seen as the essential function of public service broadcasting, informing the nation about itself in order for it to express itself in the democratic process. News was one of the principal justifications for public service broadcasting systems, and a central feature of the national public sphere. This was true even in the United States and in many parts of South American commercial broadcasting, where providing a national news bulletin was a key element in justifying a national broadcaster's credentials and right to have a broadcast licence.

The news program itself, it could be argued, was the original format transfer. The model of the speaking head, newsreader or anchor facing the public and the desk has been copied all over the world, of course, without any official format transfer (Paterson and Smith 1998). Recently, however, national television systems have increasingly been brought into question as they have been confronted by new technologies such as satellite, digitalization and multiple channels, which in turn have been linked to the global rise of commercial television and diasporic non-national viewing. The decline of public broadcasting and the centrality of the news in the broadcasting systems of Europe has been part of a broader shift associated with the rise of new forms of cultural populism, and the domination of politics by the logics of television programming (Jost 2007). In this technological and politico-cultural realignment, commercial television could be seen as a cultural form distinct from that of public television.

As it emerged, so did new forms of programs – including news parody, which has circulated within different European countries with many variations. Examples include puppet shows in Britain (*Spitting Image*), France, Spain (*Les guignols*) and Russia (*Kukly*). Many other variations of news satire are shown in other countries, from *Freitag Nacht News* in Germany and *Décodeurs de l'Info* in Belgium, to *Le Vrai Journal* in France, *Veckans nyheter* in Sweden and *Brass Eye* in Britain. All mock the news while imitating its format.

It is not surprising, in this historical climate, that national news and television markets have been confronted with these programs, which question and undermine the most serious function of national network television – particularly in state broadcasting systems: that of delivering the national news. However, the cultural and technological transformations since the 1990s have given rise to the new form of parody news. Just as national news defined the nation state, parody news is a response to a new geo-political phase where sub-national and supra-national identities have become more important. Global flows of content now play a larger role in defining viewers' identities as trans-national television consumers and weaken the force of national news programs, which now have to cope with being counter-programmed against news and news parody.

The situations in Italy and Bulgaria both conform to the general transformations of European broadcasting. In this study we examine how a format which was developed in response to legal regulations in Italy, and which became instrumental in the legitimation of commercial broadcasting, was imported into Bulgaria where it was able to perform a similar task. We thus seek to combine considerations about genre with those of political economy and law to consider the impact of format transfer.

In Italy, we have seen the end of an era: the postwar republic based on the ideological consensus of an anti-fascist state, despite a divide between the left and right, has given way to a postmodern politics dominated by the logic of communications. Consumer television accompanied a unique form of 'consumer politics', where branding has encroached upon the place formerly occupied by ideology.

In Bulgaria, we have seen a cultural political revolution with the end of communism, the rise of the consumer market economy and electoral politics. In this process, there has been a desacralization of the state in television representations. Furthermore, the language used to talk about the state on Bulgarian television has become increasingly ironic and vernacular.

State institutions had been part of a 'civic religion' in Italy, and even more so in Bulgaria. Television was both one of these institutions and the organ that celebrated state rituals. In this process of change, it is not surprising that irony and parody are employed to form a language of disenchantment, a secular idiom that resists the institutionalizing function of the official language of politics and of the official news programs.

The satirical genre and legitimacy

Since the 1980s, we have seen the rise of parody TV across the world. There has been some academic discussion of the impact of parody news on national television systems, but very little work on the international circulation of this genre. It should be noted that few, if any, of the news parody programs that emerged in the 1980s and 1990s were linked to formal format transfer agreements. There are some exceptions – for example, *Les guignols* in France on Canal Plus was formatted to Spain as *Las noticias del guiñol*. Most news satire involves copying and borrowing ideas without format transfer. The case discussed in this chapter is a regional format transfer within Europe, between one medium-sized and one small-sized television market. The Italian parody news show *Striscia la notizia* ('Tearing the News to Shreds') was exported to Bulgaria, under the name *Gospodari Na Efira* ('Lords of the Air'). In both countries, it played a significant role in political life and contributed to political change. The context of the end of communism and the need for media to take up its role in society proved conducive to the success of the show in Bulgaria. In Italy, the show appeared during the collapse of the ideological domination of Italian politics by the twin forces of Catholicism and communism. It was also a period of media deregulation that allowed Silvio Berlusconi to create his media empire and later leverage on this to start his political career. In fact, the show appeared on Berlusconi's television networks.

Satirical news programs teeter on the cusp between fiction and non-fiction genres. Parody breaks generic structure, revealing the actual form of the genre while criticizing the cultural, economic and political function of television. Parody television was the generic playground where the two underlying political-economic models of television – public service versus commercial – and their two different symbolic orders negotiated and tried to institutionalize different languages and forms. Italy in the 1980s was the world's first deregulated, or even 'a-regulated', television system. The new private networks attracted attention to themselves by breaking down the distinction between news and entertainment (Doyle 1989). Umberto Eco's (1984) famous essay made this very clear, calling this genre-bending phenomenon 'neo-television'.

In at least three cases, news parody seems to have taken on great importance at times when confidence in the national news was collapsing. In the United States, *The Daily Show* rose to prominence when mainstream media failed to question the government over the issue of weapons of mass destruction as justification for the invasion of Iraq. In Spain, *Las noticias del guiñol* became popular during Aznar's willingness to support the Iraq War. In Bulgaria as well, *Gospodari Na Efira* appeared in a climate of disappointment with the government led by the former king, Simeon Saxe-Coburg, who had presented such hopes for a transformation of Bulgaria out of the ideological divide of post-communism.This is also true of the Tangentopoli crisis, when more than half of Italy's parliamentarians went to jail for corruption. Public television suffered a severe crisis of authority since its news editors had ties with the corrupt political class in a system where different and opposing parties in parliament shared out the positions of influence on the RAI (Padovani 2004).

In Italy, news on the public channels was formal and was required by law to provide fair access to representatives of different parties. This appeared ludicrous, given that these parties were being revealed to be hotbeds of corruption (Ginsborg 2001).We argue that one of the key roles of news parody is to take away the legitimacy of national news. Canale 5's *Striscia* and ITV's *Spitting Image* or *Le Vrai Journal* on Canal Plus helped undermine the mainstream national networks' role as the providers of the real representation of the national. Meanwhile, the comic genre can accrue legitimacy. For instance, *The Daily Show* is used to gain audience share to the Comedy Central network, but it also allows the network to be seen as speaking the truth about established networks, and the fabrication and bias of their news. One could argue that parody undermined the legitimacy of national broadcasters, only to re-establish it for commercial broadcasters. Indeed, in all of these cases, we see a logic where the concept of the national is decoupled from what used to be its synonym, the concept of the public. This, in turn, is linked to broader transformations in television's audiences, which no longer need to be defined in national terms in the era of regionalization and globalization.

'*Striscia la notizia*': Tearing the news to shreds

Striscia La Notizia is in part what Jones (2007) and Baym (2005) define as a fake news program that airs daily on weekdays at 8.40 p.m. on the national private channel Canale 5, part of Silvio Berlusconi's Mediaset network. *Striscia*'s current scheduling, directly after Canale 5's main news program, fits well with its parody function, as the program 'inserts itself in the information flow established by the newscast, exploiting some of its features, upon which it performs a commentary' (Mascio 2002: 198). Under the deceptively silly appearance of a parody program, *Striscia* blends elements of different genres, such as investigative journalism, television criticism and comedy. The standard set-up of the show features two anchormen introducing correspondents and reports, with frequent entertaining intermissions, such as dance numbers by the *veline* – two girls who bring the anchors the news stories – and comic skits by the anchors. It also contains a parody of Italy's main Meet the Press-type show, *Porta a Porta*, with a puppet named Gabibbo purporting to be an investigative journalist who inquires into minor corruption and bureaucratic malfunctioning. The show gives an award called the Golden Tapir for the worst possible performance of a public figure, television journalist or bureaucrat. There is a section where celebrities' secrets are revealed to show their facelifts, surgery and makeup cover-ups. Other elements include parodies of the Swiss news, clips for the worst moments of television denounced by viewers, and also small scandals and other incidents submitted by viewers. Part of the program is devoted to revealing the corruption and inadequacy of the public service – for example, showing government disability offices with no wheelchair access or revealing hospital corruption. In a way, this redefined the notion of what public service television should be: no longer about the political, but rather exposing the inefficiency of the state in the public interest. Hence, unlike what Jones (2007) defines as 'fake news', it contains a cocktail of genres – fact, fiction and variety.

One of the most consistently successful programs of Italian television, *Striscia* started on 7 November 1988 on the youth-oriented Channel Italia 1 (owned by Berlusconi's corporation Fininvest, later to become Mediaset) as the spinoff of a successful variety show called *Odiens* (the Italian transliteration of the word 'audience'). The following year, it was moved to the more popular Canale 5 channel, programmed against the traditional timeslot of the eight o'clock news on Rai Uno, the most important program of the primary national network. The program's producer and creator, Antonio Ricci, claimed he wanted to create what he called a '*nazional-popolare*' (national popular, in his corruption of Gramsci's concept) variety show with some journalistic elements. Ricci had produced a number of successful comedy and variety shows, which were noted for their thematic and visual experimentation. *Drive-in*, his first program on a Fininvest channel, became widely popular for breaking the conventions of the *varietà* genre, with a postmodern and fast-paced show that broke the distinctions between host and guests and between actors and public.

The historical importance of *Striscia* needs to be viewed in light of the competition between public broadcaster RAI and Berlusconi's Fininvest. During the 1980s, Fininvest's status as the national network was still openly questioned, due to the peculiar conditions of its formation. As Italy in the late 1970s had gained the world's first deregulated television system, Berlusconi had been able to create and take over the private television system by virtue of a mix of political patronage, innovative management and successful programming techniques. Most of Fininvest's success was due to its ability to directly challenge RAI's undisputed authority in broadcasting, and to transform the Italian television system from a public monopoly to a duopolistic mixed system. Since the early 1980s, the competition between the two broadcasters had been played out along a two-pronged strategy based on counter-programming and parody. The first network to conceive and initiate this strategy was Berlusconi's Canale 5, which needed to legitimate itself in the eyes of the Italian audiences. Canale 5 was able to establish legitimacy through its capacity to attract large audiences by means of popular entertainment and systematic counter-programming to break up the habits of RAI's audiences (Doyle 1989). Parody programs poking fun at the competitors also played a vital role in the competition, as Ricci's *Drive-In* successfully challenged the typical RAI tradition of the *varietà*. By the mid-1980s, RAI had started to respond to the successful challenges of Fininvest by counter-programming shows that were targeting, in a humorous way, the commercial ethos of the private broadcasters.

By 1988, the competition for audience share between the private and public broadcasting monoliths had reached a point of balance, but Berlusconi was still fighting to establish the legal right to have a national television network. As stated above, a key element in legitimization of the network was the ability to broadcast news programs. However, at the time of *Striscia*'s introduction, Fininvest (together with all private television) was prohibited from broadcasting live news. The Italian Constitutional Court had previously ruled that news was the exclusive privilege of public television. The court's argument was based on the notion that only the state could provide universal access to information, and accurately reflect the political and social life of the country. Due to this legal impediment, and since the Fininvest networks were perceived as mostly entertainment based, Fininvest developed a logical strategy to introduce news interlaced with comedy, which could be defined as entertainment and not information, and thus circumvent the court ban.

At the same time, given the changes in television, there was a growing awareness of the different political agendas being followed by the public broadcaster. Competition had effectively contributed to highlight the extent to which political parties controlled the public broadcaster. The RAI was administered by the Italian parliament and reflected the political parties present in parliament. To this end, *Striscia* escalated the competition by attacking the public network on its strongest yet most sensitive spot, the legitimacy of the newscasts, drawing attention to the party political pressure and influence. To further undermine the authority of RAI, *Striscia* parodied the form of the public news and exposed its falsity and complacency with official politics. As Ricci (1998) argues: 'The television of the past was highly ideological television…You'd be watching the newscasts, thinking to simply receive news, instead they're selling you a political idea, and a car too.'

Striscia was thus essential in building of the identity of Canale 5 as a national private channel representing the interests of the people against a corrupt and inefficient state, hypocritical politicians and a lap-dog public service television station. Under the claim of offering 'everything that the other newscasts won't tell you' (Guidici 1998), *Striscia* represented a radical departure from traditional television journalism, openly paying tribute to the logic of counter-information that was popular among Italian grassroots movements in the 1970s. Unlike the formal structure of the RAI news, which requires political parties to be represented in proportion to their presence in the parliament, *Striscia* provided a more open and fresh format. Hence it went against the prevailing logic of the RAI's *lottizzazione*, of parcelling editorial positions according to political currents (Padovani 2004). From the beginning, *Striscia* attempted to redefine the notion of public service television, claiming that it was no longer about representing political traditions but rather exposing the inefficiency of the state in the public interest.

In light of this new political approach, most of *Striscia*'s reports were concerned with government and bureaucratic wrongdoing, investigating incompetence and corruption with a direct, aggressive approach. *Striscia* would show how hospitals were not working, or how petty officials were taking bribes. *Striscia* became so successful at investigative journalism that it beat newscasts at their own game, scooping stories before any other news outlet. In 1994, *Striscia* recorded a conversation between two politicians waiting to go on air that brought the first Berlusconi government close to a major political crisis. Unlike other newscasts, *Striscia* disclosed the list of the Italian manufacturers of the land mines that were used during the conflict in the former Yugoslavia. Recently, the show revealed that the Neapolitan mafia was dumping toxic waste on farmland, and as a result Korea and Japan banned the importation of mozzarella cheese. On some important occasions, *Striscia*'s political views became even more evident, as during the First Gulf War when the show took a strong anti-war position, attracting the protests of viewers and associations close to the Italian Army.

However, this model of confrontational journalism was mixed with absurd parody. Amongst a number of correspondents was the puppet Gabibbo, who became mascot of the show. Introduced in 1990, Gabibbo is a large red puppet with a thick Genoan accent. Born as a parody of the ugly face of television, 'Gabibbo…is the horrid side of television, the increasing void of content in programming' (Guidici 1998) on both public and private channels. Ricci (1998) recalls that Gabibbo was born at a time when 'loudmouths' were becoming popular on television, as the puppet stands for those television characters – such as talk shows hosts and pundits – who have a 'quarreling, threatening attitude'. From a mere parody, Gabibbo has gradually and somehow unexpectedly evolved into the avenger of the common people. On several occasions, city councils, volunteers or factory groups have called Gabibbo in support of their causes. The puppet has been the protagonist of news stories that have brought lawsuits against the program, but that also have led to investigations and arrests. *Striscia* now has a hotline, SOS Gabibbo, that viewers can use to call and notify about frauds against consumers, inefficiencies of the public administration and similar issues. As Guidici (1998) claims, 'thousands of citizens prefer to file a complaint to the Gabibbo rather to the State institutions'. Hence *Striscia* made a new appeal for legitimacy. Rather than following the RAI model of public broadcasting, representing the nation and being administered by the elected representatives of the nation, *Striscia* claimed to be the voice of the ordinary people against the establishment, and all of those who it deemed to be its puppets. This language would later be key in Berlusconi's claims to represent ordinary folk – *la gente* – and his language style would be termed *gentese*, or 'ordinary people's speech'.

According to Ricci (1998), counter-information and advocacy were simply the products of a broader and more ambitious goal of *Striscia*, which was to redefine television's pedagogic role. By critiquing television journalism, particularly on public television, *Striscia* 'attacks the whole broadcasting system, which has in journalism the main source of credibility, authority and self-legitimation' (Guidici, 1998). Ricci (1998) and the other *Striscia* authors understood ahead of time that the most sensitive target of cultural and political criticism was not politics *per se*, but the television system itself. Hence the program's content was a new mixture of genres: puppet show, Italian variety show with dancing girls, and comedy – all contained within the form of the news. This was to become a format just like other formats, where a combination of genres – elements of game, reality and fiction – are mixed together. Francois Jost (2005) has produced interesting maps which allow us to track these generic shifts in the relationship between different genres of television formats, which are to a large degree a combination of previous generic elements. In the case of *Striscia*, these were not simply innocent generic inventions but a programming innovation whose stated aim was to attack the legitimacy, credibility and authority of the state broadcasting system. Alternative journalism for *Striscia* is only important insofar as it helps question the authority of television. To Guidici (1998): 'Counter-information is only…one of the means to unmask the fictions of the television language.' Ricci (1998) takes up the rhetoric of the

Italian radical left movement of counter-information, which had been championed by many famous intellectuals from Deleuze and Foucault to Meaghan Morris (see Buchanan and Parr 2006: 52). Ricci and others were, however, able to appropriate this rhetoric of counter-information as a discourse which legitimated the anti-state broadcasting discourse of the new private media monopoly of Fininvest. The owner of this monopoly, of course, became Italy's prime minister. Ricci admitted clearly having a didactic approach to television production, teaching viewers to be sceptical about the claims of truth and objectivity of television. With this goal in mind, *Striscia* has exposed numerous examples of omissions and fabrications by television journalists. In one early example, at the time of the Gulf War, *Striscia* revealed that a CNN correspondent from Tel Aviv was wearing a fake gas mask, suggesting that the Iraqi army was using chemical weapons against Israel.

Openly disassembling the mechanisms of fiction, *Striscia* addresses viewers as savvy users of media, involving them in the deconstruction of official texts and in the production of critical texts. In turn, viewers' belief in the authority of *Striscia* and of its channel was built by inciting disbelief in the television system, particularly the public broadcaster. The work of *Striscia* against the credibility of television is again summed up in the figure of Gabibbo, which 'is able to unmask the fiction and the bad manners of the other "puppets" of television' (Ricci, quoted in Guidici 1998). However, to further prove television's capacity of constantly creating new fictions, Gabibbo went from being a parody to become a respected figure in television journalism. As Ricci comments: 'I think it is dramatic and very telling that the most believable person on television is a puppet, a fake commentator.' (in Guidici 1998)

So *Striscia* was a program developed in very specific national conditions. It was not simply a new format, but a program whose consent and form played a role in changing the political economy of television and politics itself. In the next section, we consider what happens when such a program's format is transferred to another national context.

Gospodari Na Efira

Bulgaria has undergone a twenty-year transition from an authoritarian to a liberal-democratic media system. The transition has not always been easy, and often has involved strange shifts and turns. By 2009, 98 per cent of Bulgaria's households were equipped with a television set and there were 203 licensed TV operators, of which 196 were cable or satellite operators – among them three national terrestrial networks (BNT, bTV and Nova TV) (Spassov 2008). Television had been an instrument of the Communist Party since its creation in 1959. It remained so until 1989, when the only two TV channels in the Bulgarian air became ' public' (as opposed to socialist) and were formally transformed into a state-owned and financed television network. For some years after its formal disengagement with the communist regime, television in Bulgaria remained unlike that of other European countries, still marked by its past. In the first five years of democratic government, whenever a new party or a coalition came to power, the current director of the Bulgarian National

Television (BNT) was ritually replaced by a journalist close to the ruling party. Consequently, journalists critical of certain politicians were fired (Bakardjieva 1995).

Despite large national audiences which consisted of most of the country's population, television programming and production values remained reminiscent of the communist era, due both to a lack of professionally trained journalists and the absence of a culture of free media. Indeed, the very notion of 'free media' was up for definition. In the 1990s, cable TV stations quickly emerged in many cities at the same time, and each of them exploited a temporary licence and created original programming broadcasting for a very small audience (Open Society Institute 2005: 350). At one point, there were 300 cable televisions channels in Sofia, and another 100 or so in the countryside (2005: 346). Most of these channels had very negligible ratings (CEM 2002). According to the Open Society report in 2005, this caused the creation of a 'a vibrant, unregulated, often amateurish alternative television culture in Bulgaria'. This parallels the situation in Italy in the 1970s, when what had been a television system dominated by the Christian Democrat Party was transformed into the unregulated 'Wild West of the airwaves'. The deregulation of television in 1976 by the Italian constitutional court ended in the legalization of Berlusconi's networks in the early 1990s. During this period in Bulgaria, parody programs were quick to appear on many of these new stations, including the national broadcasters, Channel 1 and Channel 2. As in many other countries, parody shows did not follow a clearly defined format transferred from elsewhere but consisted mostly of improvisations performed by actors, ridiculing politicians of the day. Judy Halvadzhian, the producer of *Gospodari Na Efira*, thought that it 'could not have occurred in the 1990s, because democracy was still very weak and such a level of parody would not have been tolerated' (quoted in Todorova 2007).

The Bulgarian mediascape began to change visibly in 1999 when the second frequency of the national television network, the former Channel 2, was sold to Rupert Murdoch's Balkan News Corporation, and the first private national channel, bTV, was created. Two years later, bTV had the leading share of over 40 per cent of the television audience (Open Society Report 2005: 346). In terms of programming, and professional and technical standards, it greatly surpassed anything previously shown on the Bulgarian airwaves. At that time, Judy Halvadzhian founded the freelance Global Vision production company which, like many others, produced original content in this rather chaotic television market.

In a recent analysis of Bulgarian television, Ibroscheva and Raicheva-Stover (2009) argue that, in Bulgaria, the lack of professional TV journalism largely distorted the division of roles in the media. These authors argue that television sought to inform, whereas newspapers commented and radio entertained:

> Over the last 10 years, newspapers and radio stations informed, whereas television usually campaigned in favor of governmental interests…The emergence of private national channels was expected to offset this peculiar configuration of the mediascape and lead to depoliticization of the broadcasting market. This, in turn, was seen as the most practical,

market-driven solution to restore both political neutrality as well as professional norms in the field of broadcast journalism.

Striscia's transfer to Bulgaria was one of the engines of this change. *Striscia* had been one of the first TV shows that Judy Halvadzhian wanted to recreate in Bulgaria upon his return from Italy in the 1990s. The Italian-educated TV producer, who founded what would later become the most successful production company in Bulgaria, saw many opportunities in the newly de-monopolized television sector. At that moment, in his words, 'it was the best of times, it was the worst of times' for making television in Bulgaria (Todorova 2007). In 2001, a demonstration version of the Bulgarian version of *Striscia* had been created, but bTV rejected it because of a budget disagreement. This delayed the appearance of the show on national TV for another two years. Instead, an agreement was worked out with 7dni, a small TV station broadcasting in Sofia only. Two years later, the show transferred to Nova TV. *Gospodari* aired for the first time on Nova TV in 2003, at a very important moment for the Bulgarian media. Ten years after the opening up of Bulgaria's media environment, Nova TV was the third channel to have the right to national coverage after a complicated lawsuit. A significant impediment for Bulgaria's media system was the lack of adequate legislation, which made acquisition of channels and licensing very difficult (Bulgarian Supreme Administrative Court Decision No. 573, 13 July 2001, case No. 2736/2001). This is, of course, reminiscent of the Italian situation in the 1980s, where there was a legislative vacuum following the Constitutional Court's liberalization of the airwaves. Although Nova TV had existed as a station since 1994, it took nine years for it to obtain a national licence and become the second private national broadcaster by the same Supreme Court decision of 2001. This took place after a complicated process where the court ruled entirely in favour of Nova TV.

In terms of programming, the first ten years of deregulated and open television allowed the Bulgarian audience to get to know different programs, some of which were imported, and develop an affinity for Western programming. These first years created the first TV stars, and the first global formats were adapted to the Bulgarian market – *Big Brother*, *Who Wants to Be a Millionaire?* and *Star Academy*. It also witnessed the rise and fall of many comedy programs, political programs and parody shows. None of them seemed to be able to capture the national imagination. *Gospodari* succeeded in doing three things: following the format of *Striscia*, it was able to keep the audience entertained, shame politicians and undertake some investigative journalism. Gradually, however, the emphasis of the show became more entertainment and less politics.

When *Gospodari* was first aired, there were many comedy programs mocking politics, and it was not regarded as a very innovative concept. The presenters were well known to the Bulgarian TV audience, and the themes the show explored were already talked about in the public sphere. The humour was something people appreciated, but humour alone was not enough to create a major impression. Shortly after its launch, however, *Gospodari* became one of the most watched programs in Bulgaria. Its ratings soon surpassed those of the news, although it aired after prime time. In 2004, *Gospodari* won the award for best entertainment program at the Albena Media Festival, the biggest and most prestigious in Bulgaria's media industry (Karbovski 2008).

Perhaps what made *Gospodari* such a sensation, and the most successful parody show on Bulgarian TV, was not the fact that it made fun of politics; rather, it was the fact that it made fun of the media. Like *Striscia,* it took away the legitimacy of its competitors. *Gospodari* used television as its primary source, and built its social critique on pointing out the gaffes of TV presenters and unprofessional journalism. It was a program that functioned as a foil to all the other programs, and consequently was able to make commercial television legitimate. The show assumed the social function of a watchdog, not only over politicians and public matters but over the media as well. This was the key innovation that *Gospodar*i brought to the Bulgarian mediascape. After ten years of a deregulated and privatized television sector in Bulgaria – where, prior to 1989, television had abided by the rules of a totalitarian media system – the show criticized the way the media worked in 'liberated' Bulgaria. *Gospodari* used television as its primary source, and built its social critique on pointing out the gaffes of TV presenters, and unprofessional journalism. It was a program that functioned as a foil to all the other programs – a type of meta-television genre.

Gospodari is the only TV format transferred to Bulgaria which could not be classified as entertainment. The format is almost identical to its Italian prototype: there are two hosts, who sit behind desks as if they were news presenters, who lead in the reports, prepared in advance, and tell jokes about the subject-matter of the reports. There are also two girls, like the *veline* in *Striscia,* who dance on top of and around the desks, and who have no other function in the show. The 'trademark' of the show is the award given each month to a public figure who has committed the most incompetent, unethical or sometimes even illegal deed. The award is in the shape of a skunk, and it is meant to symbolize the stink that they have caused, and the unfortunate consequences that people have experienced as a result of the actions of this particular person. This is, of course, the equivalent of the Golden Tapir given out by *Striscia.* The breakthrough moment of the show happened in a climate of overall disappointment with government led by the former king in exile, Simeon Saxe-Coburg, the hallmark of whose electoral campaign was the slogan 'Give me 800 days and I will improve your lives'. On day 800 of his mandate, 8 October 2003, *Gospodari* officially awarded the Golden Skunk to him. At that time, although less than a year old, the parody show demonstrated its intent to play a serious role in Bulgaria's public sphere, and claimed to be protecting the interests of 'the people', holding politicians and institutions accountable. As in Italy, we see a shift here, with commercial television claiming to represent the interests of ordinary people rather than the nation or the state. Although *Gospodari* advertises itself as a watchdog of the media, the reporters on the show often deal with subjects that are more political in nature, such as embezzlements, inadequate bureaucrats, scandals, and so on. By the symbolic gesture of the award, *Gospodari* criticizes certain elements in society without necessarily being seen to take an explicit political stance.

Gospodari is one of the few shows featuring serious investigative reporting. In its panel discussion about Bulgaria's media sustainability in 2008, the International Research and Exchange Board (IREX) concluded that Bulgaria lacked a watchdog function:

> Specialized coverage in different beats, especially investigative reporting, still fails to become a far-reaching characteristic of the whole media environment. Small and/or regional outlets are particularly handicapped by a limited workforce with insufficient experience that can be developed into beat reporters. (IREX 2008)

In an article for a national newspaper *Standart*, the most popular investigative journalist in Bulgaria, Martin Karbovski (2008), called *Gospodari Na Efira* 'the people who do the job of being the real media watchdog instead of the Council of Electronic Media'. In his analysis of their impact on Bulgarian politics, Karbovski mentions two cases when the reports of *Gospodari* were prophetic of future developments. A month after a report on the dangers of falling façades of shops in Varna, a girl was killed by one such façade. Had action been taken in time, argues Karbovski, such a tragedy could have been prevented – but 'unfortunately *Gospodar*i are the only ones who take social responsibility nowadays in Bulgaria' concludes Karbovski. The second case involved a television host who had deceived people by promising nonexistent awards for calling into the show. '*Gospodari* were the only ones to notice that this show supposedly gave away a tremendous amount of money, and that the complaints against it were increasing dramatically.' After the *Gospodari* report, the show was taken off air. Ironically, the show was broadcast on the small TV station 7dni, where *Gospodari* had aired for the first time.

When the producers of *Gospodari*, Global Vision, first adapted *Striscia*, the format of the show had not even been copyrighted; however, as the interest on the Bulgarian side increased, *Striscia*'s producers copyrighted the format and licensed it out to Global Vision. When asked why he chose this particular show to produce in Bulgaria, the producer of *Gospodari*, Judy Halvadzhian, said that the format was designed very intelligently, as it allowed for a lot of creativity in the way it mocked current events or public figures, and that the open format allowed for up-to-date jokes. However, he said that at the same time the format was tied to the concept of news and current events, which made it inexhaustible, as there would always be material on which to comment (Todorova 2007). The biggest advantage of the format, in Halvadzhian's opinion, was the space it provided for interpretation and criticism – something viewers never got from the hard news featured in the news bulletins. The serious political critiques of the day, on the other hand, were not very accessible or attractive for young audiences, as they often involved an elevated language from which youth felt alienated. Halvadzhian said the humour which was the backbone of the format of *Striscia* and *Gospodari* was the show's 'licence' for criticism and serious discussions, while keeping the audience entertained.

Conclusion

We can argue that the format was transferred in a moment where there were very similar transformations going on in the political economic media structures of Bulgaria to those that had taken place in Italy in the 1980s and 1990s. After a long period of domination of the media by ideological discourse and beliefs, both systems erupted into a frenzied period of deregulation. In Italy, the ideological domination was that of the Christian Democratic Party, but it became mixed after the 1970s with the inclusion of leftist parties. In Bulgaria, it was the stranglehold of the Communist Party. However, beyond this ideological stance, both systems venerated the state as a type of civic religion. The deregulation and chaos of freedom of broadcasting led in both cases to the establishment of large private networks, which required legitimacy while taking away the legitimacy of the state broadcasting system. In both cases, we argue, parody news was a significant element in establishing a new discourse of legitimacy for a culture of entertainment and for the new commercial television.

If *Striscia* and *Gospodari* were both examples of the same format that transferred from one country to another, we argue that it is because they both did the textual work required for a cultural transformation of audience attitudes to the state and to the media. This, in turn, was important for understanding the transformation of the national political economies of television in each country, and to the cultural acceptance of commercial broadcasting services as a system which represented ordinary people and their interests against those of the bureaucracy, the state and public broadcasting. Indeed, what was being transformed was the conception of the imagined community of the nation. *Striscia* as a format was a clever response to a legal prohibition on news programs. It broke down the distinction between news and entertainment. This generic transformation attacked the notion of information as truth. Ricci (1998) said repeatedly that television news was a fiction, but that *Striscia* was the truth because it revealed the fiction of media. Hence we could argue that *Striscia* played a vital part in installing a new regime of truth which was in turn linked to a new political economy of the media. In Italy, this then led to the transformation of the political system where Berlusconi the television proprietor could succeed in taking political power. In Bulgaria, the importation of this program was important in the success and establishment of the third national network, Nova, and provided part of its legitimacy both by establishing large audiences and shifting the regime of truth. Naturally, this also entailed a shift in power. Format transfer in this case should be understood not simply as the innocent development of generic hybrids and of their cultural adaptation, but as part of the global circulation of regimes of truth. Foucault (2001) argues:

> 'Truth' is to be understood as a system of ordered procedures for the production, regulation, distribution, circulation and operation of statements. Truth is linked in a circular relation with systems of power which produce and sustain it, and to effects of power which it induces and which extend it, a 'regime' of truth. (2001: 209)

Format transfer should also be studied and understood as a game of innovation and restraint around generic rules, a system of ordered procedures for the production, circulation and regulation of formats. *Striscia* and *Gospodari* both helped to create new regimes of truth which have had profound effects on the societies of Italy and Bulgaria. Therein lies their power.

References

Achter, Paul (2008), 'Comedy in Unfunny Times: News Parody and Carnival After 9/11', *Critical Studies in Media Communication*, 3, pp. 247–303.

Atallah, Paul (1986), *Of Homes and Machines: Television Technology and Fun in America (1944–1983)*, Montreal: McGill University.

Bakardjieva, Maria (1995), 'The New Media Landscape in Bulgaria', *Canadian Journal of Communication*, 20(1), http://www.cjconline.ca/index.php/journal/article/view/845/751. Accessed 30 October 2003.

Baym, Geoffrey (2005), '*The Daily Show*: Discursive Integration and Reinvention of Political Journalism', *Political Communication*, 22(3), pp. 259–76.

—— (2007), 'Representation and the Politics of Play: Stephen Colbert's Better Known District', *Political Communication*, 24(4), pp. 359–76.

Buchanan Ian and Parr, Adrian (2006), *Deleuze and the Contemporary World*, Edinburgh: Edinburgh University Press.

Council for Electronic Media (CEM) (2002), *Expert Report - November 2002*, no. 15-00-144, 7 November, Sofia: CEM.

Doyle, Waddick (1989), From Deregulation to Monopoly: A Cultural Analysis of the Formation of Italy's Private Television Monopoly, PhD thesis, Griffith University, Brisbane.

Eco, Umberto (1984), 'A Guide to the Neo-Television of the 1980s', *The Journal of Cinema and Media*, 25, pp. 18–25.

Foucault, M. (2001), 'Truth and Power', in C.J. Calhoun, J. Gerteis, J. Moody, S. Pfaff and I. Virk (eds), *Contemporary Sociological Theory*, Oxford: Blackwell.

Gaines, Elliot (2007), 'The Narrative Semiotics of the *Daily Show*', *Semiotica*, 166(1–4), pp. 81–96.

Ginsborg, Paul (2001), *Italy and its Discontents*, London: Allen Lane.

Gospodari website (2003) http://gospodari.com/?go=skunks&p=awards&sub=ok&year=2003.

Guidici, Silvia (1988), 'Stricia la Notizia: Molto visto e poco studiatao', *Problemi dell'informazione*, 23(3), pp. 417–26.

Hallin, Daniel and Mancini, Paolo (1984), 'Speaking of the President: Political Structure and Representation Form in US and Italian Television News', *Theory and Society*, 13(6), pp. 829–50.

Hariman, Robert (2008), 'Political Parody and Public Culture', *Quarterly Journal of Speech*, 94(3), pp. 247–72.

Ibroscheva, E. and Raicheva-Stover, M. (2009), 'Development of Digital TV in Bulgaria: Opportunities and Problems', *International Journal of Communication*, 3, pp. 87–107.

International Research & Exchange Board (IREX) (2008), *Media Sustainability Index 2004: The Development of Sustainable Media in Europe and Eurasia*, http://www.irex.org/msi/index.asp. Accessed 25 November 2008.

Jones, Jeffrey (2007), 'Media and Restyling of Politics', in John Corner and Dick Pels (eds), *Political Communication*, 24(4), pp. 444–46.
Jost, Francois (2005), *Comprendre la télévision et ses programmes*, Paris: Armand Colin.
—— (2007), *La culte du banal*, Paris: Editions CNRS.
Karbovski, Martin (2008), '"*Gospodari Na Efira*" Took the Business Away from the Council of Electronic Media', *Standart* (national newspaper, Sofia, Bulgaria) 4 February.
Mascio, Antonella (2002), '*Striscia La Notizia*: Sotto Il Segno del Tapiro', in Ugo Volli (ed.), *Culti TV: Il Tubo Catodico e i Suoi Adepti,* Milano: Sperling & Kupfer.
New Dobrudja Tribune (2005), 'Who Got the Awards of the International Media Festival in Albena', Dobrich, Bulgaria, 6 June, http://www.ndt1.com/article.php/20040606144858140. Accessed 12 February 2009.
Open Society Institute (2005), 'TV Across Europe: Regulation, Policy and Independence – Bulgaria', http://www.mediapolicy.org/tv-across-europe/the-2005-television-across-europe-reports/television-across-europe-2005-2006-individual-country-reports-and-translations/media_bul1.pdf/views. Accessed 12 February 2009.
Padovani, Cinzia (2004), *A Fatal Attraction: Public Television and Politics in Italy*, Lanham, MD: Rowman and Littlefield.
Paterson R. and Smith (1998) A. *Television: An International History*, New York: Oxford University Press.
Ricci, Antonio (1998), *Striscia la Tivu,* Torino: Einaudi.
Roe, Amanda (2006), 'Television Satire, Democracy, and the Decay of Public Language: John Clarke's Verbal Caricature', *Media International Australia*, 121, pp. 93–104.
Spassov, O. (2008), 'Public Service Broadcasting in Bulgaria at the End of the Analog Age', in S. Miklos and A. Isanovic (eds), *Public Service Television in the Digital Age*, Sarajevo: Mediacenter.
Todorova, Dimitrina (2007), Interview with Judy Halvadzhian, June.
Tunstall, J. (2008), *The Media Were American: US Mass Media in Decline*, New York: Oxford University Press.
Wiese, Danielle R. (2005), 'Entertaining the Citizen: When Politics and Popular Culture Converge', *Argumentation and Advocacy*, 41(4), pp. 239–42.
Xiaoxia, Gao and Brewer, Paul R. (2008), 'Political Comedy Shows and Public Participation in Politics', *International Journal of Public Opinion Research*, 20(1), pp. 90–91.
Zolo, Danilo (1999), From Historic Compromise to Telecratic Compromise: Notes for a History of Political Communication in Italy Between the First and Second Republic', *Media, Culture & Society*, 21(6), pp. 727–41.

Part V

National Imaginings

Chapter 13

Defining the Local: A Comparative Study of News in Northern Ireland

Sujatha Sosale and Charles Munro

While the trend in global entertainment television points to localizing strategies, the popular view of television news often points to its globalizing power. Oft-quoted cases in this instance are CNN of the United States, the BBC of the United Kingdom and Al-Jazeera of Qatar, with such claims tied mainly to technology and global corporate power. The modern news format itself is globalized in many ways – with reference to broadcast news in particular, the limitations of time, the general structuring of the information in linear order because of the temporal structuring of broadcasting (countered to an extent with different kinds of information made available in banners and crawls, in addition to the voice that attempt non-linear forms of presentation), the importance of going 'live' on air and of course the overall professional ideology of news practices (Golding 1979) all, to a large extent, factors that define the broadcast news format everywhere. This is not to say that there are no attempts at alternate definitions of the news. At various times, scholars have debated various approaches to the news, such as Asian journalism (Gunaratne 1999), development journalism (Gunaratne 1998) and peace journalism (Tehranian 2002). These approaches describe an ethos and practice that are either adopted by or advised for regions (typically, countries in the global South) or are more normative and prescriptive for an era where, increasingly, news is defined almost exclusively by war and conflict.

However, in this study we suggest that, like entertainment television, the television news industry also adopts *localizing* strategies for a reason similar to that of entertainment television – to attract maximum viewership and survive competition – but does so in ways unique to the news format, process, practice and market, taking into consideration a host of contextual factors. To illustrate this phenomenon, we use the case of the global and national news giant that is at the same time a public broadcasting service – the BBC – in Northern Ireland, a territory of the United Kingdom. The efforts of the BBC to define the concept of local news in relation to its competitor UTV (formerly Ulster Television), a subsidiary of UK's ITV, gives us an opportunity to study organizational redefinitions of the idea of the 'local' in an era where, in many cases, the costs of news-gathering and news operations have actually proved to be more benign for national and global news, through subscriptions to packages offered by global news agencies.

This study seeks to answer the research question of how, in the Northern Ireland market, the BBC is positioning itself as the best source for 'local' news. Rather than studying the BBC alone in this region, we argue that we can understand its idea of the local more effectively by studying its organizational strategies against the backdrop of its competitor, UTV. The BBC and UTV are the dominant (Rolston and McLaughlin 2004) and competing news organizations in this area of the United Kingdom, and each works to distinguish itself as the primary local broadcast news entity for the Northern Ireland market. Both organizations compete to attract the largest possible audiences. In its 2007 report, the Office of Communications (Ofcom), Britain's commercial television regulation authority, noted that UTV had a 24 per cent audience share in this region compared with a nationwide ITV average of 20 per cent for regional programming, while the BBC had a 28 per cent audience share compared with its national average of 32 per cent for regional programming (Ofcom Communications Market Report 2007). Ofcom reports that UTV, across all programs, is the most popular television entity in Northern Ireland, with the BBC in second place. The BBC has historically served the larger political entity of the United Kingdom in its capacity as a public broadcasting service (Swales 1997). The BBC draws its revenue from the licensing fees paid by UK television viewers. In Northern Ireland, that includes viewers living within the nine most northerly counties in Ireland that constitute the national borders of the United Kingdom. Overall, as Hemmingway (2008) points out, the organization considers itself a leader in the broadcasting industry in all of the United Kingdom. Organizational planning and strategy documents of the past few years show that the BBC continues to take its role as a public service news provider seriously, and has renewed efforts to keep to its original and traditional mandates for serving local populations. Its recent efforts to define and intensify local news output in Northern Ireland are a response to the competitive presence of UTV. As part of ITV, which is also a UK institution, UTV is the dominant commercial broadcasting entity in Northern Ireland, and as such has the potential to draw advertising revenue from the regional market comprising Northern Ireland and the Republic of Ireland, which is geographically and politically differentiated from the United Kingdom.

This tension between the two broadcasters in the same market arises at least in part from the differences in the types of broadcast organizations – one (the BBC) a public service institution and the other (UTV) a commercial entity dependent on advertising revenue (Swales 1997). This tension carries significant implications for programming, content, promotion and marketing for both these organizations. But, surprisingly enough, upon examining prime-time evening news for both channels, and through his long-term association with the BBC, one of the co-authors of this chapter found that both the BBC and UTV geared their news towards Northern Ireland audiences. In other words, they shared the localizing ethos. Yet one of the two channels – UTV – had drawn larger audiences. As Rai and Cottle (2007) note in their study of the globalization of the 24-hour news concept, broadcasting is a 'numbers game', and the lead that UTV enjoys in this instance has been attributed to the time factor (another critical consideration for broadcasting). Its 6.00 p.m. weeknight news program *UTV Live* precedes the BBC's 6.30 p.m. news program *BBC Newsline*, and thus captures viewer attention in the first round of news for the evening. The BBC's challenge is to build a sense that it covers more local news to draw more viewers to its newscast that airs a little later in the evening. To better understand the dynamics of BBC's efforts to define local news, we examined a variety of sources and documents produced for and by the BBC and, for some comparison, we examined some UTV sources for information. The rationale for the choice of sources is provided in the details about the study in a separate section below. Our research contributes towards a contextualized understanding of the trend towards increasing localization in news broadcasting. In the context of all of Ireland, given certain factors like the cultural identity associated with language (see, for example, Northover and Donnelly 1996, who have described broadcasting efforts in the Irish language for both television stations, and related self-identification of audiences based on cultural considerations of language rather than citizenship in a particular country), localizing news format and content pertains more to the political territory of Northern Ireland. In other words, even though cultural affinities between the two Irelands may exist, local news geared to Northern Ireland highlights the complexities that need to be considered for understanding the localization efforts in the contemporary global era.

We begin the next segment of the chapter with background and context information within which to locate BBC Northern Ireland. This discussion enables us to place the BBC's efforts to localize news in Northern Ireland in the larger regional context. Even if audiences across the border in the Republic of Ireland are able to receive some BBC channels, the BBC's efforts are directed to localize within-border programming. Therefore, understanding the broadcasting environment within which the BBC operates in Northern Ireland is important. A discussion of some concepts and definitions relevant to the study – such as global, national, regional and local – follows. We then explain the methods and data sources we have used to answer the questions raised about the BBC's local television news programming efforts in the Northern Ireland context. We conclude the chapter with observations about the merging of the news format and news content in an effort to localize news.

The greater broadcasting environment for BBC Northern Ireland

The marketplace for broadcast news in the United Kingdom is dominated by two large media players, the British Broadcasting Corporation (BBC), a quasi-governmental body funded by a licence fee paid by viewers, and Independent Television (ITV), a confederation of publicly traded corporations regulated by a separate government body. Other companies, such as the national news provider Sky News, which is part of the multi-channel satellite-delivered pay television program service of British Sky Broadcasting, and independent producers provide news programming but on a limited scale compared with the BBC and ITV television channels (Küng-Shankleman 2000; Swales 1997).

While the BBC is chartered as a non-commercial 'public service broadcaster', it schedules its television news programs to compete for viewers with the commercially funded ITV. For example, both channels present their main news programs during peak news viewing times, weeknights between 6.00 and 7.00 p.m. and 10.00 and 10.40 p.m. As Küng-Shankleman (2000) has described in her comparative study of the BBC and CNN, the BBC has had to face increasing competition over the years from privately funded television. It has had to adapt, over time, its ethos of broadcasting as a public good to a private good, and has done so by adding a commercial component to its stable of channels, though the commercial channel ventures are not seen inside the United Kingdom; the BBC's commercial component is limited to overseas program sales (like BBC America in the United States), its publishing and DVD over-the-counter sales divisions. In the case of the *BBC Newsline* program in Northern Ireland, even though the program is part of the BBC's public service broadcasting, it has had to adopt marketing strategies to compete with UTV, such as marketing and brand positioning.

However, the two organizations differ in their approach to news content. At 6.00 p.m., the BBC presents world and national news while ITV is presenting local news from regional newsrooms around the United Kingdom. This would mean that UTV, the subsidiary of ITV in Northern Ireland, presents local news at this time. Half an hour later, the two organizations reverse the process for next 30 minutes: the BBC goes to its regional newsrooms and ITV devotes that time to presenting world and national news. For the 10.00 p.m. news, both begin with national news and cut away to their regions about half an hour later.

Ironically, it is the *local* news that most exposes the distinctive *national* identities. The United Kingdom is a country that recognizes four culturally based 'nations': England, Scotland, Wales and Northern Ireland. The BBC has structured its organization to provide local newsrooms in each of what it calls 'nations and regions' to respond to these national identities in its programming and news content. ITV similarly operates local newsrooms, though these are fewer in number than at the BBC (Munro 2008).[1]

Nowhere are the concepts of competition and national identity more apparent than in Northern Ireland, a UK province that exists on an island it shares with the Republic of Ireland to its south. There, BBC Northern Ireland and the ITV company UTV compete for viewers in a politically complex environment, one that has been marked by decades of civil unrest between two communities that are both culturally Irish, but with separate religious traditions. One community identifies itself as Protestant and affirms its allegiance to the nation of Northern Ireland (and thus to the United Kingdom) while the other, which is officially Roman Catholic, wants to eliminate the international border to its south to unite with the Republic of Ireland. Political parties represent these views in Northern Ireland. This all means that presenting local news in Northern Ireland requires carefully balancing political sensitivities. News coverage must be carefully edited so as not to incense one community over the other. A news editor in Northern Ireland must, among other things, be careful not to be perceived as *over*-covering news events in the Republic of Ireland (Munro 2008).

Understanding the 'local'

In contemporary parlance, we often encounter the term 'global' in relation to an idea of a planetary whole (e.g. Albrow 1997; Appadurai 1993). The term 'local' refers to specific, microcosmic places as opposed to the vast spaces suggested by the contemporary definitions of the global. This is especially apparent in today's networked global society, where information technologies encompassing satellite and Internet communications enable such talk about the idea of the global. Global media oligopolies manoeuvre technology and capital to direct flows of cultural goods worldwide. Travelling cultures, migratory and diasporic populations and other human and cultural factors contribute equally to the creation of a large, multi-continental idea of the global. Thus it is possible to conceptualize the global as something that involves crossing national borders. Expressed in this way, globalization is an old phenomenon – less intense in networking than it is at present, but nevertheless very much present in pre-Information Communication Technology (pre-ICT) societies (Germain 2000). O'Brien (1992) defines the term 'global' as that which involves the crossing of national borders, yet retains a sense of national boundaries. Explaining it in the context of financial globalization, he points out that national characteristics are integrated closely with the cross-border structure of organizations. Theoretically, the concept of the local is tied to a particular locale (Kraidy and Murphy 2008), typically situated within national borders. In the case of the BBC in Northern Ireland, its news and other programming can be, and are, received by citizens of the neighbouring country, the Republic of Ireland. But the BBC positions itself as a Northern Irish (and hence essentially UK) broadcasting entity serving local Northern Irish audiences.

It is interesting to note that the BBC uses the term 'nation' to refer to the Northern Irish territory, and also the term 'region' – as in 'regional broadcasting'. These terminologies require some unpacking. Historically, the BBC has used the term 'nation' in its deliberations to refer to its broadcasting territories of England, Scotland, Wales and Northern Ireland (Munro 2008). In its documents, the BBC refers to Northern Ireland as a *nation* (along with Wales and Scotland) and identifies *regions* within England. Here, the BBC's *nations* can be understood as areas within national borders, but the BBC does not ignore the national borders separating them (for example, the two Irelands might be considered a region in a geographical sense but they are distinct political entities – nations in that Northern Ireland is part of the United Kingdom, and also a cultural entity within the BBC's domestic broadcasting). Technology makes it possible to cast the latter definition of 'region' as a broadcasting market since programming can be viewed on both sides of the border, but political boundaries have constrained definitions to the former (i.e. within-nation). In this study, we use the terms 'local' and 'regional' interchangeably, especially the term 'regional' as it appears in the BBC documents. In relatively early discussions of global media, Sreberny-Mohammadi (1996) identified these levels of analysis and asked for a contextual understanding and interpretation of them to render the concepts useful for studying the media in any given case. This idea has been especially helpful for our study, where sorting out the terms 'global' (crossing national borders), 'national' (single over-arching political unit designating the country) and 'local' (connections to the more immediate environs, combining geography and citizenship) helps in examining the efforts of the BBC to define the idea of local news in the context of Northern Ireland, with a focus on the BBC Northern Ireland program *BBC Newsline*, the prime-time evening news broadcast.

Definitions of the local are important in this context because they constitute a part of what Corner (1995) terms the 'social character' of television and, particularly for this study, television news. Analyses of some BBC documents show the organization's interaction with and shaping of this social character in the process of addressing competition for its main evening news broadcasts in Northern Ireland. Britain's ITV (of which, as already mentioned, UTV is a part) was introduced in 1954 (Swales 1997), some time after the introduction of the BBC, and over time it presented a challenge to the BBC with its advertising-based approach to television in the United Kingdom. Even though ITV is founded on a different model, it has shared the struggles to define local programming (Swales 1997). In response to UTV's popularity in the area, the BBC renewed efforts to localize programming, perhaps also as a continuation of the successful localizing experiments in other areas in the United Kingdom carried out between December 2005 and August 2006, though the intention of the latter was to experiment with digital production of regional television news (Hemmingway 2008).

Given this background, our research questions are as follows:

1a. What discourse of the 'local' emerges from BBC's organizational efforts to attract viewers who are now watching the more popular UTV?
1b. How do governmental (such as the Agreement to the Charter and the Green Paper) and community documents (such as the White Paper) construct a sense of the 'local' for the BBC?
2. How does the BBC-related discourse stand against UTV's self-perception and rating as the principal local television station in the Northern Ireland region?

The term 'discourse' in the research questions refers to a general sense of talk and meaning about the concept of 'local' in organizational deliberations, and is not intended to be used in its strict methodological sense as employed in textual analysis. We examined various documents about, for and by the BBC to arrive at an understanding of its definition of 'local' news in the Northern Irish context. In places where comparisons help illustrate BBC Northern Ireland's conceptualization of local news, we have consulted some documents and the website for UTV, though we do not engage in an in-depth interpretive analysis of the latter.

The study

The current broadcast scenario in Northern Ireland presents a compelling case for studying the localization of news in organizations that are global and national news giants, like the BBC, and in a complex region that contains cross-border cultural affinities but within-border political citizenship, like Northern Ireland. The purpose of the study is to understand how the BBC constructs the idea of the 'local' for news produced for Northern Irish audiences.

In a broad sense, such a study of organizational endeavours involves a political economic approach that allows us to look at appeal to the audiences as a direct way of garnering market share in the region. The issue of power enters this picture when we consider the potential broadcast organizations have to reshape content to suit what they perceive to be audience interests. While this may seem nothing out of the ordinary, the ways in which the organizations have redefined their news mandates makes for informative study, and is instructive in demonstrating the daily operations of news producers in constructing what Hemmingway (2008: 13) calls the 'news episteme'.

In one of the few works explicitly engaging with research methodology in political economic approaches to studying media, Meehan and colleagues (1993) observe that political economy is more encompassing in its study of production, distribution and consumption of communication. Ideal though that would be, in order to maintain feasibility this study addresses mainly production, or rather organizational strategies that affect the production of news. This includes the plans of the organization for localizing news in new and unique ways that set it apart from its competitors.

Meehan et al. (1993) identify an 'institutional base' as a form of data, and we adopt this idea by looking at the efforts of the organization to define the idea of local. Some of our data come from official-legal-institutional documents about the BBC; data from BBC-generated documents give us an idea of the organizational deliberations about this concept and BBC publicity as manifested on the BBC website tells us how the BBC projects itself to the regional audience. The documents were selected based on one of the authors' experiences with the BBC for over a decade, and his assessment of what would be relevant to the study. Table 13.1 provides detailed information on the documents and the purpose behind their generation. Meehan et al. (1993) acknowledge the difficulties in gathering data for studies situated in the political economic domain of the media. However, one of the co-authors could indeed articulate these different strategies for defining the local in both broadcasting institutions – the BBC and UTV – because of an intensive program of work with one that entailed assessing the other as a competitor.

One other valuable source of evidence that Meehan et al. (1993: 113) identify has to do with 'reminiscences and popular insider stories', which they observe will 'provide illustrative anecdotes'. Though they refer to more popular (as in non-specialist) sources, for this study Munro's first-hand witnessing, participation and later recall of some of the discussions in the BBC have also proved helpful. While the author does not himself become a data source, his observations as a result of his more than decade-long association with the BBC in a consulting capacity appear throughout the chapter. Although not the same as proximate access (or direct observation), as established by Scott (1990) and recommended by Meehan et al. (1993) as good methodological practice for political economic approaches to studying the media, the co-author's presence during many of these discussions, and even help with drafting the localizing strategy, provide a fairly good representation of proximate access.

Table 13.1: Data sources*

	Document	Source	Purpose
BBC	1. BBC New Agreement to accompany the Charter 2006	1. Department for Culture, Media and Sport	1. Reassessment of BBC by government in preparation for Charter renewal.
	2. White Paper 2005	2. Northern Ireland Community Relations Council	2. Public feedback prior to Charter renewal in 2006. Channelled through this office. Document provided as part of the Charter Review's consultation, and submitted to the Department of Culture, Media and Sport.
	3. Response to the Charter around the time of renewal	3. BBC	3. Review of the Royal Charter by the BBC Board of Governors and statements about the role of the BBC and its funding.
	4. BBC Northern Ireland objectives 2001**	4. BBC document	4. Plan for renewed strategy for localization.
	5. BBC Strategic Marketing Plan, 2003**	5. BBC	5. Specific plans and approaches detailed for BBC's localization of *BBC Newsline*, its prime-time news program in Northern Ireland.
	6. BBC Northern Ireland website	6. BBC	6. BBC's information and publicity portal for Northern Ireland online
UTV	1. Ofcom May 2007 report for ITV	1. Ofcom	1. Performance review
	2. Ofcom Local Content Guidelines 2008	2. Ofcom	2. Guidelines for local content – radio
	3. UTV Media plc Preliminary Results 2007	3. UTV	3. Semi-annual report
	4. UTV website	4. UTV	4. UTV's information and publicity portal for NI online

* Data sources are not presented in chronological order, since a relatively new discourse of the local has been in progress for the last eight years or so and we have treated it as a discussion across the years rather than in any strict chronological order.
** Indicates BBC document with restricted access.
The rest are publicly available.

Some documents provided general and background information while others, such as the 2001 and 2003 BBC documents, focused on organizational strategies for local programming. Special permission was obtained to refer to these two documents in the study, though some details of marketing and other strategies have been omitted here in order to maintain confidentiality in those areas.

The renewed need for localism and the BBC brand

In 2001, Munro, then a consultant for the BBC, produced a document on the objectives for Northern Ireland, where the organization had concentrated its efforts on localizing evening news, but was still not in the lead (that position rested with UTV). The larger nationally competitive environment created by the BBC and ITV formed the backdrop for strategizing for a local thrust for the BBC in Northern Ireland. UTV's prime-time evening programming strategies – a half-hour program with local appeal starting at 5.30 p.m., to help garner local audiences, followed by the half-hour *UTV Live* news program at 6.00 p.m. – posed difficulty for *BBC Newsline*, starting at 6.30 p.m., to draw audiences since viewers would already have watched the news for the evening. It was agreed that the BBC would utilize audience research more closely, and review organizational issues that could possibly stand in the way of localizing efforts. A major thrust apparent in this document is the building of the BBC's evening news in Northern Ireland – *BBC Newsline* – as a local brand. The strategies to do so involved modifications to content, title and screen presence, and the development of an advertising campaign. Taking steps to match the competition, such as building anticipation for evening news in the afternoon news, as UTV was doing, was also considered. Reminders of the evening prime-time news during other news bulletins of the day – a practice employed by UTV – were recommended for the BBC as well, with specific strategies for inserting reminders in other BBC news programs preceding *BBC Newsline*.

The idea of the local emerges here from the ways in which the BBC sought to position itself against its competitor, as well as its efforts to make intrinsic definitional changes to its content. A host of content-related ideas to claim the local emerged from this document, including developing regular features of specific interest to its Northern Ireland viewers. Additionally, cross-media platforms were also considered for both content and promotion. Finally, the document recommended drawing upon the BBC's reputation as a provider of quality television, and suggested incorporating its established brand name presence (from presence at large to presence in local news in Northern Ireland) in the content. A similar emphasis on the BBC's long-standing reputation was advised for the advertising campaign.

A detailed marketing and programming plan was laid out in the 2003 Strategic Plan Document developed by the BBC and its consulting agency. This document also emphasized the importance of the BBC brand, since its established reputation could be leveraged for attracting local audiences for its evening news program. The document specified sources of news program content, analyzed the competition (UTV) and emphasized a cross-platform approach to advertising its motto in Northern Ireland that appears in its publicity in the area today: 'Live. Local. Listens.' The concatenation of these words suggests a responsive broadcasting presence in the heart of the community. From a content point of view, the plan included the task of communicating to the Northern Irish public the benefits to watching *BBC Newsline* by identifying features on a daily basis that would address this task. The strategic plan outlined ways to differentiate *BBC Newsline* from UTV's local evening news program, *UTV Live*. For example, by maintaining continuity in the content, the plan argues for a continued presence of the BBC brand in the local top-of-mind awareness. It also discusses publicity strategies across media.

As another marketing tool, the BBC's website shows that the BBC is investing heavily in the concept of localism, beginning with the integration of the word 'local' in its Universal Reference Locator. The home page contains a UK map, and links to view its prime-time evening news program in Northern Ireland, *BBC Newsline*. Northern Ireland is identified as a 'nation', a part of the nations and regions divisions of the BBC that are geographically as well as politically defined, but not in the sense of separate political entities such as the United Kingdom and the Republic of Ireland. Nevertheless, the strategy is clearly to identify and address local audiences. Clicking on an area of the United Kingdom map takes the reader to the local news of the region. Hence the idea of the local is integrated into the national picture of the BBC, and each 'nation' has a link to it that will take the reader from the national to the local page. The URL 'local' indicates that, even though the map in the home page is the United Kingdom, it is a platform for helping the reader to enter the local.

Localizing BBC news as a public service

The BBC operates under Royal Charter that is administered by the BBC Trust, which is renewed at ten-year intervals. The current Trust document became effective on 1 January 2007. It broadly defines the purpose of the BBC. The renewed need for local programming and content can be read in the New Agreement, a document 'complement[ing]' the BBC Charter in the following statement about what BBC programming should carry: 'content that reflects the lives of different peoples and different communities within the UK' (New Agreement 2006: 4). In the same section, the Agreement also reiterates catering to minority languages. These issues may relate to diversity, but to be able to appear as viable content, such programming would have to invest considerably in localization. The larger remit for the BBC to produce quality programming and operate as a public service is clearly articulated by the Charter. In certain segments, particularly the one on the Public Value Test, the audience pulse on matters is considered first, before raising the issue of revenue. This points to the general public service ethos of the BBC, which is arguably integral to localizing its service for communities in all regions of the United Kingdom. Regional (or, for our purposes, local) audiences are identified by the Agreement as those who live in Northern Ireland, Wales and Scotland.

From the point of view of the BBC's review of the Charter around the time if its renewal, all levels are encompassed in its articulation of its 'core purpose': building citizenship (national), serving the community (local), continuing as a global leader and 'building a digital Britain' (national) (BBC's Response 2005: 4). Largely, the Green Paper has concerned itself with digitizing British broadcasting, with the BBC seeing itself as the leader in this venture. The BBC's commitment to public service broadcasting is also apparent in its attempts to 'deliver value through clearly defined public purposes' (BBC's Response, 2005: 11, 12). It renews its promise to serve its 'nations, regions and communities', and the different audiences and diverse cultures that make up its viewership. Its pledge to pay attention to local audiences is apparent in such statements. It also promises to 'form a new relationship with audiences', thereby indicating its increased sensitivity to the local.

The White Paper (the BBC Charter Review 2004), authored by the Community Relations Council of Northern Ireland prior to the renewal of the BBC's charter, offers a third different view of what the 'local' content should be in BBC programming. The Council describes itself as a 'bridge' between different sectors of society, with its keywords being 'peace…inclusiveness…stability…and reconciliation'. The document identifies the BBC as one of the important social institutions whose objectives are seen to match those of the regional government's, especially on issues of race, equality and peace. Its concern for representing Northern Ireland in a peaceful light emerges clearly at the beginning of the document. Overall, it endorsed the BBC's quality programming in the area, and reiterates the importance of programming intended for local communities. Specifically, however, the Council's observations about the past 30 years of reporting strife and conflict in Northern Ireland reflect its concerns over the perception of Northern Ireland in the minds of the UK (and perhaps even Irish, since broadcasting signals are picked up on the other side of the border as well) public. This document represents the community's expectations of the BBC, and it sees the broadcasting organization as 'play[ing] a critical role in investigating and reporting the alternative Northern Ireland'. It envisages this alternative Northern Ireland as one where diversity is embraced, and cooperative ventures rather than strife are emphasized in local news coverage. The Council sees a role for the BBC's objective of 'sustaining citizenship and civil society' in conveying a positive picture of Northern Ireland. The document provides a blueprint from a community perspective for how the BBC should localize its programming. It advocates engagement with local communities and initiatives, to help present a picture of Northern Ireland today in all its cultural diversity and peaceful coexistence of the various groups and communities, and avoiding stereotypical portrayals of a conflict-ridden Northern Ireland. It calls for the BBC to 'lodge itself in the new articulation of diversity' (Northern Ireland Community Relations Council 2006: 2), demonstrating this at the operational levels by hiring more local producers for programs intended for local audiences. In fact, the Council calls for the BBC to educate Northern Irish populations on diversity, moving away from representations of strife and problems. As a community organization entrenched in local concerns, the Council concludes the report by offering to help the BBC in this mission.

The Council's emphasis on the portrayal of a positive image of the local that is different from BBC's deliberations about localizing its programming in the area is worth noting. Understandably, the BBC is interested in inserting its presence into the local content it creates, considering the competition it has to contend with for its *BBC Newsline* program. Its long-established reputation then becomes its added value (as a brand) to the local news programming. Of course, as other documents indicate, the BBC has also worked with content and format changes to localize news in the region, besides marketing itself as a brand. The concerns of BBC Northern Ireland have not extended to or addressed the kinds of representations and portrayals involved, but rather a strong presence in the local happenings, by reporting them in a prompt and thorough manner. The Council takes a different approach, in that it calls for a re-tooling of the image of Northern Ireland for local (and presumably non-local) audiences. Such a re-tooling and communication of an 'alternative Northern Ireland' can be achieved, in the Council's collective opinion, through important institutions like the BBC. Accordingly, the White Paper calls for inserting the local in BBC programming (which suggests a different approach from the BBC's efforts to insert itself as a brand into local news programming), thereby implying that the BBC has to change its approach to local newsworthy events at times.

UTV's 'local'

Writing about the elections in 1997, Finlayson observed that Northern Ireland was treated as a periphery of the United Kingdom, and that BBC's coverage of election news in Northern Ireland at the time was more English in its approach. The article does not discuss UTV's parallel approach to the same election, but Finlayson's (1997) analysis, coupled with UTV's rating as the dominant television broadcaster in the region, hints at the magnitude of the competition with which the BBC has to contend in establishing its regional presence in Northern Ireland. UTV, originally incorporated as Ulster Television, has served the Northern Irish region for about half a century. It holds the independent television licence for Northern Ireland. On its website, UTV positions itself as the first 'indigenous broadcaster' in Ireland, now enjoying the larger market share in Northern Ireland (http://www.u.tv). Ofcom regulates UTV, but does not regulate its investments. As a commercial media concern, UTV has invested heavily in media properties, mainly radio, across the border in the Republic of Ireland. With salespeople also located in the Republic, UTV can claim a pan-Irish ownership of sorts (Munro 2008). But UTV's website makes its position in relation to the BBC clear:

> *Domestic* programmes are at the heart of this competitive strength and for this reason most are scheduled in peak viewing times. During the year they consistently attract large audiences and further extend the already substantial lead on the main competition. (http://www.utvmedia.com/television.asp?sub=au&sublk=cst&fursublk=tele; emphasis added, with 'domestic' referring to Northern Ireland)

In a recent report on local content guidelines for radio broadcasting issued by Ofcom (2008), there is a reference to 'substantial deregulation' that hints at more diverse revenue sources for UTV. In other words, it has the effect of allowing UTV to provide less UK content. This deregulatory move, though appearing in a document pertaining to radio broadcasting, frees UTV from strict requirements to provide local content and in some senses allows it to increase cross-border content. Ofcom's periodic reminders of UTV's remit to respond to local/regional needs in Northern Ireland, coupled with the deregulation, allows for some interpretation of the term 'regional' as a cross-border sense idea, and could be interpreted as allowing a different construction of the 'local' in local news and programming. Revenue sources make it necessary for UTV to cater to the audiences across the border as well. Ofcom terms its deregulatory move as a 'need for flexibility in difficult times'. The new deregulation and its effects are worth pursuing in future studies.

However, it is important to note that audience analyses for the news programs show that UTV concentrates on highly localized news content for Northern Ireland and, as mentioned in the introduction to this chapter, is the leader in overall programming in that region. UTV regards itself as a strong UK (and not Irish) company, in spite of its cross-border interests. Its prime-time evening news program is the competition that the BBC is trying to beat. This is partly due to the time of broadcast, as discussed in an earlier section, but also its campaign as an indigenous broadcaster with strong roots in Northern Ireland.

Thus UTV sees itself as a local television service provider, integrated into the community, whereas the BBC is a national (and international) broadcasting organization with a reputable brand name that it is using to garner local UTV audiences in Northern Ireland. The BBC's response to the Green Paper is a contrast to its marketing strategies for *BBC Newsline*. As a public service broadcaster, its response to the government during charter renewal expresses a clear commitment to what it sees as its institutional responsibilities towards local communities, the nation and the world. However, in its more micro, local operations, it has had to act as a commercial concern with an eye on marketing and branding, even if its revenue sources do not come from advertising.

Conclusion

The BBC and UTV share common ground in many respects. They are leading competitors in the Northern Irish region. Both organizations broadcast in the local language also and, unlike the press which is divided along religious lines in the area, BBC and UTV address all audiences (Munro 2008). The broadcasting organizations respond to what they perceive as 'local' needs (already existing), and their efforts to define these for their news operations are in turn shaping that market. This symbiosis appears on both television and radio.

The market struggles between the BBC and UTV make for an interesting case study. The BBC is a historically established broadcast giant known for its demands on quality, and the younger UTV, a subsidiary of ITV – equally regulated for quality – has to take a more commercial approach, and has the freedom to appeal to audiences without having to resort too much to mandates and remits beyond Ofcom's criteria for serving the local population. Definitions of 'local' for BBC pertain mainly to within the United Kingdom and, more closely, within Northern Ireland territories. The BBC's strategies for cutting into the competition for evening news programming involve a rethinking of both its format and content. Moran (2004: 5) provides some definitions for television format. The first refers to 'a set of invariable elements in a programme', which are then combined in various ways to produce an episode, while a second refers to consistent ways of organizing a single episode. In the case of *BBC Newsline*, both definitions are present in the planning and strategy documents. Attention to content does not appear at the expense of attention to format. The two work simultaneously to define individual newscasts as well as their overall approach to newscasts in the region.

Acknowledgement

The authors would like to thank the School of Journalism and Mass Communication, International Programs, and the Stanley-UI Support Organization, The University of Iowa, for providing travel funds to enable presentation of an early version of this chapter at the 2008 Conference of the International Association for Media and Communication Research, Stockholm University, Stockholm, Sweden.

Note

1. This citation refers to observations of co-author Charles Munro as a long-term consultant to BBC Northern Ireland. Material drawn from his experiences in this chapter have been cited as such.

References

Albrow, M. (1997), *The Global Age*, Stanford, CA: Stanford University Press.

Appadurai, A. (1990), 'Disjuncture and Difference in the Global Cultural Economy', *Public Culture*, 2(3), pp. 1–23.

British Broadcasting Corporation (BBC), website, http://www.bbc.co.uk/local. Accessed 10 October 2008.

BBC's Response to the Green Paper (2006), http://www.bbc.co.uk/info/policies/text/green_paper_response.html. Accessed 9 November 2008.

Community Relations Council (2006), *BBC White Paper*, Belfast, Northern Ireland. http://www.community-relations.org.uk. Accessed 11 June 2009.

Corner, J. (1995), *Television Form and Public Address*, London: Edward Arnold.

Finlayson, P. (1997), 'The Broadcast Media in Northern Ireland', *Historical Journal of Film, Radio and Television*, 17(4), pp. 477–80.

Germain, R. (2000), 'Globalization in Historical Perspective', in R. Germain (ed.), *Globalization and Its Critics: Perspectives from Political Economy*, London: Macmillan, pp. 67–90.
Golding, P. (1979), 'Media Professionalism in the Third World: Transfer of an Ideology', in J. Curran, M. Gurevitch and J. Woollacot (eds), *Mass Communication and Society*, Beverly Hills, CA: Sage, pp. 291–308.
Hemmingway, E. (2008), *Into the Newsroom: Exploring the Digital Production of Regional Television News*, London: Routledge.
Gunaratne, S. (1998), 'Old Wine in a New Bottle: Public Journalism, Developmental Journalism, and Social Responsibility', in M.E. Roloff (ed.), *Communication Yearbook 21,* Thousand Oaks, CA: Sage.
—— (1999), 'The Media in Asia', *International Communication Gazette*, 61(3–4), pp. 197–223.
Kraidy, M. and Murphy, P. (2008), 'Shifting Geertz: Toward a Theory of Translocalism in Global Communication Studies', *Communication Theory*, 18(3), pp. 335–55.
Küng-Shankleman, L. (2000), *Inside the BBC and CNN: Managing Media Organizations*, London: Routledge.
Meehan, E., Mosco, V. and Wasko, J. (1993), 'Rethinking Political Economy: Change and Continuity', *Journal of Communication*, 43(4), pp. 105–15.
Moran, A. (2004), 'Television Formats in the World/the World of Television Formats', in A. Moran and M. Keane (eds), *Television Across Asia*, London: Curzon, pp. 1–8.
Northern Ireland Community Relations Council (2006), *BBC Charter White Paper*, http://www.community-relations.org.uk/filestore/documents/BBC-Charter_Review_White_Paper-Final_April06.pdf. Accessed 9 November 2008.
Northover, M. and Donnelly, S. (1996), 'A Future for English/Irish Bilingualism in Northern Ireland?', *Journal of Multilingual and Multicultural Development*, 17(11), pp. 33–47.
O'Brien, R. (1992), *Global Financial Integration: The End of Geography*, London: Pinter.
Ofcom (2007), May Report, http://www.ofcom.org.uk/research/cm/cm07/uk. Accessed 9 November 2008.
—— (2008), *Local Content Guidelines*, http://www.reuters.com/article/pressRelease/idUS92778+07-Feb-2008+RNS20080207. Accessed 9 November 2008.
Rai, M. and Cottle. S. (2007), 'Global Mediations: On the Changing Ecology of Satellite Television News', *Global Media and Communication*, 3(1), pp. 51–78.
Rolston, B. and McLaughlin, G. (2004), 'All News is Local: Covering the War in Iraq in Northern Ireland's Daily Newspapers', *Journalism Studies*, 5(2), pp. 191–202.
Scott, J. (1990), *A Matter of Record: Documentary Sources in Social Research*, Cambridge: Polity Press.
Sreberny-Mohammadi, A. (1996), 'The Global and the Local in International Communication', in J. Curran and M. Gurevitch (eds), *Mass Media and Society*, London: Arnold, pp. 119–38.
Swales, V. (1997), 'Television in the United Kingdom', in J.A. Coleman and B. Rollet (eds), *Television in Europe*, Exeter: Intellect, pp. 21–34.
Tehranian, M. (2002), 'Peace Journalism', *The Harvard International Journal of Press/Politics*, 7(2), pp. 58–83.
UTV (2008), http://www.utvmedia.com/television.asp?sub=au&sublk=cst&fursublk=tele. Accessed 31 May 2008.
UTV Media (2007), 'Preliminary Results', http://www.utvmedia.com/reports.asp?sub=iv&sublk=rpt&rept_id=33. Accessed 9 November 2008.

Chapter 14

Independent Television Production, TV Formats and Media Diversity in China

Michael Keane and Bonnie Liu

The content conundrum

China is facing unprecedented challenges to how it restructures and manages its television industries. Until now, two overriding themes have organized media research on China: first, transnational media companies' aspirations to break into the Chinese market; and second, the seemingly unwavering control of information by the Chinese Propaganda Department. In recent years, however, the TV production landscape in the PRC has changed dramatically. More satellite channels are available to the viewer as provincial broadcasters seek to branch out and establish their position in relation to the national broadcaster China Central Television (CCTV). Greater consumer choice is, in turn, driving producers to look for new ideas, as well as older ideas that can be reformatted to fill an expanding content vacuum. The advent of digital TV is adding to the content conundrum. Although TV serial drama remains dominant, reality TV and infotainment programming are seen as easy ways to produce TV that is cheaper and has less risk attached. The problem, however, is that much of the current output is of variable quality.

In this emerging post-broadcasting environment, a proliferation of independent companies has emerged, all jockeying for a position in the rapidly forming TV market. In many instances, these production companies are operating with greater degrees of flexibility than was allowed over the past few decades, when production units were linked directly with television stations. In this regard, old relationships and structures are changing. A different kind of analysis is therefore needed.

In this chapter, we provide some background to the formatting of TV in China. We compare the business models of independent format producers in open media systems with the more restricted operational practices of the Chinese TV industry. The chapter begins with a snapshot of the format model. It then looks at the first instances of formatting in China, which were largely cases of program cloning. Two phases of appropriation are evident. In the first, Chinese stations took key elements from neighbouring television systems; in the second, Chinese TV producers borrowed heavily from international hit programs such as *Who Wants to Be a Millionaire?*, *Idol* and *Dancing with the Stars*. For emerging television companies in China, both the bottom line and the need to avoid risk are very important. Moreover, because the concept of copyright is undeveloped in China, revenue-sharing between the broadcaster and producer is negotiated differently. In examining these developments, we show how China's television producers have begun to understand the reality of the post-broadcasting world. What we notice, moreover, is a flow of program ideas rather than a flow of program licences. In very few instances, broadcasters have taken the format licensing option, and where this has occurred there has usually been an existing relationship of cooperation.

The format option

Albert Moran's seminal work over the past decade has established the field of TV format research (Moran 1998, 2005; Moran and Malbon 2006). In recent years this research has begun to address the spread of international formats in Asia (Moran & Keane 2004; Keane et al. 2007; Keane and Moran 2004; Moran and Keane 2008; Keane 2007; Fung 2004). Aside from this work, however, very little material exists in English in relation to formats in China. Likewise, the topic has received limited scholarly attention in China, where the topics of reality TV and program cloning both generate mixed reactions (Xie and Chen 2007; Yin et al. 2006).

It is unclear why this field has not generated more attention in China. One argument is that the concept of the traded format is unsuited to an environment where intellectual property rights are not well understood. Certainly there is a suspicion among many observers of China's media that the structure of the system does not encourage a rights-based trading system. Local producers are unable to incubate, test and finance program ideas in the same way that international media companies do. This means that original content which might attract market attention is less likely to emerge. The alternative option is to borrow and copy ideas.

In China, we observe the practice of formatting but it is rare to find a systematic process whereby an original idea is devised and progressively matured into a TV program. While the 'pie and crust' metaphor (Moran 1998) implies that formatting is basically a matter of providing local filling, in reality the process is more complex. For instance, whereas the conventional TV program industry follows a generic three-stage process (pre-production, production and post-production), the format moves through a comparable process of trailling, testing and refining. It also entails a complex process of distribution and licence negotiation across different cultural zones and markets (Moran and Malbon 2006). As Moran and Malbon (2006: 67) note, 'rights are attached to various elements, territories, production obligations and time deals'. In addition, because many formats are reality based, there is frequently a necessity to negotiate revenue-sharing between the licence-owner and the broadcaster, together with various players such as telecommunication and media companies that provide ancillary services for the promotion of branded content.

In examining the flow of content within and across television systems in China, we note two sides to formatting: the first is often conveniently expressed as localization or 'glocalization' (see Robertson 1992) – that is, the global or regional (Asian) content adapts to norms or responds to 'local' values. In other words, the pie looks similar but has different ingredients. Such filling is a means to distance the product from its origins, enough to avoid charges of copyright violation. An example would be the adaptation in July 2002 of *Who Wants to Be a Millionaire?* into China as *The Dictionary of Happiness* (CCTV2). The program was a copy of the Celador original, but it was modified just enough to avoid the international 'format police' (Keane et al. 2007). Another example is the Chinese variety infotainment show *Zhengda zongyi*, which began broadcasting in April 1990 on CCTV. For many years the show was China's window on the world; its youthful and energetic reporters visited many countries and demonstrated a variety of customs and traditions. By the end of the decade, the show's producers were attempting to radically reshape its appeal; in one revamp, this show morphed into a direct copy of the UK game show format *Dog Eat Dog*, in which a group of contestants engage in an elimination competition showcasing a variety of skill sets. After being 'contacted' by FRAPA on behalf of the format owners, the producers introduced a series of further localizations, reinserting elements of the original format (Keane et al. 2007).

The second instance of formatting is where transnational media companies localize a format as a strategy for gaining entry into the national market. This is an important consideration for two reasons. Much media research on China has suggested that Chinese television is threatened by globalization. In this field of critical inquiry, finished programs are exported to China. However, there is very little evidence to suggest that Western programs appeal to Chinese viewers. The programs that are broadcast on television channels are often B-grade movies, which are dubbed by Chinese professionals. Nor is there any evidence to suggest that international Chinese channels such as Star TV's xingkong weishi, partly owned by Rupert Murdoch's News Corporation, have succeeded with their Western-flavoured formats. Nowadays, the schedules of xingkong weishi are dominated by Korean dramas and Taiwanese entertainment shows.

Development of formats in China

Before we analyze examples of formatting in China and the business models of China's domestic production companies, it is worth briefly sketching out the relationship between the Chinese state-owned media and the people who provide creative and technical services – that is, writers, producers, actors and directors. From its inception in 1958, television was part of the state's ideological machinery. Of course, China was a typical authoritarian state until 1978 and the media were central to maintaining the hegemony of the Chinese Communist Party. Even after China adopted its wide-ranging economic reforms in the 1980s television remained state owned and heavily monitored by the Chinese Propaganda Department.

By the mid-1980s, investment in content production began to come from non-state agencies and advertisers as more channels were opened. But television remained essentially a public institution (*shiye*) not a commercial enterprise (*chanye*). This can be seen in the mode of production. From 1958 until the early 1990s, all television programs – television serial dramas, documentaries and entertainment genres – were made by professionals in dedicated production units within television stations – for instance, Beijing TV had its own TV drama production unit, its own variety show unit, and so on. The home broadcaster would screen first and then the program might be exchanged with other stations. In this model, there was no effective trading of rights and no syndication of programming. However, the lack of a trading system had another side: it encouraged the copying of formats (even though the idea of a format was seldom used). For example, if station A made a successful program, station B would follow suit. This was not seen as anti-competitive, but rather the preferred approach to programming. It was also a 'safety first approach'.

In recent years, television has gradually reformed from public institution to industry. China joined the WTO in 2001, and this further stimulated the reform and commercialization of the media. In turn, more independent companies formed, offering a range of services related to content production, advertising and distribution. At the same time, the number of TV stations began to shrink as media conglomerates formed. Provincial and city-level TV stations began to believe they could contend with the power of the national broadcaster, CCTV. The emergence of satellite TV channels in particular has enabled provincial television networks – many of which formed into conglomerates – to aspire to national reach. In order for this aspiration to succeed, however, the challenge is to produce compelling tradable content. Each provincial network is allowed one satellite television channel, and invariably it is these channels that prove to be the most innovative. Perhaps the most well known is Hunan Satellite TV, which will figure in the discussion of TV formats below.

Independent production in China

Globally, TV format production follows a 'publishing model', in which production is sub-contracted out to independent companies. Independent companies have taken the lead in defining the international TV format market. The trend towards independent production began with US network television during the 1950s. The studio system was reorganized, allowing production to be 'outsourced' to independent producers. The shift to independent TV production occurred later in Europe, but its eventual advent was noteworthy. The establishment of Channel 4 in the United Kingdom in the early 1980s was the catalyst for change. In Western Europe, the privatization of public channels and the licensing of new commercial channels during the 1990s promoted the role of independent producers. It is not altogether coincidental, therefore, that independent television format production emerged from this region. In East Asia, independent production occurred much later, due to the nature of the market and a propensity on the part of governments to regulate control of content by opting to deal with broadcasters. In Hong Kong, domestic programming was produced within TVB and ATV. As Anthony Fung (2004) notes, it has really only been in the past few years that the outsourcing model has come into practice. In Mainland China, independent production companies are a recent occurrence and have moved quickly into making television formats.

In China, there are currently three models of program production. The first is a legacy of the state-controlled media system where the program (TV serial, variety show, documentary, etc.) was produced in the television studio. As mentioned above, each TV station has its own production units. In particular, news programs that include political discussion are kept in-house. Following the maturation of the industry, under the second model the program is devised and produced by independent companies. China's national broadcaster, which once used to produce everything in-house, now cooperates with independent companies. For instance, one of CCTV's brand shows, *Lucky 52* (*xingyan 52*), is produced by an 'independent', the Qixinran company. The third model involves the program being devised and produced with no direct links to a broadcaster. In return for the content, the broadcaster trades a small amount of time to the independent companies. The independent companies provide the program content for the broadcaster and they stand to gain financially from using the advertising time to attract sponsors. Some channels have traded substantial channel time to independent companies, such as Hainan's Travel Channel and Beijing TV's Life Channel.

From the three production models, we note that TV formats in China – as elsewhere – rely on independent companies. However, we should be clear that the term 'independent' in the Chinese media landscape does not equate with the autonomous independent company in democratic media systems. The Chinese independent company remains quite conservative, aware that any discretion will result in the suspension of its production licence. Nevertheless, while most independent companies still adapt rather than pay for the rights to overseas TV formats, the resulting localization does provide an injection of diversity into the Chinese media ecology. In addition, the presence of independent producers has provided a platform for provincial TV broadcasters to compete with CCTV. Among them, Hunan TV and Shanghai Oriental TV have taken the lead in TV format innovation.

Several reality-based genres have increased the awareness of formats in China over the past decade. The first category to be widely imitated was the romantic liaison genre, often referred to internationally as the dating show. While not falling under the strict generic classification of a quiz or game show, these shows increasingly incorporate elements of reality formats. The Taiwanese program *Special Man and Woman* (*feichang nannü*), distributed by Phoenix Television (Hong Kong), was the first dating program to be broadcast in China. First shown in China in July 1997, *Special Man and Woman* was quickly followed by a mainland copy, *Romantic Meeting* (*meigui zhi yue*),[1] produced by Hunan Satellite TV. However, both these programs are an example of travelling formats. The group-date format had originated in Japan in December 1975 on NET (now ANB) on a program called *Propose Dai-Sakusen*.[2]

Hunan Satellite TV's version of screen dating mimicked the Taiwanese original, although it did exhibit some 'cultural' differences. According to one critique of the two shows, *Romantic Meeting* was more down-market and frivolous than the Taiwanese original, with the 'unsophisticated' Mainland contestants engaging in more banter and blatant self-promotion than their Taiwanese counterparts. The author attributed this difference to the fact that Taiwanese people subscribe to a more ethical code of self-presentation based upon Confucian principles (Ye 2000). The TV dating craze of the late 1990s subsequently disappeared as the Internet took over as the principal screen matchmaker.

By the early 2000s, the reality show had found its way into the lexicon of Chinese media studies (Ma 2001; Li 2002; Yin et al. 2006; see also Li 2008).[3] The Chinese nomenclature for reality television is literally 'real people show' (*zhenren xiu*). However, as elsewhere in the global television environment, the Chinese reality television 'show' is a descendant of the documentary form. The documentary was the staple of Chinese broadcasting throughout the development of Chinese television. Its form was propagandistic and its ubiquity ensured that reception was bound to suffer when confronted by the emergence of infotainment genres. Documentary was left with no alternative but to redefine its relationship with the viewer or be banished to rarely viewed timeslots and channels.

The first reality show to be screened in China was called *The Great Survival Challenge (Shengcun da tiaozhan)* (Guangdong TV). It set a precedent by incorporating ideas from international reality game shows like *Survivor* – albeit without the elimination of the weakest. The concept for the show was initially conceived as a summer holiday program targeted at young adults. A camera followed an outdoor survival challenge in the vicinity of Guangdong province. The show was subsequently expanded to a more ambitious survival challenge – following the route of the Chinese Long March (1940s) along the border regions and up into north China. The participants traced the footsteps of communist heroes such as Mao Zedong, Deng Xiaoping and Zhou Enlai. Not unsurprisingly, this political re-enactment failed to inspire the imagination of Guangdong viewers. The following season saw the *Great Survival Challenge* duly presented as an all-female survival affair. Images of young women revealing their fantasies of success and scrambling up coconut trees soon inspired another ambitious wave of reality television. *Into Shangrila (Zouru xiangelila)* was produced by a documentary filmmaker, Chen Qiang, whose previous work had included a 1990 documentary ode to the Yellow River. Two teams of young Chinese were drawn from eighteen different provinces and 30 cities. In many respects, the show was a Chinese *Survivor* minus the excessive individualism and conniving that seems to attract US audiences. Whereas the foreign *Survivor* promised the winner the mother of all prizes, the participants in *Into Shangrila* were rewarded by the glory of being seen on television.

By 2004, the success of reality TV and quiz formats such as CCTV's *Dictionary of Happiness*, a copy of Celador's *Who Wants to Be a Millionaire?*, had had shown that Western formats could take root in China with careful localization. Better still, there was little need to pay the licence fee if you were able to claim local characteristics. From the beginning of that year, a number of shows featuring amateur singing stars featured heavily on Chinese screens. The talent tsunami, as it would become, had a lot to do with the international success of the *Idol* format, which originated in the United Kingdom before climaxing in *American Idol*. Franchised copies and spinoffs had appeared in Australia, Canada and Malaysia. In reality, these shows were refashioning a format that had long featured on television in East Asia. TTV's *Five Star Prize* (*wu deng jiang*) had run for 33 years in Taiwan from 1965 to 1998, and had produced several superstars, including Jacky Wu (Wu Zong-Xian) and A Mei

(Chang Hui-Mei). In 1997, two programs appeared in Taiwan that anticipated the arrival of the global *Idol* format: they were *Super New Idol* (*chaoji xin renwang*) (ETTV) and *The Great New Singing Competition* (*xinren gechang dasai*) (San Li TV). In 1998, MTV introduced *The New Karaoke Station* (*xinsheng kawei zhan*), a singing competition with contestants from all over Asia. In 2004, the program *Super New Idol* received a new lease of life due to the global popularity of the *American Idol* format, which was televised in Taiwan.

On the Mainland, Hunan Satellite TV's *Super Girl* was the market leader. Like other Hunan hit shows, it was a calculated approximation of foreign successes. It emulated ITV's *Pop Idol* (UK) and *American Idol* (Fox Network USA). *Super Girl* quickly became a phenomenon in Mainland China, attracting the attention of cultural and industry critics who proclaimed a new stage of development in TV culture. According to some critics, the success factors of *Super Girl* indicated a road ahead for entertainment programs. Three success factors, in particular, were advanced in support of the format: the ordinary nature of the entertainers, simple sets and interactivity. In particular, the so-called non-elite (*pingmin*) character of the show confirmed the universal aesthetic that resonates with a previous era of unadorned fame: there is no dazzling stage, participants audition without a musical track, and they face a highly critical and even satirical jury. Audiences then vote for their favoured participants; the rest are eliminated and end up either as blooper material or 'worst of' out-takes that contrast with the careful grooming of the new idols.

The future of formats post-*Super Girl*

Following *Super Girl*'s breakout success in 2004, talent shows began to occupy prime time. Shanghai Oriental TV, which – along with the Hunan Media Group – recognized the advantages of formatting, produced two talent show versions called *Go! Good Boy* (*jiayou haonaner*) and *My Style! My Show!* (*woxing woxiu*). Not to be outdone, CCTV produced *Special 6+1 (feichang 6+1)/Dream China* (*mengxiang Zhongguo*), which was presented as a more appropriate civilized model of identifying emerging homegrown talent. The producers of CCTV's *Special 6+1/Dream China* saw HSTV's *Super Girl* as an upstart challenger that needed to be given a lesson. However, *Super Girl* was already the preferred brand, thanks to Hunan Satellite TV channel's extensive distribution; meanwhile, the audience figures were drawing extensive revenue. The answer was to bring in some big guns. On 24 July 2005, Alan Tam, the renowned Hong Kong singer, and Hacken Lee, one of the presenters of a Hong Kong talent show *Minutes to Fame,* known for its inane proceedings, appeared on *Dream China.* The guest appearance temporarily changed the language of the show from official Mandarin to non-official Cantonese, and the character from formal to fun. Despite the fact that the producers of *Special 6+1/Dream China* repeatedly emphasized a rejection of inanity, the hybrid phenomenon only confirmed that CCTV's serious format was undermined by *Super Girl* (*Beijing Morning Post*, 26 July 2005; see Keane et al. 2007).

By 2006, the *Super Girl* effect had produced an array of imitators. More channels were showing similar shows in prime time and audiences were expressing dissatisfaction with the never-ending parade of performing boy/girl talent. Out of all these talent shows, only Hunan STV's *Mingsheng Dazheng* took the formal road, buying the licence for *Just the Two of Us* from the BBC (Kong 2007). According to one report, the station had outlaid RMB1 million (Kang et al. 2006). While most talent shows were relatively risk averse, one show called *The First Touched* (*diyici xindong*) by Chongqing Satellite TV itself touched a nerve by serving up what the State Administration of Radio, Film and Television (SARFT) deemed low quality. The result was immediate. Not only was this program banned by SARFT, but all 'live' talent shows were subsequently regulated. The regulations took aim at the selection progress for participants, restricting the time to two and a half months. Furthermore, talent shows were not allowed to be broadcast during prime time, all contestants had to be over eighteen years old, and the hosts were barred from using certain kinds of language in the program. For example, trendy and seemingly salacious terms of address like 'sister' or 'brother' were no longer condoned among hosts, panel members and contestants; in addition, hosts and panel members were prohibited from engaging in banter and what might be deemed flirtatious behaviour.

Whether it was the effect of this government crackdown or simply that audiences had tired of the parade of similar 'wanna bes', the result was a waning of the fortunes of such amateur talent shows. In place of the amateur talent format came the dancing show. This first appeared on Fujian South-East STV in the form of a program called *Celebrities Moving With Dance* (*xingsui wudong*). However, the popularity of the dancing show peaked with Shanghai Oriental STV's *Dancing Party* (*wulin dahui*). The audience share achieved by this program nationally in 2006 reached 16 per cent (CSM Statistics).[4] The success of *Dancing Party* was reminiscent of the *Super Girl* phenomenon. The parent broadcaster, Shanghai Media Group (SMG), admitted that it had 'borrowed' the idea from *Dancing with the Stars* (ABC-US), but pointed out that it had 'localized' the idea by introducing different rules. The financial benefits were immediate. The associate director of the entertainment program department in SMG revealed that the group had recouped RMB20 million for the naming rights from a web company called JiuYou, whose business focuses on online game, music and other entertainment areas (Lu 2006),[5] while the allocated nineteen minutes of advertising time sold out even before the program was broadcast (Guo 2006). Well-known celebrities were invited from Hong Kong and the program became popular in South-Eastern Asian countries. Another celebrated dancing show is the licensed version of *Dancing with the Stars*, purchased by Zhejiang STV. However, it seems its success is mostly due to its being a franchise of the original version and a corresponding announcement by the independent television company, Beijing Shixi Media Company, condemning Shanghai's *Dancing Party*. This independent claimed it had spent a considerable amount of money to purchase the licence of the original program *Strictly Come Dancing* from the BBC (Guo 2006). Despite this, Shanghai Oriental TV's *Dancing Party* remained the audience favourite.

By 2008, it was suddenly 'back to the future'. Chinese TV screens were full of a new kind of reality show: karaoke. The idea here varied from testing memory of lyrics to testing the singer's pitch and tone. By the end of the year, nine different karaoke programs had appeared on six different channels. Zhejiang STV broadcast three while Hunan STV produced two programs. Zhejiang Satellite TV's *I Love Remembering Lyrics* (*wo ai ji geci*) was the first to offer this competition; this was soon followed by Guangdong Satellite TV's *Keep Singing Tonight* (*jinye chang bu ting*). However, the former soon became the most popular and was even exported to South-East Asia. Malaysian WaTV reportedly bought the program from Zhejiang STV at a cost of US$1,000 per episode (Li 2008). In a short space of time, Hunan STV and Jiangsu STV followed with the aptly named *Duelling Microphones* (*tiaozhan maikefeng*) and *Who Dares Sings (shui gan lai changge)*. Such programs bear a close resemblance to overseas formats; in particular, *I Love Remembering Lyrics* is a composite of NBC's *The Singing Bee* and Fox Broadcasting's *Don't Forget the Lyrics*, while *Duelling Microphones* and *Who Dares Sings* borrowed ideas directly from ITV's *Who Dares Sings*. In the case of the latter, there was some formal connection, with the producer acquiring software from ITV for testing the singing tones.

Concluding remarks: Hunan leads the way again

The formation of independent TV companies in China has witnessed a greater degree of diversity in programming. A number of these companies have opted to become involved in formatted TV, sometimes by making their own original content, sometimes by making an international format, but more often by just producing a copied show. In comparison to the international practice whereby broadcast rights are shared between the format devisor/owner and the producer (often the same entity), in China this rarely occurs. While an independent company may generate a format, the company invariably is allocated broadcast time rather than rights payment to exploit its property. Where the company simply makes the program based on an international version, the business model is similar. However, there are other ancillary rights and fees that the production company can receive, such as a share of revenue from sales of branded content and a share in the SMS revenue generated from audience votes. In addition, where the company has a stake in the talent, they may sometimes generate income from concert and public appearances.

The future of formatting may well hinge on how the industry matures, and particularly how effectively satellite broadcasters compete for national and regional markets. In other words, satellite TV stations are leading the way – notably players such as Shanghai Oriental Satellite TV and Hunan Satellite TV. As mentioned above, Shanghai Oriental Satellite TV's *Dancing Party* has captured markets in South-East Asia. An even more promising sign is interest from the BBC in Hunan Satellite TV's *Duelling Microphones*. It seems that the BBC has decided to join with Hunan in helping to license its homegrown format internationally.[6] These are interesting times, which may well herald a new era in Chinese television format trade.

Notes

1. The word *meigui* means 'rose'. A literal translation would be 'rosy meeting'.
2. The dating program concept was developed by Fuji Television a year earlier – a one-on-one scenario called *Punch de Date*. Incidentally *dai-sakusen* literally means 'big operation'. It comes from the Japanese title of *Mission Impossible*, which was very popular at that time. The Japanese title of *Mission Impossible* was *Spy Dai-Sakusen*.
3. The earliest publication is Ma (2001).
4. *China Entertainment TV Program Report 2006–2007*, Shanghai TV Festival and CSM, 06/2006, P164.
5. http://www.9you.com. Accessed 11 June 2009.
6. http://ent.qq.com/a/20090323/000386.htm. Accessed 11 June 2009.

References

Fung, A. (2004), 'Coping, Cloning and Copying: Hong Kong in the Global Television Format Business', in Albert Moran and Michael Keane (eds), *Television Across Asia: Television Industries, Programme Formats and Globalization*, London: Routledge, pp. 74–87.

Guo Chun (2006), '*Dancing Party* Involved in the Infringement Fighting: The Copyright Crisis of TV Entertainment Program' *(wulin dahui juanru qinqyuan fenzheng, zongyi jiemu banquan weiji)*, *China Press Journal*, 23 October. http://media.people.com.cn/GB/40606/4932402.html. Accessed 4 April 2009.

Kang Yanfang, Huia Long and Wang Yuyi (2006), 'Famous TV Programs Coming from Copying, CCTV and STV Both Cloning' (*zhiming jiemu doushi chaolaide, yangshi weishi douzai kelong*), *Chongqing Evening News*, 8 December, http://www.hj.cn/html/Culture/Click/2006-12/8/0612811385963369.html. Accessed 4 April 2009.

Keane, M. (2007), *Created in China: The Great New Leap Forward*, London: Routledge.

Keane, M., Fung, A. and Moran A. (2007), *New Television, Globalisation and the East Asian Cultural Imagination*, Hong Kong: Hong Kong University Press.

Keane, M. and Moran, A. (2008) 'Television's New Engines', *Television & New Media*, 9(2), pp. 155–69.

Kong Lei (2007), 'Mingsheng Dazhen: Official Cloning' (*Mingsheng Dazhen, guanfang chaoxi*), *The Wuhan Magazine*, Wuhan Provincial Daily Newspaper Group, 21 August.

Li Degang (2002), 'Analysis on the Emerging Logic of Reality Show' (*zhenrenxiu jiemu fuxing de yuanyin*), *Journal of Voice & Screen World*, 10.

Li Hongyu (2008),'Reality Show: Challenging the Current Situation in China' (*zhenrenxiu tiaozhan Zhongguo guoqing*), *Southern Weekend* (*Nanfang Zhoumo*), 18 September.

Li Junna (2008), '*Dancing Party* Popular in South-East Asia, Chinese Entertainment TV Programs Busy Exported' *(Wulin Dahui deng zouqiao Dongnanya, zongyi jiemu mang chukou)*, *Liberation Daily (Jiefang Ribao)* 17 December, http://media.people.com.cn/GB/8531923.html. Accessed 4 April 2009.

Ma, Nina (2001), 'Study on the New Movement of the Television in the Way of Television: The Overview of the Research Project Display on Reality Show' (*yi dianshi shouduan yanjiu dianshi de xinjucuo – zhenrenxiu yanjiu keti yanshihui ceji*), *Journal of Television Research*, 2.

Moran, A. (1998), *Copycat TV: Globalisation, Program Formats and Cultural Identity*, Luton: University of Luton Press.

—— (2005), 'Formats in the New Television Landscape', in Janet Wasko (ed.), *A Companion to Television*, Malden, MA: Blackwell.

Moran, A. and Keane, M. (2004) (eds), *Television Across Asia: Television Industries, Programme Formats and Globalization*, London: Routledge.

Moran, A. and Malbon, J. (2006), *Understanding the Global TV Format*, Bristol: Intellect.

Robertson, Roland (1992), *Globalization: Social Theory and Global Culture*, London: Sage.

Xie Gengyun and Chen Hong (2007), *Reality Show: Theory, Pattern and Innovation (zhenrenxiu jiemu – lilun, xingtai he chuangxin)*, Shanghai: Fudan University Press.

Ye Zhe (2000), 'Cong "jiaoyou" kan wenhua' (Looking at culture from a relationships perspective), *Southern Television Academic Journal* (*Nanfang dianshi xuekan*) 2, pp. 4–5.

Yin Hong, Ran Ruxue and Lu Hong (2006), *A Whirlwind of Entertainment: Understanding the Reality Show (yule xuanfeng – renshi dianshi zhenrenxiu),* Beijing: China Radio & TV Press.

Chapter 15

A Place in the Sun: Global Seriality and the Revival of Domestic Drama in Italy

Milly Buonanno

Historical premises

Until the mid-1990s, homegrown production of serialized television narratives – be they open or closed continuous serials – didn't exist at all in Italy. The first locally produced daily soap, *A Place in the Sun*, was first screened in 1996, when the Italian television industry was already more than 40 years old. A latecomer to the national fictionscape, on which it was destined to make a profound impact, *A Place in the Sun* was the achievement of a well-tempered cooperation between local and global. In this chapter, I reconstruct the case study of the first Italian soap opera, pointing out how players and formats from abroad proved an instrumental resource in laying the grounds for a much-awaited relaunch of the domestic TV drama.

In order to understand the sort of cultural revolution brought about by the advent of the daily soap on the TV drama scene, we need to go back a little to the history of Italian television. As previously mentioned, serialized narratives remained long absent in the national fictionscape. This happened because of two largely interrelated reasons: first, the fierce opposition to seriality, regarded by creative talents and professional circles (authors, directors, actors, producers, network executives) as a US-dominated cultural form; and second, the small size of the Italian television industry, which was built on a old and well-established tradition of short-running and movie-like formats such as TV movies, mini-series in a few parts, and series of four to six episodes. This tradition, which today enables Italy to be the leading producer of two-part mini-series among the five largest European countries (Buonanno 2000), can be traced back to the origins of Italian television. Italian State Television (RAI) came into being in 1954, and for more that two decades it was run as a public service in a monopolistic system (Buonanno 2004); these are the years that some nostalgically consider the (first) golden age of Italian TV drama.

The monopolistic phase was deeply influenced by pedagogical assumptions in tune with the public service ethos – television was conceived as a means of bringing education and culture to viewers – and by a management trained in humanities. As far as television drama was concerned, the combination of educational mission and historical-literary classic culture gave rise to a genre that soon became the hallmark and pride of Italian drama: the *sceneggiato*, a term still used by elderly people to refer to homegrown television fiction.

In terms of format, the *sceneggiato*, as a story segmented into a very few instalments leading to a narrative closure, was the equivalent of today's mini-series, even though the latter are a bit shorter (usually two parts). In terms of content, it revolved around 'serious' matters, inspired by respectable and reliable sources – often a literary work, a historical event or a biography of a figure from the past. The hugely popular *sceneggiato* (known as literary adaptation or costume or period drama in other countries such as the United Kingdom, where it flourished in the early days of public service television as well – Caughie 2000) became, and remained for more than twenty years, the 'national genre' of Italian television drama.

Over the years, the *sceneggiato* underwent substantial changes, such as addressing contemporary family and social issues; however as a basically short-running narrative, it set the standard for what has long been considered to be typically Italian. More importantly, it fulfilled a role of 'cultural legitimization' of television drama since, by introducing the more highbrow elements of literature and history, it realized a mediation between the 'aristocratic' model of the cinema, based on prototypes, and the 'popular' models of the television storytelling, based on repetition and seriality.

It was in the 1980s, at the height of the major transformation of the Italian television system, that the deeply rooted and widespread opposition to seriality – an integral part of élitist Italian culture, as pointed out by Antonio Gramsci (1985) almost a century ago – really made its presence felt. As is widely known, the Italian television scene underwent a far-reaching and turbulent change from the mid-1970s onwards, when commercial networks began to appear, first locally and then nationally (Baransky and Lumley 1990; Buonanno 2004). The most immediate consequence of this transformation, which created the preconditions of the duopoly RAI-Mediaset, was an enormous increase in television programming and an urgent need to fill the schedules with a quantity of 'volume television' that domestic production system could not satisfy. Private channels therefore gave way to heavy imports of American television drama, and public television – faced with competition – felt compelled to do the same. In consequence, Italy became, and remained for many years, the main European importer of foreign (mainly US and Brazilian) television drama. It was during this time that Italian viewers became familiar with new formats and genres such as the continuous serial, both open and closed; they experienced for the first time, and were fascinated by, the North American daily soaps and prime-time serials (Silj 1988) and Latin American telenovelas; and they were exposed to an unending stream of episodic series from the United States.[1]

In the face of the popularity earned by the foreign drama series and serials, the public broadcaster first considered producing domestic serials and long-lasting series in order to compete with the American imports. In fact, a minority group of RAI executives, mindful of the need to establish a factory-based system of domestic drama, developed a strategic project along these lines in the early 1980s (Brancato 2007). The project ignited intense discussion within and outside television milieus; there was much opposition to what was perceived as a surrender to 'alien' modes of production and narration, as an unacceptable way of becoming willingly 'Americanized'. Issues of identity and 'otherness', national and international 'ways of television', tradition and change informed the debate, both intellectually and emotionally. As a conclusion, no action was taken by RAI. The commercial channels, on their part, were scarcely sensitive to matters of original production, being satisfied with their politics of imports. It was only in the second half of the 1980s that Mediaset began producing domestic drama in small quantities, prudently choosing to follow in the footsteps of public television.

As a consequence of this situation – exploitation of foreign 'canned shows', also for their economic convenience in comparison with the more expensive domestic fiction, along with refusal to put in place a production system on industrial basis, seen as a betrayal of national tradition – Italian television drama entered a period of decline, lasting until the mid-1990s. In this regard, suffice it to say that during the television season 1995–96, scarcely 130 hours of first-run domestic fiction – more or less the equivalent of the yearly length of a single daily soap – were broadcast in Italy on the six national channels (three of them RAI, and three Mediaset). This was the lowest proportion among the big European countries. Not completely by chance, in a slightly antecedent article on *Variety* that accounted for 'the current trends in domestic TV programming across the main European territories' (April 1995, p. 45), the Italian drama was hardly mentioned.

A turning point

Ten years later, during the television season 2005–06, the offerings of first-run domestic fiction on the broadcasting channels had reached 720 hours, and amounted to about 800 hours by the time of writing in mid-2008.

In fact, the television drama has now developed into the 'central storytelling system' (Newcomb 1988: 88) of Italian society. In a country where reading books and newspapers is a barely diffused habit, and where the national cinema has ceased since the 1970s to be a medium of popular entertainment, television has assumed the role of contemporary super-narrator. The production of domestic fiction, which had dramatically decreased under the impact of foreign imports in the 1980s and the early 1990s, has significantly increased in relatively short space of time (Buonanno 2007). Therefore, an abundant supply of homegrown drama has filled the schedules of the national broadcasting channels. Taking advantage of the privileged placements in prime-time slots, from which most of the foreign (mainly US) shows have been removed, it has managed to capture the widest possible audiences. The late 1990s and early 2000s have witnessed a true rebirth of both the production capacity and the popularity of the local drama, along with the establishment and consolidation of the Italian television industry (Buonanno 2009).

The relaunch of domestic fiction was set in motion in 1996, a year now considered the threshold of the 'second golden age' (to borrow the definition from Thompson 1997) of national TV drama. It coincided with the industrial production, run by the global player Grundy International, of the first ever Italian continuous serial, the daily soap *A Place in the Sun*, which is still on air today. This was intended to be screened on Raitre, the third channel of public television.

As a reflection of the *liaison* between the local and the global which, in diverse combination, is at the origin of a wide range of contemporary television formats and contents, the encounter and deal between RAI and Grundy did not merely lay the foundation for factory-based mass production, where only a cottage industry had existed previously, or enhance a poor fictionscape by adding a certain amount of 'volume television'. Rather, it precipitated a small 'cultural revolution', in that it opened the way for the legitimization of the most popular forms of televisual storytelling, namely the continuous serials that had long been banned from the production culture and practice of Italian television drama.

The rebirth of domestic TV fiction owes much to the turning point marked by the first daily soap. In subsequent years, the serial formula proved crucial, since serials boosted the productive capacity of the infant Italian industry. They soon became popular with the viewing public, thus extending the range of domestic shows that enjoyed success, cult status and critical acclaim. In this respect, Italy represents a case of a national system of drama production and consumption that has been imbued with new life and strengthened by the processes of change set in motion by the import and adoption of foreign elements (whether they are production companies, know-how, formats or formulae).

A compelling environment

The road that eventually led Italian television to experiment with the continuous serial formula was long, difficult and obstructed by entrenched production practices and cultural elitism. It is therefore difficult to over-estimate the nature and significance of the introduction of a daily soap into the domestic fictionscape. We are dealing with a dramatic reversal in the Italian broadcasters' strategies.

Far from being an unexpected conversion along the road to Damascus, the change matured in the 'compelling environment' which was taking shape in the mid-1990s. In fact, heavy pressures were put on the broadcasters at that time to produce more original drama, as a consequence of a number of different but converging conditions:

- In the wake of the European directive, 'Television Without Frontiers', the Italian broadcasters were required by law to reinvest fixed shares of their net revenue from licence fees (public television) and advertising (commercial television) in national and European production of fiction and film. The parliamentary itinerary of the law, definitively approved in 1998, started in 1996.
- Although pay TV penetration in the mid-1990s remained at a preliminary stage, the thematic channels carried by the digital platforms (Telepiù, Stream) were already absorbing growing quantities of movies and sport events, taking them away from terrestrial networks; in consequence, the latter needed to have larger amount of drama available in order to fill the void.

- The popularity of the foreign – that is to say, US fiction – was waning at least partly due to audience saturation. As the biggest European importer of ready-made programs from the United States and from Latin American countries during the 1980s, Italy had been virtually addicted to international television content, but the foreign imports' run of luck was coming to an end, and national drama had to take its place.
- Finally, and perhaps most importantly, in the midst of the process of globalization – and possibly as a counterpoint to it – the viewing patterns of mass audiences in Italy (and elsewhere) were being reshaped by a deeper desire for storytelling infused with cultural proximity (Straubhaar 1991); demands and choices of television viewers were being driven by an intensified predilection for national, homegrown drama. This was not at all a new phenomenon – even in the *Dallas* years, domestic fiction (if it was available) proved more attractive than US imports (Silj 1988) – but it gained more weight and visibility at a time when imports were losing ground when it came to viewers' preferences.

This set of circumstances was able to convince the Italian broadcasters to put an end to what, in the early 1990s, had become an authentic escape from domestic drama (Buonanno 2002). Public television initiated the trend by taking the controversial decision to produce a daily soap. For a television industry and culture which had opposed the idea of long seriality tenaciously for decades, the decision represented a 180 degree rotation.

The close encounter of local and global

For the sake of precision, it has to be pointed out that a number of attempts to create homemade long-running drama (not a daily soap, though) had previously been undertaken by private television. Continuous serials, in the closed variant of the *telenovela*, were produced at the beginning of the 1990s for prime time on the Mediaset commercial channels. These included both Italo-Argentine co-productions (Mazzioti 1996), where the Italian partner's creative contribution was practically non-existent, and home-grown *feuilletons* such as *Ivy*, *Passions* and *Camilla* (O'Donnell 1999). Despite a few decent results, the project of opening up the spaces of prime time to serialized domestic drama was a failure, and was therefore abandoned. The idea was probably premature, at a time when the presence of a domestically produced serial would have appeared unorthodox even in daytime. But the deceptive outcome of the experiment was first and foremost due to other factors – in particular, the *mésalliance* between the foreign and the domestic, in that neither of the two was endowed with the right credentials to make such a break with tradition palatable.

The 'alien' Latin American *telenovela* adopted as a model was the least suitable narrative formula for this purpose. In Italy – indeed, probably more than elsewhere – it is difficult, if not impossible, to find a genre that is as under-valued and discredited as the *telenovela*, which has become the epitome of the lowest aesthetic and cultural level of televisual seriality. The word has come into common parlance and into journalists' vocabulary with the derisory meaning of a thing or topic that drags along inconclusively through ostensible *coups de théâtre* and a lot of standing about. Furthermore, the early 1990s saw a massive fall in the popularity enjoyed by Latin American serials in the previous decade. This was brought about by intensive programming that made the schedules of Rete 4 (Mediaset's 'female' channel) practically mono-generic. Nor, for its part, was Italian commercial television – almost an absolute beginner in drama production – in a position to deploy and impose the cultural hegemony that would have been necessary to support a similar innovation.

In order for long seriality to be turned into a constituent part of the domestic television landscape, it was imperative for the initiative to be assumed by a player that enjoyed acknowledged authority on the national television scene. A daily soap was dangerous territory to cross, riven by the apparently immeasurable gap between something seen as frivolous and culturally insignificant ('only a soap opera'), and the relevant issues that it was likely to raise and inject into public debate: cultural identity and tradition; televisual quality; and the role and destiny of the Italian television industry. The project called for a player that could reliably offer guarantees concerning the risky operation, and be robust enough to withstand the criticism and controversies that would be aroused. Public television had the sufficient patrimony of authority, credibility and strength and, unlike what had happened in the 1980s – given the pressing and inescapable necessity to expand production capacity – decided to invest this patrimony in the project of the first Italian soap opera, which was destined to introduce into the domestic fictionscape, and above all to legitimize, the continuous serial as a narrative formula and a production mode.

Since the continuous serial's narrative formula and production mode were completely alien to Italian television culture, the expertise and know-how had to be sought outside national boundaries. Like other European broadcasters, RAI turned to the global player Grundy, which had initially built in Australia a remarkable experience as a producer of television entertainment. The company had been the first to export soap formats to European markets, as well as having the required human resources and competencies for adapting the original templates in accordance with the different national contexts of the importing countries (Moran 1998; O'Donnell 1999).

The extent to which *A Place in the Sun* was adapted from the format of an Australian soap opera – namely *Neighbours* – is an issue to which I will return later. Here, however, I wish to look at the communication strategy agreed to, and put jointly into practice, by RAI and Grundy with the aim of preventing or softening criticism and disapproval of a partnership that could be perceived in Italy as a *liaison dangereuse*. This communication strategy entailed, for instance, recalling the Australianness of Grundy as the ambivalent but eventually positive feature of a foreign partner who, if nothing else, was not American. More importantly, it was centred on claims of the 'Italianity' of the soap, from the very moment of its conception; the entire promotional campaign that preceded and accompanied the launch of *A Place in the Sun* made this claim its leitmotif, insisting that 'all the stories, all the actors and all the settings' were Italian.

On the one hand, it was imperative to minimize the part played by Grundy and the contribution of the 'foreigners' (which generated unceasing polemics among Italian television producers); on the other hand, it was precisely the foreigners who offered a fundamental element of guarantee. As a matter of fact, they guaranteed production standards that local personnel at that time would not have been able to meet, because of their complete lack of experience. This argument had understandably to be handled with care, so as not to offend the sensibilities of creative talents and local producers, but it helped to forestall or tone down public scepticism. The expectations or curiosity regarding a 'completely Italian' soap opera were in fact shared by many viewers – those who had learnt to appreciate the pleasures of the continuous serial through American soaps such as *Guiding Light*, *Loving* and *The Bold and the Beautiful* – with a measure of suspicion, if not prejudice, about a homemade serial consigned to inexpert Italian hands. But the proven experience of Grundy allowed them, if nothing else, to give the concept the benefit of the doubt. Actually Grundy played an irreplaceable role. Obviously the company was able to fully master the dramaturgical model, the organization of scriptwriting and the factory-based system of production of a daily soap. It put to work its own skilled human resources, but at the same time a process of 'learning by doing' was fruitfully activated and a know-how transfer gradually occurred, from the global partner to the local personnel called to cooperate in the bilateral endeavour of the first Italian soap opera.

However, no extenuating circumstances were conceded by the critics when *A Place in the Sun* went on the air in the prime-time slot of RAI's third channel, at the beginning of the 1996–97 television season. An unprecedented barrage of merciless reviews was unleashed on what was sarcastically labelled a 'flop-opera'. In fact, the serial took more than one season to attract regular viewers and retain their loyalty. RAI stuck to its guns, exercising the privilege of a public service television station that could allow itself to keep a show on the air that was unprofitable in terms of ratings, but instrumental to growth of Italian television drama. This staying power paid off. Already, during the second season, the criticism was giving way to congratulations on an 'excellent program' of Italian television, and the feared Trojan horse of Americanization was widely acclaimed as constituting the 'first true bastion' against the American invasion. To a large extent, the *volte-face* of opinion on the first homegrown soap was due to the eloquent evidence of its Italianness.

An Italian sense of place

> If you are familiar with *Neighbours* (another Fremantle/Grundy soap) then this is like 'Ramsay Street-by-the-sea' with a bit more spice and drama thrown in for good measure. (http://bestuff.com/stuff/un-posto-al-sole, accessed June 2008)

These lines, posted on a fan forum, aptly introduce the (now-forgotten) issue which long pervaded the initial debate on *A Place in the Sun*: whether or not, and to what extent, the first Italian soap opera was a format adaptation of *Neighbours*.

The deal agreed between RAI and Grundy involved the adaptation of the hugely popular (at home and abroad – see Croft 1995; Hobson 2003) Australian soap opera, a major asset of the Grundy library. However, as mentioned before, the two players have since the beginning insisted on the 'programmatic originality' of *A Place in the Sun*, conceived and written in professional dialogue and cultural negotiation within a creative team made up of Australian and Italian authors; among these were Wayne Doyle, head writer of *Neighbours*, and the Naples-born story editor Luigi Ventriglia. Standing midway between the agreements of a formal deal and an astute communication strategy, the truth is that resemblances, echoes and resonances of *Neighbours*, or from other Grundy-branded soaps such as the German *Unter uns* (see O'Donnell 1999: 115), to be found in the concept and the early development of *A Place in the Sun* seem to corroborate the assumption that this latter was, loosely at least, shaped on pre-existing formats. But this feature did not prevent the serial from being characterized as unmistakeably Italian, an indigenous artefact from many points of view, starting from the multi-layered articulation of one of the most crucial components of every soap's world: the location.

Displaying a title that immediately conjures up the sunny Italian weather, celebrated in many popular Neapolitan songs – such as 'O' sole mio' (My sun), made internationally famous by Elvis Presley as 'It's Now or Never' and 'Chistè o paese do sole' (That's a sunny country), *A Place in the Sun* is set in the southern city of Naples, where it is also produced and shot. Naples is a highly recognizable and familiar setting for Italians, owing to its traditional presence in films, music and theatre; in fact, in the mid-1990s the city was at the height of a phase of splendour and relaunch known as the 'New Neapolitan renaissance'. *A Place in the Sun* exploits Naples as a sumptuous natural resource for the numerous scenes shot on location, giving this soap a bright airiness that is unusual for the genre, and a linguistic and stylistic cornucopia – the Neapolitan accents, the humorous tone of some of the characters and situations – which reinforces the overall effect of familiarity and recognizability.

Within the larger context of the big city, the more localized scenario of the narrative is an area in the historic centre of Naples. American, Australian and English soaps are set for preference in working-class areas or suburban residential districts. The change of location made in *A Place in the Sun* is significant in its cultural specificity. In Italy in general, and Naples in particular, suburban areas conjure up a menacing picture of rundown districts on the edge of cities, or dreary dormitory towns. Downtown areas, with their concentration of fine historical architecture – however much they may be perceived as uninhabitable because of insecurity and disorder – still condense and convey the core identity of the Italian city, in addition to being the stuff of dreams and aspirations about luxurious living.

The unexpected inheritance of a large apartment in the historic centre of Naples is the starting point of the story of *A Place in the Sun*. This leads to the most inward and important of the spatial reference points, the true social setting of the soap: a block of flats – indeed, a 'palace' – looking out to the Gulf of Naples. Here, in owner-occupied apartments on various floors of the block, live those who make up the inter-generational and socially diverse community of characters in the soap. By situating its own 'microcosm' in a setting that would be familiar to most Italians – that is to say, a condominium – the first homegrown soap thus installed itself literally and unmistakeably 'at home'. It must be added that the condominium is often referred to in Italy as a metaphor for the national social life.

Obviously the credentials of cultural belonging of *A Place in the Sun* would need to be more analytically discussed and demonstrated with reference to its characters, plotlines, situations and problems (Buonanno 1999). I have confined myself here to highlighting just a few instances to identify the requisite of Italianness as the main factor that has contributed to the reappraisal of the initial prejudices and opposition regarding the first domestic soap opera.

Without any doubt, the continuous serial and its industrial modes of production succeeded in being embodied in the originally hostile Italian television landscape because, over and above other things, they provided tangible proof that they were not the agents or conveyors of an unconditional cultural surrender to narrative and production models of 'alien provenance'. All the evidence confirmed that the specific features of Italian culture and society were perfectly capable of re-emerging from, and even taking advantage of, the serialization process – which in a relatively short time was destined to overcome the resistance of the creative talents and local producers, as well as the ill-concealed sense of shame of the cast members. (The actors who performed in *A Place in the Sun*, many of them making their debut but others coming from the traditions of theatre and radio drama, were assured from the start that they were lending their talents not to a soap opera but to a 'real drama', this definition doubtless carrying more dignified resonance.) Thus *A Place in the Sun* came to be acknowledged and enjoyed as a daily slice of genuine Italian drama.

A seminal story

The interest of this case does not rest in – or rather, is not confined to – the testing of the local's strength, of its capacity to put in place practices of adaptation, appropriation and reworking, and perhaps above all of its resilience in the face of the foreign. Although I do not underrate the theoretical and empirical relevance of everything that can be included under the heading of 'indigenization' (which I have treated at greater length elsewhere – see Buonanno 2008), I maintain that a more comprehensive account of the issues at stake needs to go beyond, or to shift, the interpretative perspective.

A Place in the Sun is not a 'success story' in the conventional sense. In its twelve years of existence, even after overcoming the difficult initial phase, the soap never achieved particularly high ratings; its loyal audience numbers an average of 2.5 million viewers, in line with the market share of RAI's third channel in prime time.

It is, rather, a 'seminal story': the case of a daily soap which marked a decisive watershed in the history of television drama, and had far-reaching influence on the subsequent evolution of the Italian fictionscape. In a short span of time, other long-running serials have followed in the pioneering footsteps of the first domestic soap opera. The daily soaps *Living* (1999–2008) and

The Shopping Centre (2001–) have appeared in the schedules of Mediaset's flagship Channel 5; the same public television later launched *Stolen Hearts* (RAI 2, 2002–03) and *Downhome* (RAI 1, 2006–07), and much seems to be expected from *Bittersweet*, planned for the 2008–09 season. Some of them have been failures from early on; others have seen their initial success fade away with the years. Whatever the fortune of each serial, it is worth emphasizing the fact that the daily soap has been naturalized within the Italian television landscape. The radical change of the status of the soap is demonstrated by the fact that fiascos and cancellations now arouse open discontent and regret – even protests from the creative and professional circles; and loyal viewers 'left as orphans' have to work through their mourning.

An undeniable standardization effect arises from this: if Italy for a long time remained different in not having homegrown soap opera, that difference has clearly disappeared – but the gains outweigh the losses. The serialization introduced by *A Place in the Sun* opened the way for a true television industry, gave stimulus to employment levels in both the creative and the technical sectors, and brought into existence a star system and a nursery of talents. Daytime schedules, filled in the past by imported series and serials, were enriched and diversified by the introduction of local drama, and the way was paved also for serialization in prime time, which happened only a few years later.

Long seriality entered prime time in the late 1990s. In June 1998, to give female viewers an alternative to the World Cup, the evening soap was tried out with *Enchantment*, a hospital serial that was first broadcast twice a week on RAI 2 and then, once it had proved to be a success, transferred to the first public channel. The cancellation of the serial, which had run its course and unsuccessfully been turned into a daily soap in its last season (2007–08), generated controversy and even a parliamentary debate.

A Doctor in the Family, a long-running serial, followed in December 1998 on the first public channel. Like *A Place in the Sun*, *A Doctor in the Family* blended both 'otherness and our-own-ness', to quote Miller (2000: 156). In fact, it was a true format adaptation – indeed, a well-adapted indigenization of the successful Spanish comedy *Médico de Familia*. Portraying the daily life of a large household of three generations, the series managed to capture a multi-generational audience, including children. The portrayal of an extended family, harmonious and united – an image with a strong resonance in the family-centred culture still dominant in Italy – played a key role in establishing the program in the viewing habits of an average of ten million viewers. Despite a degree of cultural affinity between Spain and Italy, the adaptation of the format entailed considerable work of 'cultural localization'. Greater emphasis was deliberately placed on the family group, a shift that can be perceived immediately from the title. This was changed from the original professional qualification of the protagonist – *Médico de Familia*, equivalent to family doctor or GP – to 'a doctor *in* the family', thus anchoring his role in the family community.[2]

The access to the prestigious evening slots has obviously reinforced the standing of serial drama. However, the fact remains that mini-series preserves its historical position as the 'queen' of prime time and the trademark of quality Italian drama (Buonanno 2005). Without removing or undermining the mini-series, prime-time serials have joined it, bringing to the domestic fictionscape the unquestionable benefit of an unprecedented range and diversification of narrative formulae.

Conclusion

The turn to seriality that occurred in the mid-1990s in the contexts of specific and compelling conditions has set in motion the relaunch of the Italian TV drama. This process has needed to be activated and managed in agreement between national and international players, since Italian television was in the need of importing and learning from abroad production modes and formulae of serial storytelling that were alien to local traditions – and, what is more, opposed and feared on account of their (supposed) threatening foreignness. The result of such cooperation was the soap opera *A Place in the Sun*, 'a delicious slice of daily Italian drama' according to *The Wall Street Journal* (April 1998), acknowledged and enjoyed by viewers (Capecchi 2000) as an authentic expression of native culture.

A Place in the Sun is by no means unique or exceptional in this respect. It should be added to the many cases that, in different parts of the world, testify the capacity of the local to convert contacts and contaminations with foreign or global cultures – and clearly not only televisual ones – into configurations that are broadly consonant with native culture (Buonanno 2008). It is worth pointing out that this capacity seems in some way to be exercised *against* the varying degrees of threat or risk (or *in spite of* them) that foreignness still represents or evokes. All this testifies convincingly, when the case occurs, to the flexible resilience and dynamic vitality of the local. Not only just 'against' or 'in spite of', but 'thanks to': the Italian example suggests to me the plausibility of a different interpretative hypothesis about the relationship between the domestic and the foreign, the local and the global, where this latter does not necessarily or exclusively stands as a threat to be neutralized, or an obstacle to be overcome, but – switching the perspective – as a resource to be fruitfully exploited.

The introduction of long seriality from abroad has opened to domestic TV drama unprecedented opportunities. For the first time, the Italian creative talent has been enabled to imagine and tell long-lasting and never-ending stories. And a 'popular historiography' (White 1994) of everyday national life has found stimulus and development, as never before, in the dramaturgical models that are inherent in the continuous serials. The specific circumstances in which these processes of change and growth have occurred must not be overlooked. But they suggest that, given the right conditions, global players and foreign televisual cultures can represent a vital resource for national players and local television cultures.

Acknowledgement

Translated from Italian by Jennifer Radice.

Notes

1. A significant role in this stage was played by US prime-time serials, particularly by *Dallas*. Although this lavish serial was a phenomenon whose popularity invested the whole of Europe (and beyond), arising the alarmed complaints of intellectuals and politicians about a '*Dallas*ification' of European culture, in Italy it represented a crucial occasion in the early competition between public and private channels, an occasion which ultimately favoured the latter. In the wake of its success in the United States, *Dallas* was first imported by public television, but because of the usual suspect and disdain for US productions, and moreover as a consequence of poor competencies in matters of long seriality formulae, the serial was initially neither appreciated nor understood. The first public channel broadcast it in the spring of 1981, as if it were a series made of independent and self-contained episodes, and therefore ignoring the structural feature of the serial - that is, the chronological sequence of the instalments. Under these conditions, *Dallas* could not help but be but a flop, so public television decided not to renew the option, which was instead acquired by commercial television. Announced and accompanied by an unprecedented promotional campaign which contributed to make it the event of the season, *Dallas* was successfully broadcast in prime time on Canale 5 and certainly represented a decisive step in the establishment and consolidation of private networks - indeed, a 'Trojan horse' for the dismantling of public television monopoly.
2. It can be seen that public television has been the innovator, both in daytime and in prime time. Commercial channels awaited the actions and results of their competitor before joining the trend themselves, despite the risk of losing opportunities: the format of *Médico de familia* was turned down by Mediaset before being acquired by RAI.

References

Baransky, Zygmunt G. and Lumley, Robert (eds) (1990), *Culture and Conflict in Postwar Italy*, New York: St Martin's Press.

Brancato, Sergio (2007), *Senza fine*, Napoli: Liguori.

Buonanno, Milly (1999), *Indigeni si diventa*, Milano: Sansoni.

—— (ed.) (2000), *Continuity and Change*, Luton: University of Luton Press.

—— (2002), *Le formule del racconto televisivo*, Milano: Sansoni.

—— (2004), 'Italian Television', in John Sinclair (ed.), *Contemporary World Television*, London: British Film Institute, pp. 77–80.

—— (2005), 'La masa y el relleno: La miniserie en la ficcion italiana', *DeSignis*, 7/8, pp. 19–30.

—— (ed.) (2007), *La bella stagione*, Roma: RAI-ERI.

—— (2008), *The Age of Television*, Bristol: Intellect.

—— (2009, forthcoming), 'Religion and History in Italian TV Drama', in E. Castelló, A. Dhoest and H. O'Donnell (eds), *Nation on the Screen*, Cambridge: Cambridge Scholars Publishing.

Capecchi, Saveria (2000), *Ridendo e sognando con la soap*, Rome: RAI-ERI.

Caughie, John (2000), *Television Drama*, Oxford: Oxford University Press.

Croft, Stephen (1995), *Global Neighbours?*, in Robert C. Allen (ed.), *To be continued...*, London: Routledge, pp. 98–121.

Gramsci, Antonio (1985), *Selections from Cultural Writings*, London: Lawrence and Wishart.

Hobson, Dorothy, *Soap opera*, Polity Press, Cambridge 2003

Mazziotti, Nora (1996), *La industria de la telenovela*, Buenos Aires: Paidos.

Miller, Jeffrey S. (2000), *Something Completely Different*, Minneapolis: University of Minnesota Press.
Moran, Albert (1998), *Copycat Television*, Luton: University of Luton Press.
Newcomb, Horace (1988), 'One Night of Prime Time', in James W. Carey (ed.), *Media, Myths and Narrative*, London: Sage, pp. 88–112.
O'Donnell, Hugh (1999), *Good Times Bad Times*, London: Leicester University Press.
Silj, Alessandro (1988), *East of Dallas*, London: British Film Institute.
Straubhaar, Joseph (1991), 'Beyond Media Imperialism: Asymmetrical Interdependence and Cultural Proximity, *Critical Studies in Mass Communication*, 8, pp. 1–11.
Thompson, Robert J. (1994), *Television's Second Golden Age*, Syracuse, NY: Syracuse University Press.
White, Mimi (1994), 'Women, Memory and Serial Melodrama', *Screen*, Winter, pp. 336–43.

Chapter 16

Idol in a Small Country: *New Zealand Idol* as the Commoditization of Cosmopolitan Intimacy

Barry King

In this chapter, I provide a snapshot of *Idol* as a global format finding its way through the specificities of a peripheral locality – in this case, New Zealand. My approach to the question of how *Idol*, rebranded as *New Zealand Idol*, is articulated locally draws upon a production of culture perspective as developed by Peterson and others (Peterson and Anand 2004). Such a perspective focuses on the interaction of a range of factors, both internal and external to the artwork, that govern the production, distribution and consumption of cultural symbols. In addition, in order to recognize the inextricably local, immediate and grounded nature of performance – even when projected on a national scale and within a more or less explicit transnational framework – I will have something to say about the affective dimensions of musical performance and the process of commoditization. It is also important to recognize that a number of scholars have already stressed the influence of local factors in filtering and mediating the formative influence of global formats. In such a process, the research must shift from the musical text towards the audience context (cf Manuel 1998: 26). Interestingly enough, the *Idol* format has been seen as providing an opportunity in the context of commoditization for consumers to exercise collective bargaining power as a challenge to corporate media power (Jenkins 2006: 63). Some evidence of the repurposing of the *Idol* format has been found in the Netherlands (Reijnders et al. 2007). In Finland, a parallel song contest, *Jokamiehen Idols* (*People's Idols*), invited anyone who believed they could sing better than the contestants on the official Finnish *Idol* to dial a special number and croon into their mobile. This offshoot generated more votes (and a handsome revenue for Telecoms) than the official contest (SMLXL 2006: 9). Developments such as these provide evidence for Jenkins' (2006) argument that a new affective economy is being forged by converging media.

For my concerns here, a key theoretical issue to be addressed turns on the constraints imposed on the new 'affective economy' by the *Idol* format – might there not, on closer inspection, be different kinds of affective economies with different social and political vectors of resolution? To put the matter too starkly perhaps, what is more significant about the *Idol* format is not that it imposes sentiments – or some might say even sentimentality – on popular musical expression, but rather how the format manages the politics and aesthetics of local expression. Obviously, the various terms in play (e.g. authentic) are in themselves contested and imprecise. In what follows, I will endeavour to give some stipulative precision to what I understand them to mean.

Features of the *Idol* franchise

Perhaps the most fundamental premise of the *Idol* format is that it is a supranational music franchise. As such, the prestige and legitimacy of the format rest on the claim that a globally standardized production template is an engine for the discovery of popular musical talent. One feature of the discovery process is the use of a panel of professionally experienced experts who audition the initial pool of contestants, producing a shortlist of performers to appear on the show. The on-screen performances of those who make the cut are evaluated by the experts, who make an initial determination of who will be eliminated. Variations such as immunity contests notwithstanding, the process of elimination is ultimately determined by an 'open' referendum of viewers who cast their vote through forms of premium-priced viewer interactivity, such as telephone voting and SMS texting. Thus the franchise owner, FremantleMedia, reports on its website that the global number of votes cast by audiences for the *Idol* format has now exceeded three billion. In the United States alone, it is reported that in the 2003 season the Fox Broadcasting network was receiving in excess of twenty million telephone or text messages as votes per episode (Jenkins 2006: 59). In European markets, revenues from audience votes are estimated to reach €177 million (SMLXL 2006: 8).

Such 'viewer pays' plebiscitary practices represent a significant revenue stream for the producers and their service provider partners. At the same time, they provide powerful populist credentials equating the votes cast by audiences with the expression of popular will through the ballot box. Just as the people vote for political representatives in Western democracies, so too the audiences for *Idol* can vote for those contestants whom they feel best express the sentiments contained in popular songs. Accordingly, FremantleMedia is able to link market success with the claim that *Idol* is a vehicle for expressing the authentic tastes of global audiences for excellence in pop music. Since – unlike the Eurovision Song Contest – the *Idol* format is based on pre-sold hits rather than original songs, what occurs is at least a double delegation: first, the local capacity for emotional expression in music is assumed to be amply accommodated by songs that are already global hits; and second, in any locality only a few (ultimately one) possess the talent and ability to replicate what established 'mega-stars' have already done. Inevitably, though this may be a largely tacit or hidden process, there is a local tension between notions, however amorphous, of national character and identity and the market-driven pop cosmopolitanism implicit in the *New Zealand Idol* format. This tension – a basic feature of 'peripheral' media as cheaper foreign imports displace local productions – is perhaps at its most abstract a conflict between exchange value and use-values, particularly as these relate to notions of being gifted, of giving the gift of expression back to the community. The logic of the interplay between exchange value and use-value will be explored below, but for now it can be said that the contrast between market-driven and community-driven forms of cultural expression is sharper in New Zealand than elsewhere because of the market fundamentalism that marks the political and civic culture (Jesson 1999). It may be an irony, but it is no accident given the stripped down commercial logic of the show, that *Popstars*, the inspiration for Simon Fuller's *Idol* franchise, was developed in

New Zealand in 1999. Though the basic format went on to be adopted worldwide, *Popstars* failed to attract adequate ratings to ensure its continuance after one or two seasons in most of the countries where it aired – Germany being the exception. Nor did the many bands formed on the basis of the show succeed in establishing careers – Turkey seems to be an exception here. In New Zealand, the all-girl pop group True Bliss was formed out of the series, but was disbanded in 2000. Yet there was a kind of celebrity after life for True Bliss's alumni, with band member Megan Atali being hired as one of the judges on *New Zealand Idol* in 2006. Another local celebrity and True Bliss member, Jo Cotton, was a competitor in *Pop's Ultimate Stars* – a compendium show of the former *New Zealand Idol* finalists which she won, inadvertently underscoring the lack of durability of the talents of *New Zealand Idol* winners and restoring the mantle of pop star to a white performer.

The New Zealand music market

The New Zealand popular music market is small, reflecting its population which is around four million. Of the NZ$173 million or so earned annually in the New Zealand domestic market, about 90 per cent goes to multinational companies and international artists. By contrast, New Zealand export earnings from popular music are around NZ$5 million a year compared with the world market of NZ$44 billion. The local music scene is insufficient to support full-time professional musicians, and there are limited opportunities for employment. As a result of limited local opportunities, the key element in developing a successful career is to tap into the American market via a contract with a multinational recording company. Few New Zealand bands achieve this – Bic Runga, The Datsuns and Fat Freddy's Drop are recent examples, and there is a piecemeal track record with performers and bands such as Shona Laing and Crowded House having established a more or less continuous career in the late 1980s. In addition, there is limited radio and television exposure for local artistes and very limited student radio outlets – the traditional band starter route in the United States. Although there is a strong government policy emphasis on building a distinctive New Zealand music brand, this has focused mainly on securing overseas exposure for bands already on the path to international recognition. There has been little effective action to impose quotas for locally originated music that would give local bands airtime (Shuker 2008).

Against this local background of feast and famine, it is extremely difficult to establish a professional career. Although performer networks exist in the key cities of Auckland and Wellington, these do not develop into a simplex structure of the kind found by Richard Peterson in Nashville (Peterson and White 1986). Informal craft regulation of a simplex kind, guaranteeing a flow of suitably qualified musicians by word of mouth, depends on a steady flow of engagements and sufficiently high wages to weather down-times.

New Zealand Idol, with its proclaimed purpose of a discovering 'natural talent', prizemoney of NZ$60,000 and a contract with an international recording company, Sony-BMG, offered a 'magical' resolution to the weight of local constraints. The reality turned out to be quite different. Impressed with the strong ratings for the local airing of *American Idol* and *Australian Idol*, TVNZ, seeking to reconcile its Charter obligations to program for a young audience with good ratings, commissioned a first season of *New Zealand Idol*, which was aired in 2004. This was followed by two more seasons, with the last season airing in 2006.

Owing to declining ratings, it was decided not to fund a fourth season, putting *New Zealand Idol* on indefinite hold. Sony-BMG, which offered recording contracts to the first two season's winners, Ben Lummis and Rosa Vai, withdrew the offer of a contract for the 2006 season because of lack-lustre record sales by previous winners, even in the local market. In lieu of a contract, the 2006 winner, Matt Saunoa, received a prize of NZ$50,000 and a SUV car. Saunoa subsequently released a single (rumoured to be self-financed) through an independent record company, which was even less successful than earlier winners' singles. It was rumoured that he paid for the single out of his prizemoney – which was probably not true, but is indicative of public cynicism about the process. He subsequently moved to Australia. Despite the avowed purpose of *New Zealand Idol*, none of the winners has succeeded in launching a successful recording career. Ben Lummis and Rosa Vai proved to be modest one-hit wonders who are now largely confined to paid appearances at local events and church halls. Some contestants continue to feature in woman's magazine articles (the home of tabloid journalism in New Zealand) as reference models for lifestyle matters such as marriage, pregnancy and birth, weight problems, and the like. Given that public interest in all the winners of *New Zealand Idol*, as measured by record sales, has not been sustained after the shows have concluded, their credibility as talent contests – already viewed with scepticism – continues to be questioned:

> *New Zealand Idol* does seem to be cynically viewed as a cash cow by its makers. While *Idol* contestants are fiercely promoted throughout the run of the show, the winners are not supported in their careers after the series has ended. (Longshaw 2006)

Certainly *New Zealand Idol* has produced no stars of the likes of Kelly Clarkson or Carrie Underwood, winners of *American Idol*, nor has it launched movie careers such as that of Jennifer Hudson. Although *Australian Idol* has suffered from similar criticisms, and has not shown consistent success, it has at least demonstrated with the likes of Guy Sebastian, Shannon Noll and Ricki Lee Coulter the capacity to discover talent rather than an evanescent celebrity based on publicity (Zuel 2007). Ironically, perhaps, it is not the winning contestants on *New Zealand Idol* that can claim admittance to stardom but the presenter, Dominic Bowden. In his view, the chief value of participation in *New Zealand Idol* is that it creates a media profile or a bankable name. This is vividly demonstrated by Bowden's landing the host role on *The Next Great American Band*, which positions him as a rival to Ryan Seacrest (Stuff 2007).

It is reasonable to conclude that it is not talent that is the key variable so much as the scale constraints of a small market that make stardom an unlikely outcome. For talent – always hard to define in abstract – is concretely dependent on the very economic factors that it is supposed to transcend. Nonetheless, the notion of talent is ideologically potent in *Idol*, as is the accompanying testamentary notion of authenticity on which the definition of talent ultimately rests. But, as the constraints of market size indicate (as might factors such as authenticity), talent is less a state of being than a matter of what processes and protocols certify the possession of talent – or, in short, of the nature of authentication (Moore 2002). The *Idol* format may be said to be such a process of authentication.

The interesting question in the case of *New Zealand Idol* is what the various participants defined as a successful outcome in terms of an expression of talent. If one considers the producers, South Pacific Pictures, then the publicized purpose of the show as discovering a new and exciting musical talent was arguably secondary to profits and good ratings. The program commissioning entity, TVNZ, no less interested in profits and ratings, had the additional requirement of fulfilling the public service obligation to give voice to the aspirations of the youth of the nation, securing for New Zealand its place in a global order of talent fostered by the *Idol* franchise. The attitude of established musicians was given its strongest expression by Boh Runga, who observed that she would sooner lick the inside of a toilet than appear on *New Zealand Idol*. Less exalted craft practitioners, dependent on taking whatever work came their way, were more circumspect. For the contestants, participant observation during the 2006 season revealed a much more instrumental view focused on winning the prizemoney and the prize of a car than was apparent from accompanying press interviews, where contestants emphasized their lofty ambition to be a star (Wright 2008). The withdrawal of a record contract as a prize was probably an important factor here. For the audience, the permitted interest was on defining, by SMS and dial-in votes, a preference for specific performers, challenging on occasions the 'elite' opinions of the panel of judges marshalling an apparently countervailing and more 'authentic' measure of popularity. Important as this role-set is in defining the level of conscious agency, it is clearly a site of agency that is over-determined in a deep structural sense by a veritable engine for the profitable interface of capitalist productive relationships and cultural action. I refer, of course, to the format.

Format as an engine of commoditization

> *Engine:* An instance or a product of ingenuity; an artifice, contrivance, device, plot; and in bad sense, a snare, wile…also, in weaker sense, an appliance, means. (*Oxford English Dictionary*, 2nd ed., 1989)

As the origin of the term, the *Idol* format is a semiotic and behavioural engine for the production of a specific performance commodity (Keane and Moran, 2008). On one hand, the format is a set of rules and a contest motivated plot, designed to ensure standardized performances from contestants which have an exchange value within the political economy of broadcast television. On another, it is also an engine for the production of renown and what this renown is supposed to rest on: talent and ingenuity. Initially, it is useful to apply the conceptual scheme of the Danish linguist Louis Hjelmslev (1963) in order to map the structural transformations introduced into the semiotics of musical performance by the *Idol* format. Hjelmslev's net, as it has been termed, was designed to extend the binarism of de Saussure's division of the sign into a signifier and signified – roughly, a word and its concept – by pointing out that both the linguistic signifier and the signified were composed of a form and a substance. This innovation had the advantage of emphasizing the materiality of the sign form – particularly, but not exclusively, relevant for the class of visual signs – in a manner that complemented Peirce's tripartite theory of sign forms (Parrat 1984). Graphically, the formative relationships in Matrix One were identified by Hjelmslev as shown in Table 16.1.

Matrix One maps out the logical relationships found in signification; in a given empirical case, some of these elements are given a pragmatic pre-eminence. With the *Idol* format, it is the form of content and expression that over-determines the form and substance of content.

As Matrix Two indicates, the function of the format is to ensure that a specific set of traits is imposed on the plane of content. The plane of content is the 'live' resource that is mobilized by the format. It comprises the performances given by contestants and 'wanna-bes' and is the point of engagement through which certain features from the local cultural context come into play. The formative elements are a set of generally established rules and procedures that provide the rules and prescriptions of the format – the contract signed by the contestants, the rules governing the contest, votes, immunity devices and the like as intellectual property – and the stylistic and behavioural moulding of the 'living' labour of performance to fit into pre-established exemplars as proven on the market. Analytically Hjelmslev's (model allows for the dialectical interaction of the planes of expression and content which reciprocally

Table 16.1: Hjelmslev's Matrix One and Matrix Two.

Matrix One	**Plane of content (signified)**	**Plane of expression (signifier)**
Form	Form of content	Form of expression
Substance	Substance of content	Substance of expression
Matrix Two	**Traits of content**	**Traits of expression**
Plane of expression (signifiers) – Exchange value	Form of content: Individualistic competitive themes, rules and practices of the *Idol* format	Form of expression: MOR Anglo-American pop music genres commodities, the idiomatic style of 'hit' performers as recorded
Plane of content (signifieds) – Use-value	Substance of content: 'New Zealand' national identity, local vernacular framings of experience, people and things	Substance of expression: voice qualities, gestural repertoires, dress, physique, facial expressions – the 'look' of *Idol* contestants and 'wanna-bes'

Source: Hjelmslev (1963).

enter into the moulding of the relevant discourse. This 'natural' reciprocal determination is exactly what the format is designed to prevent. The sovereignty of form over substance found in Matrix Two is the effect of the exogenous imposition of the format as a regulatory device. In *Idol*, performance as an interdependent collective process is subordinated to the forms necessary to protect the property rights of the franchise owner, FremantleMedia. This process of subordination is represented in *Idol* publicity as its opposite, as the winning contestants' triumphant ascent to professionalism, as the sublimation of amateurism and karaoke-fed delusions of talent.

A significant aspiration driving the *Idol* format is recycling established pop commodities in order to create a new set of spectacular commodity values. In order to add a new sheen to what is old, the format is designed to ensure that an appearance of singularity is constructed through the introduction of the cover of a distinctive national voice. At the most abstract level, *New Zealand Idol* is a part of this as a decommoditization and recommoditization process centred on what has been standardized by the market (Kopytoff 1986). So another way to characterize the hegemony of form over content is to define the format is an engine for determining what can ascend to the level of a marketable exchange value. As it turns out in the New Zealand case, the 'unique' values created by the contestants do not succeed in forming a new commodity but the show itself – which is, with some exceptions, the case in most local iterations of the format. In theory at least, it is through the action of the format that the use-values that inhere in the local context are congealed into performance-based exchange values. But before exploring the general features of the *Idol* format as an engine for the reproduction and recycling of pop music exchange value, a few remarks on the concepts of value are in order.

At the most abstract level, use-value and exchange value are polar differentiations in the field of value created by the actions of human labour power. Although it is possible to speak of nature as having intrinsic value, this actually means nature as a repository that can be, or has been, worked upon by human agency to become a source of value for human beings. In the case of a human being, it is clear enough that notions of natural endowment rest on human productive activities such as the nurturance and socialization of the human infant. In evolved societies such as that of late capitalism, there is already a vast presence of antecedent labour, and for the individual there is all the labour undertaken by parents and others that reaches back down the chain of care that comprises everyone's personal history.

To speak of a natural talent, then, as is the *raison d'être* of *Idol*, is actually to speak of capacities or use-values that have already been developed and have the potential to be turned into exchange value or commodities. Use-values may be defined as developed capacities that have been moulded for human purposes, whereas exchange values are use-values congealed into a marketable state or as commodities (Brown 2008). Another way to express this is to say that value in its two forms as use and exchange value is always (whether as a natural resource to be cultivated or as the goods already cultivated) the product of human labour. But the tendency under capitalist relations of production is that only some value-producing activities are recognized as productive because they create surplus value or profits for capitalist enterprise. These are the exchange values congealed by the commoditization process (Marx 1976: 1038–39). The realm of use-values is bounded on one side by useless things and on the other by use-values that have been congealed into exchange value and have a price.

Applying these categories to the empirical realities of *Idol*, we must first note that any show (and, for that matter, the series) is a single large-scale commodity whose exchange value is congealed in a series of specific visual events or performances (cf Marx 1976: 995). The performances that make up the total commodity of *Idol* are manifold and organized through editing by a differential combination of visualized and de-visualized (or 'cut') content. Each show includes musical performances and 'reality' sequences where contestants emote or talk to the camera about their reactions to the contest and other contestants. The exchange values that make up the show are implicitly distinguished from performances that lack exchange value and may even lack use-value – those performances that fail to be even worthy of being shown to audiences as ' failed' auditions or cautionary tales about the capacity of 'non-professionals' for self-delusion and their inability to even produce useful musical values. Within the show, the dramatic contrast between the professionalism of the judges and the amateurism or actual skill limitations of contestants eventuates in a process of conflict and mismatch between the judges, the contestants and premium viewer interactivity voting. In this manner, the performances that comprise a given show congeal to a greater or lesser degree as expressions of the exchange values that make up the commodity spectacle of the song contest. So it is that the production process itself – the performance labour process – becomes subject to the law of exchange value, and the derivative exchange values – the discrete products as hits or professional services (engagements) that purportedly accrue to the winner – are designed (with a certain degree of optimism, as it turns out) to nurture another cycle of production. In this sense, everything seen in the show is an exchange value, even those performances that make it to the screen as examples of shoddy and inept performances visualizing the impact of failure.

The delegation of expression

> Music expresses that which cannot be said and on which it is impossible to be silent.
>
> – Victor Hugo

In contrast to the narrowing process imposed by exchange values, the use-value of musical forms and performances is a manifold realm of potentiality. This can be empirically identified by the study of the uses and gratifications that are derived by specific sub-cultural groups and specific individuals from preferred musical genres – music is seen as helping individuals manage their emotions and connect with like-minded others, actually and vicariously, through the enjoyment of performances (Wells 1990). In the most general terms, then, the use-value of music rests on its ability to facilitate a feeling engagement with others in a shared ritual event (Frith 1989: 2002). It also nurtures self-identity and is part of the existential search for order and predictability in a chaotic or overly constrained social world (DeNora 1999; Vannini and Waskul 2007). Successful singers (and, for that matter, actors) can be regarded as privileged emotional managers, expressing through the marshalling of techniques and technologies feelings audience members lack the confidence or ability to express for themselves (Orzechowicz 2008). The Utopian dimension of music – its capacity to project, within a transitory event, a durable state of being in which the human capacity for feeling and expression transcend the weight of the divisions and inequities of condition that 'morselize' everyday experience – is the 'social origin, collectively hidden, of unhappiness in all its forms, including the most intimate, the most secret' (Bourdieu 1999: 629).

As I see it, the *Idol* format is an engine for the delegation of the capacity for a ritual expression, a capacity vested in proved hits. This delegation certainly – for that is what the contest is about – empowers some singers over others to be delegates for specific audience segments, and the audience votes are a medium – however limited and flawed – for audience preferences. But the delegation of expression in *Idol* also has a social, if not societal, framing, as marked by the interface between the national and global as sites of expression. Following Zizek (1997), we can view *Idol* as an interpassive process. In this process, the ritual, expressive functions held to be central to the experience of popular music are delegated to the *Idol* format. This delegation relies on some interwoven axioms of operation. The first is that musical talent and expressivity are adequately captured and demonstrated through a song contest. The second is that the importance of popular music to the development and regulation of personal identity, whether of the performers or the audience, is smoothly and copious expressed through the pop standards that are selected for performance. Third, American pop standards (or standards that have succeeded in the United States) are an effective vehicle for the discovery of 'raw' talent. Fourth, the specificities of national or local identity, with the associated value of authenticity, are smoothly expressed through the *Idol* format. All of these delegations are literally in contest within the show and provide, with a greater degree of energy, the stuff of the spectacle of success and failure.

Generally speaking, there are endogenous and exogenous resistances to these axioms of delegation which, if accepted, accomplish the subordination of the local to the global – or what is tantamount to the same thing, of concrete use-values to abstract exchange value. The key endogenous constraint arises from the mixing of elements of the *Big Brother* format with a song contest. In *New Zealand Idol*, contestants were heavily coached on how to emote on camera when seemingly disclosing personal hopes and fears – particularly as it was a common belief held by production staff that Kiwis were not good at expressing emotions. Similarly, contestants were coached to smile and look directly into the camera as the instructions for the numbers to be used for text or internet voting were announced. As was demonstrated long ago, these kinds of manipulations are intrinsic to the successful projection of persona on television (Horton and Wohl 1956). But the *New Zealand Idol* contestants were much more vulnerable, and lacked the protection of a successful celebrity brand, so finding the right degree of self-disclosure or of 'looking good' on camera was experienced as stressful and could lead to feelings of being exploited.

The importance of developing a successful brand was also implicit in the background preparations for performance. Much careful attention was given to makeup and costuming by production staff and by the performers themselves, in order to impart a positive personal image to the performance of pop standards. But other organizational features were also at work when it came to these image-building and sustaining activities, not to mention the vaguely articulated sense of being part of a team charged with undertaking a collaborative endeavour. The most blatant of these was the reality that, even if preparing in isolation, each contestant was mindful of competing against his or her fellow contestants. Nor was this competition solely a matter of self-image: there was a sense of being a representative of the nation, and of one hometown and family. Stresses such as these were encountered in a condensed form through the *Big Brother*-style isolation and sequestration of the ten finalists in a secret location. The tensions and anxieties – not to mention the rivalry and antipathies that develop in any production – were present in an unbroken, potentially full-time process of face-to-face interaction, and provided an ever-present source of tension/distraction from the business of preparing for performance. The fact that the performers had limited or no influence over the songs selected for performance, and limited opportunity to rehearse, added further strain to the quality of their onscreen performance in addition to the usual nerves and competitive pressures overall (Wright 2008). Similar findings were reported for the contestants on *Australian Idol* (Fairchild 2007).

For all the publicized priority on performance, the 'reality'-based exploitation of the interpersonal and personal conflicts experienced by the wanna-be and confirmed contestants was an equal, and at times a primary, source of spectacle. In relation to what the viewers saw, *as though it were a natural observation of the contestant*, such 'reality' segments provided the key to the performer as a kind of person, and in this sense constructed an identity brand that anchored the words and character provided by the song as a functioning personal statement (Fairchild 2007). The mixing of 'reality' footage and song performances meant that the latter were always semantically embroiled in a virtual showreel of back-stage 'authenticating' moments.

The politics of biculturalism

> New Zealand – our stories, our songs, our selves – *Aotearoa – a tatoukorero, a totouwaiata, koinatatou*
>
> – Motto, in English and Māori, of the New Zealand Government's Screen Production Funding Agency, New Zealand On Air

If the foregoing endogenous factors are common to any local version of the *Idol* format, the specificity of *New Zealand Idol* rests on exogenous factors. It is here that we find an implicit delegation of expressivity which is unique to New Zealand; this arises from the dominant imaged community of nationhood (Anderson 1983). In official culture, New Zealand is a postcolonial nation based on a bicultural partnership between the indigenous people, the Māori, and the descendants of European settlers. The basis of this partnership (which, in contemporary times, involves the descendants of white settlers – identified by the Māori term, Pakeha – being the numerically and economically dominant partner) rests on the Treaty of Waitangi, signed in 1840 by representatives of the British government, headed by Lieutenant Governor William Hobson and a party of Māori chiefs – the latter subsequently including over 500 Māori signatories. The implementation of the Treaty has a long and contentious history which cannot be reviewed here, but one of the significant features of the colonization process is that Western capitalist values – particularly private property, market-mediated exchange and individualism – steadily and forcibly supplanted the notions of collective ownership and kinship ties that were central features of Māori and Pasifika cultures (O'Sullivan 2007: 11–35, 56).

Although the original terms of the treaty, as the Māori understood them, were ignored by the white settlers in the drive to colonize the land, the Treaty itself survived as a significant historical and legal precedent. More than a century after its signing, it became a living – if disputed – force in national politics, largely in response to the political activism of the Māori in the 1970s and 1980s – a period identified as the Māori Resurgence (King 2003: 441–85). The Treaty of Waitangi Tribunal, set up in 1975, was empowered to examine claims for restitution of historic injustices, especially in relation to confiscations and the forced sale of Māori land. The Tribunal in principle, whatever the practical outcomes, made the concept of a bicultural partnership between Māori and Pakeha the bedrock of national identity, honoured in state ceremonies, language and cultural policy. Such a partnership not only held out the possibility of the Treaty partners being reconciled around a common framework of understanding; it also served to symbolize the end of the historic dependence on 'Mother England' which had joined the European Union, affirming a distinctive 'local' identity that would permit New Zealand to carve out a distinctive competitive niche in the global economic order (Pearson 2005: 32).

Although it could not be denied that contemporary New Zealand was increasingly becoming a more diverse society with immigrants from China, India and South Africa, as well as the traditional influx of immigrants from Polynesia and Europe, the principles of power-sharing and joint stewardship between Pakeha and Māori became a dominant motif in the projection of a national identity. For all the symbolic significance of biculturalism, as social statistics such as the rate of imprisonment, poverty, disease and educational under-achievement indicated, cultural prominence did not translate for Māori into effective economic power (Towns et al. 2004). Notwithstanding its important 'symbolic' role in state ceremonies and advertising branding, the evidence suggests that Māori culture is less a repository of deeply held horizontally shared values than an image bank for national and international tourism (Ryan 2002). Nor is biculturalism without its critics. Many Pakeha, passing lightly over the socio-economic status of Māori as an underclass, suspect that the symbolic pre-eminence of Māori culture is a vehicle for legitimizing preferential treatment for Māori and Pasifika groups. Ameliorative social policies in education and welfare, the development of a Māori Television Channel and the Treaty settlement process itself are seen as intrinsically unfair and as promoting dependency. Suspicions of affirmative action have a global pedigree, of course, as debates in the United States have repeatedly demonstrated. But in New Zealand they have a particular directness, if not stridency, given the small population, a small tax revenue base and the pervasiveness of neo-liberalism as a kind of common sense which makes even modest concessions to welfare seem egregious. Biculturalism has its critics within Māoridom, too; it is viewed as an inherently colonial policy that weakens claims for self-determination (O'Sullivan 2007: 25–35).

The particular feature of biculturalism that is salient here is that Pakeha and Polynesian people such as the Māori are perceived as having a different capacity for emotional expression:

> In New Zealand as in the United States, human relations among Pakehas are often thought to lack passion and spontaneity; the Pakeha approach to things is detached and coldly rational; Pakehas have lost the appreciation for magic and the capacity for wonder or awe inspired by the unknown; Pakeha culture is out of step with nature – it pollutes the environment and lacks a close tie with the land. Māori culture is represented as the ideal counterbalance to these Pakeha failings. Māoris cherish the dead, speaking to them and weeping freely over open caskets, while Pakehas mute the mourning process and hide the body from sight. (Hanson 1989)

Such personality stereotypes may be seen as a mundane elaboration of substantial metaphysical differences between a Western European and *Māoritanga* or Māori world-view (Patterson 2000). Their interest here rests not on their accuracy so much as the fact that they suggest another specifically *local* delegation of expressivity. All of the winners of the three *New Zealand Idol* contestants were from a Māori or Pasifika background. In *New Zealand Idol 2006*, for example, five of the ten contestants were from a Māori/Pasifika background, which is disproportionate to their numerical presence in the population at large. Certain prominent demographic groups were not represented in any of the contests – for example, Asians and Indians – so the show had a bicultural framing.

It would be rash to interpret this imbalance as being caused by an emotional deficit on the part of Pakeha performers. Other factors would have been just as important, such as the broader range of socio-economic or career opportunities available to Pakeha as opposed to Māori and Pasifika youth – or, at the more proximate level of those who were prepared to be engaged, the stronger family structure of the Māori and Pasifika communities delivering more votes. Further, as was found in *American Idol*, and held to explain the long runs of Hawaiian contestants, audience members in more populous areas of the country may have had greater difficulty in registering their vote because of high demand on the power grid (Paulsen 2008). Whether such a crowding effect was important in New Zealand is not known, but it cannot be ruled out given that some less populous areas have a higher concentration of Māori or, the converse, that the most populous area, Auckland, may have seen some votes lost through high demand. Again, although the judges – two Māori/Pasifika and one Pakeha – were held to sit at the altar of professionalism, their judgements did always lead to elimination as the audience vote presented a counter-valuation. Further, the introduction of immunity challenges also served to soften the efficacy of professional judgement by permitting the audience to make particular contestants immune from elimination. More empirical evidence is needed on the relative impact of these factors; however, as for the outcome of the shows themselves, they worked as if Māori/Pasifika contestants had an advantage when it came to adding a distinctive expressive dimension, a decisively Kiwi 'grain' of the voice to somewhat bland diet of pop standards (Barthes 1985). This testimony, if not directly an expression of a subterranean ethnically grounded authentication, certainly expressed the tacit belief that the kind of singer was more important than the performance of the song. Unfortunately, as already mentioned, once the protective zone of the contest was removed, the 'discovered' talent was found wanting.

Commoditizing intimate cosmopolitanism

> Disciplinary divides have negatively affected the discussions of cosmopolitanism even more than most terms. The normative ways of interrogating cosmopolitanism in political philosophy, for example, have involved categorizations and definitions related to world citizenship, universality, and global rights; more recently the term has been employed to signify contemporary political practices associated with globalization and the possibilities of a new global democratic order. In the latter incarnation scholars…have used it with reference to the promise of a global democracy based on liberal conceptions of human rights, tolerance, and universal standards of dignity and justice. The standpoint is a moral and ethical one, often with a prescriptive impetus of moving towards a more progressive and just social world. (Mitchell 2007: 706)

As this quote indicates, the classical formulations of cosmopolitanism have over-emphasized the faculties of reason, cognition, political and ethical principles at the expense of the emotions. Against these formulations, cosmopolitan intimacy can be characterized as a grounded engagement that can nurture the potential for revolutionary action through caring, emotional identification and empathy for others – characteristics that have been linked to a distinctive feminine world-view (Gilligan 1993: 22–23).

As an initial approximation, and as I wish to use the term here, *cosmopolitanism* refers to a disposition and impulse towards solidarity – the nurturing of an emotional engagement which fosters the exchange of ideas, beliefs and values in pursuit of cross-cultural involvement and acceptance. In this sense, it is the longing and search for a utopian community through popular cultural forms such as music that have been identified as a feature of entertainment (Dyer 2002). At the same time, I would also underscore another outcome that seems closer to what was reproduced by *New Zealand Idol*. Under the guise of a celebration of talent and the pop universalism, there steadily emerged an ambivalent embrace in which the values celebrated within the show were not embraced in the wider social context (Skrbis and Woodward 2007).

As I have suggested, a significant aspiration underlying *New Zealand Idol* – and, I believe, *Idol* in general – is to reclaim singularity through the introduction of the 'grain' of a distinctive national or Kiwi voice. Should this process succeed, then TVNZ would have satisfied its public service obligation whilst having produced, cheaply, a world-class program. Moreover, the format could be seen as providing a potential, within the framework of corporate popular music and its exchange values, for the expression of popular as a realm of use-values, nurturing the development of grassroots cultural production and the values of cosmopolitan intimacy. But this poaching within the corporate bailiwick turned out to be a comforting wish rather than a sociological reality. As the programs unfolded, the imparting of a distinct and singularizing voice was increasingly delegated to Māori/Pasifika contestants. This development meant that the inclusive potentiality of popular song was compromised by the imposition of a racialized hierarchy of expressivity. From within the contest itself, it was demonstrated that only a specific kind of person could fully claim to sing the songs the world has sung. This binary framing around the powers to claim ownership of the national voice was at odds with *Australian Idol*, where:

> The program came to represent all of Australia, according to the producers, from town to country. The sharp contrast in background and experience between the two finalists played on vague notions of 'togetherness' and 'diversity' while papering over some fairly significant social cleavages in the wider society. In this respect, *Idol* proved itself to be incapable of explanatory nuance not restricted to an individual's life history and ignorant of cultural politics that were not resolutely affirmative. (Fairchild 2007: 371)

In the case of *New Zealand Idol*, it was less that social cleavages were, within the narrow confines of the show, papered over so much as 'eroticized'. So the process of exchange formation within the discursive frameworks and practices of the show ran an uncertain course between demonstrating that particular individuals had a greater share of natural talent (always an empirical possibility) and declaring through its voting procedures that a whole category of people was naturally more talented. Further, given that this 'talent' veered towards adding emotional tone rather than 'vision' – which were pre-given by the established hits that provided the prototypes of local activities – then the show came close to endorsing, by default, the stereotype that non-white people are more musical, and possess greater powers of rhythm and swing, because they are more imbued with sensuality than intellect (Radano 2001).

To be sure, for many (including me), it is a positive development when a disadvantaged and disparaged racial category can celebrate a moment of triumph over the assured hegemony of whites. It did, after all, express some of the features of the self-image of Māori and Pasifika peoples and, conversely, of whites as inherently arrhythmic and uncool (Diawara 1998). But this ascendancy was marked as transitory, as a holiday from normality. This triumph of Māori and Pasifika expressivity soon acquired the image of unsustainability, being exposed post-contest as little more than a highly context-specific condescension. As the winners, lauded within the show as the field commanders of global musical exchange values, struggled to exercise their talents independently, the local market proved indifferent, and there was only a minor interest in exploiting the 'stars' as personality brands. Moreover, the following winners-only show, *Pop's Ultimate Stars*, restored the crown of national stardom to a white performer. As it happens, *Idol* graduates, for the most part, had little after-life in Australia too (Perez 2008). But while, across the Tasman, 'white' served as the unmarked norm – Guy Sebastian's background notwithstanding – against which the singularities of the personae were exercised, in New Zealand, white and Māori/Pasifika became the authenticating markers of differential powers of expression (Dyer 1999). It was no surprise, then, that in Australia the contest was seen as a self-contained exercise in marshalling audience attention (Fairchild 2007: 372). In New Zealand it was that too, but there was an unmistakable – if implicit – expectation that *New Zealand Idol* was yet another nation-defining moment, a sort of subterranean, shamefaced Eurovision song contest.

Conclusion

In sum, in *New Zealand Idol* the potential for cosmopolitan intimacy transpired into a postcolonial expression of dependency, less a challenge to corporate pop values than a kind of self-indulgent karaoke. Yet it is not my intention to assert that no 'utopian' space is possible within the framework of commoditized music production. Rather, this opening out of expressive possibilities for the subaltern depends on exogenous factors: on the cultural relations of the people themselves, specifically on a shared rather than divided sense of condition that can nurture the affective undercurrents of loss that power through the weight of existing social divisions (Tadiar 2008: 13). Such undercurrents are difficult to articulate in the bicultural framing of New Zealand national culture, even if they fuelled the competitive relationships that drove the contest. So it was that the format as a device for congealing exchange value in all and any local contexts worked its magic of sublimation on the popular uses of music in a small country at the bottom of the world.

References

Anderson B. (1983), *Imagined Communities: Reflections on the Origin and Spread of Nationalism*, London: Verso.

Barthes, Roland (1985), *The Grain of the Voice: Interviews 1962–1980*, trans. Linda Coverdale, New York: Hill and Wang.

Bourdieu, P. (1999), *The Weight of the World: Social Suffering in Contemporary Society*, trans. Priscilla Pankhurst Sullivan, Stanford, CN: Stanford University Press.
Brown, Andrew (2008), 'A Materialist Development of Some Recent Contributions to the Labour Theory of Value', *Cambridge Journal of Economics*, 32, pp. 125–46.
DeNora, Tia (1999), 'Music as a Technology of the Self', *Poetics*, 27, pp. 31–56.
Diawara, M. (1998), 'Homeboy Cosmopolitan', *October*, 83, pp. 51–70.
Dyer, R. (1997), *White: Essays on Race and Culture*, London: Routledge.
—— (2002), *Only Entertainment*, London: Routledge.
Fairchild, Charles (2007), 'Building the Authentic Celebrity: The *Idol* Phenomenon in the Attention Economy', *Popular Music and Society*, 30(3), pp. 355–75.
FremantleMedia (2007), *Pop Idol* website, http://www.fremantlemedia.com/our-programmes/view/Global+Hit+Formats/viewprogramme/Idols. Accessed 22 September 2007.
Frith, Simon (1989), 'Towards an Aesthetic of Popular Music', in R. Leppert and S. McClary (eds), *Music and Society: the Politics of Composition, Performance and Reception*, Cambridge: Cambridge University Press.
—— (2002), 'Music and Everyday Life', *Critical Quarterly*, 44(1), pp. 35–48.
Gilligan, C. (1993), *In a Different Voice*, Cambridge, MA: Harvard University Press.
Hanson, Allan (1989), 'The Making of the Māori: Culture Invention and Its Logic', *American Anthropologist, New Series*, 91(4), pp. 890–902.
Hjelmslev, Louis (1963), *Prolegomena to a Theory of Language*, trans. Francis J. Whitfield, Madison, WI: University of Wisconsin Press.
Horton, D. and Wohl, R.R. (1956), 'Mass Communication and Para-social Interaction: Observations on Intimacy at a Distance', *Psychiatry*, 19, pp. 215–29.
Jesson, Bruce (1991), *Only Their Purpose is Mad: The Money Men Take Over New Zealand*, Wellington: Dunmore Press.
Jenkins, Henry (2006), 'Buying into *American Idol*: How We are Being Sold on Reality Television', in *Convergence Culture: Where Old and New Media Collide*, New York University Press, pp. 59–90.
Keane, M. and Moran, A. (2008), 'Television's New Engines', *Television and New Media*, 9(2), pp. 155–69.
King, Michael (2003), *The Penguin History of New Zealand*, Auckland: Penguin.
Kopytoff, Igor (1986), 'The Cultural Biography of Things: Commoditization as a Process', in A. Appadurai (ed.), *The Social Life of Things: Commodities in Cultural Perspective*, Harvard, MA: Cambridge University Press, pp. 64–91.
Longshaw, J. (2006), 'NZ Idol 2006 Ends on Sour Note', http://www.kiwiherald.com/NZIdol2006.html. Accessed 16 December 2008.
Manuel, Peter (1998), 'Gender Politics in Caribbean Popular Music: Consumer Perspectives and Academic Interpretation', *Popular Music and Society*, 22, p. 2.
Marx, Karl (1976), *Capital: A Critique of Political Economy, Volume One*, trans. Ben Fowkes, London: Penguin.
Mitchell, Katharyne (2007), 'Geographies of Identity: The Intimate Cosmopolitan', *Progress in Human Geography*, 31(5), pp. 706–20.
Moore, Alan (2002), 'Authenticity as Authentication', *Popular Music*, 21/2, pp. 209–23.
O'Sullivan, Dominic (2007), *Beyond Biculturalism, The Politics of an Indigenous Minority*, Auckland: Huia Press.
Orzechowicz, David (2008), 'Privileged Emotion Managers: The Case of Actors', *Social Psychology Quarterly*, 71(2), p. 143.

Parrat, Herman (1984), 'Peirce and Hjelmslev: The Two Semiotics', *Language Sciences*, 6(2), pp. 217–27.

Patterson, John (2000), *People of the Land: a Pacific Philosophy*, Wellington: Dunmore Press.

Paulsen, Wade (2008), 'Distorted *American Idol* Voting Due to Overtaxed American Phone Grid?', http://www.realitytvworld.com/index/articles/story.php?s=2570. Accessed 16 December 2008.

Pearson, David (2005), 'Citizenship, Identity and Belonging: Addressing the Mythologies of the Unitary Nation State in Aotearoa/New Zealand', in James H. Liu, Tim McCreanor, Tracey McIntosh and Teresa Teaiwa (eds), *New Zealand Identities: Departures and Destinations*, Wellington: Victoria University Press, pp. 21–37.

Perez, J. (2008), 'The *Australian Idol* Journey: A Guaranteed Road to Ruin', http://www.livenews.com.au/Articles/2008/11/21/The_Australian_Idol_journey_a_guaranteed_road_to_ruin. Accessed 16 December 2008.

Peterson, R.A. and Anand, N. (2004), 'The Production of Culture Perspective', *Annual Review of Sociology*, 30, pp. 311–44.

Peterson, R.A. and. White, H.G. (1981), 'Elements of Simplex Structure', *Urban Life*, 10(1), pp. 3–24.

Radano, R. (2001), 'Hot Fantasies: American Modernism and the Idea of Black Rhythm', in R. Radano and P. Bohlman (eds), *Music and the Racial Imagination* (Chicago Studies in Ethnomusicology), Chicago: University of Chicago Press, pp. 459–82.

Reijnders, S., Rooijakkers, G. and van Zoonen, L. (2007), 'Community Spirit and Competition in *Idols*: Ritual Meanings of a TV Talent Quest', *European Journal of Communication*, 22(3), pp. 275–92.

Ryan, Chris (2002), 'Tourism and Cultural Proximity: Examples from New Zealand', *Annals of Tourism Research*, 29(4), pp. 952–71.

Shuker, Roy (2008), 'New Zealand Popular Music, Government Policy, and Cultural Identity', *Popular Music*, 27(2), pp. 271–87.

SMLXL (2006), '*Pop Idol*: The Fake Plastic Trees of Reality TV, or Participatory Democracy in Close-up?' http://www.smalxtralarge.com. Accessed 16 December 2008.

Skrbis, Zlatko and Woodard, Ian (2007), 'The Ambivalence of Ordinary Cosmopolitanism: Investigating the Limits of Cosmopolitan Openness', *The Sociological Review*, 55(4), pp. 730–47.

Stuff (2007), 'Dominic Bowden Loves LA', *Sunday Star Times*, 17 December. http://www.stuff.co.nz. Accessed 15 December 2008.

Tadiar, N.X.M. (2009), 'Popular Laments: Affective Literacy, Democratization and War', *Cultural Studies*, 23(1), pp. 1–23.

Towns, Cindy et al. (2004) 'The Orewa Speech: Another Threat to Māori Health', *The New Zealand Medical Journal*, 117(1205), pp. 1–7, http://www.nzma.org.nz/journal/117-1205/1145. Accessed 14 March 2008.

Trevett, Claire (2006), 'Record Giant Scratches *NZ Idol*', http://www.nzherald.co.nz/nz/news/article.cfm?c_id=1&objectid=10384486. Accessed 16 December 2008.

Vannini, Phillip and Waskul, Dennis (2006), 'Symbolic Interaction as Music: The Esthetic Constitution of Meaning, Self and Society', *Symbolic Interaction*, 9(3), pp. 5–18.

Wells, Alan (1990), 'Popular Music: Emotional Use and Management', *Journal of Popular Culture*, 2(1), pp. 105–17.

Wright, Rebecca (2008), *New Zealand Idol*: Performance, Talent and Authenticity in a Song Contest, unpublished MA thesis, Auckland University of Technology.

Zizek, S., (1997), 'The Supposed Subjects of Ideology', *Critical Quarterly*, 39(2), pp. 39–59.

Zuel, B. (2007), 'Will *Idol* Graduates Ever Get Any Respect?' *Sydney Morning Herald*, 6 September, http://www.smh.com.au/news/music/will-idol-graduates-ever-get-any-respect/2007/09/05/1188783289280.html. Accessed 20 December 2008.

Chapter 17

From Global to Glocal: Australianizing the Makeover Format

Tania Lewis

Since the breakthrough success of the British home makeover show *Changing Rooms* on prime-time UK TV in the early 1990s, the past few years have seen the growing popularity of the lifestyle makeover format around the world (Lewis 2008b). Emerging as part of the broader rise of formats in the TV industry, the makeover represents a complex blend of TV genres – combining conventions and concerns borrowed from lifestyle advice television, daytime talk shows and reality TV with a transformational 'before and after' narrative. Focusing primarily on ordinary people (although occasionally dealing with wayward celebrities), everything from homes (*Extreme Makeover Home Edition*) and gardens (*Backyard Blitz*) to pets (*It's Me or the Dog*), parental skills (*Supernanny*), personal etiquette (*Ladette to Lady*), cars (*Pimp my Ride*) and bodies (*The Biggest Loser*) are put under the spotlight and transformed – with the guidance of various life experts – under the gaze of the watching public.

The ubiquity of the makeover format today is reflected in the way it has, like reality TV more broadly, become a thoroughly globalized format—travelling not just within linguistically congruent TV markets but across various geolinguistic regions. The translatability of lifestyle shows across cultural boundaries is due to a range of factors including the fact that the makeover show readily lends itself to format franchising as well as the growing global appeal of lifestyle-oriented forms of consumer culture. However, while the makeover format has been embraced globally, what also distinguishes lifestyle TV as a mode of programming is its strong connection to local lifestyles and modes of consumption. Part of lifestyle TV's appeal as a global format is precisely its ability to be moulded and shaped to suit local/national conditions.

This chapter uses lifestyle makeover formats in Australia as a generative case study through which to explore some of the complex dynamics at work in relation to the global dissemination and the local production and reception of format TV. It draws upon in-depth interviews the author conducted with a range of pivotal figures in the TV industry in Australia over the period from June to August 2007. The essay examines questions related to the global influences on local TV format markets and the localization of global formats, along the way touching on a range of issues raised by the globalization of makeover formats, including how both global trends and cultural difference shape format travel and reception.

Ordinary lifestyles on television

One important context for the rise of lifestyle makeover formats has been a broader shift on television screens around the world to a focus on the lifestyles and everyday concerns of ordinary people. As Frances Bonner (2003: 28) points out, since the 1980s television has been marked by a growing concern with the mundane and 'the ordinary', as reflected in its increasing focus on domestic space and the lives of members of the public. Likewise, writing in the 1990s about the growing role of 'true life story' genres in the United States, United Kingdom and Europe, Ib Bondeberg (1996) argues that this has occurred as part of a broader embrace of privatized modes of discourse, with the camera increasingly turning to focus on the intimacies of people's lives and relationships.

The reasons for this focus on ordinary people's lifestyles on TV are complex and multifaceted. Representing more than just a convenient new moniker for the TV industry, the rise of lifestyle television can also be seen as part of a broader shift to a strongly consumer-centred 'lifestyle culture'. As Jonathan Bignell notes in his book, *Big Brother* (2005: 40), the transnational mobility of reality and makeover TV can be seen as marking an increasingly global preoccupation with 'personal confession, modification, testing and the perfectibility of the self'. Such a notion of the self is very much a product of a lifestyle culture that foregrounds personal choice and the malleable nature of the self, seeing ordinary people as being able to reinvent their own life 'biographies'. In this cultural and ideological context, the makeover show can be seen to literally extend the DIY rubric of home renovation to every aspect of one's life, from health and fitness to interpersonal and familial relationships.

While the growing global hegemony of lifestyle and consumer culture forms an important cultural and ideological backdrop to the rise of makeover TV, the prime-time emergence of these formats is also, of course, linked to a range of pivotal developments within the global TV industry itself. In particular, the shift since the 1980s towards modes of relatively cheap, 'unscripted' television focused on ordinary people can be seen as an attempt to deal with an increasingly deregulated market and a fragmented audience, with free-to-air networks now competing with pay TV for viewers' attention, offering audiences an abundance of programming choices (Bonner 2003; Ellis 2000). In a post-broadcast setting, 'water cooler' TV shows like *The Biggest Loser* and *Trinny and Susannah Undress the Nation*, which purport to speak to a national community of viewers, have a strong appeal to networks and advertisers. Often packaged as a multi-platform franchise complete with a website, spinoff books and other merchandise, popular lifestyle formats and their associated lifestyle experts (figures like Carson Kressley, Jamie Oliver and Trinny and Susannah) also offer a degree of 'branding' that gives them a strong edge in a competitive, converged media market.

Another important reason for the global success of makeover TV has been its ability to travel as a format into a range of different television markets. The emergence of a multi-channel environment has produced a situation where the pressure for product has encouraged local producers to create programs that can potentially move across a range of markets (Moran 1998; Waisbord 2004). This situation has seen a relative challenge to US hegemony in global TV traffic and trade as TV formats increasingly emerge from the United Kingdom and Western Europe as well as from smaller players such as Australia and Mexico (Magder 2004; Moran and Keane 2006; Waisbord 2004).

As Waisbord (2004: 359) comments, the rise and rise of format television has resulted in a situation whereby '[a]round the world, television is filled with national variations of programs designed by companies from numerous countries'. For instance, Endemol, a company that originated and continues to be based in Holland, first created the global reality TV phenomenon *Big Brother* for the Dutch market, going on to sell the format to numerous countries. Reality lifestyle programs offered up as format 'shells', such as the highly popular garden makeover format *Ground Force*, first aired in the United Kingdom, and the US plastic surgery format *Extreme Makeover*, have been shown to have considerable transnational mobility and selling power, they are amenable to being readily 'indigenized', even in the case of programs emerging from non-English markets (such as the Dutch market), and are relatively risk free, having previously been tried out on an audience (Waisbord 2004).

The global rise of the makeover show

Over recent years, makeover TV has become a globally successful format, appearing on prime-time schedules around the world. As noted, the format business has seen a relative shift away from American domination of TV production and dissemination. While US makeover formats like *Extreme Makeover* and *Queer Eye for the Straight Guy* have proved popular in a range of territories, many countries around the world are now producing and at times exporting their own makeover formats. Singapore's Mediacorp, for instance, has produced an extremely popular Chinese-language home makeover series called *Home Décor Survivor*, which has run to several series and has also produced a spinoff series called *Junior Home Décor Survivor*, while the format rights to the New Zealand reality-based green lifestyle show *Wasted* have been sold to a number of countries, including the United States and Spain.

While format production then has become a relatively globalized affair, two countries in particular – the United Kingdom and the United States – have been associated with the production and dissemination of makeover shows, with the United Kingdom playing an important early role in shaping the format. Here I want briefly to discuss the lifestyle makeover format in the United Kingdom and United States before going on to discuss Australia's lifestyle TV industry.

The first successful makeover show to air on prime-time TV was the British home renovation game show format *Changing Rooms*.[1] First broadcast on the BBC in 1996, it was later sold into a number of international markets, and is seen in the industry as a breakthrough show in terms of bringing the makeover on to prime-time TV. In the United Kingdom and elsewhere, makeovers had previously featured on daytime TV as segments on magazine programs and talk shows aimed at women. However, *Changing Rooms* saw the lifestyle makeover expand into a full-length reality game show format aimed at a broad prime-time audience, including male viewers. It was a model adapted and copied by local TV producers around the world.

Daytime TV makeovers, reflecting their largely female audiences, had often focused on issues of personal style and fashion. The first successful makeover formats in the United Kingdom, however – including the hugely popular format *Ground Force* (2007), which sold to the United States and Australia – were shows oriented towards investing in and improving the home rather than the self. The format subsequently evolved to embrace a range of other full-length makeover formats, including shows like *What Not to Wear* (BBC 2001) fronted by the now globally successful fashion makeover gurus Trinny and Susannah.

While these earlier makeover formats were strongly entertainment-oriented shows, the lifestyle makeover format can be seen to be linked to more 'educational' TV genres – for example, British daytime advice TV and social observational documentary forms such as Paul Watson's *The Family* (BBC 1974). More recently, the reality lifestyle show in Britain – and, as Ouellette and Hay (2008) note, to a certain extent the United States – has been marked by something of a return to the educational and social concerns of the social observational form. For instance, the past couple of years have seen a variety of shows emerge out of the United Kingdom around the intersection of health, lifestyle and parenting issues, including *Honey We're Killing the Kids* and the highly successful *Supernanny*.

While the makeover format is often associated with the United States, American free-to-air networks were somewhat slower to embrace the makeover show as a prime-time format compared with the United Kingdom, focusing instead in the 1990s on a range of (early) reality-style formats from the low budget, actuality-based television of the *COPS* variety to shows like MTV's *The Real World* (1992). The first makeover show on US television was the home renovation show *Trading Spaces*, a US adaptation of the BBC's *Changing Rooms*. It first appeared on a cable channel, The Learning Channel (TLC), in 2000, achieving high ratings which rivalled those of the free-to-air networks.

Despite the popularity of *Trading Spaces* and other DIY and hobbyist shows on cable TV, however, arguably US makeover culture has been more oriented towards personal makeover shows (Kavka 2006). Thus the first breakthrough makeover show on US network TV was the surgical makeover program *Extreme Makeover*, which first aired on the ABC in 2002, while subsequent highly popular US formats have included *Queer Eye for the Straight Guy* and *The Biggest Loser*. While the United States was relatively slow to pick up the prime-time makeover format, it has subsequently become a major producer and global disseminator of a wide range of makeover formats, from car makeover shows (*Pimp My Ride*) to 'greenovation' programs (*The EcoZone Project*).

The rise of lifestyle formats in Australia

Another television market that has embraced the makeover format is Australia. Like the British, Australians have had a long-running interest in lifestyle (or what used to be termed 'infotainment') programs. Over the past couple of decades, Australian prime-time TV has been populated by a variety of lifestyle programs. Magazine shows such as the long-running *Better Homes and Gardens* (produced alongside a magazine of the same name) and the holiday show *Getaway* have had sizable prime-time audiences of both male and female viewers. In the 1990s, however, something of a lifestyle programming 'boom' took place on Australian TV, with a range of innovative lifestyle formats appearing in prime time, including shows like *Sex* and *Money* which aimed to vamp up the magazine format to target a younger audience.

It was against this backdrop that Australians embraced the makeover format, which took off from the late 1990s onwards. While, prior to the 1990s, Australian house and garden-oriented magazine shows would often feature a segment where property was transformed (2005), Australia had never produced a full-length makeover show. In Australia (as in the United States), the UK *Changing Rooms* program was a pivotal influence on the industry. As executive producer for the ABC, Erik Dwyer, notes:

> *Changing Rooms* was the first reality observational show. Before then they were all structured magazine style shows like *Better Homes and Gardens* and *Our House* where the host throws to a story, etc. So *Changing Rooms* was the first off your shoulder reality lifestyle show. (Interview with author)

Building upon its existing lifestyle TV industry. Australia made a number of homegrown house and garden makeover shows. For instance, the popular Australian garden makeover show *Backyard Blitz* (2000) originally started out as a small segment on the pioneering Australian lifestyle show *Burke's Backyard* (1987), but due to popular response was turned into a standalone 30-minute weekly show. As Dwyer notes, however, the shift between magazine makeover and the prime-time home and garden makeover format involved a dramatic shift in focus:

> Seventy per cent of the story wasn't the bricks and mortar but the interaction and reaction of the people and getting into their heads, so that was the transformation between [magazine shows and makeover formats]. We started to turn the camera on the people not what they were putting together. So that was a big change. (Interview with author)

In subsequent shows like *Renovation Rescue* (2004), the melodramatic element of the show was further heightened. Drawing hosts from a range of previous makeover shows, it showed them renovating 'for good', making over the homes of 'deserving' people – a motif that has become a common feature of Australian makeover shows. Although focusing on very attractive, camera-friendly couples rather than 'deserving Aussies', *The Block* (2003), in which four couples competed to each renovate a flat in the iconic beachside suburb of Bondi, also drew upon the conventions of melodrama and soap opera combined with a competitive game show element. The show was hugely popular in Australia, and the format rights sold to a variety of countries around the world, including Scandinavia, the United Kingdom and the United States (see also Chapter 10 in this volume).

While Australia has produced numerous homegrown makeover formats, most of which have been home and garden makeover shows, it has also produced a number of local versions of international formats, including more recently the US personal makeover shows *Queer Eye for the Straight Guy* and *The Biggest Loser*. Both were made after airing the original version of the show, a process that in the case of *Queer Eye* saw the local show flop, while by contrast *The Biggest Loser* has run to four locally made series. Numerous international formats have also been aired without local versions, from the UK and US versions of *Supernanny* to the UK fashion makeover show *What Not to Wear*, again with mixed results in terms of audience reception.

The Australian TV industry

The difficulty of predicting what foreign formats will work in the Australian market points to the ongoing role of local influences on shaping transnational format flow. Australia in many ways has a rather distinct televisual landscape, which I would argue has played a strong role in determining the kinds of formats that get produced in Australia and also, to a certain extent, their reception. The Australian TV industry is small and has been marked until recently by a relative lack of competition from pay TV and digital television, which for various reasons have been slow to take off there. Compared to the multi-channel environments of the United Kingdom and United States, the Australian TV market has largely been dominated by free-to-air networks. While over the past couple of years the combined audience of subscription television has started to rival the commercial networks in relation to audience share, as Trevor Eastment, Head of Programming at Foxtel's Lifestyle Channel, notes:

> We've got a culture of free TV here…we've had five TV stations for nothing. We're one of the very few countries in the world that's never paid anything for television. In England you pay a licence fee. The culture there is that you pay for TV and in the states they've had cable forever. So it's just not part of the culture here – audiences have this idea that TV should be free. (Interview with author)

The dominance of the free-to-airs means that, until recently, format commissioning and development in Australia have been shaped strongly by the networks. Australia has three commercial networks, Seven, Nine and Ten, which tend to dominate audience share, and two publicly subsidized channels, the ABC (Australian Broadcasting Company) and SBS (Special Broadcasting Service). SBS, with its charter to represent 'multicultural Australia', is a relatively minor player in terms of audience share, airing a range of foreign and niche-oriented programming. In recent years, however, it has bought the rights to produce local versions of a range of international formats, including the hugely successful UK show *Top*

Gear (*Top Gear Australia* is now being made into a second series), as well as commissioning local formats such as *Eco-House Challenge*, an innovative green makeover format made by Prospero Productions, an independent production company in Western Australia. The main public broadcaster, the ABC, which has continued to adhere to a fairly traditional 'public service' model, is a rather embattled and under-funded public institution (although it has a considerably larger audience share and budget than SBS). While the ABC was something of a pioneer in early lifestyle TV, unlike the BBC it has not embraced reality lifestyle formats. In recent years, it has commissioned the low-budget personal makeover show *Agony Aunt* and the green-oriented 'observational documentary' *Carbon Cops*, as well as airing the odd glossy international lifestyle format such as Channel Four's *Grand Designs*; overall, though, its focus has stayed on more traditional forms of documentary programming.

The majority of reality makeover formats have thus appeared on the commercial networks. Channels Nine and Seven, which have traditionally appealed to an older demographic, have produced the lion's share of local home and garden makeover shows, as well as continuing to air a range of magazine-style lifestyle shows such as *Better Homes and Gardens*, *The Great Outdoors* and *What's Good for You*. Nine has also produced some reality-based personal makeover shows such as *Celebrity Overhaul* (2004), and more recently a local version of ITV's *Ladette to Lady*. In general, though, Network Ten – which aims at a younger demographic, similar to that of the UK's Channel Four – has been the leader in the Australian market in terms of airing reality-based shows. Drawing upon its success with the local version of *Big Brother*, Ten has commissioned a range of local versions of US and UK reality and lifestyle formats, including *Australian Idol*, *The Biggest Loser*, *Queer Eye for the Straight Guy* and *Honey We're Killing the Kids*, exposing Australian audiences to a much wider range of makeover formats than the usual home and garden renovation shows associated with Seven and Nine. While subscription TV has been a relatively minor player on the scene, more recently it has also been making inroads into the format market with Fox 8 producing the highly successful *Australia's Next Top Model* and the Lifestyle Channel also airing a number of foreign makeover formats, including home makeover shows and personal and relationship makeover shows such as *Supernanny* and *How to Look Good Naked*.

Global influences on the Australian market

Despite a relatively small, and at times parochial, TV market with a limited number of channels (although this situation is starting to change with digitalization and the growing popularity of subscription TV), the format industry is alive and well in Australia, with audiences exposed to a variety of original foreign, localized versions and homegrown formats. Network programmers and production companies alike have a strong awareness of global trends in format development, and local production increasingly occurs with an eye to the global market. As Carl Fennessy, co-head (with brother Mark) of FremantleMedia Australia, comments:

> The TV creation and production world is pretty small these days. There's probably been more communication between international producers of all sizes in the last three years than in the previous twenty. TV is so instant today – if you talk to people at the networks, they're aware of what's new coming out of the UK, even what's being pitched, because of that drive to find the next big thing or the next format that's going to work. They have reps on the ground everywhere looking…so they can leap onto it and perhaps option the format before their competitors because really now the speed with which a format can go multi-territory is incredibly fast. (Interview with author)

Cathie Scott, an executive producer at Network Ten, likewise reiterates the importance to the networks of having good international 'intelligence':

> We've got links with companies in the UK and the US and we've also got people who work for Ten who are based there so we get kept up with all the new formats that are coming through. What is working and what isn't and while they are very different markets it certainly gives you a good indication of what may or may not be successful here. Everyday we get a report from our person in LA and our person in London about what's been on the night before, how it's done, any press articles, any trends within the business coming up…And we get a format report which actually tables all the formats that are currently on around the world so we try and keep abreast of what's happening everywhere. (Interview with author)

As Scott also notes, formats are sometimes offered directly to the networks by multinational production companies (such as FremantleMedia or Endemol), many of which now have arms in Australia. Indeed, a feature of the Australian production scene (and a reflection of the broader industry globally) is the fact that small, independent, locally based companies are increasingly being absorbed into large multinational production companies. As many in the industry agree, with only three major commercial networks commissioning formats (although subscription TV is starting to make inroads here), Australia is a particularly risk-averse industry, with the networks often looking to buy formats with a track record in large markets like Europe, the United Kingdom and the United States, leaving independent producers relatively dependent on the ABC and SBS for commissions and sales.

However, while the industry people I interviewed commented on the globalized industrial context in which Australian format producers now work, they took pains to emphasize that producing content for the local Australian market is the primary focus of much of their work. As Carl Fennessy put it in relation to making local formats:

> FremantleMedia Australia is creating primarily for the local market – both for free to air and cable. If something local happens to work globally then that's great but that's not necessarily the focus…We would certainly never intentionally internationalize a show in the hope that it will travel. I think you have to be true to your audience and to the broadcaster who's commissioning you. (Interview with author)

Likewise, as a senior executive at another production company notes, in looking to and purchasing from the global format market, one has to be attuned to local concerns:

> Television is tribal – what a lot of people watch in Sydney is not necessarily what they'll watch in Melbourne or Brisbane, never mind on the other side of the world. The great fallacy is network television. I look at the ratings every day and there are often shows that rate well in Sydney but not in Melbourne. Some big shows, dramas like *CSI*, do well for networks but a lot of shows don't travel outside of their little market. So with formats while something may have done well in your market they have to be thoroughly reworked for other markets. We say we have to Oz-ize formats to make them work here. You look at pace, etc. and some things just don't translate and that's not just across world markets that's also across boundaries within markets.

Cultural and market specificity of formats

Despite the growing international exchange of formats across a range of genres from comedy to game shows to reality and lifestyle formats, formats seldom travel between markets without some kind of local adaptation, indicating the ongoing role of nationally based cultural and industry influences. For instance, at a generic level, certain territories have embraced certain types of formats. In broad terms, the United Kingdom is associated in particular with lifestyle formats and with popular factual programming, while the United States and Europe have been particularly interested in social observation-style reality shows. Meanwhile, Australia has, as noted, had a long tradition of lifestyle TV – particularly home shows but more recently also popular factual formats (*Border Security*, *Bondi Rescue*, *Find My Family*) and some reality shows (*Big Brother* proved extremely popular in the Australian market).

Alongside these differences in generic preferences, there are distinct cultural differences in terms of scheduling, program aesthetics and audience preferences. As a senior executive at a major production company notes:

> In the UK they structure their content hours differently – they run things for longer, have less commercial breaks. UK shows tend to be slower while the US shows tend to be a lot faster, almost frenetic. So cultural styles come into it to a great degree. And Europe is different again. For whatever reason, I don't think there's the depth or volume of lifestyle programs in the European market as there is in Australia, US or UK markets. (Interview with author)

Further, as noted earlier, within the lifestyle genre home and garden shows have been hugely popular on prime-time network TV in the United Kingdom and Australia, while in the United States such shows have tended to be associated with specialized cable channels.

Likewise, while personal makeover shows have been highly popular in the United States and United Kingdom, despite the recent success of localized versions of global formats such as *The Biggest Loser*, Australia has never had a successful homegrown personal makeover format.

Within genres, program styles and other cultural differences also come into play. Tim Cobbin, executive producer for Network Nine, observes:

> On American TV everything is huge – in the UK and here in Australia we'll do up a room, show a before and after and it's great, whereas on [the US home renovation show] *Extreme Makeover Home Edition* it's 'let's rebuild a whole house, stuff it let's rebuilt the whole street!' (Interview with author)

Trevor Eastment of the Lifestyle Channel also points to the cultural differences that determine the reception of a show:

> *Survivor* didn't do well in the UK but *The Weakest Link*, which did incredibly well in the UK, didn't do so well here or in the States. If you are physically cruel to people it works in the States and here. If you're mentally cruel to people it works in the UK, but not here…I've no idea what that says culturally. In the UK they like that schoolmarmish, cruel-to-be-kind approach. (Interview with author)

Likewise, as Tim Cobbin notes:

> While America since *Survivor* has been really into reality shows, many of them don't translate for us. Even *Survivor*, which did well for two series here – it's still big in the States but is now on late-night TV here. (Interview with author)

In relation to makeover formats in particular, Australia's approach to and reception of these formats has been shaped by distinctive cultural concerns and TV traditions.[2] For example, while Australian audiences have recently embraced personal makeover shows like *The Biggest Loser*, they tend to be less comfortable with the aggressive competitive individualism that is often central to US game show-style makeover formats. Australia also has historically had much less of a confessional culture than the United States, although the increasing popularity of reality TV and personal makeover shows in Australia suggests a growing acceptance on behalf of both audiences and the contestants on these shows of personal revelation and 'therapy speak' on television.

While sharing the British obsession with home makeover shows, Australian lifestyle TV has also tended to be less concerned with class issues than its UK counterparts. As Peter Abbott at Freehand Productions noted in relation to translating British lifestyle formats for Australian audiences (in an interview I conducted with him in 2006):

> A lot of the drama of UK TV is underpinned by class struggle or, for me, a disconnect between the viewer and the people on the show. There's a lot more, 'these are people you can laugh at because they're not like us'. There's a certain meanness in that to me…That's why a lot of this programming doesn't translate. (Interview with author)

In contrast, Australian makeovers tend to be concerned less with humiliation and class conflict and more with constructing a familiar, neighbourly mode of address and focusing on more ordinary types of people. As Rick Maier, Head of Programme Development at Ten, notes:

> Shows about rich people don't really work for us because culturally we don't look up to rich people. For some reason we relate to the battlers [a colloquialism for struggling, working class Australians]. So that's a significant cultural difference, I think.

Reflecting these concerns, the hosts and experts that feature on Australian lifestyle shows tend to be positioned as resolutely average, often speaking with broad Australian accents. As one TV executive puts it:

> The image we show to the world is more working class – figures like Scott Cam [a carpenter who has appeared on a number of lifestyle shows in Australia]. Pretty much all of our presenters are comfortable and down to earth. (Interview with author)

This is not to say that there are no issues of social distinction or competitive individualism at work in Australian makeover formats – aspirationalism is a key mantra in Australian lifestyle culture, and lifestyle TV is often referred to in the industry as aspirational TV. The discourse of 'getting ahead', however, tends to be framed in terms of aspiring to a kind of average-ness, a preoccupation which speaks to a broader cultural mythos of 'mateship' and social egalitarianism.

As Craig Walsh, executive producer at Seven, sums up the Australian makeover ethos:

> We like to do things for people who are deserving. Why are they getting that kitchen? Why do they deserve it? On my show I'd be looking not for places with a harbour view but for places in the western suburbs [of Sydney – an area generally associated with more ordinary, working-class people], where I grew up and much of our audience probably come from. So we do a kitchen for three thousand dollars.

In conclusion: Glocal formats

Makeover TV programs – whether sold as format shells to be localized for a domestic market or aired in their original form – do not necessarily succeed in all TV markets. In part, this is due to the fact that, even as program shells or blueprints, TV formats are often shaped by and speak to certain types of cultural values and concerns. In the case of lifestyle television, while lifestyle culture and consumption are increasingly becoming globalized, as Bonner (2005) argues, the content of lifestyle TV has traditionally been rather inward looking, reflecting everyday concerns and national beliefs and values. Australian home makeover shows, for instance, tend to assume universal home ownership and are often framed by a distinctly Australian lifestyle culture centred on indoor–outdoor living and the quarter-acre block.

As I've noted more broadly, the development of the lifestyle makeover format in different contexts has very much reflected its ties to the 'national ordinary' while also being shaped by different nationally inflected industry histories and modes of reception, or 'television makeover cultures' as Mischa Kavka (2006) has termed them. These different makeover cultures have meant that certain kinds of shows – such as surgical makeover shows, which have flourished in the United States and South America – have not readily translated to the Australian context. Local versions of foreign makeover formats such as *The Biggest Loser* have succeeded, but have been considerably reworked to fit into the Australian market. *The Biggest Loser*, for instance, was a one-hour, once-a-week format in the United States but was refigured by FremantleMedia Australia (working with Cathie Scott from Network Ten) into a nightly format. As Scott comments, 'the show is strongly narrative driven, rather soap opera like, and we extended that element for the stripped version'. The format was also localized through the use of an Australian host and the introduction of Australian trainers to the show – a move that proved extremely popular.

At the same time, makeover shows – like other formats – are a complex mix of global and local influences, and they often succeed locally in part ironically because of their global branding. Domestic versions of shows like *The Biggest Loser*, for instance, often do well because audiences have first been prepared for the show by viewing the original US or UK version. Adapting local versions of high-rating foreign formats can be a fraught process, however. As one Australian TV executive pointed out, in certain cases 'showing the original format here can poison the water for the local version'. Central here is the cast contingency of lifestyle shows where figures like Jo Frost from *Supernanny* and the Fab Five from *Queer Eye for the Straight Guy* become such global icons that it is hard to make a local version of the format with local hosts and experts. The Australian version of *Queer Eye* shown on Network Ten, for instance, was a flop and is held up by Australian producers as a cautionary tale regarding remaking highly visible, branded foreign formats without using the original cast. Arguably one of the reasons why the local version of *The Biggest Loser* has been such a success is that, as part of its deal with NBC, it wrote the charismatic US trainers Bob and Jillian (who were by then major international celebrities) into its first few series before later introducing Australian trainers, producing a format that was essentially a blend of US and Australian influences – in other words, a 'glocal' format.

Even localized versions of makeover formats, then, are never completely domesticated, while supposedly homegrown formats such as the extremely successful Australian competitive renovation show *The Block* can often work in local and global markets. While set in the iconic Australian location of Bondi, *The Block* sold as a format across a range of territories including rather colder climes such as the United Kingdom and Scandinavia (where, according to one executive, they put a fish in a bowl as part of a renovation only to find it had frozen overnight!). The point to make here is that, while TV markets and cultures are still strongly national, the rise of the format points to the growing way in which TV markets are inextricably connected to transnational industrial processes and cultural influences. The makeover format speaks neither solely to the 'national ordinary' nor to a purely universalizing televisual culture of Euro-American lifestyles and consumption, but rather to a television industry and culture marked by increasingly complex negotiations between globalizing forces and domestic concerns and contexts (Moran 1998).

Notes

1. *Changing Rooms* was the brainchild of British lifestyle TV guru Peter Bazalgette, who also created groundbreaking lifestyle formats such as *Ready Steady Cook* and *Ground Force*. Bazalgette's TV production company eventually became part of Endemol UK, and as chairman of the company he introduced *Big Brother* to British television audiences.
2. For a more in-depth examination of these issues, see the chapter on the making of the Australian version of the BBC lifestyle makeover format *Honey We're Killing the Kids* in my book *Smart Living: Lifestyle Media and Popular Expertise* (Lewis 2008a).

References

Bignell, J. (2005), *Big Brother: Reality TV in the Twenty-First Century*, Basingstoke: Palgrave Macmillan.

Bondebjerg, I. (1996), 'Public Discourse/Private Fascination: Hybridization in "'True-life-story" Genres', *Media Culture & Society*, 18(1), pp. 27–45.

Bonner, F. (2003), *Ordinary Television: Analyzing Popular TV*, London: Sage.

—— (2005), 'Whose Lifestyle is It Anyway?' in D. Bell and J. Hollows (eds), *Ordinary Lifestyles: Popular Media, Consumption and Taste*, Maidenhead: Open University Press, pp. 35–46.

Ellis, J. (2000), *Seeing Things: Television in the Age of Uncertainty*, London: I.B. Tauris.

Kavka, M. (2006), 'Changing Properties: The Makeover Show Crosses the Atlantic', in D. Heller (ed.), *The Great American Makeover: Television, History, Nation*, New York: Palgrave Macmillan, pp. 211–29.

Lewis, T. (2008a), *Smart Living: Lifestyle Media and Popular Expertise*, New York: Peter Lang.

—— (ed.) (2008b), *TV Transformations: Revealing the Makeover Show*, London: Routledge.

Magder, T. (2004), 'The End of TV 101: Reality Television, Formats and the New Business of TV', in S. Murray and L. Ouellette (eds), *Reality TV: Remaking Television Culture*, New York: New York University Press, pp. 137–56.

Moran, A. (1998), *Copycat TV: Globalisation, Program Formats and Cultural Identity*, Luton: University of Luton Press.

Moran, A. and Keane, M. (2006), 'Cultural Power in International TV Format Markets', *Continuum*, 20(1), pp. 71–86.

Ouellette, L. and Hay, J. (2008), *Better Living Through Television*, Oxford: Blackwell.

Waisbord, S. (2004), 'McTV: Understanding the Global Popularity of Television Formats', *Television & New Media*, 5(4), pp. 359–83.

Afterword

Manuel Alvarado

Albert Moran's *TV Formats Worldwide: Localizing Global Programs* is a very important book.

Of the three stages of commodity existence, 'circulation' is, in the fields of cinema and television studies, the least researched. In terms of priority, 'consumption' has always come first, understood on the one hand in terms of 'effects studies', audience research and the concomitant 'moral panics' which are inevitably the result of such research and, on the other hand, in terms of critical analysis.

Accounts and analyses of 'production' came much later, largely because producers did not want researchers and academics sniffing around their underbellies, uncovering and revealing their working practices (and maybe malpractices!). This now seems strange in the twenty-first century, when everyone in the media industries – from studio and production bosses to 'runners' – wants to explain the significance of their role and contribution to the production under analysis. One only has to look at the end-credits of the latest Hollywood blockbuster in comparison to, say, those of *Citizen Kane* to realize that fact.

So 'circulation' has been the ignored and enigmatic field. Historically, the 'costs' of production may have been considered a confidential matter, while 'consumption' obviously had no choice but to be open and transparent. But 'circulation' is all about money and profit and gain, and most people – not unlike British politicians – are usually shy about discussing such matters.

This is why the work of Professor Moran and his colleagues around the world is so important. Professor Moran was an important pioneer in production studies – note his groundbreaking volume *Making a TV Series – The Bellamy Project* (Currency, 1982) – but it is his work on the circulation and distribution of television worldwide over the last fifteen years that will prove to be his enduring legacy. This book extends significantly his invaluable work on the globalization of media products which are still – and I suspect always will be – rooted in the local; these publications include *Film Policy: International, National and Regional Perspectives* (Routledge, 1996), *Copycat TV: Globalisation, Program Formats and Cultural Identity* (University of Luton Press, 1998), *Television Across Asia: Television Industries, Programme Formats and Globalisation* (Routledge, 2004), *Understanding the Global TV Format* (Intellect, 2006), *New Television: Globalisation and the East Asian Cultural Imagination* (Hong Kong University Press, 2007) and *New Flows in Global TV* (Intellect, 2009).

The local/global distinction in TV is remarkably similar to the same dichotomy in language. Everyone speaks their mother tongue first (obviously) but in most regions of the world, their second language is likely to be English. Apart from any other factors, the dominant language of the media, pop music and computers is persuasively English. Similarly, as Alessandro Silj and his colleagues (1988) demonstrate, every country which produces soap operas will see them coming at the top of the domestic ratings, but the second most popular will almost invariably historically be the American ones such as *Dallas* or *Dynasty*.

The globalization of TV these days has largely come to mean 'formats', as many of the essays in this collection will attest. And, as Professor Moran outlines, these can take a number of forms, which his collaborators attempt to define. Intriguingly, Professor Moran emanates from an ideal environment within which to undertake these analyses. As an (Irish) Australian, he has lived in a unique televisual environment. Australia has fiercely commercial TV, radio and press industries (one merely has to cite the name Rupert Murdoch amongst a number of media barons) that also coalesce with a state broadcaster (the ABC – the Australian Broadcasting Corporation) which is based on the BBC and a film industry largely set up by the Scottish founder of the British Documentary Movement, John Grierson. The result of this interesting confluence – in my experience – is as follows.

When I first experienced the privilege of being invited to Australia more than 30 years ago to give a keynote address at an at an international conference followed by a four-week national tour, I encountered an intriguing television system. Apart from the local (state) and national programming, I experienced local versions of both UK and US game shows and the original versions of these programs – that is, I could watch the UK, US and Australian versions of *Sale of the Century*! What is more, they were all repeated, so that my Australian hosts could say – 'wait for the next bit – it's hilarious'! I was bemused if not dumbfounded. What I also found intriguing in this early globalization of local formats were the prizes – what in the UK would have been, say, a three-piece lounge suite was, in the Australian case, translated into a barbecue and surfboard.

This book about the local and the global is largely about formats. Professor Moran identifies, non-exclusively, five formats. The first is the 'free copying over the years of TV news formats'. The second is the copying of documentary styles – for example, the BBC's *Panorama* and the ABC's *Four Corners*. Third, there is the selling and reconstruction of sitcom formats (e.g. *Hancock's Half Hour, Till Death Us Do Part, Steptoe and Son, Are You Being Served?, The Office*). Fourth, there is the very different area of soap operas. From a British perspective, this provides an intriguing and enigmatic terrain. In the United Kingdom and the United States, soaps such as *Dallas, Dynasty* and *Knot's Landing* were all about wealth, power and control. They were hugely popular peak-time viewing. Daytime soaps were Australian, such as *Neighbours, Home and Away, E Street* and *Heartbreak High*, which were all about suburban (middle-class) life. Early peak evening soaps, however, were/are provided by the relentlessly working-class or rural British serials such as *Coronation Street, EastEnders, Brookside, Emmerdale*, and so on. Attempts in the United Kingdom or Europe to produce more American-style soaps – for example, *The Cres* or *Chateauvallion* – were huge failures.

The fifth, and most important, category for formatting is obviously game shows, reality TV programs and all the other makeover and cookery programs which endlessly bombard our screens. These should probably be dealt with as separate categories. I will not comment about these partly because a significant amount of this book looks at these phenomena. However, what I will do is close with one anecdote. I was invited to be interviewed for half an hour on ABC radio in Tasmania in late 2002, and at one point I mentioned the British reality TV show that was currently being recorded in a remote part of Queensland, entitled *I'm a Celebrity – Get Me Out of Here!* The extremely well-informed interviewer and her producer had never heard of it…So we have a situation where I might have been 'acting' globally but appearing on a local radio station, although the interview was subsequently transmitted nationally, while British commercial television was making a program internationally in another country (which seemed to have little sense of the production) but for local, domestic consumption in the United Kingdom.

Local – national – international – global…this book provides fresh insights into the complex interrelations of these concepts.

Reference

Silj, Alessandro with Alvarado, Manuel (1988), *East of Dallas: The European Challenge to American Television*, London: British Film Institute.

Notes on Contributors

Klaus-Dieter Altmeppen is a Professor of Journalism in the Department of Journalism at the Catholic University Eichstaett in Germany. He focuses his research in the area of media (economics, management and organizations). He also works on journalism structures and ethics as well as on entertainment acquisition and production, and is Vice President of the German Communication Association (DGPuK).

Manuel Alvarado has authored, co-authored and edited many books and articles about the mass media over a career in which he has spent half his time working in universities and the other half working for organizations like the BBC, the British Film Institute and UNESCO. He is now retired, but is still Visiting Professor at City University, London, Associate Publisher with Intellect Books, Bristol and Chair of Grants for Sir John Cass's Foundation, which is the largest educational charity in the City of London.

Doris Baltruschat is a media producer and teacher with extensive experience in the distribution of international film and television programs. She has a Masters degree in Mass Communications from the University of Leicester in the United Kingdom and a PhD from Simon Fraser University in Canada. Her research interests include globalization and culture, film and TV coproduction, interactive media, Aboriginal communications and social movements. She has published on these topics in various international books and journals, including *Media Organization and Production* (Sage, 2003), *Cross-Border Cultural Production: Economic Runaway or Globalization?* (Cambria Press, 2008), the *Canadian Journal of Communication* and the *International Journal of the Humanities*. Her research has been presented at the Media in Transition conferences at the Massachusetts Institute of Technology in the United States and Cambridge University in the United Kingdom. She has been on the board of directors for the Canadian Association of Media Educators, and, as part of the Campaign for Press and Broadcast Freedom, organized the Media and Democracy Day event in Vancouver, Canada. Currently, she is teaching in the School of Journalism and Communication at Carleton University in Ottawa.

Raymond Boyle is a Senior Lecturer at the Centre for Cultural Policy Research at the University of Glasgow in Scotland. He has published widely on media and sports issues and sits on the editorial board of *Media, Culture and Society*. He is the principal investigator on a two-year AHRC-funded project on the Public Understanding of Business: Television, Representation and Entrepreneurship.

Milly Buonanno is Professor of Television Studies in the Faculty of Sciences of Communication at La Sapienza University of Rome. She is the founder and director of Osservatorio Fiction Italiana (1988–present) and coordinator of the Eurofiction Project (1996–2004) on the European television industry. Professor Buonanno has extensively researched and written on television storytelling, journalism, gender and news, and is the author and editor of more than 50 books, the most recent being *The Age of Television* (Intellect/University of Chicago Press, 2008). She is currently working on a social history of Italian TV drama.

Gabriele Cosentino is a PhD candidate in the Department of Media, Culture and Communication at New York University. His main area of research is the relation between politics and popular culture. He has presented his work at international conferences, and taught in colleges in the United States and Europe. His dissertation concentrates on the intermeshing between entertainment and politics on Italian television.

Waddick Doyle is the Director of the Division of Global Communications and Film, and of the Masters in Global Communications program, at the American University of Paris. He has published extensively on French and Italian television and also on semiotic theory. He is also a member of the board of the Centre pour les Etudes des Communications Internationales (CECI) in Paris and the Global Media Research Center at the University of Southern Illinois in the United States.

Sonia Jalfin is a Lecturer in Media and Politics at the University of San Andres and Cultural Advisor at Telefe, a leading television broadcaster in Argentina. She is a media consultant for the United Nations Development Program and regularly publishes on media and communications. She has also worked as a media and political commentator on radio and TV. She has received a Merit Award from the London School of Economics.

Pia Majbrit Jensen is Assistant Professor at Aarhus University, Denmark. Her research revolves around the role of media in globalization processes and her research topics include international TV program formats and genres, local media systemic conditions and production analysis. Besides contributions to media journals, her main academic scholarly input is the PhD thesis 'TV Format Adaptation in a Transnational Perspective', a comparative, transnational and historical case study of the use and extent of TV formats in Australia and Denmark.

Michael Keane is a Centre Fellow at the Australian Research Council Centre of Excellence for Creative Industries and Innovation and an Associate Professor at Queensland University of Technology, Brisbane, Australia. His research interests include innovation policy and creative clusters in China, audio-visual media in China, South Korea and Taiwan, and television formats in Asia. His most recent book is *Created in China: The Great New Leap Forward* (Routledge, 2007).

Barry King is Professor of Communications at Auckland University of Technology. He has taught at universities in the United Kingdom and the United States, and was recently a visiting Professor at Malmo University in Sweden. He is an internationally recognized researcher in the areas of communications and cultural theory. His publications encompass popular photography, the sociology of acting and performance, American media culture, stardom and celebrity, violence and the media and visual semiotics. He is the co-author of *Studying the Event Film: Lord of the Rings* (Manchester University Press, 2008) and is completing a book on contemporary stardom.

Marwan M. Kraidy is an Associate Professor at the Annenberg School for Communication at the University of Pennsylvania. His research focuses on global communication and Arab media. His books include *Global Media Studies: Ethnographic Perspectives* (Routledge, 2003), *Hybridity, or the Cultural Logic of Globalization* (Temple University Press, 2005), *Reality Television and Arab Politics: Contention in Public Life* (Cambridge University Press, 2009) and Arab Television Industries (British Film Institute, 2009).

Katja Lantzsch was a research associate in the Department for Media Management at Ilmenau University of Technology in Germany. She completed her dissertation about international TV format trade and inter-organizational networks in September 2007. Since 2008, she has worked as a consultant for organizational development in the publishing industry. Her research interests include media management and media marketing.

Edward Larkey is Professor of German Studies and Intercultural Communication at the University of Maryland in the United States. His recent book, *Rotes Rockradio: Populäre Musik und die Kommerzialisierung des DDR-Rundfunks* (Red Rock Radio: Popular Music and the Commercialization of GDR Radio), was published by LITVerlag in Germany in 2007. He is currently conducting trans-cultural narrative analyses of adaptations of global television formats in Germany and the United States in preparation for a new book.

Tania Lewis is a Senior Research Fellow in Sociology at La Trobe University, Melbourne, Australia. She is the author of *Smart Living: Lifestyle Media and Popular Expertise* (Peter Lang, 2008). Her current research is on green lifestyles and ethical consumption, and lifestyle television in Asia.

Bonnie Liu is a PhD candidate in the Creative Industries Faculty of Queensland University of Technology, Brisbane, Australia with CSC-QUT scholarship. She is doing research on the innovation and competition of television production in China, and her current research aims to find out what the emergence of independent television companies means for the diversity and quality of content in the Chinese television industry. She graduated with a Masters degree in Communication and Journalism from the Communication University of China in Beijing and was formerly a Lecturer in Communication at the University of China.

Albert Moran is Professor in the School of Humanities at Griffith University in Brisbane. His research interests have to do with Australian film and television history, media and place, and cross-border flows in TV formats. His recent publications include the book *New Flows in Global TV* (Intellect, 2009) and the collection edited with Michael Keane, 'Cultural Adaptation', which appeared as a special issue of *Continuum: Journal of Media and Cultural Studies* in 2009 and is also being published as a book by Routledge.

Charles Munro is a broadcast journalism professional who was a producer and manager in television news departments in Detroit, Cincinnati and New York. He was Senior Director of International Media for Iowa-based Frank N. Magid Associates, where he provided news and strategic consultation to networks and television companies in North America, Europe, the Middle East and Asia. He is currently an Adjunct Lecturer in the University of Iowa's School of Journalism and Mass Communication.

Yngver Njus obtained his Masters degree in 2004 from the University of Oslo. Currently, he is a doctoral candidate in the Faculty of Film and Television Production Studies at Lillehammer University College in Norway, and studies collaborative media production practices. He has previously worked as media analyst in NRK, the Norwegian public service broadcasting company.

Sujatha Sosale is an Associate Professor in the School of Journalism and Mass Communication at the University of Iowa, United States. Her research interests include media and social change in the global South, particularly in former Anglophone and Francophone colonies in the East African and South Asian regions, and globalization and the news. Her professional experience includes work in multinational advertising agencies and freelance journalism for area and regional newspapers in South India. The chapter was finalized when the author was an Obermann Scholar at the Obermann Center for Advanced Studies, the University of Iowa.

Amos Owen Thomas is currently Visiting Professor of Marketing at the University of Botswana. His research interests include globalization of media industries, political economy of trade and business ethics. Prior to an eighteen-year academic career at six universities internationally, he worked for fourteen years in MNCs, NGOs and government.

Dimitrina Todorova is Bulgarian and about to graduate in Global Communications from the American University of Paris where she is an Annenberg Fellow. She previously worked at the Bulgarian News Agency and Balkan Bulgarian Television. In France, she worked for Disney Publishing's emerging markets in Eastern Europe and Africa. Currently, she is interning at the Brand Communications and Quality Department of BNP Paribas, working extensively on Internet communications. She is planning to go on to higher studies in political communications, focusing on media in Eastern Europe.

Silvio Waisbord is Assistant Professor in the School of Media and Public Affairs at the George Washington University, Washington, DC. He is also the Editor in Chief of the *International Journal of Press/Politics*. Previously, he was Associate Professor in the Department of Journalism and Media Studies and Director of the Journalism Resources Institute at Rutgers University, New Brunswick, NJ, United States. He is the author and co-editor of four books and articles on journalism, media industries and international development. He holds a PhD in Sociology from the University of California at San Diego, California.

Andreas Will is a Professor and Head of the Department of Media Management at Ilmenau University of Technology in Germany. He holds a Diploma Degree from Karlsruhe University of Technology and a PhD from Augsburg University. His research interests include innovation, management and marketing in the media industry. Current projects concern the acquisition and production of TV entertainment, the Internet economy (online music distribution, video on demand) and business models in the games industry.

Index

www.ingramcontent.com/pod-product-compliance
Lightning Source LLC
LaVergne TN
LVHW060728310826
846742LV00016B/49